# China and Maritime Europe, 1500–1800

*China and Maritime Europe, 1500–1800*, looks at early modern China in some of its most complicated and intriguing relations with a world of increasing global interconnection. New World silver, Chinese tea, Jesuit astronomers at the Chinese court, and merchants and marauders of all kinds play important roles here. Although pieces of these stories have been told before, these chapters provide the most comprehensive and clearest summaries available, based on sources in Chinese and in European languages, making this information accessible to students and scholars interested in the growing connections among continents and civilizations in the early modern period.

John E. Wills, Jr., is Emeritus Professor of History at the University of Southern California. He is the author of many books, articles, and chapters on China.

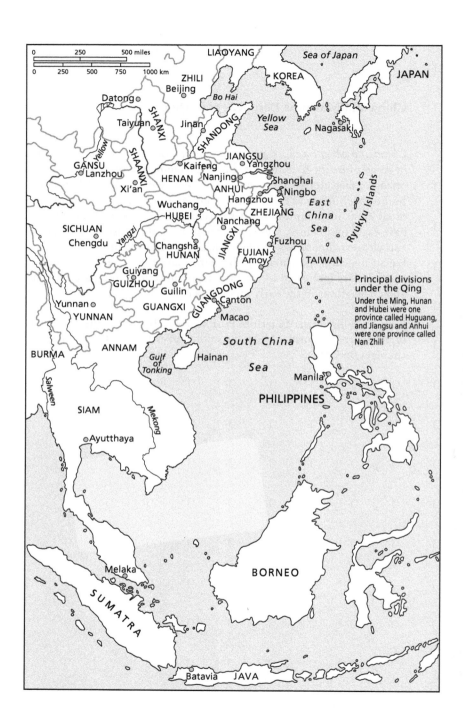

| | 0 | 250 | 500 miles |
| 0 | 250 | 500 | 750 | 1000 km |

LIAOYANG

*Sea of Japan*

JAPAN

ZHILI
Beijing

*Bo Hai*

KOREA

Datong

SHANXI

Taiyuan

Jinan

SHANDONG

*Yellow Sea*

Nagasaki

Yellow

GANSU
Lanzhou

SHAANXI

Kaifeng

JIANGSU
Yangzhou

Xi'an

HENAN

Nanjing

Shanghai

ANHUI

Ningbo

Wuchang

Hangzhou

*East China Sea*

HUBEI

ZHEJIANG

Nanchang

Ryukyu Islands

SICHUAN
Chengdu

Yangzi

JIANGXI

Changsha
HUNAN

Fuzhou

FUJIAN
Amoy

TAIWAN

Guiyang
GUIZHOU

Guilin

Yunnan

GUANGDONG

Principal divisions
under the Qing

YUNNAN

GUANGXI

Canton

Macao

Under the Ming, Hunan
and Hubei were one
province called Huguang,
and Jiangsu and Anhui
were one province called
Nan Zhili

BURMA

ANNAM

*South China*

Salween

Hainan

*Sea*

Gulf
of
Tonking

Manila

SIAM

Mekong

PHILIPPINES

Ayutthaya

Melaka

BORNEO

SUMATRA

Batavia   JAVA

# China and Maritime Europe, 1500–1800

## Trade, Settlement, Diplomacy, and Missions

Edited by

**JOHN E. WILLS, Jr.**
*University of Southern California*

with contributions by

**JOHN L. CRANMER-BYNG**[†]
*University of Toronto*

**WILLARD J. PETERSON**
*Princeton University*

**JOHN E. WILLS, Jr.**

and

**JOHN W. WITEK, S. J.**[†]
*Georgetown University*

CAMBRIDGE
UNIVERSITY PRESS

# CAMBRIDGE
## UNIVERSITY PRESS

32 Avenue of the Americas, New York NY 10013-2473, USA

Cambridge University Press is part of the University of Cambridge.

It furthers the University's mission by disseminating knowledge in the pursuit of education, learning and research at the highest international levels of excellence.

www.cambridge.org
Information on this title: www.cambridge.org/9780521179454

© Cambridge University Press 2011

First published 2011

*A catalogue record for this publication is available from the British Library*

*Library of Congress Cataloguing in Publication data*
Wills, John E. (John Elliot), 1936–
China and maritime Europe, 1500–1800 : trade, settlement, diplomacy, and missions / John E. Wills, Jr.
   p.   cm.
ISBN 978-0-521-43260-3 (hbk.) – ISBN 978-0-521-17945-4 (pbk.)
1. Europe – Relations – China.   2. China – Relations – Europe.   3. China – History – Ming dynasty, 1368–1644.   4. China – History – Qing dynasty, 1644–1912.   5. China – Commerce – Europe.   6. Europe – Commerce – China.   7. Missions – China – History.   8. Europe – History, Naval.   I. Title.
D34.C6W55   2010
303.48´251040903–dc22        2010031361

ISBN  978-0-521-43260-3  Hardback
ISBN  978-0-521-17945-4  Paperback

# Contents

# Contributors

**John L. Cranmer-Byng** (1919–1999) was Professor of History at the University of Toronto.

**Willard J. Peterson** is Gordon Wu '58 Professor of Chinese Studies and Professor of East Asian Studies and History at Princeton University.

**John E. Wills, Jr.,** is Emeritus Professor of History at the University of Southern California.

**John W. Witek, S. J.** (1933–2010), was Professor of East Asian History at Georgetown University.

# Preface

The essays collected in this volume are revised versions of chapters originally prepared for publication in volumes 8 and 9 of *The Cambridge History of China*. The authors have undertaken this separate publication because they believe their subjects are connected with each other in ways that might not be apparent in the contexts of the two *Cambridge History* volumes and because they wish to make them more accessible to scholars who might not notice their appearance in those volumes and would appreciate having access to them in this more compact and convenient format. We have particularly in mind our colleagues in various areas of study of early modern European relations with Asia who do not specialize in the study of China – scholars of the Islamic world, South Asia, Southeast Asia, Japan, and Korea – including historians of Christian missions elsewhere in Asia. All of these studies are in the midst of vigorous revivals. Specialized conferences and publications abound, so that we are likely to meet these intellectual collaborators at a meeting in Macao or Pondicherry, at a Vasco da Gama quincentenary conference in Australia, or at a meeting in Europe focused on the career of a particular missionary. Our studies and those of all these colleagues are contributing more or less deliberately to the very exciting efforts to develop a non-Eurocentric historiography of the early modern world.

Our chapters offer much context, data, and bibliographic guidance for those who wish to make further contributions to the already flourishing literature on early modern world trade, in which China's provision of high-quality manufactures and tea and its nearly insatiable appetite for silver were important driving forces. They will also be of use to others working on world history topics that have been energetically discussed only very recently, such as the comparison of the internal authority structures and foreign relations of state systems, the indigenization of religions of foreign origins, and the dynamics of multiethnic societies, especially those in port cities. We hope that our colleagues working on all these themes in relation to China and other parts of Asia will find in this book some small payment on the great debt we owe them for their recent sophisticated studies and summaries. Finally, we have enjoyed contacts with and encouragement from colleagues in the People's Republic of China in ways we could scarcely imagine when we began work on these chapters in the 1980s. Chinese scholars long were frustrated by the difficulties of learning foreign languages and obtaining access to non-Chinese sources, but a younger generation is overcoming these obstacles and becoming full participants in the international networks of scholarship on the topics discussed in this volume. Here too we hope the volume will be of use in maintaining dialogue and establishing some sound basic narratives.

Versions of the first and second chapters of this book appeared in volume 8 of *The Cambridge History of China*. The author of Chapter 1 has taken advantage of this second publication to add a few references to recent scholarship and to include one paragraph of exposition that was unaccountably omitted from the volume 8 text. The authors of Chapters 2 and 3 have added some references to recent scholarship. We have made every effort to keep our bibliographies up to date and to revise our expositions and analyses in the light of the most recent scholarship. We hope readers will use these pointers to explore further and to keep up with emerging work. For missionary-related topics, we are especially happy to be able to refer readers to the treasures of information and interpretation in Nicolas Standaert, ed., *Handbook of Christianity in China: Volume One: 635–1800*.

Many other chapters of *The Cambridge History of China*, volumes 7, 8, and 9, will be of great importance to readers of the present work. We would mention especially William Atwell's "Ming China and the Emerging World Economy, c. 1470–1650," in volume 8. Other chapters in volumes 8 and 9 provide excellent accounts of basic contexts of economic, social, and cultural change and of Ming China's foreign relations with other areas. Volumes 7 and 9 include in their reign-by-reign summaries of Ming and Qing politics many excellent passages on foreign relations.

The authors have exchanged drafts and comments at many stages. The editor has taken responsibility for coordination and interaction with

Cambridge University Press. We are grateful for the advice and encouragement of Frederic Wakeman, Denis Twitchett, C. R. Boxer, and John King Fairbank, and we mourn the deaths of all these eminent colleagues. We are very sorry that our friends and collaborators John L. Cranmer-Byng and John W. Witek, S. J., did not live to see their contributions to this volume in print. Father Witek was active until the final editing stages. This book is dedicated to the memory of these two colleagues in gratitude for their contributions and in token of our respect and friendship.

John E. Wills, Jr.
Pasadena

# Conventions

Pinyin romanization is used throughout except for the conventional Western usages of Canton (Guangzhou) and Amoy (Xiamen). Non-Chinese place names appear in modern forms, e.g., Melaka, not Malacca; Banten, not Bantam. We use the local English standard, Macao, not the Portuguese Macau.

## MING AND QING REIGN PERIODS, 1368–1820

Throughout the Ming and Qing dynasties, years were counted by year designations (*nianhao*) that were adopted at the beginning of each reign and, unlike the case in earlier dynasties, were not changed until a new emperor came to the throne. Thus the identification of an emperor with his reign period was very strong. It is common and correct to refer to "the Qianlong emperor" using his reign period; to write "Qianlong" as if it were a personal name or title of an individual is not correct but not rare. Volumes 7 and 9 of *The Cambridge History of China* contain excellent reign-by-reign summaries.

## MING DYNASTY

Hongwu, 1368–1398
Jianwen, 1399–1402
Yongle, 1403–1424
Hongxi, 1425
Xuande, 1426–1435
Zhengtong, 1436–1449

Jingtai, 1450–1456
Tianshun, 1457–1464
Chenghua, 1465–1487
Hongzhi, 1488–1505
Zhengde, 1506–1521
Jiajing, 1522–1566
Longqing, 1567–1572
Wanli, 1573–1620
Taichang, 1620
Tianqi, 1621–1627
Chongzhen, 1628–1644
(Omitted: Reign periods of "Southern Ming" loyalist regimes after 1644 and of Qing before 1644.)

QING DYNASTY

Shunzhi, 1644–1661
Kangxi, 1662–1722
Yongzheng, 1723–1735
Qianlong, 1736–1795
Jiaqing, 1796–1820

# Introduction

## John E. Wills, Jr.

The essays in this volume seek to give connected and reliable accounts of the relations of China with Europeans who came by sea (thus not the Russians and their occasional foreign associates), from the arrival of the Portuguese early in the sixteenth century to about 1800. There is no strong historiographical rationale for breaking off the narratives at this point; the main late-eighteenth-century themes of trade in tea and opium and the clandestine Roman Catholic presence could be carried right down to the Opium War (1839–1842). But two of these essays were originally prepared for publication in the volumes on the Qing before 1800 of *The Cambridge History of China*; the first of the nineteenth-century volumes of that series, with excellent chapters on the Canton trade and on Christian missions, was published in 1978.[1] Moreover, by breaking off around 1800, we end our summaries at a period when the basic policies of the Qing state toward maritime Europeans still seemed reasonably functional and successful, and thus undercut to a degree the teleological narrative of dysfunction and cultural arrogance leading straight to the Opium War that has afflicted many summaries of these topics. Recent scholarship on Qing China, emphasizing the sophisticated achievements of "High Qing" state and society and the contingency of the nineteenth-century "great divergence" between China and the West, strengthens our interest in seeing the eighteenth century for itself. New accounts

---

[1] Frederic Wakeman, Jr., "The Canton Trade and the Opium War," and Paul A. Cohen, "Christian Missions and Their Impact to 1900," in John K. Fairbank, ed., *The Cambridge History of China* (hereafter cited as CHOC), Vol. 10: *Late Ch'ing, Part 1* (Cambridge, 1978), pp. 163–212 and 543–590, respectively.

of "strange parallels" among Eurasian polities down to the nineteenth century and of the "transformation of the world" in that century offer riches of citation and interpretation that will keep all of us busy with long thoughts in both directions from 1800 for years to come.[2]

In any case, we feel no shortage of challenges in our assignments for this volume. The developments and events discussed here once were over-emphasized in the Eurocentric histories of Henri Cordier, H. B. Morse, and others, but in recent decades they have received only erratic scholarly attention, so that we have not always been able to draw on scholarship that meets current standards of interpretation and documentation and sometimes have had to piece our summaries together from primary sources and a scattered and multilingual secondary literature. Moreover, we have found it immensely exciting and challenging to try to keep up with the dramatic recent changes in the historiography of early modern China and of the European presence in maritime Asia. Some summary of the latter may be helpful for China scholars not familiar with these litera-tures. A background sketch of current understandings of "late imperial" or "early modern" China is called for, not only for the benefit of read-ers who are not China scholars, but also because our expositions and interpretations frequently require complex contextualizations of foreign encounters in aspects of Ming–Qing China not ordinarily discussed in accounts of its foreign relations.

## CONTINUITIES AND TRANSFORMATIONS IN MING–QING CHINA

In these essays we give full accounts of a number of occasions when envoys of European rulers were received at the Ming or Qing court as ambassadors bearing tribute from rulers of lower rank. The handling of the Portuguese embassy under Tomé Pires as a tribute embassy, the uni-lateral decision in 1656 that the Dutch might send an embassy only every eight years, at a time when trade in Chinese ports was allowed only in connection with tribute embassies, and the clash with Lord Macartney over the protocol of his reception by the Qianlong emperor all seem to point toward a mode of management of foreign relations in which every-thing was governed by a single set of hierarchical concepts and bureau-cratic precedents, a "tribute system" in the full sense of the word.

---

[2] Victor Lieberman, *Strange Parallels: Southeast Asia in Global Context, c. 800–1830*, 2 vols. (Cambridge, 2003, 2009); Jürgen Osterhammel, *Die Verwandlung der Welt: Eine Geschichte des 19. Jahrhunderts* (Munich, 2009).

But we also make note of many important facets of Chinese relations with maritime Europeans that had little or nothing to do with this tribute system: Macao, the eighteenth-century trade at Canton, policy toward Catholic missionaries, and the regulation of the trade of Chinese merchants to European-ruled ports like Manila and Batavia. If we take a longer view of the history of Chinese foreign relations, we find that the Ming–early Qing tribute system reflected persistent tendencies toward the unilateral and bureaucratized control of relations with foreigners and toward the assertion of the ceremonial superiority of the Son of Heaven over all other sovereigns, but that the years from about 1425 to 1550 were the *only* time in all of Chinese history when a unified tribute system embodying these tendencies was the matrix for policy decisions concerning all foreigners. I have argued elsewhere that it would help to clarify our thinking if we would reserve the term "tribute system" for this Ming system and not use it loosely to refer to the less systematic and more varied diplomatic practices of other times.[3] Even for the Ming, a study of the chapters on other foreign relations in volume 8 of the *Cambridge History* and of a growing but still inadequate scholarly literature reminds us that there was considerable variation; the Jurchen chieftains of the northeast presented tribute and were given military command titles formally within the Ming hierarchy, and the rulers of Burma and from 1520 the Mac rulers of Annam were given titles, such as "pacification commissioner," comparable to those of tribal chieftains within the empire.[4]

We have tended to make the tribute system a master concept for the interpretation of premodern Chinese foreign relations in part because some of the first great studies of Chinese foreign relations to use Chinese sources focused on the middle decades of the nineteenth century, when bookish statecraft scholars were restudying the regulations of the Ming–early Qing tribute system and statesmen in the capital were frequently citing such precedents and were worrying a great deal about how to

---

[3] John E. Wills, Jr., "Tribute, Defensiveness, and Dependency: Uses and Limits of Some Basic Ideas about Mid-Ch'ing Foreign Relations," *Annals of the Southeast Conference of the Association for Asian Studies*, Vol. 8 (1986), pp. 84–90, reprinted in *American Neptune*, Vol. 48, No. 4 (Fall 1988), pp. 225–229; Wills, "Did China Have a Tribute System?" *Asian Studies Newsletter*, Vol. 44, No. 2 (Spring 1999), pp. 12–13. For a sketch of the history of the tribute system see Wills, *Embassies and Illusions: Dutch and Portuguese Envoys to K'ang-hsi, 1666–1687* (Cambridge, MA, 1984), pp. 14–23.

[4] Morris Rossabi, "The Ming and Inner Asia," and Wang Gungwu, "Ming Foreign Relations: Southeast Asia," in Denis Twitchett and Frederick W. Mote, eds., CHOC, Vol. 8: *The Ming Dynasty, 1368–1644, Part 2* (Cambridge, 1998), pp. 221–271 and 301–332, respectively.

defend the ceremonial supremacy of the emperor against the intrusive Western order that had been announced by Macartney. The magisterial early works of John King Fairbank focused on this period; he directed a major conference and volume on "the Chinese world order"; and his views remained somewhat colored by his deep knowledge of early-nineteenth-century sources.[5]

In the hands of writers less steeped in the sources and less wary of generalization than Fairbank, the tribute system concept has helped to sustain a simplified, essentialized picture of a very late "late imperial China," "traditionalist," unable to change, and arrogant in its attitudes toward the outside world, that is incompatible with our present understanding of the internal history and foreign relations of Qing China. The focus on the tribute system might also be seen as one of many examples of the tendency of students of Chinese history inside and outside China to privilege the view from the imperial center or from the studies of scholars and vicarious officials, with their focuses on official values and bureaucratic systems, and underemphasize the immense variety of regional developments and pragmatic arrangements throughout the empire. In many of these arrangements, both at the capital and in the provinces, we see a tendency toward *defensive* and restrictive policies regarding foreign contact; this defensiveness is a much more satisfactory master concept for the interpretation of these relations and can be related in rich ways to our rapidly evolving sense of Ming–Qing China as an arena of immense and restless economic and cultural energies, in which political order was highly valued but perceived as fragile and constantly at risk, and the dangers of foreign linkages to these restless energies were especially feared.

From about 1000 CE on, China passed through a series of "economic revolutions" in grain production, iron production, water transport, and currency that immensely increased productivity, shifted the center of economic gravity to the rice lands of the center and south, and made possible the steady commercialization of the economy and the continued push of Chinese settlement into the far south and southwest.[6] Some scholars

[5] John K. Fairbank, *Trade and Diplomacy on the China Coast* (Cambridge, MA, 1953), Ch. 2; Fairbank and S. Y. Teng, "On the Ch'ing Tribute System," *Harvard Journal of Asiatic Studies*, Vol. 4 (1939), pp. 12–46, reprinted in Fairbank and Teng, *Ch'ing Administration: Three Studies* (Cambridge, MA, 1960); Fairbank, ed., *The Chinese World Order: Traditional China's Foreign Relations* (Cambridge, MA, 1968).
[6] Mark Elvin, *The Pattern of the Chinese Past* (Stanford, CA, 1973); Mark Edward Lewis, *China's Cosmopolitan Empire: The Tang Dynasty* (Cambridge, MA, 2009), esp. Chs. 3, 6; Lieberman, *Strange Parallels*, Vol. 2, Ch. 5.

would see in various regions and features of Song China a very early "early modernity." A much broader elite emerged, its energies directed to modes of status seeking controlled by the imperial center – validation of local social domination by examination success and talented provincials rising to high office through the examination system. This new elite was dedicated to the realization, through local organization and education even more than through imperial fiat, of a harmonious, hierarchical, agrarian society rooted in Confucian texts and values and cleansed of the foreign influence of Buddhism. But the economic shifts made the kinds of total control of trade and agriculture attempted by the Tang impossible, and led to tacit and sometimes overt positive evaluations of commerce and consumption, including foreign trade, trends that continued in Ming and Qing times.[7]

For foreign relations, the consequences of the long and gradual victory of the scholar-officials and their Neo-Confucian cultural program were contradictory. Since Han times scholar-officials frequently had opposed military expansionism and state efforts to increase revenue as offenses against the paternal care the ruler should show toward his people; of course, the power and prestige of military officers and revenue-enhancement specialists also threatened the political dominance of the scholar-officials. The ruling house of the Tang (618–907) and many close associates had combined a love of horses, hunting, and war with patronage of Confucian scholarship, profound allegiance to Buddhism, and fascination with foreign peoples and their exotic goods. Only in the 800s did segments of the elite begin to elaborate linked attacks on Buddhism as an antisocial teaching of foreign origin and on military influence in politics.[8] Buddhism became much more deeply indigenized in East Asia, with its own texts and holy sites owing nothing to India, so that the traffic in monks, texts, and relics that had sustained earlier maritime trade between China and India was replaced by a complex trade in spices, incense woods, and other consumer goods.[9] Under the Song (960–1279), despite a huge and expensive military establishment, military officials and organization were more thoroughly marginalized politically. Chinese models of rulership and bureaucratic organization helped to catalyze

---

[7] See especially the sweeping survey of this trend in Gang Zhao, *Geopolitical Integration and Domestic Harmony: Foreign Trade Policy in Qing China, 1684–1757* (typescript, 2009).

[8] Charles Hartman, *Han Yü and the T'ang Search for Unity* (Princeton, NJ, 1986).

[9] Tansen Sen, *Buddhism, Diplomacy, and Trade: The Realignment of Sino-Indian Relations, 600–1400* (Honolulu, 2003).

the formation of powerful states of mixed ethnicity and culture around the Song frontiers, in which Buddhism, under Neo-Confucian attack in the Song realm, remained very powerful. Song resistance to the military threats of these powerful neighbors was awkward and expensive. All of north China was lost to the Jurchen invaders in the 1120s. Thereafter, scholar-officials would neither give military men enough power to have a chance of success against the Jurchen Jin Dynasty nor accept the diplomatic parity forced on the Southern Song state (1125–1279) by the Jin. These contradictions were resolved, after a fashion, by the unification of East Asia under the Mongol Yuan (1279–1368). Commercial prosperity, urbanization, and local elite cultural activism continued. Neo-Confucian orthodoxy gained some government favor. But the ruling elite of Mongols and their Khitan, Jurchen, and Central Asian associates was conspicuously alien, and Chinese scholars in office were far less numerous and influential than under the Song.[10]

The collapse of the Yuan and of the pan-Asian *Pax Mongolica* after about 1345 led to decades of civil war. By 1368 the Ming founder had defeated his rivals in the Yangzi valley and driven the Mongols out of the north China plain. Commerce and agriculture were badly disrupted and took decades to recover. Later Ming scholars and statesmen looked back and saw in the first reigns of the dynasty the creation of a magnificent systematic bureaucratic order, the work of sagely rulers and of scholar-officials at last able to put into practice their Confucian ideals. Some of the innovations of the founders, like the integration of an empire-wide system of Confucian schools into the first level of the examinations leading to eligibility for office, did prove amazingly durable and effective props of political stability and cultural unity. But modern scholarship sees in these first reigns not so much rulers and ministers with common ideals and goals as a series of conflicts and contingent changes in which the scholar-officials won occasional and incomplete victories when it suited the needs of two formidable warrior-despots, the Hongwu (r. 1368–1398) and Yongle (r. 1402–1424) emperors.[11] Thereafter, scholar-official dominance of policy

---

[10] Herbert Franke and Denis Twitchett, eds., CHOC, Vol. 6: *Alien Regimes and Border States, 907–1368* (Cambridge, 1994).

[11] This summary is under the spell of the innovative views presented in Richard Von Glahn and Paul Jakov Smith, eds., *The Song–Yuan–Ming Conjuncture in Chinese History: Theoretical and Historical Perspectives* (Cambridge, MA, 2003). Excellent summaries of these reigns are to be found in Frederick W. Mote and Denis Twitchett, eds., CHOC, Vol. 7: *The Ming Dynasty, 1368–1644, Part 1* (Cambridge, 1988); in Edward J. Dreyer, *Early Ming China: A Political History, 1355–1435* (Stanford, CA, 1982); and in Timothy Brook, *The Troubled Empire: China in the Yuan and Ming Dynasties*

making was more often the norm, broken by revivals of imperial military adventurism and the associated power of the court eunuchs, which in their turn were likely to last until the death of a willful emperor allowed the literati to regain control. The Portuguese were baffled witnesses and victims of such a political reversal after an imperial demise in 1522.

In late Ming compilations, which provided precedents to guide early Qing practice and continued to influence the thinking of Qing statesmen, the Ming founders were portrayed as having established a uniform matrix for the management of all the empire's foreign relations. All rulers who wished to communicate formally with the imperial court had to acknowledge that they were subordinates of the Son of Heaven, dependent on his appointment or confirmation as a successor, received at the imperial capital as tributaries, their ambassadors as *pei chen*, ministers of ministers. The early Ming state brought together in singularly systematic union long-standing tendencies toward the assertion of the supremacy of the Son of Heaven over all other rulers and the unilateral, bureaucratic control of foreign relations. Active efforts to extend Ming hegemony were especially conspicuous under the Yongle emperor – the famous maritime expeditions of Zheng He (described later), major military expeditions into the Mongol homeland, an abortive conquest of Annam (modern Vietnam), and diplomatic initiatives to the northeast, to the northwest, and to Tibet and Nepal.[12] After 1425 the ceremonial supremacy of the Son of Heaven was carefully guarded, but the impulse to assert hegemony by force appeared only rarely, despite much bellicose rhetoric.[13] Foreign relations were more and more exhaustively bureaucratized – trade only in connection with embassies, strict rules on the frequency of embassies, the size of their suites, the presents they were to bring, and those they would receive. This system, the tribute system in the full sense of the word, had some successes in limiting contacts with smaller neighbors and giving them incentives to stay on good terms with the Ming. Unlike the situation under Song and Yuan, there was no legal residence or travel of foreigners within the empire except in connection with tribute embassies. This was defensive policy at its apogee.

---

(Cambridge, MA, 2010). One can open up an immense range of new perspectives on these and later periods of Ming history by browsing and following "q.v." citations in L. Carrington Goodrich and Chaoying Fang, eds. *Dictionary of Ming Biography*, 2 vols. (New York, 1976).

[12] Hok-lam Chan, "The Chien-wen, Yung-lo, Hung-hsi, and Hsüan-te Reigns, 1399–1435," in *CHOC*, Vol. 7, pp. 182–304, pp. 221–236; Wills, *Embassies and Illusions*, pp. 16–17.

[13] Alastair Iain Johnston, *Cultural Realism: Strategic Culture and Grand Strategy in Chinese History* (Princeton, NJ, 1995).

For two especially important and dangerous relations, the fundamentals of the tribute system could be maintained only when supplemented by other defensive measures, and the results were mixed or counterproductive. With respect to the Mongols, scholar-officials tended to oppose any step toward permitted trade and stable relations with "insincere" savages, so that there seemed to be no alternative to the vast expenses of border garrisons and the construction of the present Great Wall.[14] The threat of "Japanese pirates," many of them renegade Chinese, was partially contained not by effective diplomacy or by naval action but by drastic prohibitions of all maritime trade except that in connection with tribute embassies.

The most notable phenomenon of the foreign relations of the Yongle period has special relevance to our study of maritime relations. Almost all of the ports where the Portuguese made their connections and attempted their conquests in the early 1500s had been visited about eighty years previously by one or another of the seven great fleets the Ming sent into the Indian Ocean under the command of the eunuch Zheng He.[15] The largest of them had more than sixty large ships, some of them six-masted "treasure ships" over 100 meters long; more than 200 lesser craft; and 28,000 men. If such forces had still been on the Malabar coast in 1498, Dom Vasco da Gama and his three little ships would have been very lucky to avoid annihilation until the shift of the monsoon allowed them to flee to East Africa. But the Zheng He expeditions were fundamentally limited and defensive in purpose. In the wake of the nearly total prohibition of maritime trade by Chinese, it was advisable to encourage its replacement

---

[14] Arthur Waldron, *The Great Wall of China: From History to Myth* (Cambridge, 1990).

[15] In addition to Hok-lam Chan's excellent survey, see Louise Levathes, *When China Ruled the Seas: The Treasure Fleets of the Dragon Throne, 1405–33* (New York, 1994), and Edward L. Dreyer, *Zheng He: China and the Oceans in the Early Ming Dynasty, 1405–1433* (New York, 2006). Still important are the pages on this theme in one of the great intellectual monuments of the twentieth century, Joseph Needham, *Science and Civilization in China*, Vol. 4: *Physics and Physical Technology*, Part 3: *Civil Engineering and Nautics* (Cambridge, 1971), pp. 379–699. One of the most useful of the more specialized studies is Ma Huan, *Ying-yai Sheng-lan: 'The Overall Survey of the Ocean's Shores,'* ed. and trans. by J. V. G. Mills (London, 1970; reprint, Bangkok, 1997). See also Goodrich and Fang, *Dictionary of Ming Biography*, pp. 194–200, 355–365, 440–441, 522–523, 531–534, 661–665, 804–805, 958–962, 1026–1027, 1198–1202, 1364–1366. The study of Zheng He has been set back some years by the confusion generated by the amateur speculations of Gavin Menzies, *1421: The Year China Discovered the World* (London, 2002). An excellent exposé is provided by Quentin McDermott, "Junk History," broadcast by the Australian Broadcasting Corporation on July 31, 2006, transcript available at http://www.abc.au/4corners/content/2006/s1702333.htm.

by trade brought to China in ships based abroad, in connection with tribute embassies from foreign rulers.

The expeditions also gave crucial decades of employment to thousands of shipwrights, suppliers, and sailors who otherwise might have been extremely restive as the prohibitions of maritime trade began to bite. They were hugely successful in bringing tribute envoys and their exotic gifts, including ostriches, zebras, and giraffes, to enhance the mystique of the Son of Heaven. They followed trade routes more or less well known to Chinese mariners of Song and Yuan times.[16] At Palembang on Sumatra they crushed a nest of Chinese pirates and left a substantial garrison behind. They intervened rather haphazardly but effectively in the politics of Ceylon (modern Sri Lanka) and of Samudera on Sumatra. When part of a fleet settled down to wait for a change of monsoon, the Chinese built big stockades and buildings, but apparently always of wood, and they always left – a stunning contrast to the Portuguese, who from the beginning intended to stay and built fortifications out of hard coral rock that have withstood five hundred years of tropical heat and rain.

The Zheng He expeditions certainly reinforced local rulers' sense of the power of China and the political and commercial advantages of the tribute relationship. A substantial number of Chinese merchants and sailors accompanying the expeditions must have settled in Southeast Asian ports, contributing to the expansion of local trade and providing much of the expertise and manpower for tribute voyages to Chinese ports. Thereafter, there were numerous cases of tribute embassies from Melaka and from Siam staffed and even headed by Chinese.[17] The Portuguese would seize a key point in this Chinese diaspora, Melaka, with the aid of

[16] Some of the latest contributions to a complex literature on Song–Yuan maritime history are Billy K. L. So, *Prosperity, Region, and Institutions in Maritime China: The South Fukien Pattern, 946–1368* (Cambridge, MA, 2000); Angela Schottenhammer, ed., *The Emporium of the World: Maritime Quanzhou, 1000–1400* (Leiden, 2001); Schottenhammer, *Das songzeitliche Quanzhou im Spannungsfeld zwischen Zentralregierung und maritimem Handel* (Stuttgart: Steiner, 2002); Sen, Chs. 4, 5; Derek Heng, *Sino-Malay Trade and Diplomacy from the Tenth through the Fourteenth Century*, Ohio University Research in International Studies, Southeast Asia Series, No. 121 (Athens, OH, 2009).

[17] Chang Pin-ts'un, "The First Chinese Diaspora in Southeast Asia in the Fifteenth Century", in Roderick Ptak and Dietmar Rothermund, eds., *Emporia, Commodities and Entrepreneurs in Asian Maritime Trade, c. 1400–1750*, Beiträge zur Südasienforschung, Südasien-Institut, Universität Heidelberg, No. 141 (Stuttgart, 1992), pp. 13–28; Sun Laichen and Geoff Wade, ed., *Southeast Asia in the Fifteenth Century: The China Factor* (Singapore, 2010). A key set of references on tribute embassies from Southeast Asia is available in Geoff Wade, "Southeast Asia in the Ming Shi-lu," electronic resource, 2005, http://www.epress.nus.edu.sg/msl.

the local Chinese and then would ride the network of Chinese shipping on their first probes to Siam and the China coast.

Why, then, did the Ming abandon this remarkable projection of its wealth and power into the Indian Ocean? Scholar-officials pursuing Neo-Confucian agendas of cultural orthodoxy, limited government, and noncommercial agrarian stability had opposed most of the diplomatic and military initiatives of the Yongle reign, including the expeditions in Mongolia and Vietnam and the Zheng He expeditions. After the death of the Yongle emperor, efforts to hold on in Vietnam, where Ming forces were being trounced, soon were abandoned. Hardly anyone disagreed with the need for massive troop deployment and fortification against the Mongols, highly mobile warriors who had been driven out of China just fifty years before. Yongle had come to the throne as the victor in a revolt against his nephew and had moved the capital from Nanjing in the Yangzi valley to Beijing, his old base and the old Mongol imperial capital, reinforcing the centrality of the confrontation with the Mongols in Ming foreign relations and marginalizing the nexus of Nanjing shipyards, lower Yangzi commercial interests, and Fujian seafarers that supported the Zheng He expeditions. Xia Yuanji, one of the most eminent of the scholar-officials punished by Yongle and returned to power after the great despot's death, had vehemently opposed the vanity and waste of resources of the Zheng He expeditions. It is a bit surprising that even one more was sent, in 1432–1434. There are stories, not altogether reliable, that in the 1470s a scholar-official successfully aborted consideration of a renewal of the voyages by destroying many of the records of the earlier ones.[18]

The Zheng He voyages had integrated the attractions of China as an economic and political center, the skills of Chinese seafarers and merchants, and even a promising connection with the world of Islam; Zheng and several of his key commanders were Muslims, some with a good knowledge of Arabic. After 1435 small Muslim communities in Chinese ports were involved in trade, and some Chinese settled abroad became Muslim, especially on Java, but on the maritime Silk Road as on the continental one mutual ignorance and suspicion were the rule in relations between the Chinese and Islamic worlds. All Chinese who settled abroad had gotten there in violation of Ming prohibitions of maritime trade and could expect no acknowledgment or support from the Ming state. This strengthened their tendency to assimilate to local cultures and serve local

---

[18] Goodrich and Fang, *Dictionary of Ming Biography,* pp. 958–962.

rulers, in Melaka, in Java, in Siam, and even in the Ryukyu Islands, where Chinese émigrés and other merchants managed a thriving tribute connection with the Ming and voyaged as far as Melaka.

From 1425 to 1435 an alliance of a strong and effective emperor with some of the great scholar-officials who had been dismissed and imprisoned in the last years of the Yongle reign seemed to promise a stable and effective political system. Thereafter, alternation between domination by scholar-officials and by despots and their eunuchs became the general rule, masked and negotiated by narrow Neo-Confucian rhetorics of imperial sagehood and ministerial selflessness. This political culture frequently was short on realistic assessment of policies but still sufficiently stable to provide a peaceful environment for economic expansion. Throughout the 1500s, with a vital contribution from silver imports (discussed later in this essay and in Chapter 1), the commercial economy grew steadily. The resulting commercialization of culture and corruption of officials weakened the enforcement of restrictive, defensive policies toward foreigners while increasing the perceived need for them.

From 1500 to after 1800, the strength and variety of the commercial economy and the widening of the area settled by Han Chinese were not accompanied by anything like a proportional expansion of the apparatus of the state. Under the Qing an ethic of administrative efficiency and canny use of the special solidarity of an ethnically alien ruling house produced some administrative successes and masked this basic structural problem until about 1800. Ming–Qing society was marked by immense and diverse cultural energies and capacities for religious commitment, as well as by great entrepreneurial and commercial achievements, none of which were very well channeled or controlled by the cautious and thinly spread apparatus of the state. The dangers that these energies would be captured by foreign connection, commercial or religious, or by networks of subversive Chinese living overseas, seemed very great. In many episodes characterized by anti-Christian policies and efforts to control the coast and its trade, as in many other episodes in the long history of Chinese foreign relations, it is very clear that the real worry was not about the foreigners, who could be controlled, watched, and if necessary expelled, but about the "Chinese traitors" (*Han jian*) who would ally with them.

We will note in Chapter 1 a spasm of effort in the 1520s to revive traditional tribute system limits on foreign trade, which contributed to the failure of the first Portuguese efforts to establish relations. In the 1550s these restrictions, and their analogues in relations with the Mongols, collapsed in turmoil and small-scale invasion, and the tribute system was tacitly abandoned as a matrix for many branches of foreign relations. It was in this new situation that the Portuguese were permitted to settle at Macao and Chinese traders were permitted to sail to Manila and other Southeast Asian ports.

The peak years of the Spanish and Portuguese commercial connections with China, around 1590–1610, represented one facet of a time of immense commercial vitality in the empire, which was accompanied by a mounting political, cultural, and military crisis.[19] In Chapter 1 some estimates are offered of the inflow of silver from Japan and Spanish America in the late Ming. The sums were very large and the consequences profound. This massive flow of specie was, of course, made possible by the immense low-cost production of the mines of the Spanish Empire and by the opening of many new mines in Japan. But it would have been smaller and much shorter in duration without the enormous *demand* for silver created by Ming China's long and difficult search for an adequate medium for large transactions and empire-wide revenue transfers to replace the paper currency destroyed by excessive issue at the beginning of the dynasty. Theories that tie price rises and fiscal crises to year-to-year fluctuations in silver imports are increasingly called into question in the historiography of early modern Europe[20] and now are largely discredited for China by the work of Von Glahn, Flynn, and Giráldez.[21]

We can see a succession of phases in the effects of political change on the pace of the transition to silver: moderate until after 1500 as the state and the elite focused on the recovery of rural society and production from the civil wars of the 1300s; speeding up in the 1500s as private wealth was drawn into the vortex of empire-wide factional politics; and

---

[19] Willard J. Peterson, *Bitter Gourd: Fang I-chih and the Impetus for Intellectual Change* (New Haven, CT, 1979); Timothy Brook, *The Confusions of Pleasure: Commerce and Culture in Ming China* (Berkeley, CA, 1998). On the military challenge most important to our maritime story see Kenneth Swope, *A Dragon's Head and a Serpent's Tail: Ming China and the First Great East Asian War, 1592–1598* (Norman, OK, 2009).

[20] Jack A. Goldstone, *Revolution and Rebellion in the Early Modern World* (Berkeley, CA, 1991), pp. 87–89, 359–375; Michel Morineau, *Incroyables gazettes et fabuleux métaux. Les retours des trésors américains d'après les gazettes hollandaises (XVIe–XVIIIe siècles)* (Cambridge, 1985), pp. 78–90.

[21] Dennis O. Flynn, *World Silver and Monetary History in the 16th and 17th Centuries* (Aldershot, 1996); Dennis O. Flynn and Arturo Giráldez, eds., *Metals and Monies in an Emerging Global Economy* (Aldershot, 1997); Richard Von Glahn, *Fountain of Fortune: Money and Monetary Policy in China, 1000–1700* (Berkeley, CA, 1996). For the most recent salvo in long-running debates see Dennis O. Flynn and Arturo Giráldez, "Born Again: Globalization's Sixteenth Century Origins (Asian/Global Versus European Dynamics)," *Pacific Economic Review*, Vol. 13, No. 3 (2008), pp. 359–387.

a final phase after 1580 when the state could not control the use of silver, commercialization and corruption fed on each other, and silver imports reached their peak. The inflow of silver ceased to grow after about 1620 but did not decline sharply until about 1660, as Qing economic warfare on the south coast and Japanese export restrictions both began to bite. The inflow grew again after 1700 but reached a peak about 1750; by that time much of the growth of the Qing economy was sustained by improved mechanisms of commercial credit and by vigorous state support of the copper currency.[22]

In the late Ming, Confucian scholars were ill at ease with a society that was increasingly commercialized, urbanized, and tolerant of unconventional behavior. Prices were rising, so that everyone from the common soldier to the high official needed more income, and got it by demanding raises, taking bribes, and so on. Corruption enhanced inequities and shortfalls in revenue collection, while the government's need for revenue increased steadily. Scholarly proposals for reform were not implemented, and when the court dispatched eunuchs to the provinces to seek new sources of revenue, they encountered vehement and well-organized local resistance involving both the elite and commoners. Both the first Dutch approach to the China coast and the crisis at Manila in 1603 involved local intriguers allied with eunuchs. Reform-minded officials out of office, living in retirement in their home places, kept a close eye on local affairs in some areas, so that the Chinese documentation of the changes of these years is unusually good. Most intriguing, a sense of a culture that could not live up to its own highest values, that had lost its solidity or substantiality of scholarship and of moral commitment, led many scholar-officials to a revived interest in Buddhism,[23] a smaller number to an interest in the new teachings brought by the Jesuits, and a few able and earnest seekers to the great leap of conversion to Roman Catholicism.[24]

---

[22] Richard Von Glahn, "Money Use in China and Changing Patterns of Trade in Monetary Metals, 1500–1800," in Dennis O. Flynn, Arturo Giráldez, and Richard Von Glahn, eds., *Global Connections and Monetary History, 1470–1800* (Aldershot, 2003), pp. 187–205.

[23] Timothy Brook, *Praying for Power: Buddhism and the Formation of Gentry Society in Late-Ming China* (Cambridge, MA, 1993).

[24] For some further development see John E. Wills, Jr., "Brief Intersection: Changing Contexts and Prospects of the Christian–Chinese Encounter from Ricci to Verbiest," in John W. Witek, S.J., ed., *Ferdinand Verbiest, S.J. (1623–1688): Jesuit Missionary, Scientist, Engineer and Diplomat*, Monumenta Serica Monographs Series, No. 30 (Nettetal, 1994), pp. 383–394.

In some important ways, the long process of the Ming–Qing transition was a major interruption in, but not a transformation of, "early modern" trends toward commercialization, urbanization, population growth, and cultural diversity.[25] The long depression of economic activity was the result of the rebellions of the 1620s, the wars of the dynastic transition, and the continued wars along the coast and against Wu Sangui and other rebellious generals. The flow of silver into China did reach a low ebb in the 1670s and 1680s, but the downturn seems to have come too late to have *contributed* to the dynastic crisis. Once peace was fully restored, China enjoyed a century of remarkable internal order, which facilitated an unprecedented growth of commerce and population. European exports of tea and imports of silver were involved in this growth but, except in the Canton area and a few tea-growing counties, were not among its fundamental causes.[26]

In other respects the new Qing elite really was new.[27] With a Manchu imperial house and military establishment at its core, it provided firm and coherent control far beyond that of the Ming, including an effective end to the millennial threat of nomadic raids from Mongolia. Unwilling to expand its revenues or bureaucracy to keep pace with the expansion of population and settled area, in part because if the number of officials increased a higher proportion of them would be Han, not Manchu, it kept a wary eye on a vast empire in which its highly sophisticated systems of control were stretched extremely thin. Unlike their counterparts in the late Ming, the Chinese elite experienced a loss of autonomy but

[25] Jonathan D. Spence and John E. Wills, Jr., eds., *From Ming to Ch'ing: Conquest, Region, and Continuity in Seventeenth-Century China* (New Haven, CT: 1979); Frederic Wakeman, Jr., *The Great Enterprise: The Manchu Reconstruction of Imperial Order in Seventeenth-Century China*, 2 vols. (Berkeley, CA, 1985); Lynn A. Struve, *The Southern Ming, 1644–1662* (New Haven, CT, 1984); Struve, ed., *The Qing Formation in World-Historical Time* (Cambridge, MA, 2004); Struve, ed., *Time, Temporality, and Imperial Transition: East Asia from Ming to Qing* (Honolulu, 2005).

[26] The literature on Qing social and economic history is large and constantly growing. An excellent synopsis, which emphasizes differences among macroregions and assigns to foreign trade a somewhat larger causative role than I do, is Susan Naquin and Evelyn Rawski, *Chinese Society in the Eighteenth Century* (New Haven, CT, 1987).

[27] Jerry Dennerline, "The Shun-chih Reign," Jonathan Spence, "The K'ang-hsi Reign," Madeleine Zelin, "The Yung-cheng Reign," and Alexander Woodside, "The Ch'ien-lung Reign," in Willard J. Peterson, ed., *CHOC*, Vol. 9, Part 1: *The Ch'ing Dynasty to 1800* (Cambridge, 2002), pp. 73–309; William T. Rowe, *China's Last Empire: The Great Qing* (Cambridge, MA, 2009); Mark C. Elliott, *Emperor Qianlong: Son of Heaven, Man of the World* (New York, 2009).

a gain in opportunities for effective participation in the management of an orderly and productive society.[28] The sense of cultural and moral crisis that had propelled a few late Ming intellectuals into the Roman Catholic Church produced a few more distinguished converts, of whom the painter and poet Wu Li is the best known,[29] but their conversion in no way marked the beginning of a growing trend. A few high-ranking Manchus, products of a quite different culture, were the most important new group of Catholic converts in the early Qing. The survival and even growth of centers of Catholicism among the common people in places as widely separated as Fuan in Fujian province and parts of the great inland Sichuan basin, taking forms sometimes strikingly similar to those of such subversive religious groups as the White Lotus, demonstrated that the kinds of response to the alien religion that aroused so much antagonism amid the new surge of missionary activity after 1860 already were present in the eighteenth century.

The Manchu Qing rulers were intelligent and effective in maintaining a coherent status quo despotism in the face of residual resentment of their alien rule and ever more striking expansion of population, commerce, and settlement area.[30] Some of the organizational accomplishments of state and society, such as the provision of famine relief even for rural populations,[31] were quite beyond the capabilities of their European contemporaries. As late as 1800, the standard of living in the most prosperous parts of the Qing Empire and that in western Europe were roughly equal.[32] This prosperity and organizational sophistication can be seen in the continued growth of the great tea trade at Canton. Qing policies on China's Inner Asian frontiers sought to project conquest and control,

[28] For a vivid example of wide-ranging and thoughtful ministerial competence in an official of remote provincial origins, see William T. Rowe, *Saving the World: Chen Hongmou and Elite Consciousness in Eighteenth-Century China* (Stanford, CA, 2001).

[29] Jonathan Chaves, *Singing at the Source: Nature and God in the Poetry of the Chinese Painter Wu Li* (Honolulu, 1993); John E. Wills, Jr., *1688: A Global History* (New York, 2001), pp. 136–139.

[30] A rich range of sophisticated summaries and guides to the literature on "High Qing" are now available. See Willard J. Peterson, ed., *CHOC*, Vol. 9, Part 1: *The Ch'ing Dynasty to 1800* (Cambridge, 2002); Rowe, *China's Last Empire*; Elliott, *Emperor Qianlong*.

[31] Pierre-Étienne Will and R. Bin Wong, with James Lee, contributions by Jean Oi and Peter Perdue, *Nourish the People: The State Civilian Granary System in China, 1650–1850* (Ann Arbor, MI, 1991).

[32] R. Bin Wong, *China Transformed: Historical Change and the Limits of European Experience* (Ithaca, NY, 1997), Ch. 1–5; Kenneth Pomeranz, *The Great Divergence: China, Europe, and the Making of the Modern World Economy* (Princeton, NJ, 2000).

not to establish a defensive perimeter. Here we see a masterful, empirical, multicultural face of the Qing that scarcely was visible at Canton. Tibetan Buddhism, personally important to the great Qianlong emperor (r. 1736–1796) and to many at his court, was astutely managed as a major source of influence among the Mongols. The formidable military strength of the Manchu Banners were dispatched on one expensive expedition after another. Tibet, modern Xinjiang, and what is now the Mongolian People's Republic became parts of the Qing Empire. Multicultural cities were managed, political exiles put to work, law and order maintained through diverse systems of indirect rule.[33] But in the relations we deal with in this book, Qing policies maintained Ming defensiveness and even made it more effective; their wariness of any new source of organized dissidence or cultural heterodoxy among their Han Chinese subjects was reinforced by their particular animus toward the maritime Chinese, perhaps the most thoroughly distrusted of all the varieties of "Chinese traitors."

In tracing the theme of the effects of relations with the maritime Chinese on Ming and Qing policy toward foreigners, we will be constantly drawn away from a capital-centered history into the distinctive histories of several macroregions that had important coastal zones, of the ports of south China and those where Chinese settled overseas.[34] In Ming times, Chinese merchants, craftsmen, and sailors became vigorous participants in building a new world of trade and settlement around the South China Sea. The sixteenth and early seventeenth centuries were the peak of an "age of commerce" in maritime Southeast Asia, in which indigenous rulers and elites, traders from all around the Indian Ocean, Europeans, and Chinese were active participants.[35] The rise of Nagasaki and other

---

[33] Peter C. Perdue, *China Marches West: The Qing Conquest of Central Eurasia* (Cambridge, MA, 2005); Peter C. Perdue, "Empire and Nation in Comparative Perspective: Frontier Administration in Eighteenth-Century China," in Huri Islamoğlu and Peter C. Perdue, eds., *Shared Histories of Modernity: China, India, and the Ottoman Empire* (London, 2009), pp. 21–45; Evelyn S. Rawski, *The Last Emperors: A Social History of Qing Imperial Institutions* (Berkeley, CA, 1998); James A. Millward, *Beyond the Pass: Economy, Ethnicity, and Empire in Qing Central Asia, 1759–1864* (Stanford, CA, 1998); Piper Rae Gaubatz, *Beyond the Great Wall: Urban Form and Transformation on the Chinese Frontiers* (Stanford, CA, 1996).

[34] John E. Wills, Jr., "Maritime China from Wang Chih to Shih Lang: Themes in Peripheral History," in Spence and Wills, eds., *From Ming to Ch'ing*, pp. 204–238; Wills, "Contingent Connections: Fujian, the Empire, and the Early Modern World," in Struve, ed., *The Qing Formation*, pp. 167–203.

[35] Anthony Reid, *Southeast Asia in the Age of Commerce, 1450–1680*, 2 vols. (New Haven, CT, 1988–1993); Reid, ed., *The Last Stand of Asian Autonomies: Responses*

ports of Kyushu, the beginnings of Chinese settlement of Taiwan, the sudden emergence of Haicheng and then Amoy, the flourishing of Macao, Manila, Banten, Batavia, Ayutthaya, Melaka, and many more depended heavily on their activities.

The south coast of China was the scene of the longest-lasting resistance to Qing consolidation of power, until the Qing conquest of Taiwan in 1683, which left the Qing rulers and their ministers determined to control the south coast, permanently distrustful of the maritime Chinese and extremely aware of the difficulties of bureaucratic control and military action in their world. The maritime Chinese preserved memories of the long struggle and heroism of Zheng Chenggong and other resistance leaders, and were drawn toward the Heaven and Earth Society (Tiandihui) and other anti-Qing organizations by their usefulness for community organization overseas as well as by Ming loyalist heritages.[36] The mutual mistrust of Manchus and maritime Chinese prevented any reach of Chinese dynastic power farther into the rapidly changing maritime world. New studies of Southeast Asia in the eighteenth century and of the roles of the maritime Chinese in it are beginning to suggest trends, in which the Chinese participated vigorously, of commercial and demographic expansion away from the major capitals and entrepôt cities.[37] This more spread out and indigenized Chinese presence may have provided fewer centers for anti-Qing intrigue in the short run, but did not reduce Qing wariness and led in the long run to the far larger and more openly anti-Qing overseas Chinese presence of the late nineteenth century. Within the Qing Empire, the south coast ports and capitals were under thorough central control after about 1680, while Taiwan was dealt with warily and not allowed to become a center of foreign trade.

Qing attitudes toward this maritime world were full of contingencies and apparent contradictions. The Qing conquest elite, the product of a northeastern milieu of rapid urbanization, vigorous commerce, fluid ethnic identity, and diverse religious expression, could scarcely give full

---

to *Modernity in the Diverse States of Southeast Asia and Korea, 1750–1900* (London/ New York, 1997).

[36] Dian H. Murray, in collaboration with Qin Baoqi, *The Origins of the Tiandihui: The Chinese Triads in Legend and History* (Stanford, CA, 1994).

[37] Leonard Blussé and Femme Gaastra, eds., *On the Eighteenth Century as a Category of Asian History: Van Leur in Retrospect* (Aldershot, 1998); Li Tana, *Nguyen Cochinchina: Southern Vietnam in the Seventeenth and Eighteenth Centuries* (Ithaca, NY, 1998).

assent to the anticommercial, antireligious, and antiforeign strands in the Chinese tradition. The Qing rulers abandoned restrictions on maritime trade and confinement of that trade within the tribute system as soon as the south coast was pacified, but remained wary of the maritime Chinese and learned little about the Europeans trading in the ports of south China and ruling many of the Southeast Asian ports where Chinese settled. The Kangxi emperor and many at his court were interested in the new learning of the Jesuits, employed them in astronomy, cartography, and diplomacy, and declared that their religion was not heterodox. Sophisticated discussions of European astronomy became important in the subtle rapprochement of the Kangxi emperor and the Jiangnan literati.[38] A few members of the capital elite became Christians. But the Chinese Rites Controversy revealed to the outraged emperor the extent of foreign control over Roman Catholics within China and the intolerance of some church authorities for basic features of the Chinese tradition, ending the best chance Christianity had before the twentieth century for genuine toleration and indigenization in China. Late Kangxi domestic political anxieties revived perceptions of threat from "Chinese traitors" along the coast and led to a revival of restrictions on maritime trade.

In the Yongzheng (1722–1735) and Qianlong (1736–1796) reigns, prohibitions of Roman Catholicism were intermittently enforced, but given the thinly spread nature of the imperial bureaucracy, they were never more than partially effective in eliminating Christian communities or forbidding missionary access to the empire. Wariness toward the maritime Chinese and the "Chinese traitors" associated with the forbidden Christian religion contributed to a growing defensiveness toward foreign contact in general, especially after about 1740. As a result, the Qing state regulated but did not substantially impede the steady growth of European trade at Canton, from which the court drew impressive revenues. There were a few new signs of trouble at Canton after 1780. The wariness and insistence on correct ceremony with which the Qianlong court received the Macartney embassy were products not so much of changes in relations with the Europeans as of the court's general preoccupation with orthodoxy and symbolism in these years, intensified for foreign relations by the fiasco of the invasion of Annam/Vietnam in 1788, and the

[38] Minghui Hu, "Provenance in Contest: Searching for the Origins of Jesuit Astronomy in Early Qing China, 1664–1705," *International History Review*, Vol. 24, No. 1 (March 2002), pp. 1–36; Benjamin A. Elman, *On Their Own Terms: Science in China, 1550–1900* (Cambridge, MA, 2005), Chs. 3–5.

elaborate face-saving ceremonies surrounding Qing recognition of the new Tây Sơn regime.[39]

## A CHANGING MARITIME WORLD

Our understanding of the maritime world that impinged on China and that the maritime Chinese helped to create is changing rapidly, in ways that are very helpful for thinking about the specific developments studied in this volume.[40] The basic change is from a "European expansion" approach, in which the eventual European dominance of long-range maritime trade was thought of as inevitable and rapidly achieved once Europeans entered the Indian Ocean, to an "Asian maritime history" view, in which Asian rulers, merchants, and seafarers are seen to have been active and effective participants in the shaping of maritime Asia throughout this period. Today the study of maritime Asia is strongly indigenized, rooted in the historiography of various areas of Asia and frequently the work of Asian scholars. It sees many important maritime developments as "interactive emergences," results of interactions between characteristics of Asian civilizations and those of the European intruders, made possible largely by Asian productivity and sophisticated commercial networks, in such a way that it does not make sense to try to divide our analyses into "European impact" and "Asian response." The essays in this volume, written by students of Chinese history and deeply indebted to the great progress in studies of Ming–Qing history in recent decades, are very much a part of this trend.

Sixteenth-century Europeans frequently viewed social change and economic growth with almost as much misgiving as their Ming contemporaries, but for them their eruption into the Indian Ocean was a vast opening toward new possibilities of profit, conquest, and conversion. The disruption and the death – including that of many Europeans who fell in battle or died of disease – were far from the eyes of the rulers

---

[39] Truong Buu Lam, "Intervention versus Tribute in Sino-Vietnamese Relations, 1788–1790," in John K. Fairbank, ed., *The Chinese World Order: Traditional China's Foreign Relations* (Cambridge, MA, 1968), pp. 165–179, 321–326.

[40] For surveys and introductions to a rapidly developing literature see John E. Wills, Jr., "Maritime Asia, 1500–1800: The Interactive Emergence of European Domination," *American Historical Review*, Vol. 98, No. 1 (February 1993), pp. 83–105; Wills, "Interactive Early Modern Asia: Scholarship from a New Generation," *International Journal of Asian Studies* (Japan), Vol. 5, No. 2 (July 2008), pp. 235–245; and Markus P. M. Vink, "Indian Ocean Studies and the 'New Thalassology'," *Journal of Global History*, Vol. 2, No. 1 (2007), pp. 41–62.

and the writers of celebratory chronicles. We sense only obliquely in the pages of those chronicles that the Indian Ocean into which Vasco da Gama's ships sailed as they rounded southern Africa, attacked the Swahili ports, and crossed to Calicut in 1497–1498 was largely a Muslim realm, united by religion and common principles of law, its trade reinforced by the pilgrim traffic to Mecca and the demand for Indian and Southeast Asian goods in the prosperous Muslim heartlands. Especially in south India, the Portuguese learned common idioms of interaction and understanding with Hindus and Muslims, of which we can find traces in their writings, including those of Tomé Pires, who plays a prominent role in Chapter 1.[41] The Portuguese carried the ancient Christian–Muslim war all the way from the Mozambique channel to the Spice Islands, but they also frequently found Muslim advisers and allies.[42] The role of Chinese seafarers was not as prominent in this world as it had been eighty years before Da Gama's arrival, when the great fleets under Zheng He crossed and recrossed the Indian Ocean. Once they reached Melaka, however, the Portuguese entered a maritime world in which the Chinese were major participants and sometimes useful advisers or allies. The Portuguese who reached the China coast before 1524 were products of the internal anarchy and external anti-Muslim ferocity of the early Estado da Índia. The men who found their way to the arrangements for Chinese toleration of Macao thirty years later had been shaped by a changed world of "controlled conflict" and frequent close cooperation, especially at the local level, between Portuguese and Indians, both Hindu and Muslim.[43]

For the first generations of Portuguese in Asia, Christianity was expressed largely by its battle against Muslims. Sustained and intelligent missionary efforts did not really begin until the arrival of the first Jesuits in the 1540s. The stories of the great Jesuit pioneers – Xavier in Japan, Nobili in India, Ricci in China – have been told often and well. The Jesuits brought to Asia the renewed commitment and discipline of the Catholic

---

[41] Joan-Pau Rubiés, *Travel and Ethnology in the Renaissance: South India through European Eyes, 1250–1625* (Cambridge, 2000); on Pires see esp. pp. 202–210.

[42] Sanjay Subrahmanyam, *The Portuguese Empire in Asia, 1500–1700: A Political and Economic History* (London, 1993), Ch. 3; Subrahmanyam, *The Career and Legend of Vasco da Gama* (Cambridge, 1997). For up-to-date analyses and references to the energetic recent literature see Francisco Bethencourt and Diogo Ramada Curto, eds., *Portuguese Oceanic Expansion, 1400–1800* (Cambridge, 2007) and A. R. Disney, *A History of Portugal and the Portuguese Empire: From Beginnings to 1807*, 2 vols. (Cambridge, 2009), Vol. 2.

[43] Sanjay Subrahmanyam, *The Political Economy of Commerce: South India 1500–1650* (Cambridge, 1990), Ch. 5.

Reformation; a concentration on education, intellectual rigor, and ministry to the social and political elite; an astute use of all the resources of the European visual arts,[44] which characterized their work throughout Europe; and a deep learning of the Greek and Roman classics that predisposed many of them to the respectful study of the non-Christian classics of Asian cultures and to efforts to articulate ways in which Christ and Confucius could be as compatible as Christ and Cicero. Many of these efforts bore the stamp of the broad tendency in early modern European intellectual life that has been labeled "Hermetic," which gave primacy to the articulation and interrelation of structures of meaning. South Indian encounters and debates, in a world where Hindus, Muslims, and Christians met in the courts and markets and none could expel the others, sharpened the quest for strategies of respectful encounter.[45] Efforts to show how this background was expressed in missionary efforts still are not common; they include studies of Ricci's uses of the Renaissance arts of memory and of the tendency of French "Figurist" Jesuits to find anticipations of Christian revelation everywhere, even in the *Yi Jing*.[46] The Jesuits, of course, were not the only missionaries in China. We are just beginning to study the European backgrounds of the Spanish Dominicans and Franciscans and of the French priests of the Missions Étrangères, and the important ways in which the Spanish missionaries were shaped by their experiences in the Philippines.[47]

The Spaniards who founded and ruled Manila were not entirely free of conquistador ideas, but got almost no opportunity to try them out on the China coast, and in general remained uneasily dependent on the trade and the organizing skills of the maritime Chinese. The main engine of the prosperity of Manila was the fragile link provided by the Manila galleons between China's thirst for silver and the immense new supplies

[44] Gauvin A. Bailey, *Art on the Jesuit Missions in Asia and Latin America, 1542–1773* (Toronto, 1999).

[45] Rubiés, *Travel and Ethnology*, Ch. 9.

[46] The link with the Hermetic tradition is made explicit in D. P. Walker, *The Ancient Theology: Studies in Christian Platonism from the Fifteenth to the Eighteenth Century* (Ithaca, NY, 1972), Ch. 6. For case studies in Jesuit cultural synthesis in China and creativity in defining Jesuits' roles in China and Europe, see esp. Jonathan D. Spence, *The Memory Palace of Matteo Ricci* (New York, 1984); John W. Witek, S.J. *Controversial Ideas in China and in Europe: A Biography of Jean-François Foucquet, S.J. (1665–1741)*, Bibliotheca Instituti Historici S.I., Vol. 43 (Rome, 1982); and Florence C. Hsia, *Sojourners in a Strange Land: Jesuits & Their Scientific Missions in Late Imperial China* (Chicago, 2009).

[47] Eugenio Menegon, *Ancestors, Virgins, and Friars: The Localization of Christianity in Late Imperial China* (Cambridge, MA, 2009).

available from the Spanish Empire in the Americas. The Dutch East India
Company's assault on the Fujian coast and on Chinese shipping in the
1620s brought to East Asian waters a degree of efficient organization
of violence and integration of war and commerce far beyond that of the
Portuguese Estado da Índia.[48] But not even the Dutch could "force the
Chinese to trade," and soon they had to accept a position on Taiwan that
was strikingly similar to that of the Spanish at Manila. After their expulsion from Taiwan in 1662, they, and the English after them, came to the
China coast for trade, not war, and for most of the eighteenth century
they were reasonably satisfied with conditions of trade at Canton, while
the efficient communication structures of the great East India Companies
coordinated the unprecedented growth of purchases in China of tea for
European markets.

Two final shifts of offshore contexts in the late eighteenth century
were the rise in Indian and Southeast Asian waters of a dynamic network
of European private "country trade" and the closely related rise of British
political power in parts of India, which eventually washed up on China's
shores in the forms of impatient Bengal bullyboys and opium.[49] As we
end our studies around 1800 we see these transformations, including the
effects of a succession of Anglo-French wars, very much in midcourse.
Although Chinese settled in Southeast Asia interacted with these newcomers everywhere, little or no sense of these changes is apparent in the
writings of the Qing court and elite. Siam and Annam/Vietnam passed

---

[48] Excellent starting points for reading and thinking about the great companies include
Holden Furber, *Rival Empires of Trade in the Orient, 1600–1800* (Minneapolis, 1976);
[J.] L. Blussé and F. Gaastra, eds., *Companies and Trade: Essays on Overseas Trading
Companies during the Ancien Régime* (Leiden, 1981); and Om Prakash, *European
Commercial Enterprise in Pre-Colonial India*, in *The New Cambridge History of
India*, II. 5 (Cambridge, 1998). On the Dutch company see F. S. Gaastra, *The Dutch
East India Company: Expansion and Decline*, trans. Peter Daniels (Zutphen, 2003), and
Els M. Jacobs, *Merchant in Asia: The Trade of the Dutch East India Company during
the Eighteenth Century*, trans. Paul Hulsman (Leiden, 2006). On the English East India
Company and its contexts see W. Roger Lewis, ed., *The Oxford History of the British
Empire*, 5 vols. (Oxford, 1998), Vols. 1, 2. On eighteenth-century transformations espe-
cially as viewed from London, with full citations of the recent literature, see H. V. Bowen,
*The Business of Empire: The East India Company and Imperial Britain, 1756–1833*
(Cambridge, 2006).

[49] Furber, *Rival Empires*, Ch. 6; C. A. Bayly, *Indian Society and the Making of the
British Empire*, In *The New Cambridge History of India*, Vol. 2, Part 1 (Cambridge,
1988); P. J. Marshall, *Bengal: The British Bridgehead – Eastern India, 1740–1828*, In
*The New Cambridge History of India*, 2, II (Cambridge, 1987); Søren Mentz, *The
English Gentleman Merchant at Work: Madras and the City of London, 1660–1740*
(Copenhagen, 2005).

through huge breakdowns of internal order but then emerged with stronger monarchies that sought tribute relations with the Qing, so that from the perspective of Beijing it did not seem that much was changing in the distant "Southern Seas."[50]

The following chapters, then, offer for the most part some fairly narrow slices of the histories of Ming–Qing China and of an emerging interconnected world, along the lines where these two massive histories intersected. Sometimes, usually because European-language sources have been preserved, we can study these slices in great detail – prices, quantities of trade, individual human interactions in their day-to-day complexity. Poised in these moments of interaction, we stand outside each culture, looking into it from the vantage point of the other with which it intersected. Seen in this light, we believe, our non-Eurocentric studies of European relations with China have much to offer to the tentatively emerging study of the early modern world. For us, "early modern" includes not only Europeans but Chinese merchants supplying reliably one of the great global trades of the eighteenth century, Chinese intellectuals and religious seekers finding ways to be Christian and Chinese, and an emperor who learned how to measure the latitude of his camp as well as how to shoot a heavy bow and study the *Yi Jing*.

---

[50] John E. Wills, Jr., "Functional, Not Fossilized: Qing Tribute Relations with Annam (Vietnam) and Siam (Thailand)," 1700–1820, *T'oung Pao*, in press.

I

# Maritime Europe and the Ming

## John E. Wills, Jr.

THE MARITIME MATRIX

The Portuguese conquered Melaka, a loyal Ming tributary, in 1511. Among the many kinds of merchants they encountered there were some who came all the way from the Ryukyu Islands, another small state flourishing on the funneling of trade with China through its tribute embassies. The Chinese were everywhere, even though the Ming state forbade all maritime voyages by Chinese. By this time, the whole structure of prohibitions was bending, but not breaking. The expansion of Chinese illegal maritime trade had produced a flourishing outlaw entrepôt at Yuegang near Zhangzhou in Fujian.[1] In the Zhengde period (1506–1521) ships from Southeast Asian tributary states were allowed to come as frequently as they wished, without regard for the limitations of time and number in the regulations of the tribute system, and their trade was taxed. The Superintendencies of Maritime Shipping (*shibosi*) were directed by eunuchs, who were especially interested in obtaining rare imports for the palace. The Guangdong Superintendency had a tax-collection station at the distant coastal point of Dianbai in Gaozhou to accommodate this trade,[2] and apparently later at Tunmen in the Canton estuary, the scene of the first encounters with

---

[1] Chang Pin-ts'un, *Chinese Maritime Trade: The Case of Sixteenth-Century Fu-chien (Fujian)* (Ph.D. dissertation, Princeton University, 1983), Ch. 3; Lin Renchuan, *Mingmo Qingchu siren haishang maoyi* (Shanghai, 1987).

[2] Zhang Weihua, *Mingshi Folangji, Lüsong, Helan, Yidaliya sizhuan zhushi* (Beiping, 1934), p. 52. This work, far more than a commentary on the *Mingshi* chapters, is the best available collection of Chinese sources on the topics of this chapter. For the Portuguese see also Zhou Jinglian, *Zhong-Pu waijiao shi* (Shanghai, 1936).

the Portuguese, or at Macao itself. This trade, officially approved but in violation of the basic rules of the tribute system, provided the matrix for the flourishing trade between Siam and Melaka and South China within which the Portuguese began their relations with China. The eunuch superintendents used their positions to obtain extra illicit income for themselves and foreign rarities for the court; the relative openness to maritime trade in the Zhengde reign was very much connected with the domination of a restless nonconformist emperor by his eunuchs, which also was behind the initial acceptance of the first Portuguese embassy and then its rejection after the death of the Zhengde emperor.

## THE PORTUGUESE ENTRY, 1514–1524

Vasco da Gama's voyage around the Cape of Good Hope and the arrival of his ships at Calicut on the west coast of India in 1498 opened a new phase in the history of Asia and, in conjunction with the Columbus voyages to the Americas in the same decade, of the world.[3] The effects of the European intrusion into the Indian Ocean were by no means as overwhelming as those of the Spanish on the Caribbean, Mexico, and Peru; in particular, there was no catastrophic mortality as a result of non-immunity to Eurasian diseases. Asian maritime traders remained effective competitors of the Europeans on most routes and in most goods until the age of steam, and European political power was confined to small islands and coastal enclaves until the Dutch advances in Java from the 1670s on and the rise of English power in India after 1750. Still, the Portuguese and their successors could be very disruptive. European ships were better gun platforms than those of the Indian Ocean, but it is not clear how often this led to clear naval superiority. More important was the projection of state power onto the high seas, the combination of piracy, naval gunnery, and aggressive efforts to monopolize lines of trade that the Portuguese brought with them from the Mediterranean world. The prosperous and sophisticated network of Muslim maritime trade linking the Red Sea and the Persian Gulf with India and Southeast Asia was only sporadically supported by Ottoman power, and much later by Oman. The Portuguese seriously inhibited the trade of their Muslim rivals until after 1550, when they became more interested in their own intra-Asian trade and more

---

[3] Sanjay Subrahmanyam, *The Career and Legend of Vasco da Gama* (Cambridge, 1997); Subrahmanyam, *The Portuguese Empire in Asia, 1500–1700: A Political and Economic History* (London, 1993), Chs. 1– 3.

accommodative toward their Muslim competitors. This pattern was mirrored in their relations with China, where early aggressiveness, and no naval superiority at all, led to disaster, while commercial accommodation after 1550 was a brilliant success.

At Calicut on the southwest coast of India, Vasco da Gama heard stories of pale, bearded men on big ships who had sailed along that coast several generations before; the Portuguese did not realize that these were allusions to the great fleets of Zheng He.[4] If the Ming state had not abandoned its great maritime venture eighty years before, the Portuguese adventure probably would have come to a quick and unpleasant end at this point. Melaka became the key to the Portuguese advance toward China. The first Portuguese expedition there was instructed to find out as much as possible about the "Chijns" and their trade. Chinese merchants trading at Melaka, somewhat at odds with the local rulers, were friendly to the Portuguese in 1509, and in 1511 loaned Albuquerque's invasion force a large junk, which he used in a key landing that led directly to the final rout of the Melakan forces.[5] The Chinese merchants sought to remain on good terms with the conquerors, transporting a Portuguese ambassador to and from Siam on their junks. We have only shadowy knowledge of the first two visits to China under Portuguese auspices, by Jorge Alvares in 1514 and by the Italian Rafael Perestrello in 1515–1516. The latter went on the junk of a Melaka merchant, and it is likely that the former also took advantage of Melakan or Chinese shipping. Both traded at Tunmen in the Canton estuary and brought back highly profitable cargoes.[6]

The scope of the Portuguese effort altered dramatically with the arrival in the Canton estuary in August 1517 of eight ships under Fernão Peres de Andrade, bearing Tomé Pires as ambassador from the king of Portugal to the Ming court. Peres de Andrade had been sent from Lisbon in 1515 expressly for this mission, along with the Florentine merchant Giovanni da Empoli, who already had been in India and Melaka and had transmitted to his Medici masters what he had learned about that

[4] Donald Ferguson, "Letters from Portuguese Captives in Canton, Written in 1534 and 1536. With an Introduction on Portuguese Intercourse with China in the First Half of the Sixteenth Century," *Indian Antiquary*, Vol. 30 (1901), p. 421.

[5] Ibid., p. 422; Geoff Wade, "Melaka in Ming Dynasty Texts," *Journal of the Malaysian Branch of the Royal Asiatic Society*, Vol. 70, Part 1 (1997), pp. 31–69; Luis Filipe Ferreira Reis Thomaz, "The Malay Sultanate of Melaka," in Anthony Reid, ed., *Southeast Asia in the Early Modern Era: Trade, Power, and Belief* (Ithaca, NY, 1993), pp. 69–90.

[6] J. M. Braga, *China Landfall, 1513: Jorge Alvares' Voyage to China* (Hong Kong, 1956).

"cosa grandissima" called China.[7] The choice of Pires as ambassador was a brilliant, unconventional one; in a society where noble blood was usually a prerequisite for important office, he was a bourgeois pharmacist, albeit a rich one with excellent court connections, recently charged with investigating and collecting Asian drugs to send home to King Manuel. He was the best European collector of information on Asia in his time; his *Suma Oriental* is the most important source in any language on the trade of maritime Asia at the beginning of the Portuguese intrusion.[8] Progress toward China was delayed in the Straits of Melaka by the loss of a ship and by the discussion of an alternative venture to Bengal, then accelerated by the glowing report on the China trade brought by Rafael Perestrello in 1516.

Upon his arrival in June 1517, Peres de Andrade, with Empoli serving as factor (commercial agent) and frequent intermediary with the Chinese authorities, made every effort to establish good relations with them, and was reasonably successful, but in the process provided first instances of some perennial sources of trouble in premodern Sino-European relations: European impatience and assumptions of reciprocity in foreign relations against Chinese bureaucratic delays and unilateral management, as well as the Europeans' tendency to reject Chinese explanations of their decisions and to interpret them instead as the result of the corrupt self-interest of the officials.[9] Dealing at first with the naval commander at Nantou near the mouth of the Pearl River, Peres de Andrade sought for more than a month permission to take his ships up the river to Canton. When he threatened to go without written permission, the naval commander gave way and passed his troublesome guest on to the Canton authorities, offering the assistance of pilots.

Arriving before the city without written permission, the Portuguese caused more alarm and indignation by discharging their cannon in

---

[7] Giovanni da Empoli, *Lettere di Giovanni da Empoli*, ed. A. Bausani (Rome, 1970), pp. 77, 157.

[8] Tomé Pires, *The Suma Oriental of Tomé Pires*, ed. and trans. Armando Cortesão, Hakluyt Society, New Ser., Vol. 89–90 (London, 1944); for biographical information see pp. xviii–lxiii. See also Pires, *O Manuscrito de Lisboa da "Suma Oriental" de Tomé Pires (Contribução para uma edição crítica)*, ed. Rui M. Loureiro (Macao, 1996).

[9] The main Portuguese sources for this account of the Tomé Pires embassy are the passages on it in João de Barros and Diogo de Couto, *Da Asia de João de Barros e Diogo de Couto* (reprint, Lisbon, 1973–1975), III:I:I; III:II:VI, VII, VIII; III:VI:I,II; III:VIII:V. (The Roman numerals refer to *decadas*, *livros*, and *capitulos*, respectively; individual notes in the present chapter for passages not easily found in this chronological sequence also give page numbers of this reprint.) On the attributing of all delays to private interests of the officials see III:II:VIII, p. 209.

friendly salute. Their explanation that the Chinese merchants did the same thing when they arrived at Melaka and their avowal that in taking Melaka they had avenged the local ruler's tyrannies against the Chinese could only have added to Ming official concerns, since Chinese overseas trade was illegal and the deposed king of Melaka a loyal Ming tributary. The ships were closely watched, the Portuguese were not allowed ashore, and no one was allowed to come to them. After the high provincial officials arrived at Canton to deal with the strangers, the Portuguese were received ashore with considerable pomp, and lodgings were provided for Tomé Pires and the seven Portuguese (and probably some slaves) who were to accompany him on the embassy. Trade goods were brought ashore bit by bit, trade being conducted "in the most orderly fashion possible." One ship was detached to reconnoiter trade prospects on the Fujian coast. Prospects were excellent, but reports of this voyage stirred Chinese fears of spying. Peres de Andrade may not have been fully aware of the imperative need to leave before the end, about March, of the north monsoon winds. He missed the 1517–1518 north monsoon and left in September 1518 at the very beginning of the next north monsoon, having made a very good impression (a Portuguese chronicler tells us) by posting a notice at Tunmen that anyone who had been injured by a Portuguese or to whom a Portuguese owed money should see him for redress.

In August 1519 Simão de Andrade, brother of Fernão Peres de Andrade, arrived from Melaka with three junks and soon destroyed the fragile accommodation Fernão had worked so hard to build. At Tunmen, the island center for the trade of all foreigners, he built a small fort, ceremoniously executed a Portuguese, and barred the other foreigners from trading ahead of him. He and his men knocked the hat off an official who tried to assert Ming authority on the island. They bought Chinese children, some of whom, sons and daughters of good families, were found several years later by the Portuguese authorities at Diu in western India.[10] Buying and selling of children was scarcely unknown in Ming China, but the large new demand of the Portuguese may have stimulated kidnappings from good families and also contributed to the stories that soon were circulating of how the Portuguese were buying the children to cook and eat. Simão and his party stayed over the winter and left in September 1520; there is no record of local action to stop or punish their abuses, but reports soon must have been on their way by various channels to Beijing, where their impact would combine with other factors to doom the Pires

[10] Ibid., III:VI:II, p. 17.

embassy and relegate Portuguese relations with China to an outer margin of illegal private trade for more than thirty years.

The embassy party left behind in Canton in 1518 left for the north only in January 1520. By that time, Portuguese sources tell us, there had been three exchanges of communications about it between Canton and Beijing. In contrast to the willingness of Qing rulers and ministers to accept new tributaries and to celebrate them as evidence of the far-reaching charisma of the dynasty, many Ming statesmen seem to have believed that no embassy should be accepted from a ruler who had not been enrolled among the tributary states in the first reigns of the dynasty.[11]

This viewpoint did not immediately prevail in these last years of the Zhengde emperor, with the eunuchs' interest in the exploitation of commerce and the emperor's fascination with all kinds of exotic people.[12] The embassy reached Nanjing, where the emperor was residing, in May 1520, but soon was ordered to go on to Beijing and await the emperor's return there. It is probable that whoever had control of the Portuguese party deliberately avoided an imperial interview, which would have had unforeseeable consequences, considering the emperor's delight in exotic foreigners and the corruption and viciousness of his entourage. Portuguese sources tell us that while they were waiting in Beijing they had to go on the first and fifteenth of every lunar month to prostrate themselves before a wall of the Forbidden City; I know of no Chinese source on such a ceremony.[13] They heard of the emperor's arrival at Tongzhou in January 1521 and the execution there of the captured rebel prince of Ning. (The silly emperor fancied himself a general and had barely been dissuaded from leading the expedition against the prince of Ning in person.)[14] They knew that ambassadors had arrived from the exiled king of Melaka to report on the Portuguese conquest and to ask Chinese assistance in driving out the invaders and restoring the city to its rightful lord. They knew of memorials by two censorial officials, Qiu Daolong and He Ao, condemning the Portuguese conquest of Melaka and urging that the embassy be rejected, and a further memorial from the Canton officials reporting that the Portuguese were troublesome people and were asking to be granted a trading post. They were told that after these negative reports about the

---

[11] Zhang Weihua, *Mingshi Folangji*, pp. 9, 32.
[12] James Geiss, "The Cheng-te Reign, 1506–1521," in Frederick W. Mote and Denis Twitchett, eds., *The Cambridge History of China* (hereafter cited as *CHOC*), Vol. 7: *The Ming Dynasty, 1368–1644, Part 1* (Cambridge, 1998), Ch. 7.
[13] Ferguson, "Letters," p. 467.
[14] Geiss, "The Cheng-te Reign," pp. 423–436.

Portuguese had been received in the capital, the interpreters were summoned and questioned one by one, and at least one of them confessed that the interpreters had not actually seen the letter from the king of Portugal, since the Portuguese had expected to deliver it sealed into the emperor's hands, but had made up an appropriate "tribute memorial" text. There is no mention of this in Chinese sources.

The Portuguese no longer were summoned to the twice-monthly ceremonies outside the palace, but there was no conclusive rejection of the embassy until after the death of the emperor on April 19, 1521, which was followed by major political changes, as scholar-officials turned against eunuch influence at court and struggled among themselves over ceremonial proprieties within the imperial family.[15] Mourning for the emperor apparently required the temporary suspension of all ceremonial and other dealings with foreigners. In the changed political atmosphere, with the temporary ascendancy of Grand Secretary Yang Tinghe and the general turn against eunuch influence, a decision to reject the embassy and forbid all relations with the Portuguese, already probable before the emperor's death, was a foregone conclusion.[16] The embassy was hurried out of Beijing the day after the emperor died and arrived in Canton in September.

In April or May 1521, in the early weeks of the south monsoon, about five Portuguese ships and junks arrived at Tunmen and began trading. When news of the emperor's death arrived, all foreigners were ordered to leave the country at once. The Portuguese refused, since they had not finished taking in their export cargoes. The Chinese assembled a substantial squadron and attacked the Portuguese and some junks from Siam and Patani that had Portuguese aboard; one ship was sunk and many Portuguese and other foreigners were killed or taken prisoner. When two more Portuguese junks arrived in June, another Chinese attack was beaten off, a lull followed, and in September three Portuguese ships barely managed to beat off another attack and get away. Thus by the time the Tomé Pires embassy arrived back in Canton on September 22, 1521, these sea battles had reinforced the determination of the Ming authorities to exclude the Portuguese. The embassy party was kept separate from the prisoners taken in the sea fights. The authorities made inventories, the

---

[15] Ibid., pp. 440–450.
[16] Carney T. Fisher, *The Chosen One: Succession and Adoption in the Court of Ming Shizong* (Sydney, 1990); James Geiss, "The Chia-ching Reign, 1522–1566," in Mote and Twitchett, eds., *CHOC*, Vol. 7, pp. 440–466.

Portuguese thought dishonestly,[17] of the embassy's presents and of the trade goods taken from the captured ships.

The final chapter of this story was the arrival at Tunmen in August 1522 of three ships under Martim Affonso de Mello Coutinho, who had a royal commission to conclude peace with China and enough men to garrison a fort he hoped to establish, presumably with Chinese consent. The commanders of these ships knew nothing of the breakdown of relations and lost two of their ships to an unexpected Chinese attack. The survivors managed to get away on the third ship after only fourteen days in Chinese waters. The prisoners taken in the sea fights were treated harshly, put in cangues (heavy wooden collars), and executed after the autumn assizes of 1523. Tomé Pires was forced to write letters to the king of Portugal, the viceroy of Portuguese India, and the governor of Melaka conveying the emperor's command that Melaka be returned to its rightful sovereign. He and his party were held hostage, to be released only when the Ming authorities were informed that the Portuguese had returned Melaka to its legitimate ruler. Pires died in 1524. Two of his party were still alive in 1534–1536, sending letters to Melaka and Goa full of good information and wild plans for the conquest of Canton.[18] The Ming authorities mustered fleets every year until 1528 to guard against the return of the Portuguese. The taxed nontribute trade that had flourished in the Zhengde reign was prohibited in Guangdong to all foreigners, and Southeast Asian trade shifted to illegal entrepôts in the Zhangzhou area of Fujian, to the great detriment of Guangdong's revenues and commercial economy. Even after Guangdong's taxed nontributary trade was reopened in 1530, the Portuguese were completely excluded.

These episodes had attracted a good deal of attention in the Canton area, and set there a tone of fear and contempt toward the Portuguese that persisted throughout the flourishing of Macao. In the court and among the high bureaucratic elite, they left, to judge by surviving Chinese sources, only fragmentary and ambiguous impressions. The cannon and ships of the Portuguese were appreciated, one ship was built in Portuguese style in the Canton estuary, and one official, Wang Hong, made a name for himself promoting the copying and use of Portuguese-style cannons as far away as the Great Wall forts. The Portuguese were known in the

---

[17] Ferguson, "Letters," p. 469.
[18] Armando Cortesão, in his introduction to the *Suma Oriental* of Tomé Pires, pp. xlvii–xlviii, argues that these letters were written in 1524. See, however, Ferguson, "Letters," p. 478, for a clear reference in one of these letters to the maintenance of defense fleets along the coast until 1528.

records of this time as Folangji, after the Indian–Southeast Asian term "ferengi," referring to any Latin Christian and ultimately derived from the Franks of the Crusades. "Ji" also meaning "device," the same characters were used for the cannons, and soon some were confused as to whether the Folangji were guns or people. In the *Ming Shi* account of the Portuguese and a few of its sources, one of the foreign hangers-on at the imperial court, Huozheyasan, appears as the Portuguese ambassador or interpreter; this probably is a confusion involving someone from Hami or Turfan, Muslim city-states near China's northwestern frontier that had extremely tangled tributary relations with the Ming court at this period, but may reflect some kind of intrigue involving a Melakan Chinese interpreter. Geoff Wade has pointed to a Khoja Husain or Hasan in the Malay sources who might have been partly of Chinese origin, hospitable to the Portuguese arrival in Melaka, and subsequently attached to their embassy to China. If such a person had begun to have second thoughts about the newcomers who had come to stay and rule in Melaka, and then had seen which way the winds were blowing in Beijing after the death of the Zhengde emperor, he would have been in an ideal position to change sides and tell all about the bogus "tribute memorial."[19]

## FROM LIAMPO TO MACAO, 1530–1572

The debacle of the 1520s thrust the Portuguese back into the margins of the Southeast Asian trade with China, traveling as individuals on Southeast Asian shipping and eventually sending their own ships to the ports where the Melakans, Siamese, and others traded. There are stray references in the 1530s to royal or viceregal grants of voyages to China, and the first Portuguese ship to reach Japan, in 1542, was blown there on a voyage to "Liampo," presumably the Shuangyu trading center on Liangang Island in the Zhoushan Archipelago on the Zhejiang coast.[20] In the 1540s this area became a flourishing center for illegal or semilegal trade between China and Japan and between China and Southeast Asia. Portuguese also were involved in the illicit trade centered on Yuegang harbor in the Zhangzhou estuary of Fujian, the "Chincheo" of the European sources, including the nearby island of Wuyu. This illicit trade

---

[19] Paul Pelliot, "Le Hoja et le Sayyid Husain de l'Histoire des Ming," *T'oung Pao*, Vol. 38 (1948), pp. 81–292; Wade, "Melaka," pp. 50–53.
[20] Zhang Zengxin, "Shiliu shiji qianqi Putuoyaren zai Zhongguo yanhai di maoyi judian," in *Zhongguo haiyang fazhanshi lunwen ji (er)* (Taipei, 1986), pp. 75–104.

was in a way a revival of the marginally legal trade on the Guangdong coastal islands in the Zhengde period and similarly served to quarantine dangerous foreigners far away from the major cities. But since they had no legal sanction and no official presence, they were more prone to violence and vulnerable to government hostility than the earlier centers had been.

In the rise and fall of these centers the Portuguese were not so much independent actors as they were marginal participants in a Sino-Japanese process.[21] Reports of illegal trade and of the piracy that sometimes accompanied it finally led in July 1547 to the appointment of Zhu Wan as a special grand coordinator with wide authority to stamp out smuggling and lawlessness on the Zhejiang and Fujian coasts. In November 1547 Zhu already was investigating the situation in the Zhangzhou area and recommending measures to improve defenses and to control the activities of the coastal Chinese.[22] In April 1548 he was in Hangzhou coping with the irregularities of the Japanese embassy under Sakugen Shuryō and assembling forces for an all-out assault on Shuangyu. From April to June of that year the Shuangyu area was occupied and devastated. Chinese sources report only a few hundred casualties, and there is no reliable record of any Portuguese casualties; clearly many Chinese and foreign ships and traders had managed to get away. It was very convenient for the denizens of Shuangyu that this attack came at the beginning of the south monsoon, the season for departures of trading ships to Japan. Given the conspicuous preparations for an attack on their island bases, it cannot have been too difficult for the outlaw traders to assemble export cargoes and get their ships and people out of harm's way.

Zhu Wan already had been in Fujian in 1547 and had ordered measures to cut off illegal trade there. He returned in the summer of 1548, undeterred by rising opposition to his policies and a reduction of his authority in August. The Portuguese trading on the Fujian coast that summer at first found their trade almost entirely cut off but later were able to bribe some of the coastal commanders and obtain their export cargoes. Lin Xiyuan, a former high official now deeply involved in maritime trade, apparently had abetted their trade by various maneuvers

[21] For an excellent summary and full citations of sources see Jurgis Elisonas, "The Inseparable Trinity: Japan's Relations with China and Korea," in John Whitney Hall, ed., James McClain, assistant ed., *The Cambridge History of Japan*, Vol. 4: *Early Modern Japan* (Cambridge, 1991), pp. 235–300.

[22] L. Carrington Goodrich and Chaoying Fang, eds., *Dictionary of Ming Biography*, 2 vols. (New York, 1976), pp. 372–375; Geiss, "The Chia-ching Reign," pp. 494–495.

to delay enforcement of Zhu's rigid orders and by arguing that the Portuguese had traded peacefully for the previous five years and even had helped the authorities attack a pirate.[23] Early in 1549 Portuguese traders, probably coming from Japan, found it impossible to trade and left their goods in the hands of Chinese agents. In February or March, one or two junks were lured to the shore and attacked at Zoumaqi in Zhaoan near the Fujian–Guangdong border. Several hundred were killed on the spot or died soon afterward; ninety-six prisoners were taken to Quanzhou, where Zhu Wan ordered the Chinese among them executed. Four Portuguese prisoners were labeled kings or princes of Melaka. Zhu's executions on his own authority, especially those not at the scene of the battle, were just what his enemies needed to secure his downfall; he was dismissed and imprisoned, and apparently committed suicide. The fraud of the "Melakan nobles" was uncovered, leaving the Portuguese very much impressed with the thoroughness and impartiality of Chinese justice. The Portuguese spent several years in exile in various parts of China, and some eventually joined their compatriots trading on the Guangdong coast.[24]

The downfall of Zhu Wan was followed by years of upheaval and antipirate campaigns on the coasts of Jiangnan, Zhejiang, and Fujian. Deprived of their livelihoods and unable to collect trade debts in China, Chinese and Japanese maritime traders turned to large-scale attacks on Chinese cities and even to great expeditions inland or up the Yangzi River; to the Chinese state all these people were "pirates," and although many of them were Chinese, they usually are referred to as the *wokou*, "Japanese pirates." Militias were recruited and tribal troops were brought in from the southwest who were as destructive as the pirates. The richest areas of China were thrown into chaos for several years; only very gradually did the Ming officials manage to negotiate splits in the pirate forces, defeat some in battle, and bring the situation under some control. But there was no formal legalization of Chinese maritime trade until 1567. The Portuguese sometimes were victims of this violence and of official hostility to all maritime traders, but they and a few pragmatic officials found their way to accommodations in Guangdong while most official attention was focused farther north. Successive pirate–trader coalitions found

[23] Zhang Weihua, *Mingshi Folangji*, pp. 43–47; Goodrich and Fang, *Dictionary of Ming Biography*, pp. 919–922.

[24] C. R. Boxer, ed. and trans., *South China in the Sixteenth Century, Being the Narratives of Galeote Pereira, Fr. Gaspar da Cruz, O.P., Fr. Martín de Rada, O.E.S.A.* (London, 1953), pp. xxvi–xxxvii, 190–211.

it harder to do business in Ming harbors and sought bases and plunder as far away as Taiwan and Manila. The legalization of maritime trade at Haicheng, Fujian, discussed later, made it possible to engage in maritime trade without outlaw collusion.[25]

Looking for peaceful trade, the Portuguese turned again to the coast of Guangdong. Everywhere along the Chinese coast, old restrictions were shattered, and military men, sometimes in alliance with elements of the local elite, were very influential. This was the changed situation in which the Portuguese partially overcame the legacy of their first rupture in the 1520s and worked out an astonishingly useful and durable accommodation of Chinese and Portuguese interests – Macao. Several early sources say that the officials allowed the Portuguese to settle at Macao in 1557.[26] By the 1620s the Portuguese of Macao had built up an elaborate story of the extermination by the Portuguese in 1557 of a large force of pirates that had occupied Macao and of the consequent cession of Macao by the emperor to Portuguese sovereignty, confirmed by a "golden chop" preserved in the Macao city hall. However, the Macao authorities repeatedly acknowledged that the Chinese state retained ultimate sovereignty over Macao, and we will see that some elements of this foundation myth probably are reflections of well-documented events in 1564–1565. In Chinese sources the 1557 date has been found only in a recently noted document from 1628 in which the "Weiliduo," that is, the vereador, or Crown attorney, of the Portuguese local government, is represented by his Chinese amanuenses as listing a long series of services of Macao to the Ming, beginning with the driving out of the Macao peninsula in 1557 of "Ama and other pirates." "Ama" was part of the popular name for the goddess Mazu, worshipped on the "Amagao," "cape of Ama," before the Portuguese arrived there.[27]

---

[25] Geiss, "The Chia-ching Reign," pp. 494–504; John E. Wills, Jr., "Maritime China from Wang Chih to Shih Lang: Themes in Peripheral History," in Jonathan D. Spence and John E. Wills, Jr., eds., *From Ming to Ch'ing: Conquest, Region, and Continuity in Seventeenth-Century China* (New Haven, CT, 1979), pp. 210–213; Charles O. Hucker, "Hu Tsung-hsien's Campaign Against Hsu Hai, 1556," in Frank A. Kierman, Jr., and John K. Fairbank, eds., *Chinese Ways in Warfare* (Cambridge, MA, 1974), pp. 273–307; Lin Renchuan, *Mingmo Qingchu siren haishang maoyi* (Shanghai, 1987), pp. 85–111.

[26] One of the earliest surviving references to this date is that of Mendes Pinto; Fernão Mendes Pinto, *The Travels of Mendes Pinto*, ed. and trans. Rebecca D. Catz (Chicago, 1989), p. 508.

[27] Tang Kaijian, *Weiliduo "Baoxiao shimo shu" Jianzheng* (Guangzhou, 2004), pp. 2–4, 49–59; the text was preserved in Han Lin, *Souyu quanshu*, and was first noticed by Huang Yinong. I am grateful to Professor Tang for bringing this important work to my attention.

Still better documented is the first phase of the acceptance of the Portuguese, before 1557.[28] Portuguese private trade on islands off the Guangdong coast probably had begun immediately after the debacles in Zhejiang and Fujian in 1548 and 1549. The first initiative toward a more formal presence was taken by the viceroy at Goa in 1552, with the dispatch at the suggestion of the Jesuit Francis Xavier of one Diogo Pereira as ambassador to China.[29] The Portuguese governor at Melaka did not allow Pereira to proceed beyond that point, perhaps out of fear that he might intrude on the dominance of Melaka merchants in Portuguese trade with Japan and China. Xavier, who had accompanied Pereira and had hoped to gain entrance to China in connection with the embassy, went on without it and died on Shangchuan Island off the Guangdong coast a few months later.

A much more successful initiative was taken by a private Portuguese merchant named Leonel de Sousa, who also arrived on the Guangdong coast in 1552. His own letter of 1556 is our main source on this episode and one of the most important documents in the history of Sino-Portuguese relations.[30] Sousa's success was a result of his own recognition, consonant with his own preoccupation with trade and distance from the absurd bellicosity of the first generations of Portuguese in Asia, that profitable trade with China would require accommodation with Chinese interests and authorities, especially in view of the reputation for violence the Portuguese had acquired in the past. He was lucky to find a counterpart equally distant from past Chinese preoccupations, and ready to work out a local accommodation, in "the haidao," the vice-commissioner for the maritime defense circuit, Wang Bo, who is identified in Chinese sources as having accepted bribes from the Portuguese and allowed them to land their goods "to dry them out" and to pay taxes and trade at Canton.

---

[28] A pioneering English-language synthesis of much of the following was provided in J. M. Braga, *The Western Pioneers and their Discovery of Macau* (Macao, 1949).

[29] Rui Manuel Loureiro, *Fidalgos, Missionários, e Mandarins. Portugal e a China no Século XVI* (Lisbon, 2000), pp. 556–560.

[30] This letter first was published in 1910 by Jordão de Freitas. See Freitas, *Macau: Materiais para a sua História no Seculo XVI* (reprint, Macao, 1988); on the "ground rent" issue see pp. 20–21. It is also available in Arquivo Nacional da Torre do Tombo, ed., *As Gavetas da Torre do Tombo*, 12 vols. (Lisbon, 1960–1977), Vol. 1, pp. 909–915. For Chinese references to Wang Bo "concealing the name" of the foreigners and permitting their trade, see Li Qingxin, *Mingdai haiwai maoyi zhidu* (Beijing, 2007), pp. 262–263; the most complete study of Chinese sources on Macao under the Ming can be found on pp. 236–267, 346–432.

In 1552 Sousa learned that all foreigners were being allowed to trade upon payment of duties "except the Ferengi, who were people with filthy hearts ... whom they took for pirates." He urged the other Portuguese trading in the area to keep the peace, secured their agreement to pay duties if they were allowed to trade, and arranged to "change their name" so that they would no longer be identified with the hated Ferengi. He told Wang Bo they would pay only 10 percent duty; Wang said that the imperial duty was 20 percent but that he would accommodate them for the time being by levying that duty on only half their goods. Many Portuguese went to Canton and traded there with no difficulty, concealing so many of their goods from the tax collectors that they paid duty on only about one-third of them. Wang was received ceremoniously on the Portuguese ships, to his great satisfaction. He granted Sousa jurisdiction over the people on all sixteen ships, Portuguese and Southeast Asian, that were trading in the area. In all this Sousa was helped by a wealthier merchant, Simão d'Almeida, who got things done much more quickly by giving gifts to Wang Bo and his subordinates. It may have been at this time that it was agreed that the vice-commissioner for the maritime circuit would be paid 500 taels per year; according to Macao local tradition, this remained a private payment to "the haidao" until 1571 or 1572, when, the payment being made in the presence of other officials, a quick-witted commissioner saved himself from suspicion by identifying it as a "ground rent" payment to the imperial treasury for the settlement at Macao. When Simão d'Almeida left, Wang suggested that an embassy be sent to regularize the status of the Portuguese. Thus when Sousa sailed for Melaka in the fall of 1554, secure foundations had been laid for the accommodation of the Portuguese on the Guangdong coast, without any reference to the court in Beijing or to any aspect of its policies other than the taxation of foreign trade.

Between 1552 and 1557 there was a gradual shift of the center of Portuguese activity from Shangchuan, where Francis Xavier had found Portuguese trading in 1552, to "Lampacao" (Langbaigao), farther east and much closer inshore, and on to Macao. The best description from this period is provided by the Jesuit Belchior Nunes, who spent the winter of 1555–1556 at Lampacao on his way to Japan.[31] There were three to four hundred Portuguese there that winter, in rude thatched dwellings, so disorderly that the Jesuits had all they could do to keep them from

---

[31] Antonio Francisco Cardim, S.J., *Cartas que os Padres e Irmãos da Companhia de Iesus escreverão dos Reynos de Iapao & China*, 2 vols. (Evora, 1598; reprint, Tenri, Japan, 1972), Vol. 1, fol. 32v–37.

killing each other. Father Belchior went to Canton, probably along with Portuguese merchants trading there, in a vain attempt to procure the release from captivity of a Portuguese captured in Fujian several years earlier. No doubt the shift of the center of Portuguese activity to Macao continued in 1557. A letter from Father Gregorio González, only recently noticed and still unpublished, describes his staying there to minister some Portuguese traders and perhaps Chinese converts and, in 1557, for the first time being allowed to stay there for the winter and not being forced to tear down their temporary wood and straw houses. This is probably as close as we will ever come to confirming that 1557 was in some way Macao's date of birth as a permanent Portuguese settlement.[32]

By 1562 it was estimated that there were eight to nine hundred Portuguese at Macao. They had two modest churches and some houses more comfortable and substantial than the straw sheds of Lampacao. Francis Xavier had written to the viceroy at Goa deploring the blocking at Melaka of Diogo Pereira's embassy and urging that it be sent; this finally was done, Pereira reaching Macao in 1563. Initial reactions by the Canton officials suggested that it might be accepted as a tribute embassy; the presents were very carefully inspected, and a high official who came to Macao to check on the embassy seemed very pleased by his splendid reception. The officials suggested that some additional presents be sent from Goa, including two elephants, and the Jesuits took this seriously enough to write to Goa urging compliance. But nothing came from Goa, there were "many delays," and finally the Chinese authorities asked two key questions: Had they brought the document given to the previous embassy? (This probably referred to the order to the Portuguese to give up Melaka.) Why had they taken Melaka? With these questions, which seem to have come some time in 1565, it was clear that the embassy was not going to be received. Macao would continue to develop completely outside the rules and precedents of the tribute system. But just at that moment, a Jesuit letter tells us, "God opened an unexpected path, which Diogo Pereira in his vigilance knew how to use." Mutinous soldiers from farther up the coast occupied an area near Guangzhou and terrorized shipping. An official asked for Portuguese help, and Macao sent three hundred men, concealing their guns on Chinese junks for greater surprise; the mutineers fled as soon as the Portuguese opened fire.[33] The broad outlines of this story are confirmed by Chinese sources; the official was Yu

---

[32] Loureiro, *Fidalgos*, pp. 543–545.
[33] Freitas, *Macau*, pp. 30–35.

Dayou, a prominent commander in Ming coastal pacification efforts in these years. Another distinguished official, Pang Shangpeng, submitted in these years an analysis suggesting that it was futile to try to expel the foreigners from Macao, and it would be better to keep troops near them and under close control.[34] Macao would be outside the tribute system, tolerated but closely watched, its usefulness tacitly recognized.

A stronger and more surprising base in the 1560s for the Portuguese master narrative of pirate chasing and the "golden chop" in 1557 is found in the stories an able soldier named Tristam Vaz da Veiga told a local historian of the island of Madeira in the Atlantic about 1585–1590.[35] (Vaz had gone on from Macao to participate in two defenses of Melaka against Aceh attack in the 1570s and to make a prudent decision to surrender a fortress in Portugal to the new Spanish monarch, for which he was rewarded with command over all military forces on Madeira.) Returning early in 1568 from a voyage to Japan, Vaz found his trade at Macao delayed because some of the Portuguese had not paid their tolls, "and no trade is done without that." So he was not able to continue on the north monsoon, and on June 12, 1568, was present when a fleet of about a hundred Chinese pirate ships, forty of them large, appeared off Macao. The next day the pirates started to land, at least three thousand of them, half carrying muskets. Vaz led against them fewer than ninety Portuguese "and their slaves." African slaves could be formidable warriors, even in defense of their masters, and there may have been more than three hundred of them, but still the pirates outnumbered the defenders by eight or ten to one. Vaz thought it surely was God's work that the defenders repelled the pirates four times that day, with thirteen or fourteen dead on their side and forty to fifty pirates. Over eight days they repelled more attacks on land and at least one on Vaz's ship, and estimated that as many as six hundred pirates had been killed. An official came down and arranged a truce, and the pirates withdrew to Nanao; later they may have attacked up the river, even to the city of Canton. Vaz and Belchior Carneiro, the newly arrived bishop, now organized the entire population, rich and poor, Portuguese, Chinese, and slaves, in constructing in just eighteen days a mud-brick wall around Macao. This was the first time

[34] Zhou Jinglian, *Zhong Pu waijiao shi* (Shanghai, 1936), pp. 64–65, 72–73; Fei Chengkang, *Aomen sibai nian* (Shanghai, 1988), pp. 27–28.

[35] Gaspar Frutuoso, *Livro 2°das Saudades da Terra. Em que se Trata do Descobrimento da Ilha de Madeira e suas Adjacentes e da Vida e Progenie dos Illustres Capitães Dellas*, introduction and notes Damião Peres (Porto, 1926), pp. 151–156. I owe my knowledge of this valuable and out-of-the-way source to Loureiro, *Fidalgos*, pp. 581–582, 587.

the Ming authorities had tolerated any fortifications. The officials now recruited about fifty Portuguese and some slaves and Christian Chinese to go on the war junks to attach the pirates; they took eleven of their twenty-three ships. Vaz recalled that after this the captains-major had to find ways to turn aside many Chinese requests for such assistance.

## MACAO AND NAGASAKI, 1572–1640

In 1567 a carefully limited and controlled maritime trade in Chinese ships, based at Haicheng in the Zhangzhou estuary, Fujian, was legalized. Haicheng was the new name for Yuegang, which had been the center of a never-suppressed illegal trade, some of which now flowed into the new legal channel. Quotas were established for the number of ships allowed to sail to each foreign port each year. Fairly soon, if not immediately, taxes were levied on this trade in two forms: "measurement" fees on each ship according to its size and tariffs on various kinds of goods according to an elaborate schedule of rates. The precedents for this mode of taxation are obscure but seem to be entirely domestic, in tolls collected around Beijing and at Shanhaiguan early in the sixteenth century.[36] A further consolidation of this opening took place at the end of 1578, in the midst of Zhang Juzheng's efforts to strengthen provincial administration and tax collection, on the initiative of his man in Guangdong, Ling Yunyi; foreign trade in Chinese shipping was explicitly permitted and taxation of it regularized.[37] Manila soon became one of the destinations. Trade to Japan was never legal, but some of it was probably carried on under the small quotas for Danshui and Jilong on Taiwan. Once the Portuguese were well settled at Macao, their ships going up to trade at the Canton fairs seem to have been taxed under a similar system; Ljungstedt places the permission of Portuguese big ships going up to anchorages near Guangzhou and

---

[36] *Ming Shi*, 81:19, entry for Jiajing eighth year (1529); Wada Sei, ed., *Minshi shokkashi yakuchū*. 2 vols., Tōyō bunko ronsō, No. 44 (Tokyo, 1960), 867–871; Eduard B. Vermeer, "Up to the Mountain and Out to the Sea: The Expansion of the Fukienese in the Late Ming Period," in Murray A. Rubinstein, ed., *Taiwan: A History, 1660– 1994* (Armonk, NY, 1999), pp. 73–74; Li Qingxin, *Mingdai haiwai maoyi zhidu*, pp. 257–259. Taxation of ships by measurement as early as 1550 is mentioned cryptically in the important text of Fr. Gaspar da Cruz, O.P., who even notes the same practice in Siam, where émigré Chinese were already influential; Boxer, *South China*, p. 204. Gang Zhao, "Geopolitical Integration and Domestic Harmony: Foreign Trade Policy in Qing China, 1684–1757" (Typescript, 2009), pp. 70–73, notes the tentative and local nature of this opening. But precedents were established, and in any case much trade was completely out of official control.

[37] Li Qingxin, *Mingdai haiwai maoyi zhidu*, pp. 383–384.

being taxed there in 1578–1579.[38] The Haicheng opening looks modest and tentative, but it set the stage for the entire development of administration of foreign trade discussed in these chapters; the "measurements" and tariffs applied to the great Canton trade in the eighteenth century were its direct derivatives, also often linked to policy for the taxation of domestic trade, and having no connection with the precedents for trade of tribute embassies and the old Superintendencies of Maritime Trade.[39]

Between 1572 and 1590 an institutional framework emerged both in the Guangdong bureaucracy and within the little Portuguese settlement that made Macao controllable and tolerable in the view of the Chinese bureaucracy. These changes are poorly documented in Chinese sources, and the Portuguese sources on them are largely second- or third-hand, but the general pattern seems clear enough, and its efficacy in actual operation can be seen in many well-documented instances from later decades. We have almost no evidence on connections with Chinese political contexts, but it may be useful to notice that these developments began in the years of Zhang Juzheng's efforts at fiscal reform and revived central control and continued at a time when there was a sharp decline in administrative energy at the center but still many instances of competence and reforming energy in the provinces.[40] In sharp contrast to the Fujian bureaucracy's conflicts with Manila, the Dutch, and the Chinese merchants of Haicheng after 1600, there is no evidence that the activities of eunuch tax collectors and mining intendants caused any substantial difficulty in Macao–Guangdong relations; when the notorious Gao Cai who caused so much trouble in Fujian tried to extend his depredations to Guangdong, he was met by firm resistance with excellent court connections and was recalled to the capital.[41]

[38] Sir Andrew Ljungstedt, *An Historical Sketch of the Portuguese Settlements in China* (Boston, 1836), pp. 66–72.

[39] Pin-tsun Chang, *Chinese Maritime Trade*, pp. 261–290; Charles W. MacSherry, *Impairment of the Ming Tribute System as Exhibited in Trade through Fukien* (Ph.D. dissertation, University of California at Berkeley, 1956), Ch. 4; Lin Renchuan, *Mingmo Qingchu siren haishang maoyi*, pp. 142–153, 287–303; Li Qingxin, *Mingdai haiwai maoyi zhidu*, pp. 312–345; Bodo Wiethoff, *Die chinesische Seeverbotspolitik und der private Überseehandel von 1368 bis 1567*, Mittelilungen der Gesellschaft für Natur- und Völkerkunde Ostasiens, Hamburg, No. 45 (Wiesbaden, 1963), pp. 104–125; Timothy Brook, "Communications and Commerce," in Denis Twitchett and Frederick W. Mote, eds., *CHOC*, Vol. 8: *The Ming Dynasty Part, 1368–1644, Part 2*, pp. 619, 695–699.

[40] For a vivid picture of these years at the imperial court see Ray Huang, *1587, A Year of No Significance: The Ming Dynasty in Decline* (New Haven, CT, 1981). See also Ray Huang, "The Lung-ch'ing and Wan-li Reigns, 1567–1620," in Mote and Twitchett, eds., *CHOC*, Vol. 7, pp. 511–584.

[41] Li Qingxin, *Mingdai haiwai maoyi zhidu*, pp. 423–432.

We already have noticed the story that a customary bribe became a fixed ground rent payment in 1571 or 1572. The next step, and a crucial one, was taken in 1573, when a wall and gate, the "Circle Gate" (Porta do Cerco), were erected at a narrow point on the peninsula on which Macao stands, and the Portuguese and other foreigners were forbidden to go beyond it.[42] Almost no agricultural land was left on the Macao side of the barrier. Macao thus was instantly and permanently reduced to dependence on a food supply that the Chinese officials could cut off at any time. Further steps toward regularization of the status of Macao were taken in the next decade. Although it is clear that the Portuguese had been trading at Canton long before this, it is likely that as their trade grew new regulations were worked out for their trade at the two annual "fairs" there.[43] In 1582 Alonso Sanchez, S.J., came from Manila to announce the accession of Philip II of Spain to the Crown of Portugal, news that was far from welcome to the Portuguese of Macao but did not really have much effect on their control of the local situation. Nonetheless, Chen Rui, the governor-general of Guangdong and Guangxi, became suspicious and summoned representatives of Macao to his seat of government at Zhaoqing. At first, say our sources, they were severely reprimanded for using foreign laws to govern themselves on Chinese territory, but later explanations and gifts did their work.[44] It probably was after this confrontation that the Crown attorney (*procurador*) at Macao was recognized by the Guangdong authorities as "supervisor of foreigners" (*yi mu*) there.[45] Under these circumstances it is understandable that the Portuguese residents felt the need to formalize as far as possible their right to govern themselves, dealing with the Chinese officials as they saw fit and minimizing interference from their overlords in Goa or in distant and alien Madrid. In 1583 an assembly of residents presided over by the bishop agreed to petition the authorities in Goa and Madrid for the grant of a formal charter of municipal government.[46] A charter granting Macao all the privileges of the city of Évora in Portugal was granted by the viceroy in Goa in 1586 and confirmed by the king in 1595.[47]

---

[42] Zhang Rulin and Yin Guangren, *Aomen jilue* (1751), 1:2, 1:23.

[43] T'ien-tse Chang, *Sino-Portuguese Trade from 1514 to 1644* (Leiden, 1933; reprint 1969), pp. 102–103.

[44] Ljungstedt, *Historical Sketch*, p. 79; George H. Dunne, S.J., *Generation of Giants: The Story of the Jesuits in China in the Last Decades of the Ming Dynasty* (Notre Dame, IN, 1982), pp. 19–22.

[45] T'ien-tse Chang, *Sino-Portuguese Trade*, p. 101.

[46] C. A. Montalto de Jesus, *Historic Macao* (Hong Kong, 1902), pp. 36–37.

[47] The most reliable source for this is *Instrução para o Bispo de Pequim, e Outros Documentos para a História de Macau* (Lisbon, 1943), p. 142.

The municipal government established elaborate customary proce-
dures for the indirect election of three aldermen, two magistrates, and
the attorney, who formed the famous Loyal Senate (Leal Senado). Every
three years, three pairs of electors were chosen by a presiding magistrate
or judge after consultation with all citizens. Each pair of electors then
compiled a list of three names for each office to be filled. These lists were
sorted by the presiding officer into three lists for the three years, each of
which was sealed in a ball of wax, and the balls of wax placed in a bag
in a locked chest. On New Year's Eve or New Year's Day, one of those
lists was drawn at random by a small boy, and the individuals listed
in it were to hold office for the next year; vacancies owing to death or
absence were filled by election at that time. Former magistrates and other
worthy people would be summoned to a general assembly, especially during crises in municipal finance or relations with the Chinese.[48] Down to
1623 the captain-major in charge of the Japan–China voyage had some
authority when he was present in Macao; thereafter there was a resident
royally appointed captain-general, but his only sphere of real authority
was the little garrison.

Thus decision-making power was almost entirely in the hands of
resident merchant oligarchs with a vested interest in the long-run survival and prosperity of Macao, who knew how to deal with the Chinese
authorities and knew, despite the indignant trumpetings of captains-major
and captains-general about Portuguese honor and craven submission to
the mandarins, that Macao was completely at the mercy of the Chinese
state. Any time they forgot, the officials would bring them to their senses
by leaving the gate closed for a few weeks. The merchant oligarchs also
administered the Holy House of Mercy (Santa Casa de Misericórdia), a
powerful lay brotherhood for charity that cared for many of the poor and
ill and invested its capital, derived from bequests, in Macao's maritime
trade.[49] The city expressed its Catholic piety in large and fervent processions and in the support of many churches, monasteries, and convents
and many missionaries. The most powerful religious establishment, that
of the Jesuits, was a great asset in diplomacy with the Chinese and controlled so much wealth that it became a major investor in foreign trade.

---

[48] C. R. Boxer, *Portuguese Society in the Tropics: The Municipal Councils of Goa, Macau,
Bahia, and Luanda, 1510–1800* (Madison, WI, 1965), pp. 6–7, 42–71, 167–176.

[49] George Bryan Souza, *The Survival of Empire: Portuguese Trade and Society in China and
the South China Sea, 1630–1754* (Cambridge, 1986), pp. 27–29; Isabel dos Guimarães
Sá, "Charity, Ritual, and Business at the Edge of Empire: The Misericórdia of Macau,"
in Liam Matthew Brockey, ed., *Portuguese Colonial Cities in the Early Modern World*
(Burlington, VT, 2008), pp. 149–173.

Between 1590 and 1610 Macao was at the heyday of its prosperity, serving as a key linking point between the growing worldwide network of European sea routes and the overheated energies of the economy and society of late Ming China, playing an especially crucial role in the export of raw silk and silk fabrics to Japan in return for large quantities of silver. In peak years in the early 1600s it seems likely that about 1,000,000 taels of silver per year flowed from Japan to China in Portuguese and Chinese ships, with a few peak years more than 2,000,000. If something close to half of this silver arrived in Portuguese ships at a Guangdong port instead of in Chinese ships at some point on the coast of Fujian or Zhejiang, this certainly was a substantial contribution to the commercial growth of Canton and its hinterland.[50]

Despite the benefits of this trade, there was much about Macao that made the people of Guangdong uneasy. Any Chinese who went there found the streets full of strange-looking people of all types and colors, European Portuguese and slaves and mestizos from all around the Indian Ocean. The alien architecture, the religious processions, the ringing of the church bells all told him he wasn't in China. The streets were unsafe at night and sometimes in broad daylight. Elsewhere in Guangdong, the presence of Catholic converts in many localities probably aroused antagonism, which in turn affected attitudes toward Macao. Episodes of African slaves escaping from their Portuguese masters into Guangdong were another source of aversion. Already around 1580, Matteo Ricci had discovered that he had to carefully disassociate himself from Macao if he wanted to be welcomed by the Guangdong elite.[51] Around 1600 an anonymous Guangdong man was quoted as saying that Macao no longer was part of Guangdong.[52] Poets wrote about the dangers of "dragons in the water," quite different from the rain-bringing thunder dragons of the northern plains.[53]

In the 1590s Hideyoshi's invasions of Korea distracted court attention from the south coast, but reinforced perceptions of the Japanese

[50] C. R. Boxer, *The Christian Century in Japan, 1540–1650* (Berkeley, CA, 1951), pp. 105–109, and Boxer, The *Great Ship from Amacon: Annals of Macao and the Old Japan Trade, 1555–1640* (Lisbon, 1859; reprint, 1988), pp. 6, 153, 183, 196. The question of the effects of silver imports and silk exports on the Ming economy in general is discussed later in this chapter, in connection with the Manila trade.
[51] Jonathan D. Spence, *The Memory Palace of Matteo Ricci* (New York: Viking, 1984), pp. 192–193.
[52] Shen Yourong et al., *Minhai zengyan*, Taiwan wenxian congkan, No. 56 (Taipei, 1959), p. 34.
[53] Li Qingxin, *Mingdai haiwai maoyi zhidu*, pp. 396–397.

as dangerous enemies.[54] Thereafter, Japanese expansion of trade with Southeast Asia, probes toward Taiwan, and the Satsuma conquest of the Ryukyus in 1609 shifted attention back toward possible Japanese threats on the south coast. At the same time, around 1600, court-centered factional strife was strongly echoed in local struggles between eunuch mine and tax commissioners and out-of-power officials involved in the politics of their home areas and frequently allied with merchant interests. The revived perception of a Japanese threat enhanced Macao's attractiveness as a neutral channel for obtaining Japanese silver without allowing Japanese on the Chinese coast or worrying about Chinese traders to Japan colluding with the Japanese. This attractiveness, however, could be very easily offset by any hint that the Portuguese were tolerating a Japanese presence in Macao.

For policy toward Macao in these years, a key figure was Dai Yao, governor-general of Guangdong and Guangxi from 1597 to 1610. The *Ming Shi* blames him for "valuing the precious goods [of the Portuguese], pretending to forbid but secretly allowing the evil to continue to grow." Dai was a native of Changtai *xian* in Zhangzhou, Fujian, and it is likely that connections with the Fujian traders who had been in the Macao area longer than the Portuguese influenced his attitudes. Dai was praised for reducing taxes and labor services; there even was a reduction in the tax quota on Macao's trade in 1606.[55] It also is important to notice that in 1600 Zhang Dayou, the magistrate of Xiangshan *xian*, in which Macao was located, managed to turn away an effort of the eunuch tax commissioner Li Feng to settle in Xiangshan, arguing that "the nature of the foreigners is unfathomable; if by any chance they should attack the bearer of imperial orders, what could be done [to avoid an insult to] the awesome virtue of the Court?"[56]

In Dai Yao's years in power, events and rumors repeatedly reinforced Chinese negative attitudes toward Macao, but no changes in policy resulted. In 1598 the Spanish of Manila attempted to establish their own trading post in the Canton estuary. They were well received in Canton, spent about 7,000 reals on presents, and were told they could establish themselves at a place they called El Piñal, "Pine Grove," the location of which is unknown. The Portuguese, having failed to persuade the Canton

---

[54] Kenneth M. Swope, *A Dragon's Head and a Serpent's Tail: Ming China and the First Great East Asian War, 1592–1598* (Norman, OK, 2009).

[55] Zhang Weihua, *Mingshi Folangji*, pp. 52–53, 62–63; Fei Chengkang, *Aomen sibai nian*, p. 92.

[56] Zhou Jinglian, *Zhong Pu waijiao shi*, p. 93.

authorities that they should exclude the Spanish, took direct action, launching an unsuccessful fireship attack, but desisted after the Chinese reduced Macao's food supply. Later they attacked a storm-damaged Spanish ship elsewhere in the estuary. When a larger ship came from Manila to El Piñal in 1599, the Macaenses reportedly traded with it. Nevertheless, the Spanish did not leave anyone behind at El Piñal at the end of that trading season and did not repeat the experiment.[57]

In 1601, when the first Dutch ship to appear in Chinese waters anchored near Macao, the Portuguese captured a party sent to sound the coastal waters and executed seventeen of the twenty Dutch captives. The Ming authorities might have concluded from this and the El Piñal episode that the Portuguese presence at Macao was likely to draw conflicts among foreigners to their coasts. They did not; Macao was controllable when necessary, and perhaps even of some use in controlling other foreigners. The Dutch probe is noted in Ming records, but no trace has been found in them of the El Piñal events.

Much more worrisome to the Chinese were signs of Japanese infiltration at Macao and the effects of the tricky relations among Japanese, Jesuits, and Portuguese in this period. New fortifications of Macao, stimulated especially by the likelihood that the Dutch would return, alarmed the Chinese; the Portuguese might be less controllable if they were more able to defend themselves. The great Jesuit church of São Paulo, which was built in these years and on which much of the work was done by Japanese Christian artisans, looked to the Chinese very much like a fortification. Even more alarming was the rise of a thick-walled Jesuit church on Ilha Verde (Qingzhou), a small island at the inner end of Macao's Inner Harbor. The Portuguese were ordered to destroy their buildings on Ilha Verde, and some walls may have been pulled down. Then in 1606 the people of nearby regions of Guangdong were alarmed by rumors that the Portuguese planned to invade China, relying on Japanese and Malay auxiliaries and on the many Chinese who would join them. It was said that the invaders planned to set up the Jesuit Father Lazaro Cattaneo as emperor.[58] There was rioting in Macao, and a Chinese Christian was tortured to death as a spy in Canton. In 1607 Dutch ships attempting to

---

[57] Boxer, *Great Ship*, pp. 61–62; Barros and Couto, *Da Asia*, XII.II.XI; Antonio de Morga, *Sucesos de las Islas Filipinas*, ed. and trans. J. S. Cummins, Hakluyt Society, Second Series, No. 140 (London, 1971), pp. 136–138, 148–149.

[58] These rumors were started as a result of a nasty personal quarrel among Macao churchmen; Dunne, *Generation of Giants*, pp. 118–120.

trade not far from Macao were treated warily by the Chinese because of rumors that they had two hundred Japanese warriors aboard, and then were chased away by the Portuguese. In 1608 it seemed that the worst fears of the Chinese had come true. Japanese sailors and warriors returning from a trading voyage to Vietnam walked through the streets of Macao heavily armed, and finally serious fighting broke out in which many Japanese were killed.[59]

The Portuguese had had to tread carefully in dealing with the Japanese intruders because they were closely connected with the powerful Nagasaki officials on whom Portuguese trade in Japan depended. The 1608 incident led directly to a series of conflicts at Nagasaki in 1609–1610 that ended in the blowing up of the great ship *Madre de Deus*, but at Macao the violence did not continue. In 1606 a Cantonese scholar in Beijing for the metropolitan examination had proposed that the "various foreigners" be moved from Macao to Lampacao, but his proposal had been rejected.[60] Debate revived after Zhang Minggang replaced Dai Yao as governorgeneral in 1610. Some advocated driving the Portuguese away entirely. We have a text of the memorial of one Guo Shangbin advocating the expulsion of all Japanese and blacks and ordering the Portuguese to leave Macao and "trade at Lampacao as before," which probably implies no permanent settlement. With its references to Portuguese evasions of customs duties and harboring of Japanese, blacks, and Chinese desperadoes, Guo's memorial is the fullest reflection we have of Ming negative attitudes toward Macao.

In 1613, according to a Portuguese translation of a lost Chinese text, Macao was forced to expel ninety-eight Japanese and was forbidden to allow any more to come.[61] Beyond that, Governor-General Zhang did not accept Guo's drastic proposals, arguing that it was easier to control the Portuguese where they were, with Ming troops close by on several sides and easy control over the city's food supply. Late in 1614 he sent officials to proclaim a full set of regulations that the Portuguese were to obey to the letter in the future. They were engraved on a stone tablet, which was set up in front of the hall of the Loyal Senate, probably in 1617, which is the date given in an accurate Portuguese summary. Their five points

[59] Boxer, *Christian Century*, pp. 269–271, 287–288; Boxer, *Fidalgos in the Far East* (1948; reprint, Oxford, 1968), pp. 53–62; see later in the chapter on the Dutch voyages.
[60] Zhang Weihua, *Mingshi Folangji*, p. 61; Zhou Jinglian, *Zhong Pu waijiao shi*, p. 95.
[61] *Instrução para o Bispo de Pequim*, pp. 115–116, misdated 1579 but with the correct date of Wanli 41 in the text.

were as follows: (1) Macao must not harbor Japanese. (2) The buying of Chinese people is forbidden. (3) All ships, including warships, must pay duties and must come into Macao's Inner Harbor; anchoring and trading in the outer islands are strictly forbidden. (4) Trade must be conducted at Canton, not at Macao, and duties on goods must be paid there. (5) New construction in Macao is strictly forbidden; old structures may be repaired or rebuilt to match their previous condition. These regulations, and their revisions and expansions in the 1740s, were fundamental to Chinese policy toward Macao down to the nineteenth century, Macao's charter for survival through submission.[62]

For the next few years tension focused on Portuguese building in Macao, especially of anything that could be viewed as a fortification. The Chinese bureaucracy and elite were viewing the alien presence at Macao in the contexts of the deepest eunuch–scholar-official conflicts of the entire dynasty and the emergence of the military threats of Chinese pirates on the coast, mounted Chinese rebels in the northwest, and the rise of the Manchu state in the northeast.[63] In 1621 the Jesuits were forced to demolish their church on Ilha Verde, and the Ming garrison at the Circle Gate was strengthened somewhat and placed under a higher-ranking officer.[64] In 1622 the Dutch attempted to conquer Macao and were driven off by a lucky shot into a Dutch powder barrel and a wild charge of Portuguese and slaves.[65] We have *nothing* in Chinese on this episode, but we do have a Jesuit report on a defense of Macao that the Jesuits insisted had been offered in the capital by the distinguished convert Ignatius Sun Yuanhua. Sun argued, according to the Jesuits, that the city of Macao had maintained peace with the Chinese for many years and had offered its cannoneers for service against the Manchus (as described later). Now the seas were full of European pirates (referring to the Dutch). That Macao had been built was the fault of those who had been enticed by petty profits and had permitted it. "But at present there was no other way to defend the empire on that side against the Dutch pirates."[66] Another clue to the reactions of provincial officials is to be found in a Portuguese document

[62] Zhang Weihua, *Mingshi Folangji*, pp. 64–67; Zhang and Yin, *Aomen jilue*, 1:24v–25v; *Instrução para o Bispo de Pequim*, pp. 116–118.
[63] William S. Atwell, "The T'ai-ch'ang, T'ien-ch'i, and Ch'ung-chen reigns, 1620–1644," in Mote and Twitchett, eds., *CHOC*, Vol. 7, pp. 590–640.
[64] Zhang Weihua, *Mingshi Folangji*, p. 68; Zhang and Yin, *Aomen jilue*, 1:1v.
[65] Boxer, *Fidalgos*, Ch. 5.
[66] *Histoire de ce qui s'est Passé au Royaume de la Chine en l'Année 1624* (Paris, 1629), pp. 22–24 (anonymous, attributed to V. P. Kirwitzer, S.J.).

of 1623, which tells us that in the course of efforts to persuade the Ming authorities to keep some new fortifications, "more bribes were given and some mandarins came to see the great ships of the enemy and the dead who lay on the field of battle, from which they took some heads back to Canton to prove that the walls we wanted to build were only to defend the city which was the territory of the King of China."[67] A Chinese text states, however, that the Chinese did force the destruction of some walls in these years.[68]

Macao may have won some toleration for itself by obediently expelling the Japanese and by fending off the Dutch, but when the Portuguese sought to solidify their position by sending troops to aid the Ming against the rising Manchu power, they encountered much more intricate political difficulties. In 1623 the distinguished Catholic converts Xu Guangqi and Li Zhizao proposed that the Portuguese train Ming soldiers in the use of cannons. A small group of Portuguese artillerymen were brought to Beijing, but at one of their demonstrations a cannon exploded, killing a Portuguese and three Chinese. Shen Que and other opponents of the Jesuits and their converts took this opportunity to denounce this effort, and soon the gunners were sent back to Macao. In 1630 a small group of gunners again were sent and apparently participated effectively in the defense of Zhuozhou against a Manchu attack. Now the project expanded to the enlistment of several hundred Macao soldiers to serve the Ming. They got as far as Nanchang in Jiangxi, then were turned back; they may have been stopped by the efforts of the Guangdong trading interest and its bureaucratic allies, who did not want the Portuguese to have any channels of trade and communication in China that they did not control. A few went on to join the garrison of Dengzhou, Shandong, where most of them were killed when the city was taken by the northeastern warlord Kong Youde in 1632.[69]

Macao's ambivalent relations with the people and officials of Guangdong rarely imperiled its survival or even its prosperity. The main

---

[67] "Relação sobre a fundação e fortificação de Macau," November 27, 1623, published in Francisco Paulo Mendes da Luz, *O Conselho da India. Contributo ao Estudo da História da Administraçao e do Comércio do Ultramar Portugués nos Principios do Século XVII* (Lisbon, 1952), pp. 614–615.

[68] Zhou Jinglian, *Zhong Pu waijiao shi*, p. 89; Zhang and Yin, *Aomen jilue*, 2:22v–23.

[69] C. R. Boxer, "Portuguese Military Expeditions in Aid of the Mings Against the Manchus, 1621–1647," *T'ien-hsia Monthly*, Vol. 7, No. 1 (August 1938), 24–50; Goodrich and Fang, *Dictionary of Ming Biography*, pp. 414, 1147; Arthur W. Hummel, ed., *Eminent Chinese of the Ch'ing Period*, 2 vols. (Washington, DC, 1943–1944), pp. 435–436; Dunne, *Generation of Giants*, pp. 215–218.

determinant of the latter was the attitude of the Japanese toward Catholicism and by extension toward the Portuguese, who always had been so closely associated with it. The spectacular rise of Macao had depended on the great desire of various territorial lords to attract the "black ships" to their realms, as well as on the expanding silver production that made their purchases of Chinese goods possible. This unambiguously hospitable phase had an early peak, in the granting of Nagasaki to the Society of Jesus in 1580. Signs of an anti-Christian reaction began with Hideyoshi's anti-Christian edicts of 1587 and became really serious with the measures taken in 1612–1614.[70]

However, the Chinese, the Dutch, and the English still offered no adequate alternative channel of supply of Chinese goods to the burgeoning Japanese market. As late as the early 1630s, as the Japanese took increasingly severe measures to forbid their own maritime trade and to repress Catholicism, turmoil on the China coast and Dutch bungling of their relations with the Japanese inhibited the emergence of alternative sources of supply. About 1637 both the Dutch and their Chinese competitors and trading partners were settling down to peaceful trade. In a rapidly changing situation, the Portuguese were borrowing both in Japan and in China to maintain their competitive position, and their experience and established connections made them formidable rivals. It was not commercial change but the Shimabara rebellion of 1637 that doomed Portuguese trade in Japan and thereby doomed Macao to irremediable decline and poverty. The Portuguese were expelled from Japan in 1639 and forbidden to return, but only after the Japanese authorities made sure that alternative channels of foreign trade, especially Dutch and Korean, would continue.[71] When Macao sent an embassy in 1640 to plead for reconsideration, the entire embassy party was executed except for a few who were to carry the news to Macao.[72]

Macao never recovered from the loss of this leading line of trade. Dutch attacks on Portuguese shipping in the Straits of Melaka were followed in 1641 by the Dutch conquest of Melaka, depriving Macao of a key link for its trade to India. Macao sent a party of soldiers to aid the Ming loyalist Yongli emperor and suffered severely from all the wars and dislocations

[70] Boxer, *Great Ship*; Boxer, *Christian Century*; Jurgis Elisonas, "Christianity and the Daimyo," in Hall, ed., *The Cambridge History of Japan*, pp. 301–372.

[71] Ronald P. Toby, *State and Diplomacy in Early Modern Japan: Asia in the Development of the Tokugawa Bakufu* (Princeton, NJ, 1984), p. 9.

[72] Benjamim Videira Pires, S.J., *Embaixada Martir* (Macao, 1965).

of trade of the Ming–Qing transition, but the blow from which it could not recover, and never did, was the loss of the Japan trade.[73]

## MANILA

Chinese merchants had made trading voyages to the archipelago that became the Philippines long before the Spanish arrived. However, the Spanish–Chinese connection and the expansion of Chinese settlement and enterprise on Luzon owed little to those antecedents, and almost everything to the exchange across the Pacific of Chinese silks and other consumer goods for Spanish American silver. References to Chinese trade with Luzon can be found in the records of the first Spanish voyages to reach the archipelago, those of Magellan in 1521 and of Loaysa in 1527. It was a combination of a magnificent harbor, a rich agricultural hinterland, and an already established trade with China that brought the Spanish under the leadership of Miguel López de Legazpi to conquer Manila in 1570–1571, to immediately establish there the full institutional frame-work of a Spanish city, and to move the Spanish headquarters in Asian waters to the new city. The local people had just begun to develop, under Muslim influence, large-scale monarchical institutions, and offered no sustained resistance to Spanish domination once the Spanish had burned the king's town and begun building a Spanish walled town in its place.[74] Already there were Chinese settled in an area that had been granted to them by the Muslim king, across the Pasig River from Manila, roughly in the Binondo area that was a frequent center of Chinese settlement from that time to our own day.[75] Chinese awareness of the new opportunities at Manila and of the likelihood of a friendly reception was increased when Legazpi's ship rescued the crew of a disabled Chinese junk off Mindoro in 1571. Some of the rescued people came to Manila with a big cargo in

---

[73] On Macao from the late 1640s to the late 1660s see John E. Wills, Jr., *Embassies and Illusions: Dutch and Portuguese Embassies to China, 1666–1687* (Cambridge, MA, 1984), pp. 83–101 and Chapter 4, this volume.

[74] Robert R. Reed, *Colonial Manila: The Context of Hispanic Urbanism and Process of Morphogenesis* (Berkeley, CA, 1978).

[75] On the Chinese at Manila good summaries and guides to the sources are W. L. Schurz, *The Manila Galleon* (New York, 1939; reprint, 1959), Ch. 1, and the various essays in Vol. 1 of Alfonso Felix, Jr., *The Chinese in the Philippines, 1570–1770*, 2 vols. (Manila, 1966). On the Chinese presence before the Spanish arrival see especially Alberto Santamaria, O.P., "The Chinese Parian (El Parian de los Sangleyes)," in Alfonso Felix, Jr., *The Chinese in the Philippines, 1550–1770*, Vol. 1, p. 106, citing testimony in 1640 of an aged son of the former king of Manila.

1572, and in 1573 the first cargo of Chinese goods was sent off across the Pacific to Acapulco. Six junks came in 1574, twelve or more in 1575. It was precisely in these years that the exploitation of the great silver lode at Potosí in what is now Bolivia was getting well under way and a market for Chinese silks and other fine craft products was emerging in the settled and luxurious cities of Spanish America. The matching flows of Chinese goods and New World silver became Manila's overwhelming raison d'être; there was not even much done to explore the gold resources of Luzon or to develop the magnificent agricultural potential of the area around Manila. At Manila the Chinese brought almost all the goods that would be shipped to the New World, and did almost all the mercantile and skilled craft work of the city.

Before this process was well under way, the Spanish presence was almost extinguished by a Chinese attack; this was followed by an abortive opening to direct relations with the Ming that seemed for a short while to present the possibility that Sino-Spanish trade might be centered not at Manila but at a Spanish Macao on the coast of Fujian. The pirate Lin Feng had been driven off the Fujian coast in 1574 and had taken refuge in the Penghu (Pescadores) Islands. His fleet entered Manila Bay on November 29 of that year, and a first landing was driven back on the next day. On December 2 Lin himself led a larger attack by about a thousand men, but it too was driven back and about two hundred of his men were killed. He then withdrew from the Manila area and fortified himself at Pangasinan farther north on the coast of Luzon. In March 1575 a force of Spanish soldiers and Filipino auxiliaries pursued him there, burned his ships, almost took his stockade, and settled down to wait for his surrender. But Lin's men were able to get food and firewood from nearby settlements and eventually assembled enough timber to clandestinely build thirty-seven small junks and escape out to sea.[76]

Not long after the Spanish force arrived at Pangasinan, it had been joined by a Ming officer, Wang Wanggao, sent to track down Lin Feng. The Spanish seemed to have the situation well in hand, so Wang was sent on to Manila, where he was cordially received, and soon set out for Fujian, taking with him two lay Spanish envoys, Miguel de Loarca and Pedro de Sarmiento, and two priests, Martín de Rada and Jerónimo Marín, who would seek to make a trade agreement with the Fujian authorities and to obtain permission to preach the gospel in China. They were cordially

---

[76] Goodrich and Fang, *Dictionary of Ming Biography*, pp. 917–919; Boxer, *South China in the Sixteenth Century*, pp. xliv–xlvii.

received in Tongan, in Quanzhou, and finally by the governor of Fujian in Fuzhou. They were told that no answer could be given to their requests until the emperor's response to them had been received. As they sailed for Manila in September 1575, their Chinese hosts pointed out to them the little island of Wuyu on the south side of the Zhangzhou Estuary as one place where they might be given a trading post. In Chinese records their mission is recorded as a would-be tribute embassy, and it is said that they were given gifts and their presents were forwarded for them, but they were not allowed to establish any more permanent relation. Some argued for a positive response to their initiative even though they "were not a tributary country," but still it must have weighed against them that they were not to be found in the early Ming lists of tributaries.[77] Returning to Manila with the envoys, Wang Wanggao was dismayed to learn that Lin Feng had escaped. He was treated rudely by a new governor at Manila. The two priests still pressed him to take them back to Fujian, and they finally embarked on his ship but were put ashore on northern Luzon.[78] As late as 1589 the governor told Bishop Salazar he was trying to obtain an agreement with the Zhangzhou officials for a trading post on an offshore island.[79] The 1593 prohibition of Spanish trade with China mentioned later in the chapter should have put an end to these projects; the El Piñal episode described in the section on Macao would seem to represent a final effort to dodge this restriction, and its unexplained end its definitive enforcement. Thereafter, the Spanish settled down to mutually profitable but uneasy and occasionally violent relations with the Chinese who came to Manila. The great massacres of 1603, 1639, and 1662 are relatively well known and well documented, but they must be set against a background of the organization and taxation of the Chinese community that still is not well known.

Only occasionally do the Seville archives yield detailed (and hard to understand) information on the types and quantities of goods imported from China.[80] The figures assembled by Pierre Chaunu on taxation of Chinese trade and on the head taxes paid by Chinese residents can be

---

[77] Zhang Weihua, *Mingshi Folangji*, pp. 75–77.

[78] Goodrich and Fang, *Dictionary of Ming Biography*, pp. 1131–1136.

[79] Bishop Domingo de Salazar, O.P., Letter of June 24, 1590, as reprinted in Felix, *Chinese in the Philippines*, Vol. 1, p. 121.

[80] John E. Wills, Jr., "China's Farther Shores: Continuities and Changes in the Destination Ports of China's Foreign Trade, 1680–1690," in Roderick Ptak and Dietmar Rothermund, eds., *Emporia, Commodities, and Entrepreneurs in Asian Maritime Trade, c. 1400–1750* (Stuttgart, 1992), p. 70, n. 56.

used to trace general trends and volumes of trade, but clearly are tainted by changing collection practices and levels of corruption. The Chinese–Spanish trade at Manila, dependent on the annual voyages of the galleons to and from Acapulco, the longest regular voyages out of sight of land in the age of sail, has fascinated students of history for many years. Through it China found an utterly new market for its silks and a substantial new source of silver. Imports of silver to China by this route probably averaged more than 1,000,000 taels per year from 1590 to 1630, and 3,000,000 or more from 1600 to 1605.[81] As noted in the Introduction, much now is understood and much remains to be learned about the effects of the inflow of silver. Silk was widely produced and widely consumed within China; the new export markets in Spanish America, Europe, and Japan linked with the European trade probably did affect some specific regional economies and lines of production, but it is not likely that they had any major effect on the empire-wide volume of silk production. The influx of silver, and the prosperity associated with the trade, certainly set off a boom in maritime Fujian, led to the widespread use there of Spanish silver coins, and contributed to the widespread commercialization, fiscal distortion, and corruption of late Ming China.

Raw silk and silk goods always were the mainstays of Chinese sales at Manila. By 1586 concerns over the drain of specie into China, the tough and intelligent bargaining of individual Chinese traders, and the presence of a large number of Chinese at Manila throughout the trading season and even staying over to the next year led the city of Manila to petition the king for the institution of a negotiated bloc trade at fixed prices for all imports, which came to be called the *pancada*; it received royal approval in 1589. Although it seems to have been a Spanish initiative, it may have owed a good deal to proposals from the resident Chinese, since it also met Chinese needs to dispose of all goods in time for the return voyage to Fujian and to keep the trade moving as smoothly as possible.[82] In 1593 this restrictive policy was extended to a limit on the volume of trans-Pacific trade, the closing of Peru to Chinese imports, and prohibitions of Spanish trade to China and of importation of Chinese goods consigned to specific Spaniards. It seems likely that the *pancada* was never free of leaks. Soon it was confined

---

[81] Pierre Chaunu, *Les Philippines et le Pacifique des Ibériques (XVIe, XVIIe, XVIIIe siècles). Introduction methodologique et indices d'activité* (Paris, 1960), pp. 32–34, 78–79, 200–205, 268. For more discussion and bibliography see the introduction to this volume.

[82] Further evidence for a Chinese role in shaping this practice is the use by the Dutch of the word *pancado* to refer to a similar practice at Nagasaki; the Chinese traders in both places would seem to be the only possible transmitters of the practice.

to finer goods, and by the late 1600s it had completely broken down and was replaced by a free-market *feria* after the Chinese ships arrived.

A more persistent concern was the large number of Chinese who settled in the Manila area. Already in 1586 it was estimated that there were ten thousand, compared with a Spanish population of less than two thousand. General prohibitions of Chinese retail trade and permanent residence were little enforced. It is not clear when the practice of selling residence permits to the Chinese began. Around 1600 the rule was that only four thousand would be sold, for two reals each, but by that time the issue of the certificates had become a venal source of income, granted by the responsible officer to his cronies, who profited not only from sale up to the quota and beyond but from extra extortions; Chinese who were found without a permit after the annual trading ships departed had to buy one for six reals.[83] The result was that there was only very erratic enforcement of limits on numbers, and the extra burdens fell more on recent arrivals than on established Chinese merchants.

The first location of the Parian, or Chinatown, was within the walls of the city. In 1583 the Chinese were moved to a swampy area northeast of the city walls, which they rapidly turned into a thriving town of orderly streets with a large central pond, accessible to substantial ships, with an island in the center where punishments were administered to Chinese criminals. The Chinese were briefly moved from this location during several periods, and separate Christian Chinese settlements soon grew up in Tondo and Binondo north of the Pasig River, but this was the prime center of Chinese settlement down to the nineteenth century. Traces of the location are still to be found in the name of the Parian Gate of Intramuros, the old walled city, and in Arroceros Street, the location of the street of the rice merchants in the Parian.[84]

By 1590 the domination of local trade and artisanal production by the Chinese was striking, from bread baking to bookbinding to tavern keeping to stone masonry. The Dominicans built a church in the vicinity of the Parian soon after their arrival in 1587, and soon were deeply involved in learning the Chinese language and seeking converts among this population, making intelligent use of pageantry, charity, and learning.[85] Earlier

[83] H. de la Costa, S.J., *The Jesuits in the Philippines, 1581–1768* (Cambridge, MA, 1961), pp. 205–206.
[84] Santamaria, "The Chinese Parian," pp. 67–118.
[85] John E. Wills, Jr., "From Manila to Fuan: Asian Contexts of Dominican Mission Policy," in D. E. Mungello, ed., *The Chinese Rites Controversy: Its History and Meaning* (Nettetal, 1994), pp. 111–127.

Chinese converts had been expected to adopt Spanish clothing and to cut their long hair. It is not clear to what extent the Dominicans modified these policies, but two of their letters from 1589 and 1590 show considerable interest in the Chinese and willingness to consider the need to adapt to their culture.[86] The 1590 letter also gives us our first reference to a Christian Chinese, "Don Juan Zanco, Governor of the Christian Chinese."[87] It is not clear if he was given any authority over his non-Christian countrymen, but it is likely that he was an important intermediary in their relations with the Spanish. In 1603 there was a royal confirmation of what seems to have been well-established practice by that time, that a Christian Chinese was appointed mayor, *alcalde*, also referred to as *capitan*, over all the Chinese, that the other regional *alcaldes* had no jurisdiction over them, and that in legal cases and other important matters the mayor of the Chinese was required to seek the advice of the Crown attorney, *fiscal*, of the Audiencia.[88]

In 1593 the Chinese rowers of the galley of Governor Gomez Perez Dasmariñas mutinied and killed him. The mutineers headed west, most of them remaining on the Vietnam coast; thirty-two reached China, where their deed was reported to the court and their leader was punished. At Manila further attacks were feared, and the local Chinese were forced to move their Parian to the north side of the Pasig. The appearance in 1594 of seven Chinese warships, ostensibly searching for Chinese outlaws, heightened tension. Soon the Chinese were allowed to move back across the river. In 1596 twelve thousand were sent back to their homeland, but many more remained.

In 1603 this stew of fear, mutual dependence, flourishing trade, and unstoppable emigration exploded in a massacre in which more than twenty thousand Chinese were killed. The catalyst was the arrival of an official mission sent by the Fujian provincial authorities. Two Fujian adventurers, Yan Yinglong and Zhang Yi, had told Gao Cai, the notorious eunuch tax and mines commissioner in Fujian, that there was a mountain of gold on Cavite Peninsula in Manila Bay. It seems that plans were made for a mission with Ming naval backing to attack Manila or otherwise seek the mountain of gold. After a number of censors protested to no avail, the provincial authorities decided they had to send an expedition

---

[86] Reports by Bishop Salazar and Juan Cobo, O.P., in Felix, *Chinese in the Philippines*, Vol. 1, pp. 119–142.

[87] Ibid., p. 129.

[88] Milagros Guerrero, "The Chinese in the Philippines, 1570–1770," in Felix, *Chinese in the Philippines,*, Vol. 1, pp. 30–31.

of some kind, but clearly planned it to show up Zhang Yi's hoax. An assistant *xian* magistrate, Wang Shihe, and a company commander, Yu Yicheng, were sent, bringing Zhang Yi in chains, to check on the truth of his story.

The delegation arrived in March 1603 and was promptly received by Governor Pedro Bravo de Acuña, their procession with its music, heralds, and standard bearers making a great impression. They were given comfortable accommodations. When they began to administer justice in the Chinese community, they were immediately ordered to desist. At a second meeting with the governor in May, they made it clear that they were skeptical about Zhang Yi's report but had to obey the commands of their emperor. The governor then arranged for them to go to Cavite and see for themselves that there was no gold. They did so, and soon left for China, taking with them a basket of earth from Cavite and the unfortunate Zhang Yi, still in chains.[89]

Unaware of the political tensions behind this expedition, the Spanish could not believe that the search for the mountain of gold had been its real purpose. Soon rumors were spreading that the expedition had been sent to spy out Manila for a major Chinese invasion, in which the local Chinese would cooperate. Defensive measures were taken, and many Spaniards, Filipinos, and resident Japanese began to threaten the Chinese. The established merchants of the Parian remained quiet and conciliatory, but new arrivals, especially settlers in the semirural areas north of the Pasig, were not as well controlled, had less to lose, and probably were suffering more from the abuses of license fee collection described earlier. North of the river a large group of Chinese began to plan a first strike, and some Parian residents began to join them. The mayor of the Parian, Juan Bautista de la Vera, whose Chinese name was transcribed as Eng Kang, tried to dissuade them, but found his adopted son in command of the rebels. They tried to persuade him to become their leader, but he escaped back to the Parian, promptly reporting the danger to the Spanish. When gunpowder was found in his house, possibly intended for fireworks, he was arrested and eventually executed.

On the night of October 3 the Spanish shut the gates of the walled city and prepared for an attack. North of the Pasig one Spanish family was

---

[89] This account of the events of 1603 relies on De la Costa, *Jesuits in the Philippines*, pp. 203–215; de Morga, *Sucesos de las Islas Filipinas*, pp. 206–225; Francisco Colín, S.J, *Labor Evangélica de la Compañia de Jesús en Filipinas*, 3 vols., ed. Pablo Pastells, S.J. (Barcelona, 1900–1902), Vol. 2, pp. 428–432; and Zhang Weihua, *Mingshi Folangji*, pp. 90–101.

killed and many houses were burned. A Chinese attack on the church in
Tondo was beaten off by Spanish soldiers, who then foolishly pursued
the Chinese into a swampy area and were surrounded and cut down.
The rebels now rested, arguing among themselves and casting lots (probably the divining blocks still ubiquitous in southern Fujian culture) to
determine their next move. On October 6 they crossed the Pasig, occupied the Parian, and prepared for an attack on the walled city, building
ladders and rolling siege towers. They had taken some firearms from
the Spaniards cut down in the swamp, but still were no match for the
musket and cannon fire that now was trained on them from the walls
of the city. Their disorderly assaults on the wall were broken up, their
ladders and towers demolished by cannon balls. In a day or two disci-
plined Spanish and Japanese soldiers began to mount sorties from the
city, and as Filipino auxiliaries arrived from outlying areas the Chinese
broke and fled in any direction they could. They were pursued in the
countryside in the following weeks, and whenever Spaniards or Filipinos
caught up with them no prisoners were taken. Estimates of the total
number of Chinese slaughtered range from fifteen thousand to twenty-
five thousand.

The Spanish now quickly realized that however much they feared
and despised the Chinese, they could not survive without their trade
and industry. Surviving Parian merchants were assured that the trade
would continue as usual. The Manila authorities wrote to the rulers of
Guangdong and Fujian to explain what had happened. The Fujian officials were inclined to fix much of the blame on Zhang Yi. They replied,
according to the *Ming Shi*, that the Spanish should not have killed
Chinese criminals on their own initiative and that they should send the
widows and orphans back to China, but no chastising expedition was
sent. Because so much of the Parian had been burned, Chinese merchants
coming to trade in 1604 were lodged in fine houses in the walled city.
The revival of the trade was so rapid that Chaunu's figures on taxes on
Chinese trade suggest that the average value of the trade for 1606–1610
was more than 3,000,000 pesos per year, the highest five-year average in
the history of the trade.[90]

Spanish jurisdiction over the Chinese community remained tangled
and venal, with the governor supposedly having final jurisdiction and
the Crown attorney (fiscal) of the Audiencia serving as "protector" of

---

[90] Based on Chaunu, *Les Philippines*, pp. 34, 92, dividing the average collection of 46,390
pesos by the 3% rate and doubling to allow for untaxed and undertaxed trade.

the Chinese and adviser of their mayor on all legal matters. The Chinese were exempted from labor service and petty personal dues required of the Filipinos but paid a stiff license fee of eight pesos per year, with added extortions and harassments by the sellers. Chinese resentment of Spanish extortion and misrule was manifested in a series of petitions to the king of Spain to allow the Chinese to be governed solely by their own people, which were rejected in 1630.[91] The sale of the licenses remaining a venal privilege of Spanish appointees, new efforts to limit the Chinese population to 6,000 had no chance of success; estimates in the 1620s and 1630s ranged from 15,000 to 21,000, and at the time of the 1639 revolt, 33,000 to 45,000, the majority rural. The license fees became a greater source of government income than the tax on the trade of the Chinese.[92] A larger proportion of this population was now engaged in farming in outlying areas, independently, on estates of the religious orders, and at least in one case in a forced settlement project. It was these rural Chinese who rose against the Spanish and brought another massacre down on their heads in 1639.

The 1639 rebellion of the Chinese of Luzon was largely a rural affair, which only briefly occupied the Manila Parian and threatened the Spanish walled city. It was ill armed but well organized; Spanish soldiers searching camps from which they had expelled the Chinese found large stocks of rice, written notice boards, and evidence of thorough organization into squads of ten, kept track of by cashlike counters collected at the end of each fighting day. The uprising must have been prepared for some time in its rural centers. There were rumors, not very detailed or convincing, that the leaders were in touch with Zheng Zhilong, the dominant sea lord and trader on the Fujian coast, and that a coordinated rising had been planned for December 24 but botched by the earlier rural rising. This took place on November 20 at Calamba on the south shore of Laguna de Bay east of Manila, where a large number of Chinese, probably several thousand, were engaged in developing paddy rice agriculture. Many of them had been compelled to settle there, and all paid a substantial rent to the Spanish Crown. The site was very unhealthy; about three hundred had died. The rebels advanced rapidly toward Manila, and on November 22 took the church at San Pedro Makati on the eastern outskirts. They broke and fled when substantial Spanish and Filipino forces arrived. Risings

[91] Charles H. Cunningham, *The Audiencia in the Spanish Colonies, as Illustrated by the Audiencia of Manila (1583–1800)* (Berkeley, CA, 1919), p. 253.
[92] Chaunu, *Les Philippines*, p. 92.

now were reported in other areas, and from November 26 to December 2 the rebels controlled the north bank of the Pasig River. [93]

On December 2 some elements in the Parian revolted and started fires, and the Spanish began firing on it from the walls of the city. Estimating that there were 300 Spaniards capable of bearing arms against 26,000 Chinese, the Spanish took drastic action to make sure that the Chinese would never be able to assemble their forces. On December 5 the governor sent out orders to all outlying Spanish settlements to kill all the Chinese they could find, offering a reward for every Chinese head. Spaniards and Filipinos needed little urging. In some places the Chinese were rounded up and decapitated ten at a time; in others parties fanned out into the countryside to hunt them down. The total slaughter has been estimated at 17,000 to 22,000. Some fortified themselves in the mountains but eventually were dislodged. A final army of 6,000 to 7,000 held out on the eastern shore of Laguna de Bay until they surrendered on March 15, 1640, were marched back to Manila, and lodged in a stockade north of the Pasig.

Chaunu's figures on taxes on the trade of the Chinese and on the Chinese license fees both show striking declines after 1650. It was precisely at this time, not in the 1640s, that Qing efforts to deny mainland connections to their Zheng enemies began to bite, followed by the far greater disruptions of the coastal evacuations of the 1660s. In this pinched setting there was a final upheaval, which might be seen as a distant echo and continuation of the farce tragedies of the Southern Ming.[94] On April 24, 1662, less than three months after the capitulation of the Dutch at Casteel Zeelandia on Taiwan, Zheng Chenggong sent Victorio Riccio, O.P., who had had a mission at Xiamen in the 1650s, to bear a letter to Manila summoning the Spanish to acknowledge his suzerainty and pay him tribute, and threatening to lead his fleet to conquer them as he had the Dutch. If he had anything in mind other than megalomania, he may have had his eye on the rice production of Luzon, some of the surplus of which would have helped to feed his hungry soldiers on the still little-cultivated plains of Taiwan.

Riccio arrived in Manila on May 5. Zheng's threat was taken very seriously. The garrisons in Maluku and on Mindanao were withdrawn

[93] This account is based on De la Costa, *Jesuits in the Philippines* pp. 389–392; Santamaria, "The Chinese Parian," pp. 103–105; and Emma H. Blair and James A. Robertson, eds., *The Philippine Islands*, 55 vols. (Cleveland, 1903–1909), Vol. 29, pp. 201–258.

[94] Lynn A. Struve, *The Southern Ming, 1644–1662* (New Haven, CT, 1984); Struve, "The Southern Ming, 1644–1662", in Mote and Twitchett, eds., *CHOC*, Vol. 7, pp. 641–725.

to reinforce Manila; the loss of a Spanish presence in Maluku was permanent, and the Mindanao posts were not reoccupied for many years. Harsh levies of building supplies, food, and Chinese and Filipino labor were ordered, and a great deal of new work was done on the walls of the Spanish city.[95] Many argued for killing or sending away all the non-Christian Chinese. The Chinese of the Parian were more inclined to flee than to revolt, but the Spanish governor was still trying to reassure them and keep them quiet. On May 25, however, a confused melee near the Parian Gate ended with casualties on both sides and a Spanish cannonade of the Parian. More and more fled north of the Pasig. The governor now negotiated an understanding with the Chinese that those who submitted peacefully would not be harmed and that the non-Christians among them would leave Manila on the trading ships then present. We are not told how many left, but it is mentioned that 1,300 crammed themselves on one ship. None of this satisfied the widespread desire for slaughter. The governor gave way to it, ordering that any Chinese who had not come down to the assembly areas by June 4 be killed. Some were killed; others fled to the mountains, where they died of hunger or were killed by the Negritos. Father Riccio had been sent away with a defiant reply, but by the time he returned on April 8, 1663, with a conciliatory message from Zheng Chenggong's son Zheng Jing, the Spanish were ready to once again recognize their need for good relations with the Chinese.[96]

## MISSIONARIES AND THE MING STATE

The Roman Catholic missionary enterprise in Ming China led to some fascinating interactions in religion, scholarship, science, literature, and art. It also was intricately intertwined with the policies and institutions of the Catholic Church and of the Catholic monarchies and especially of their outposts at Manila and Macao and, on the other hand, with the shifts of Ming politics and the political fortunes of its patrons and protectors in the bureaucracy. Here I am concerned only with the political

---

[95] Domingo Abella, "Koxinga Nearly Ended Spanish Rule in the Philippines in 1662," *Philippine Historical Review*, Vol. 2, No. 1 (1969), pp. 301–302, 321–322.

[96] De la Costa, *Jesuits in the Philippines*, pp. 450, 483–484; Blair and Robertson, *The Philippine Islands*, Vol. 36, pp. 213–266; John E. Wills, Jr., "Les missions aventureuses d'un Dominicain, Victorio Riccio" (The hazardous missions of a Dominican: Victorio Riccio, O.P. in Amoy, Taiwan and Manila)," in *Actes du IIe Colloque International de Sinologie, Chantilly, 1977* (Paris, 1980), pp. 231–257.

dimensions of the missionary presence, not the complex story of the religious/cultural encounter.

We have noted the effort of Dominican and Augustinian missionaries to gain entry to China in connection with the Spanish embassy of 1574–1575. There were a number of later Dominican and Franciscan attempts to enter the empire from Manila, but until the 1630s all led to immediate expulsion. During its first half-century, the effective missionary enterprise was entirely the work of members of the Society of Jesus coming to the Far East under Portuguese patronage and entering China via Macao. From Francis Xavier on, Jesuits were constantly involved with Portuguese efforts to trade and settle in the Guangdong islands. An important step forward was taken by Michele Ruggieri, S.J., in his visits to Canton with the Portuguese merchants in 1580 and 1581. He studied and practiced Chinese etiquette with great care, and was asked to be present at all meetings between the foreign merchants and the officials. Ruggieri was also experimenting with having expositions of Christian doctrine translated into Chinese.[97] Matteo Ricci in a number of ways walked through doors Ruggieri had opened.

Ruggieri accompanied the Macao mission to negotiate with the governor-general at Zhaoqing in 1582, made an excellent impression on that high official, and was invited to stay. In 1583 he went to Macao and brought Matteo Ricci, S.J., back with him. As hostility surfaced there, he moved on to Shaozhou in 1589. The complex story of Ricci's gradual discovery of the possibilities of dialogue with the Chinese elite has been told many times. He also learned that the key to being able to move around the empire was the protection of high officials in whose large entourage a single foreign priest could travel without getting into difficulties with local crowds or officials. In 1598 Ricci was able to travel to Nanjing with Shi Xing, president of the Board of War. He immediately sensed Nanjing's great potential as a center for his efforts, but also great difficulties, especially when the Hideyoshi invasion of Korea had increased suspicion of all foreigners. He settled at Nanchang, where he was exposed for the first time to the sophisticated moral and philosophical debates of the late Ming academies and study societies.[98]

In 1598 Ricci paid a brief visit to Beijing in the retinue of another high official. He did not stay, but settled in Nanjing. His world map was

[97] Joseph Sebes, S.J., "The Precursors of Ricci," in Charles E. Ronan, S.J., and Bonnie B. C. Oh, *East Meets West: The Jesuits in China, 1582–1773* (Chicago, 1988), pp. 19–61.
[98] The exposition in this section is based primarily on Dunne, *Generation of Giants.*

spreading his reputation in scholarly circles. In the rich intellectual life of the city he found many to learn from and argue with. In developing his strategy to appeal to the Chinese elite he would draw on the controversies about Chinese classical texts, the criticisms of Buddhist taints in Confucian culture, and the search for more earnest and substantial forms of moral commitment that he encountered in these years. Above all, it was in these Nanjing years that he met Xu Guangqi, the most influential convert and supporter of the Jesuits in the late Ming.

In 1600 Ricci set out for Beijing again, this time in the retinue of a eunuch of the Imperial Silk Manufactories. At Linqing he came under the control of the court eunuch Ma Tang. In Beijing he was treated as a tribute envoy and the gifts he had brought for the court were treated as tribute presents. Since the emperor gave no audiences, it is not clear what kind of ceremony was conducted. Ricci noted the farcical condition of the "tribute system," exploited by scores of Central Asian merchants as a means of gaining access to the markets of the capital.[99] He managed to stay on in Beijing, although the Board of Ceremonies pointed out that tribute envoys were supposed to depart soon after their audiences.[100] He was helped by the impression his clock, spinet, and other gifts had made in the palace, as part of the vast network of pleasures and distractions the eunuchs wove around the emperor. Chinese friends old and new were assisting him in putting his writings into good Chinese, writing prefaces for his works, and reprinting them in the provinces. Sometimes searching for new spiritual insight, sometimes simply curious, visitors to the capital for examinations or other official business came to see him in a steady stream. The imperial gift of a burial ground after Ricci's death in 1610 was a further indication of the solid and respected position he had established at the court.

Unlike the Catholic missions under the Qing, which experienced repeated reversals of fortune as a result of changes in court power and policies, the missionaries under the Ming were little affected by central government policy, but gradually expanded their enterprise on the basis of a very Chinese network of publishing, friendship, and patronage. By 1628, despite two episodes of antimissionary policy, they had, in addition to the places already listed, mission outposts at Shanghai, Jiading, and Changshu in Jiangsu, at Hangzhou, and in Fujian, Shaanxi, and Shanxi.

---

[99] Joseph F. Fletcher, "China and Central Asia, 1368–1884," in John K. Fairbank, ed., *The Chinese World Order* (Cambridge, 1968), pp. 208–209, 346–347.
[100] Zhang Weihua, *Mingshi Folangji*, pp. 171–180.

Most had begun quietly with a missionary priest living in the household of a sympathetic great man whom he had met in Nanjing, Beijing, or another mission. In the early years much had depended on the favor of a few great men who converted and others who were sympathetic; a telling sign of this favor is the large number of prefaces to Jesuit works in Chinese written before 1616.[101]

Political opposition to the missionaries was instigated largely by Shen Que, who became vice president of the Nanjing Board of Ceremonies in 1615, a post that combined a minimum of actual responsibilities with a maximum of implied obligation to protect orthodoxy. In his memorial and those of his supporters we already find allegations that the missionaries were forming a secret society like the White Lotus, were serving as spies and developing a fifth column of Chinese adherents for the aggressive purposes of the Europeans, and were enticing people with monetary rewards. Closer to his duty to defend the traditional ceremonial order, Shen condemned the use of the term *Daxiyang* (Great Western Ocean), which seemed to belittle China, its different calendar, its apparent encouragement of unfilial feeling and behavior, and its buying of property near the tomb of the first Ming emperor.[102] In response, in 1617 an imperial edict ordered that all the missionaries be sent back to their own countries. Shen had a good deal of power and support in Nanjing, and there the missionaries were imprisoned and sent to Macao, while their converts suffered much imprisonment and mistreatment. There were signs of elite and popular anti-Christian feeling in a number of other places, but the elite protectors managed to keep the missionaries safe in their households. In Hangzhou, Yang Tingyun even took in and sheltered a number of missionaries who had been forced to leave their posts in Beijing and elsewhere.[103]

In 1622 there was a brief revival of Shen Que's career and his policies, abetted by the fiasco of the Macao cannoneers mentioned earlier and by the fears aroused by the large White Lotus rebellion in Shandong, but

---

[101] Ad Dudink, "Sympathising Literati and Officials," in Nicolas Standaert, ed., *Handbook of Christianity in China: Volume One: 635–1800*, Handbook of Oriental Studies, Section Four, China, 15/1 (Leiden, 2001), p. 480.

[102] Chapter 2, this volume; Ad Dudink, "Opponents," in Standaert, ed., *Handbook*, pp. 503–533; Goodrich and Fang, *Dictionary of Ming Biography*, pp. 1177–1178; John D. Young, *Confucianism and Christianity: The First Encounter* (Hong Kong, 1983), pp. 60–61.

[103] Nicolas Standaert, *Yang Tingyun, Confucian and Christian in Late Ming China: His Life and Thought* (Leiden, 1988), p. 92.

Shen soon fell from power and the missionaries once again were allowed to live in Beijing. A major breakthrough came in 1629 with the appointment of Xu Guangqi as vice president of the Board of Ceremonies and his promotion to president of that board in 1630. In 1629 he arranged a competitive comparison of predictions of a solar eclipse by the traditional Chinese, Muslim, and newly introduced European methods. The European method proved to be the only accurate one. Imperial approval was obtained for reform of the calendar according to the European methods of calculation, and a team of Jesuits and Chinese scholars set to work under Xu's direction on a large program of manufacture of instruments and translation of scientific books. The best Jesuit scientist, Johann Terrenz, died in 1630, and Johann Adam Schall von Bell and Giacomo Rho continued the work. The first calendar calculated according to the new methods was promulgated in 1634. The astronomical and calendrical work of the Jesuits turned out to be their most secure justification for a presence in Beijing and a connection with the court, allowing them to maintain the visibility in the capital of which Ricci already had made good use, to use their connections on behalf of other missionaries and of Macao, and even to make a few converts among the eunuchs and women of the palace.

I have suggested elsewhere that beginning in the political crises of the 1620s the Chinese elite found highly traditional ways to enact their dramas of selfless resistance to corrupt power, and no longer were so likely to be led by deep tensions within their own values to the desperate leap of conversion to an alien religion.[104] Such tensions may have been especially acute for members of the lower gentry, highly committed to traditional moral values but finding those values betrayed and their own zeal for action blocked in late Ming society; many Ming converts came from this stratum, and they were very influential in forming Christian communities in several provinces.[105] Late Ming practices of voluntary association fused with Catholic practices in a proliferation of catechists, sodalities, and so on that were vital to the health of Christian communities rarely visited by a missionary.[106] Liam Brockey has pointed out that as the

---

[104] John E. Wills, Jr., "Brief Intersection: Changing Contexts and Prospects of the Christian–Chinese Encounter from Ricci to Verbiest," in John W. Witek, ed., Ferdinand Verbiest, S.J. (1623–1688): Jesuit Missionary, Scientist, Engineer and Diplomat, Monumenta Serica Monographs Series, No. 30 (Nettetal, 1994), pp. 383–394; in Chinese translation of volume, Nan Huairen (1623–1688) (Beijing, 2001).

[105] Nicolas Standaert, "Well-Known Individuals," in Standaert, Handbook, pp. 420–428.

[106] Nicolas Standaert, "Associations for Lay-People," in Standaert, Handbook, pp. 457–461.

umbrella of Jesuit prestige and elite conversion became a bit less leaky, the Jesuits and soon other missionaries were more able to pursue their deepest vocation in the evangelization of the Chinese common people.[107] Nicolas Standaert has given us an excellent analysis of improvisation and "interweaving" in Chinese Christian funeral ceremonies, a matter of great importance for both traditions, beginning with the funerals of Xu Guangqi's father in 1607, Ricci in 1610, and the parents of Yang Tingyun in 1618 and 1619.[108]

The missionaries' efforts prospered in Shaanxi and Shanxi and extended into Huguang, Sichuan, and Shandong. Spanish Dominicans and Franciscans entered China via the Spanish outposts at Keelung and Tamsui on the north end of Taiwan. Although frequently they were vehemently at odds with the Jesuits on mission policy, they too profited from the acceptance of the Jesuits in the capital, particularly from the reputation and political skills of Schall, and established long-lasting mission centers in Shandong and in Fuan, Fujian. Missionaries were more or less involved witnesses of several of the dramas of the Ming–Qing transition. Two Jesuits had a harrowing ordeal as captives of the Sichuan rebel Zhang Xianzhong.[109] Another was summoned by the Ming loyalist Longwu emperor and sent off to Macao in search of military aid.[110] The Ming loyalist Yongli court, where the empress and the eunuch Pang Tianshou were converts, sent Michał Boym, S.J., to Rome as its envoy.[111] Jesuits reported on rural turmoil near Shanghai[112] and on the Qing conquest of Canton.[113] Victorio Riccio, O.P., left a long and fascinating record of his experiences at Xiamen under Zheng Chenggong.[114]

---

[107] Liam Matthew Brockey, *Journey to the East: The Jesuit Mission to China, 1579–1724* (Cambridge, MA, 2007), pp. 89–107.

[108] Nicolas Standaert, *The Interweaving of Rituals: Funerals in the Cultural Exchange Between China and Europe* (Seattle, 2008).

[109] Louis Pfister, S.J., *Notices biographiques et bibliographiques sur les Jésuites de l'ancienne mission de la Chine, 1552–1773* (Shanghai, 1932; reprint, San Francisco, 1976), pp. 232–236, 250.

[110] Goodrich and Fang, *Dictionary of Ming Biography*, p. 1151.

[111] Ibid., pp. 20–22.

[112] Archivum Romanum Societatis Iesu, Archives of the Japan–China Province, Vol. 122, fols. 204–242, Antonio Gouvea, S.J., to Father General Vitelleschi, August 16, 1645, at fols. 212–213.

[113] Antonio Francisco Cardim, S.J., *Batalhas da Companhia de Jesus na sua Gloriosa Provincia do Japão*, ed. Luciano Cordeiro (Lisbon, 1894), pp. 37–40.

[114] Wills, "Hazardous Missions."

## THE DUTCH ONSLAUGHT

The Dutch East India Company brought to Asian waters a level of centralized political and commercial decision making and bureaucratization of violence far beyond that of the Portuguese Estado da Índia. Its impact on some areas of Indonesia and on the company's Portuguese adversaries was devastating. In its relations with China, its centralized decision making, dominated by lessons learned in Southeast Asia, made it harder for the company to learn how to get along with the Chinese. That and the way in which it brought its war with the Spanish–Portuguese monarchy to Far Eastern waters produced a string of pointlessly violent onslaughts that left the "red hairs" (*hongmao*) with a bad reputation to match that of the Folangji. Later it settled down to an uneasy symbiosis with the maritime Chinese in the opening up of trade between Fujian and Taiwan and Chinese settlement on Taiwan, a process of immense importance to the history of maritime China but hardly noticed by most of the elite or by the Ming rulers, preoccupied with the terrible dramas of the collapse of the dynasty.

In 1601 a ship sent by one of the precursor companies before the founding of the United Dutch East India Company was blown past Patani on the Malay Peninsula and eventually anchored near Macao. Two parties sent ashore were taken captive by the Portuguese. Unable to send any more messages ashore, the Dutch finally left the captives behind. One of them, according to the *Ming Shi*, was questioned by the eunuch tax commissioner Li Dao. Seventeen of the twenty were executed by the Portuguese. That such a small disturbance should be noted in the *Ming Shi* should remind us that the relatively rich Chinese documentation of European relations in the decade 1600–1610 is a by-product of the elite's preoccupation with its struggles against the eunuch mine and tax commissioners and of the large number of former officials out of office and paying attention to the affairs of their home places.[115]

In 1604 the company commander Wijbrand van Waerwijck met in Patani some Fujian merchants, who told him they could arrange for the Dutch to trade if they would give rich presents to the officials. Apparently

---

[115] This section is based on W. P. Groeneveldt, *De Nederlanders in China, Eerste Deel: De Eerste Bemoeiingen om den Handel in China en de Vestiging in de Pescadores (1601–1624)* (The Hague, 1898), and Zhang Weihua, *Mingshi Folangji*, pp. 113–147. On former officials with local preoccupations see John E. Wills, Jr., "Contingent Connections: Fujian, the Empire, and the Early Modern World," in Lynn A. Struve, ed., *The Qing Formation in World-Historical Time* (Cambridge, MA, 2004), pp. 177–179.

they had the eunuch Gao Cai particularly in mind. The Dutch squadron anchored in the Penghu Islands in August and messengers went back and forth. Gao Cai sent word that permission to trade could be obtained for 40,000 to 50,000 reals. In October, however, the naval officer Shen Yourong arrived at the head of a fleet of fifty war junks and told the Dutch they would have to withdraw from Penghu, which was Ming territory, but that some kind of trading arrangement could be worked out if they would anchor on the coast of Taiwan.[116] The Dutch could find no suitable harbor there, and finally gave up and returned to Patani, leaving several of their Fujianese middlemen in Chinese prisons; at least one was executed. To the scholars and civil officials this had been just another case of collusion between eunuchs and seagoing Chinese desperadoes, so closely parallel to the 1603 events at Manila that the two were discussed in the same memorial.

When the Dutch tried to trade near Macao in 1607, they aroused Chinese fears that they might be in collusion with the Japanese and finally were driven off by the Portuguese. Thereafter, they were preoccupied with consolidating their positions in the Spice Islands and on Java, and had to get along with the supplies of Chinese goods that Chinese ships brought to Southeast Asian ports. Their attacks on Chinese shipping to Manila, 1619–1621, as part of their world war on the Iberian monarchy, must have left a few more "red hair" horror stories circulating in Fujian ports but left no trace in surviving Chinese sources.

The Dutch returned to the offensive on the China coast in 1622 with the unsuccessful attack on Macao described earlier. Their fleet then went on to occupy the Penghu Islands in July; they began to build a fort and sent a messenger to Xiamen with their amazing demands: Chinese merchants must be allowed to come to Penghu or Taiwan to trade. They also would be given Dutch passes for voyages to Batavia and perhaps also to Siam and Cambodia, but not to Manila. Any Chinese vessel sailing to Manila would risk capture and confiscation by the Dutch. Any delay in agreeing to these proposals would lead to attacks on Chinese shipping and coastal towns. The Dutch officers on the scene soon came to understand that they could not bully the Ming Empire as they often did some small Southeast Asian port kingdom, but the Batavia authorities learned slowly or not at all, and over and over again their orders licensed

---

[116] This is obliquely confirmed by a Chinese text, Zhang Weihua, *Mingshi Folangji*, p. 120, which quotes Shen saying to the Dutch, "The four seas are very wide, and there is no place where you cannot live."

episodes of irrational violence against those with whom they would have to cooperate to obtain trade.[117]

On September 29, 1622, the Dutch on Penghu received a letter from Shang Zhouzuo, governor of Fujian. It said nothing, as far as the Dutch could tell, about permission to trade. When the Dutch began to talk about attacking the coast, the bearers of Shang's letter suggested that something could be worked out if the Dutch would withdraw to some port on the coast of Taiwan. The Dutch rejected this, the solution already offered them in 1604 and that they eventually would be forced to accept, and in October and November they plundered towns and burned junks in the area around Xiamen. Chinese captives were put to work on the fort in Penghu, and some of the survivors later were shipped off to Batavia. Even so, Shang wrote to renew the suggestion that his envoys had made informally; something could be worked out, but not as long as the Dutch were occupying Penghu. Early in 1623 the Dutch commander Cornelis Reijersen visited Shang in Foochow, and they quickly came to an understanding. In the presence of a representative of the Fujian authorities, the Dutch would make a token beginning in the demolition of their fort on Penghu, which then would be reported to Beijing with a recommendation that Chinese merchants be given passes to trade with the Dutch at a port on Taiwan. The Dutch might stay in Penghu until they found a suitable port on Taiwan, but no longer. Chinese envoys would be sent to Batavia to secure confirmation of this agreement.

In June 1623, however, Reijersen and Shang learned that their superiors in both Batavia and Beijinghad rejected the proposed agreement. Shang was dismissed from his office. The Dutch sent ships to cruise off Guangdong and Fujian for Chinese shipping bound for Manila. Later instructions from Batavia, received in August, were somewhat more conciliatory, and Reijersen made further probes for renewed negotiations in August and in October, but on the latter occasion some of the Dutch envoys were imprisoned and their ships were attacked by fire ships. In January 1624 Dutch ships again raided ports along the coast south of Amoy. Beginning in February 1624, a force of forty to fifty war junks carrying more than five thousand men gradually assembled in the northern part of the Penghu Islands. On July 30 it advanced to occupy all of the

[117] On the Penghu episode see also Leonard Blussé, "The Dutch Occupation of the Pescadores (1622–1624)," *Transactions of the International Conference of Orientalists in Japan*, No. 18 ( 1973), pp. 28–44, and *Mingji Helanren qinju Penghu candang, Taiwan wenxian congkan*, No. 154 (Taipei, 1962).

main island except the point where the Dutch fort stood. The Dutch were cut off from their drinking water and had to negotiate in earnest. Li Dan, headman of the Chinese community in Hirado, Japan, and his young agent, Zheng Zhilong, were actively involved as intermediaries.[118] By the end of 1624 the Dutch had completed their withdrawal from Penghu and were beginning to establish themselves in the area of modern Tainan. After much loss of life and property on both sides, they had accepted the solution that had first been offered them in 1604.

## THE DUTCH AND THE SPANISH ON TAIWAN

In 1620 Taiwan was inhabited almost entirely by the various Malayo-Polynesian peoples whom we call the "aborigines," some of them quite closely related to some of the peoples of Luzon a hundred miles to the south. They lived comfortably off the abundant fish and game and the modest harvests of their shifting cultivation. Chinese pirates occasionally based themselves on the coast, and Chinese and Japanese traders met regularly in some of the harbors. To the Chinese and Japanese, the Dutch were intruders and competitors, but might turn out to be tolerable or even welcome neighbors if they provided new and stable trade links among China, Japan, Southeast Asia, and even the distant markets of Europe. But if they tried to have everything their own way without consideration for the interests of their Chinese and Japanese trading partners, they would make themselves most unwelcome. And they did. In 1627 and 1628 their efforts to collect tolls from the Japanese, who had been trading there before the Dutch arrived, led to a dangerous quarrel, and the Japanese authorities retaliated by prohibiting Dutch trade with Japan until 1632.[119]

---

[118] Iwao Seiichi, "Li Tan, Chief of the Chinese Residents at Hirado, Japan in the Last Days of the Ming Dynasty," *Memoirs of the Research Department of the Tōyō Bunko*, Vol. 17 (1958), pp. 27–83.

[119] The most thorough study of the Dutch period in Taiwan is Tonio Andrade, *How Taiwan Became Chinese: Dutch, Spanish, and Han Colonization in the Seventeenth Century* (New York, 2007). Other useful summaries are John E. Wills, Jr., "The Seventeenth-Century Transformation: Taiwan under the Dutch and the Cheng Regime," in Murray A. Rubinstein, ed., *Taiwan: A History, 1600– 1994*, (Armonk, NY, 1999), pp. 84–106, and John R. Shepherd, *Statecraft and Political Economy on the Taiwan Frontier, 1600–1800.* (Stanford, CA, 1993), Chs. 2–4. Pioneering and still definitive in Chinese is Cao Yonghe, *Taiwan zaoqi lishi yanjiu* (Taipei, 1979). Much of the Dutch manuscript source base is now accessible in J. L. Blussé et al., eds., *De Dagregisters van het Kasteel Zeelandia, Taiwan, 1629–1662*, 4 vols. (The Hague, 1986–2000).

The Dutch difficulties with their Chinese trading partners down to 1636 resulted from their repeated overreactions to any Chinese trading practice that they suspected interfered with their "free trade" with all Chinese merchants, and a great deal of conflict among the would-be Chinese sea lords. In particular, the Dutch repeatedly made plans to assist the Ming authorities against one "pirate" or another, their help to be rewarded by "free trade." This led to much Dutch naval activity on the coast, which usually was on balance unwelcome to the authorities and to coastal residents, especially after the brutal Dutch raids of 1622–1623. The only stable solution was for the Dutch to stay away from the coast, stay out of coastal politics, and make the best they could of whatever trade came to them. That had been, after all, the terms of the original understanding of 1624.

Between 1628 and 1636 Zheng Zhilong maneuvered and fought his way among old enemies and past and present allies to a dominant position on the Fujian coast. The Dutch usually supported him against his enemies but were always disappointed by the trade they got in return. Zheng simply was not yet in sufficient control of the situation to give them what they wanted. In 1633 a bellicose Dutch commander delivered an ultimatum to Zheng demanding relaxation of restrictions on trade, sailed off to Batavia without waiting for his reply, which was conciliatory, and returned in July to attack the fleet of the astonished Zheng. After two months of naval skirmishes and Dutch marauding along the coast, Zheng finally assembled his fleet for a full-scale attack on a Dutch squadron off Jinmen on October 21. One Dutch ship was blown up and the rest retreated to Taiwan. The Dutch had been trying to cooperate with Zheng's rivals, especially one Liu Xiang, but now rejected new overtures from him; he attacked the Dutch fort on Taiwan in April 1634 but was beaten off.[120]

Surviving sources indicate that occasional reports of these conflicts were noted by an increasingly distracted Ming court, so that there too the "red hairs" were viewed as a bizarre and dangerous people. The last "red hairs" to come to the attention of the court were in fact English,

[120] J. L. Blussé, "The V.O.C. as Sorcerer's Apprentice: Stereotypes and Social Engineering on the China Coast," in W. L. Idema, ed., *Leyden Studies in Sinology* (Leiden, 1981), pp. 87–105; Blussé, "Minnan-jen or Cosmopolitan? The Rise of Cheng Chih-lung Alias Nicholas Iquan," in E. B. Vermeer, ed., *Development and Decline of Fukien Province in the 17th and 18th Centuries* (Leiden, 1990), pp. 245–264; C. R. Boxer, "The Rise and Fall of Nicholas Iquan," *T'ien-hsia Monthly*, Vol. 11, No. 5 (April–May 1939), pp. 401–439.

the merchants and crews of four ships commanded by John Weddell, sailing under a royal charter to the "Courteen Association," not for the East India Company. Arriving off Macao in 1637, alternately led on and then blocked by the Portuguese, Weddell's ships exchanged a few shots with the fort at the mouth of the Pearl River, got into a skirmish ashore, ultimately left having obtained only very limited trade and having been ordered never to return. No doubt the Portuguese wanted to use the fierce reputation of the Dutch to block their trade, and when the Chinese found that some of the Englishmen did indeed have red and blond hair, they had no hesitation about recording this little conflict as another "red hair" intrusion.[121]

A less dangerous challenge to the Dutch position on Taiwan than the Japanese or Liu Xiang came from the Spanish settlements on the north end of the island. The outpost at Jilong (Chi-lung, Kelang, Keelung) was established in 1626 as a strategic move against Dutch power and as an effort to provide a center where Chinese merchants might come to trade with the Spanish without Dutch interference. Another post was founded at Danshui (Tan-shui, Tamsui) in 1629. The Spanish built a solid stone fortress at Jilong and fairly substantial fortifications at Danshui, and in 1628 were reported to have two hundred Spanish and four hundred Filipino soldiers at Jilong, probably more than the Dutch could have mustered in the south. The Chinese did come to Jilong to trade, but in 1630 they found the Spanish had very little silver on hand with which to buy their silk. In 1633 the Spanish were able to buy as much silk as the Dutch had in some of their first years in Taiwan, but they were finding Jilong so unhealthy that about 100 Spanish and 20 Portuguese left for Manila later that year. Danshui faced a good deal of aborigine hostility and was abandoned in 1638. In August 1642 a force of 591 Dutchmen took the Jilong fortress, encountering little resistance from a decrepit garrison of 115 Spaniards and 155 Filipinos.[122]

By 1636 Zheng Zhilong had no really dangerous rival for naval supremacy on the Fujian coast, the Japanese conflict was settled, and the Dutch East India Company, now that its Chinese and Japanese

---

[121] Peter Mundy, *The Travels of Peter Mundy in Europe and Asia, 1608–1667*, ed. Sir Richard C. Temple, Hakluyt Society, New Ser., Vols. 17, 35, 45–46, 55, 78 (Cambridge, 1907–1936), Vol. 3, pp. 159–316; Zhang Weihua, *Mingshi Folangji*, pp. 147–148.

[122] F. R. J. Verhoeven, *Bijdragen tot de Oudere Koloniale Geschiedenis van het Eiland Formosa* (The Hague, 1930), Chs. 4–7; José Antonio Borao Mateo et al., *Spaniards in Taiwan: Documents*. 2 vols (Taipei, 2001– 2002).

connections seemed to promise profit, had sent more than four hundred fresh soldiers to Taiwan. These troops in a series of marches to the north and south in 1635–1636 established firm Dutch domination over many more aborigine villages and vastly increased the zone that was safe for Chinese agriculture and commerce. A formidable stone fortress, Casteel Zeelandia, was completed and dedicated in 1639. Welcome reductions in competition for China–Japan trade resulted from the Japanese exclusion of the Portuguese and prohibition of all Japanese ocean voyages. Trade expanded very rapidly; in nineteen months, from late 1637 to early 1639, the Dutch received Chinese goods worth well more than 1,000,000 taels.[123] A large part of these goods was paid for in Japanese silver. The volume of trade remained in this range until production and trade in China were disrupted by the Ming–Qing wars. This Dutch trade and the flourishing trade of Zheng Zhilong and his associates very probably fully replaced the volume of trade lost by the expulsion to the Portuguese from Japan.

The growth of Chinese settlement and agriculture on Taiwan was a slower process. Chinese traders had been in the coastal aborigine villages when the Dutch arrived. Particularly welcome to the Dutch was the growing supply of deer hides, hunted or trapped by frontier Chinese or bought from the aborigines, which the company bought for the Japanese market.[124] A very different mode of Chinese settlement emerged as rice and sugar cultivation expanded in the plains near the Dutch forts. Several big Chinese merchants did a great deal of investing and organizing. The most interesting figure among them was Su Minggang, the first chief of the Chinese community at Batavia, who resigned that position and moved to Taiwan in 1635.[125] After 1644 a wave of refugees from the Ming–Qing wars came across the Taiwan Strait. Some of them returned to the mainland as the fighting in the southeast began to die down, but there was another surge in the 1650s as Zheng Chenggong consolidated his power base on the Fujian coast and the Qing increased their efforts to drive him out. The Chinese population was less than four thousand in 1640 but more than fourteen thousand in 1648.

[123] Blussé et al., *Dagregisters*, Vol. 1, p. 451.
[124] Thomas O. Höllman, "Formosa and the Trade in Venison and Deer Skins," in Roderich Ptak and Dietmar Rothermund, eds., *Emporia, Commodities, and Entrepreneurs in Asian Maritime Trade, c. 1400–1750*, Beiträge zur Südasienforschung, Südasien-Institut, Universität Heidelberg, No. 141 (Stuttgart, 1991), pp. 263–290.
[125] B. Hoetink, "Soe Bing Kong: Het eerste hoofd der Chinezen te Batavia." *Bijdragen tot de Taal-, Land-, en Volkenkunde van Nederlandsch Indië*, Vol. 73 ( 1917), pp. 344–415.

In striking parallel to the Spanish at Manila, the Dutch levied a head tax on every Chinese. Beginning in 1645 monopolies of trade with various aborigine villages were distributed to local Chinese under a competitive bidding system that produced considerable revenue for the Dutch Company and much trouble for everyone in the 1650s. Around 1650 half of the company's income from Taiwan came from profits of trade and half from tolls, head taxes, and so on. As the payments for the various monopolies rose as a result of competitive bidding, the tax collectors were often in arrears or in debt. The rough practices of head-tax collectors, and especially their intrusions into household where the women were kept secluded, were bitterly resented.

In September 1652 all these tensions exploded in a large but poorly armed rebellion led by Guo Huaiyi. The Dutch, warned by seven of the headmen of the Chinese community, had only one night to muster their forces. The next morning Guo's forces, more than 4,000 strong, plundered the Dutch settlement at Saccam (Chikan) across the harbor from Casteel Zeelandia, and killed and mutilated eight Dutchmen and some slaves. But then they broke and fled before the discipline and firepower of only 150 Dutch musketeers, and never again offered coherent resistance. The Dutch and aborigines hunted out the fugitives, including one large group that was camped in the mountains, and "killed between 3000 and 4000 rebel Chinese in revenge for the spilled Dutch Christian blood." There are striking parallels here with the rebellions at Manila: the split between the rural population and the leaders who informed the Dutch, the resentment of tax collection practices, and the enthusiastic participation of indigenous troops in the slaughter.[126]

In the 1650s the profits of the Dutch Company from Taiwan became smaller and less consistent, largely as a result of Zheng Chenggong's efforts to establish tight control over trade and shipping in the Taiwan Strait. Overproduction in the growing sugar industry was aggravated by a decline in European demand for Taiwan sugar as production revived in Brazil.[127] The company authorities in Batavia were more and more inclined to view Taiwan as a dubious asset, thus less inclined to take serious measures to deal with the possibility of an invasion by Zheng Chenggong. Nothing they could have done, however, would have enabled

---

[126] Johannes Huber, "Chinese Settlers against the Dutch East India Company: The Rebellion Led by Kuo Huai-i on Taiwan in 1652," in Vermeer, ed., *Development and Decline*, pp. 265–296.

[127] Kristof Glamann, *Dutch–Asiatic Trade, 1620–1740* (Copenhagen / The Hague, 1958), p. 156.

them to withstand the large and well-disciplined army with which Zheng finally landed on Taiwan on April 30, 1661.

When Zheng's troops landed, Dutch rule in most of Taiwan ended in a few days. In view of the many conflicts and irritations already described, it is not surprising that most of the Taiwan Chinese seem to have welcomed him as a liberator. The defenders of Casteel Zeelandia could do nothing but fend off Zheng's attacks, receive some reinforcements from Batavia, and wait as Zheng Chenggong consolidated his control of the island, put many of his soldiers to work farming, and even collected from the Taiwan Chinese the debts they owed the Dutch. On February 1, 1662, the Dutch capitulated and were allowed to march out in good order and depart, leaving to Zheng the company's stores of money, arms, and trade goods. The Dutch presence on Taiwan had stimulated and accelerated the process of Chinese settlement there, but the Dutch had long ago worn out their welcome. Taiwan had a Chinese ruler for the first time. But coming in the years of dynastic collapse and transition, the dramas on Taiwan had been little noticed on the mainland except in Fujian, and source material in Chinese is fragmentary.

## THE WORLD OF THE MARITIME CHINESE

The structure of this chapter would imply a set of topics on relations between European nations or peoples and such vast and undifferentiated entities as the Chinese state or the Chinese people. Most of these relations took place, however, in a special group of environments dominated by a distinctive variant of Chinese culture, economy, and politics, that of the maritime Chinese. In addition to the renowned Zheng family, we have encountered only a few named individuals, like Su Minggang and Guo Huaiyi on Taiwan and the hapless Juan Bautista de la Vera in Manila. The fate of the latter is an excellent example of the hazards of the mediation across cultural and linguistic barriers that was a maritime Chinese specialty. We have seen many maritime Chinese take on more or less of the clothing, customs, and religion of the Europeans under whom they settled.[128]

---

[128] Studies of the Chinese in the South China Sea and Southeast Asia before 1800 are developing rapidly. The multiplicity of political and cultural situations to which they had to adjust makes summary extremely difficult. For starting points see Blussé, "Minnanjen or Cosmopolitan?" in Anthony Reid, ed., *Sojourners and Settlers: Histories of Southeast Asia and the Chinese* (Honolulu, 2001); Sucheta Mazumdar, *Sugar and Society in China: Peasants, Technology, and the World Market* (Cambridge, MA, 1998), Ch. 2; Timothy Brook, *The Troubled Empire: China in the Yuan and Ming Dynasties*

The first Portuguese ventures east of India, we have seen, owed something to the Chinese who already were trading at Melaka when they arrived and who aided their efforts to go on to Siam and the China coast. In the 1540s and 1550s they shared a maritime world in crisis with a host of Chinese leaders who raided, traded, and negotiated with the government as opportunities shifted; our sources hardly ever allow us to identify a specific interaction. In 1600–1605 offshore intriguers and entrepreneurs brought the Dutch to the Fujian coast for the first time and brought agents of the Ming state to Manila. And of course the Zheng family dominated Dutch relations with China as it dominated much of maritime China after 1625. By that time Chinese sources reflect a well-developed knowledge of routes and trading practices along an "Eastern Sea" (Dongyang) route passing from Manila down to the Spice Islands and Timor, and a "Western Sea" (Xiyang) route passing the coast of modern Vietnam and the Malay Peninsula and on to Java and Sumatra.[129]

The achievements of the maritime Chinese away from the south China coast can be traced, frequently through the records of the Dutch or other Europeans, in many other ports of East and Southeast Asia: Nagasaki, Batavia, Banten, Ayutthaya, Melaka, Makasar, and so on. Of these, in addition to Manila, the most important for our story, the most thoroughly studied, and perhaps the best documented is Batavia. There had been a small Chinese settlement at Jakarta before the Dutch conquered it in 1619. Immediately after the Dutch victory, the formidable Governor-General Jan Pietersz Coen appointed Su Minggang, "Captain Bencon" to the Dutch, as headman of the Chinese community. Su and another highly capable leader whom the Dutch called Jan Con and whose Chinese name we do not know almost immediately began contracting with the Dutch to collect taxes on various forms of trading and activity, of which the tax on Chinese gambling was one of the earliest and most lucrative. Jan Con also began supplying lumber and stone for the new buildings and fortifications, hard work made more dangerous by attacks by the Banten-based enemies of the Dutch, and contracting with the Dutch to supply Chinese labor for the construction of the buildings, walls, and canals. There thus was a remarkable congruence of interest among the leaders of the Chinese community, profiting from labor contracting, supply

(Cambridge, MA, 2010), Ch. 9; and Leonard Blussé, *Visible Cities: Canton, Nagasaki, and Batavia and the Coming of the Americans* (Cambridge MA and London, 2008).

[129] Leonard Blussé, "No Boats to China: The Dutch East India Company and the Changing Pattern of the China Sea Trade, 1635–1690," *Modern Asian Studies*, Vol. 30, No. 1 (1996), pp. 56–59.

of building materials, and tax farming, and the substantial number of poor Chinese who were getting steady work on the building projects. In 1625, at Jan Con's suggestion, the Dutch began to levy a special tax of three reals on each Chinese, the proceeds of which were earmarked for construction projects and thus came back to the Chinese as wages, labor contracting profits, and payments for supplies of building materials. In addition the Chinese paid a capitation tax to obtain exemption from service in the local militia, which was farmed by the Chinese headmen. These two taxes came to provide more than half the revenue from tolls and taxes at Batavia. By 1644 the Chinese headmen farmed nineteen of the twenty-four tolls, levies, and monopolies instituted by the Dutch at Batavia.

By the deaths of Jan Con in 1639 and Su Minggang in 1644, the Chinese community at Batavia was so prosperous that it no longer provided much of the heavy labor at Batavia. They maintained a complex network of trade with many ports, including quite a few where the Dutch were not allowed or could not afford to maintain a presence. They were making first efforts in salt production and sugar cultivation around Batavia, which would lead to large-scale production later in the century. In the tense and intricate diplomacy of the Dutch with their Javanese enemies of Banten and Mataram, Chinese advisers on both sides frequently served as intermediaries. Batavia, like Manila and Casteel Zeelandia on Taiwan, was in many ways very much a "Chinese colonial town."[130]

The energetic meetings of two worlds described in this chapter, the evolution of such complex Sino-European accommodations as Macao, Manila, and the early network of missionaries and converts, owed a great deal to maritime Chinese both on the China coast and in foreign ports, to astute and realistic officials, and to statesmen and intellectuals who were much more open to novelty and to interaction with foreigners than some clichés about Chinese culture would have us believe. In our increasingly interactive and transnational world, the study of the achievements and frustrations of these Chinese and of the amazing variety of brutal, devoted, astute, obtuse, brave Europeans with whom they interacted can provide rich food for thought.

[130] Blussé, *Strange Company*, Chs. 4–6.

**2**

# Learning from Heaven

## *The Introduction of Christianity and Other Western Ideas into Late Ming China*

### Willard J. Peterson

Of the alternatives represented in the intellectual scene in late Ming, the Westerners' Learning from Heaven (*Tianxue*) was the least well precedented.[1] In spite of efforts to assimilate some of it to vocabulary and concepts in classical texts, the Learning from Heaven could not escape also being labeled Western Learning (*Xixue*). It was foreign, whereas the other main intellectual alternatives to the Learning of the Way (*Daoxue*), including Buddhism, were only different (*yi*). Although critics of the missionaries cited foreign origins in attempts to discredit the Learning from Heaven, its foreignness remained less an issue in late Ming than it became in the Kangxi period in early Qing. With no obvious detriment to his contemporary reputation, Matteo Ricci was well known under the name Li of the Far West (Li Xitai). He and his confreres published books about that different part of the world, the Far West, from which they had come. Ricci reported being told in 1599 by a censor in Nanjing that, having lived in Jiangxi and other places, he was "no longer a foreigner in China. Can there be any objection to his residing in Nanjing, where there are so many Huihui [Moslems]?"[2] Ricci had been proceeding since 1595 with

---

[1] Christians and forms of Christianity had been present and recognized during the Tang dynasty and again under the Mongols. For useful introductory summaries, see Nicolas Standaert, ed., *Handbook of Christianity in China, Volume One: 635–1800* (Leiden, 2001), pp. 1–111. The *Handbook* provides extensive bibliographical and thematic guidance that supplements what is offered in this chapter.

[2] Matteo Ricci, *Fonti Ricciane. Documenti originali concernenti Matteo Ricci e la storia delle prime relazioni tra l'Europa e la Cina 1579–1615*, 3 vols., ed. Pasquale D'Elia, S.J. (Rome, 1942–1949), Vol. 2, p. 47, n. 536, as translated in George Harris, "The Mission of Matteo Ricci, S.J.: A Case Study of an Effort at Guided Cultural Change in China in the Sixteenth Century," *Monumenta Serica*, Vol. 25 (1966), p. 69.

the tactic of acting "as though we were men of China" (*come uomini già della Cina*).³ Especially in the early phase of the mission, there was a self-conscious effort by a few of the missionaries to be Chinese, but an important aspect of their impact on literati with whom they had contact was that they were from a distant, unknown place.⁴

At the same time, they presented the essentials of their learning as universal. One of Ricci's converts wrote in 1608 that the missionary not only was not different (*yi*) or strange, but also that his conduct and his learning were compatible with Heaven.⁵ The word "heaven," which the Westerners used to distinguish the learning they sought to disseminate in China, was nicely ambiguous in its referents, pointing both to the religious Lord of Heaven (*Tianzhu*), or the Christian God, and to secular knowledge of patterns of heaven (*tianwen*), or astronomy in particular and science in general. The understanding of some of the converts moved from calculations involving celestial phenomena, through the realization that "the same minds and the same principles [are] in the Eastern and Western seas,"⁶ to recognition of an eternal, universal Lord of Heaven who was behind the religious truths as well as the regular "laws of Nature."

Although the so-called laws of Nature were represented by the missionaries as being universally so, from our current point of view the learning about patterns of heaven that they circulated in late Ming was culture bound and partial. Fewer than a dozen missionaries were involved in the publication of some fifty titles on topics in mathematics, astronomy, geography, and what was known then as natural philosophy.⁷ Almost without exception, the writings were expressions of the Aristotelian scholasticism that still prevailed in European universities' curricula. Aristotle, Ptolemy, and Galen were repeatedly cited as authorities at the moment that the vanguard of scientific knowledge in Europe was abandoning

---

³ Ricci, *Fonti Ricciane*, Vol. 1, p. 378, n. 491. Cf. Harris, "The Mission of Matteo Ricci," pp. 32, 70.
⁴ See the insightful discussion of the ambiguities in "The Problem of Nationality" in Harris, "The Mission of Matteo Ricci," pp. 49–70.
⁵ Li Zhizao, Preface to Ricci's *Jiren shi pian*, in Li Zhizao, ed., *Tianxue chu han* (1628; reprint, Taipei, 1965), 2a, p. 103. Cf. Willard J. Peterson, "Why Did They Become Christians?" *East Meets West: The Jesuits in China, 1582–1773*, ed. Charles E. Ronan, S.J., and Bonnie B. C. Oh (Chicago, 1988), p. 138, and Jonathan D. Spence, *The Memory Palace of Matteo Ricci* (New York, 1984), p. 127.
⁶ Li Zhizao, quoted in Peterson, "Why Did They Become Christians?" p. 142.
⁷ For further bibliographical and biographical details, see Willard J. Peterson, "Western Natural Philosophy Published in Late Ming China," *Proceedings of the American Philosophical Society*, Vol. 117, No. 4 (1973), pp. 295–296.

them for new assumptions, methods, and authorities. Copernicus and Galileo were mentioned, but the heliostatic or heliocentric hypothesis was not conveyed in other than Tycho Brahe's compromise system, which still centered on the earth.[8] Without judging the merits or the motives of the Jesuit missionaries' teaching Aristotelian scholasticism rather than the new science associated with men such as Copernicus, Kepler, Galileo, Vesalius, and William Harvey, we might bear in mind that the Learning from Heaven offered to Chinese readers in late Ming was only one of the sets of competing ideas explaining the phenomenal world.

A similar point applies to the religious ideas presented as part of the Learning from Heaven. The missionaries were Roman Catholic, not Protestant. In late Ming, they had to embark from Lisbon to reach China by way of Goa and Macao and thus were subject to the control of the Portuguese and then, from 1580, to the authority of the Spanish kings. Nearly all of the missionaries who participated in the late Ming intellectual milieu through their writings and conversations with literati were Jesuits. All of that is well known and not problematic, but the effect was that the religious ideas presented to their Chinese readers were not ascribed to universally in western Europe or on the Spanish peninsula or in the order of the Society of Jesus, even among its representatives who labored in China.[9] A germane example is the controversies centering on the theological ideas of Luis de Molina (1535–1600), a Jesuit at the university in Évora, Portugal. Writing in the decades after the Council of Trent came to its inconclusive end in 1564, Molina sought to reconcile the Thomist doctrine on the necessity of divine grace that was defended especially by Dominicans and the Spanish king, with the stress placed in the *Spiritual Exercises* of Ignatius Loyola on the capacity, and even the need, for each person to commit himself to being saved.[10] Even before Molina's book, *Concordia*, was published in Lisbon in 1588, debate on this issue was intense. It continued through the 1580s and 1590s and was halted only in 1607 with a papal decree that called for a truce on

[8] See the summary in ibid., pp. 298–300. Also see Nathan Sivin, "Copernicus in China," *Colloquia Copernica*, II, *Études sur l'audience de la théorie héliocentrique* (Warsaw, 1973), esp. pp. 76–82.

[9] See A. D. Wright, *The Counter-Reformation: Catholic Europe and the Non-Christian World* (London, 1982), pp. 30–31, 138. For some of the complexity of the missionaries' views, see Liam M. Brockey, *Journey to the East: The Jesuit Mission to China, 1579–1724* (Cambridge, MA, 2007).

[10] T. M. Parker, "The Papacy, Catholic Reform, and Christian Missions," in R. B. Wernham, ed., *The New Cambridge Modern History*, Vol. 8: *The Counter-Reformation and Price Revolution, 1559–1610* (Cambridge, 1968), pp. 68–69.

both sides until a decision, never forthcoming, was made in Rome.[11] Although leading Jesuit thinkers, such as the influential Robert Bellarmine (1542–1621), who had been one of Matteo Ricci's teachers at the Jesuits' Collegio Romano, did not wholly accept Molina, he gained popularity among Jesuits concerned with pastoral practice and foreign missions.[12] By the end of the seventeenth century, Jesuits were being "accused of favoring lax standards of spirituality at home, with indiscriminate access to the sacraments, ready absolution, and too frequent communion; and of being ready to compromise true Catholic teaching abroad."[13] At the beginning of the Jesuits' activities in China, however, the same practices were being glossed positively as accommodation to local cultural practice and encouragement of the early stages of true belief based more on effort than on grace.[14]

Another controversial area with important implications for the accessibility of the Jesuits' religion to potential converts in China was argued out narrowly in terms of the perennial struggles between adherents of teachings traced back to either Aristotle or Plato and more broadly in terms of the acceptability of pagan authors.[15] In 1593, one of the prolific scholars and translators of the day, Francesco Patrizi (1529–1597), published his *New Philosophy of the Universe* (*Nova de Universis Philosophia*) with a dedication to Pope Gregory XIV urging him to order that the Platonism associated with the tradition of Hermes Trismegistus displace the dangerous teachings of Aristotelian scholasticism in Christian schools, particularly those operated by Jesuits.[16] Patrizi was invited from Ferrara to teach Platonism in Rome, but his book was eventually condemned. Nevertheless, about the time Jesuits were entering China there were strong, sometimes well-received arguments for a more open stance toward pagan religious expression, and these sentiments continued to be expounded and criticized through the seventeenth century. The proponents of what was called the Ancient Theology finally lost the battle within the Roman Catholic Church,

[11] Ibid., pp. 68–69.
[12] Ibid.; Joseph Sebes, "The Precursors of Ricci," in Ronan and Oh, eds., *East Meets West*, pp. 36–37.
[13] Wright, *The Counter-Reformation*, p. 35.
[14] See Harris, "The Mission of Matteo Ricci," p. 155.
[15] D. P. Walker, *The Ancient Theology: Studies in Christian Platonism from the Fifteenth to the Eighteenth Century* (Ithaca, NY: 1972), pp. 128–130.
[16] Ibid., pp. 111–112, and Frances A. Yates, *Giordano Bruno and the Hermetic Tradition* (Chicago, 1964), pp. 181–183. For a summary of the *Nova Philosophia*, see Paul O. Kristeller, *Eight Philosophers of the Italian Renaissance* (Stanford, CA, 1964), pp. 118–125.

but in the meanwhile their arguments provided justification for any Jesuits who would choose to presume "writings ascribed to Confucius, and other ancient Chinese classics, were compatible with Christian ethics and monotheism, with good, 'natural' religion."[17] Perhaps the extreme expression of this attitude came in the *Nouveaux mémoires sur l'état présent de la Chine*, which a China missionary, Louis Le Comte, published in Paris in 1696. He offered the propositions that

the Chinese during two thousand years up to the time of Christ had known the true God, had honoured Him in a way that can serve as an example to Christians, had sacrificed to Him in the most ancient temple in the world, had had faith and all the Christian virtues, and of all the nations had been the most favored by God's graces.[18]

LeComte and others were willing to implicate Matteo Ricci posthumously as their ally in the claim that the Ancient Theology had been present in earliest China.[19] There is no good evidence that the early Jesuit missionaries wholly participated in these radical inferences, but there is at least circumstantial evidence that the ferment of such ideas at the end of the sixteenth century opened the possibility of taking an accommodative stance toward ideas that they began to call Confucianism and making expedient use of more prudent presentations of Christian theology.

## PUTTING ON NEW CLOTHES

In 1557 Portuguese merchants were granted the privilege of maintaining permanent residence at what came to be called Macao. It became a small settlement on a peninsula in Xiangshan district, south of Canton, which they officially were allowed to visit twice a year for trade. Portuguese ships had reached the China coast by 1513 and an embassy visited Beijing in 1520.[20] Missionaries traveled with the merchants and, like them, were restricted in their opportunities by the Chinese authorities, although both

---

[17] Walker, *The Ancient Theology*, p. 197.

[18] Ibid., p. 199, drawn from Virgile Pinot, *La Chine et la formation de l'esprit philosophique en France (1640–1740)* (Paris, 1932), p. 98. Also see the similar ideas in Philippe Couplet, ed., *Confucius Sinarum Philosophus* (Paris, 1687), as cited in Paul A. Rule, *K'ung-tzu or Confucius? The Jesuit Interpretation of Confucianism* (Sydney, 1986), p. 118. See also the reservations expressed in George H. Dunne, *Generation of Giants: The Story of the Jesuits in China in the Last Decades of the Ming Dynasty* (London, 1962), pp. 26–27.

[19] Walker, *The Ancient Theology*, pp. 200–201.

[20] Ricci, *Fonti Ricciane*, Vol. 1, p. 149. See Chapter 1 of this volume.

groups hoped to pursue their goals in China. After two or three years of mission work in Japan, the Jesuit Francis Xavier (1506–1552) determined that converting China was the key to converting Japan. He proposed to travel with another Portuguese embassy to Beijing as a papal envoy and there persuade the emperor to allow Christians to live, travel, and preach in the empire. Portuguese rivalries thwarted the plan in Melaka, and Xavier attempted to proceed on his own. He was taken as far as a small island southwest of what was to become Macao and, his plans aborted, died there in the winter of 1552.[21]

Over the next thirty years, more than fifty priests and lay brothers – mostly Jesuits and Franciscans, but also a few Augustinians and Dominicans – vainly attempted to establish residence in Ming territory for purposes other than trade.[22] After decades of frustration, a major change was initiated by Alessandro Valignano (1539–1606), who was appointed the visitor for all Jesuit activities east of Africa. On his way from Goa to Japan he stopped in Macao in 1577–1578. Against the predilections of Jesuits who ministered to the Macao community, Valignano agreed to permit missionaries for China to learn Chinese customs and the spoken and written language. In response to his order, Michele Ruggieri (1543–1607) was sent from Goa.[23]

Ruggieri arrived in Macao in the summer of 1579 and began an intensive course in Chinese. He progressed enough with his tutors to try putting the "Great Learning" into Latin,[24] and in 1580 he began to go with the merchants on their regular trips to Canton.[25] At this time Ruggieri reported that his study of Chinese was being criticized in Macao, even by fellow Jesuits. According to him, some asked, "What is the sense of this Father occupying himself with this sort of thing when he could be of service in the other ministries of the Society? It is a waste of time for him to learn the Chinese language and to consecrate himself to a hopeless enterprise."[26]

---

[21] Sebes, "The Precursors of Ricci," pp. 23–27.
[22] Ibid.," pp. 27–30. For summaries of the organization of the Catholic missions in Asia see Donald F. Lach and Edwin J. Van Kley, *Asia in the Making of Europe* (Chicago, 1993), Vol. 3, Book 1, pp. 130–298, and Claudia Von Collani, "Missionaries," in Standaert, ed., *Handbook*, pp. 286–354.
[23] Ricci, *Fonti Ricciane*, Vol. 1, p. 147; Harris, "The Mission of Matteo Ricci," pp. 36–37; Sebes, "The Precursors of Ricci," pp. 32–33; Dunne, *Generation of Giants*, p. 17.
[24] Knud Lundbaek, "The First Translation from a Confucian Classic in Europe," *China Mission Studies Bulletin*, Vol. 1 (1979), pp. 1–11.
[25] Sebes, "The Precursors of Ricci," pp. 29, 34.
[26] Letter by Ruggieri in Pietro Tacchi Venturi, ed., *Opere storiche del P. Matteo Ricci S.J.* (Macerata, 1911–1913), Vol. 2, p. 397, as translated in Dunne, *Generation of Giants*, p. 19. Also see Harris, "The Mission of Matteo Ricci," p. 55.

Valignano protected him and, in 1582, ordered that instead of trying to make converts more like Portuguese (in dress and manners, for example), the strategy was to recognize Chinese Christians as Chinese. In response to a suggestion by Ruggieri, Valignano also had the Goa authorities dispatch two more Jesuits to study Chinese in Macao. They arrived in the summer of 1582.[27]

Just prior to this, Ruggieri went with the Portuguese officials of Macao to Zhaoqing, the seat of the provincial governor of Guangdong, to be told of the violation of Ming rules by a Spanish group led by a Jesuit from the Philippines. They had landed in southern Fujian and were brought to Canton as spies.[28] Supposedly Ruggieri made a favorable impression on the governor, who sent for him after his return to Macao with the "spies." Ruggieri accepted the invitation and took one of the newly arrived Jesuits, Francesco Pasio (1554–1612), with him to take up residence in a Buddhist temple.

Instead of the European garb and full beard in which he had presented himself to the governor earlier in the year, Ruggieri wore Buddhist robes and had shaven his head and face. According to Ruggieri, the governor "wanted us to dress in the fashion of their priests which is little different from ours; now we have done so and, in brief, have become Chinese in order to win China for Christ."[29] A few years earlier, at Valignano's direction, the Jesuit missionaries in Japan had adopted Zen Buddhist robes, and Ruggieri and Pasio were adopting them as part of the strategy to gain permission to reside in Zhaoqing.[30] However, they were ordered back to Macao almost immediately. Pasio then went on to Japan. When the invitation was renewed, perhaps by the prefect at Zhaoqing, Ruggieri went back in the summer of 1583. Still with Buddhist robes and a shaven head, this time he was accompanied by the other recently arrived Jesuit, Matteo Ricci.[31]

In a nice coincidence, Matteo Ricci (1552–1610) was born in Italy a few months before Francis Xavier died off the south coast of China.[32]

---

[27] Dunne, *Generation of Giants*, p. 19; Sebes, "The Precursors of Ricci," p. 34; Harris, "The Mission of Matteo Ricci," p. 7.

[28] Sebes, "The Precursors of Ricci," pp. 29–30; Dunne, *Generation of Giants*, pp. 19–20.

[29] As translated in Harris, "The Mission of Matteo Ricci," p. 83, from Venturi, ed., *Opere Storiche*, Vol. 2, p. 416. The final phrase is "siamo fatti Cini ut Christo Sinas lucrifaciamus."

[30] Harris, "The Mission of Matteo Ricci," pp. 82, 84. See Sebes, "The Precursors of Ricci," p. 58, n. 72, for testimony by a Jesuit newly arrived in Japan that he was starting life anew.

[31] Harris, "The Mission of Matteo Ricci," pp. 55–56; Sebes, "The Precursors of Ricci," pp. 35–36.

[32] For brief biographical summaries, see the entry by Wolfgang Franke on Matteo Ricci in L. Carrington Goodrich and Chaoying Fang, eds., *Dictionary of Ming Biography*,

After studying law in Rome for three years, he joined the Society of Jesus in 1571 as a novice and met Alessandro Valignano. Valignano, who left in 1574 for Goa and East Asia, helped draw Ricci to China.[33] In his studies under the Jesuits in Rome, he was exposed to Christopher Clavius (1537–1612), a leading academic mathematician who was instrumental in the formulation of the Gregorian calendar announced in 1582, and to Robert Bellarmine (1542–1621), the celebrated Jesuit theologian who arrived to teach in Rome in 1576 and whose views eventually won papal support.[34] To prepare for his mission in the East, Ricci went, in 1577, to the university at Coimbra in Portugal, where what were to become the authoritative versions of Aristotelian natural philosophy were being developed for eventual publication in the 1590s.[35] Thus Ricci, in his early twenties, was exposed to the rapidly evolving idea of a Jesuit mission in Asia under Portuguese control, to the most up-to-date established concepts in mathematics and astronomy, to the new ideas in technical theology that were intended to win arguments with Protestants and, conceivably, pagans, and to the latest exposition of an elaborate, systematic account of natural phenomena that was to be the standard in most Catholic universities in the first half of the seventeenth century. It was a heady experience.

Matteo Ricci sailed from Lisbon in 1578 for Goa with twelve other Jesuits, among them Michele Ruggieri. There, Ricci completed his theological studies and was ordained a priest in 1580.[36] He then was sent to Macao, where he began to learn Chinese immediately after his arrival in the summer of 1582.[37] A year later, Ricci went back with Ruggieri to Zhaoqing. Ruggieri had been granted permission to reside there, presumably with the support of the district magistrate, Wang Pan, a *jinshi* from Shaoxing, Zhejiang. They had a residence and chapel built, continued

---

*1368–1644* (New York, 1976), Vol. 2, pp. 1137–1144, and Harris, "The Mission of Matteo Ricci," esp. pp. 6–18. The central, indispensable source on Ricci in China is his own account, available in *Fonti Ricciane*. Full accounts of his life in English are in Vincent Cronin, *The Wise Man from the West* (New York, 1955), and Dunne's *Generation of Giants*. A richly detailed reconstruction of aspects of Ricci's experience is in Spence, *The Memory Palace of Matteo Ricci*. All of these items include further bibliographic information relevant to Ricci.

33 Sebes, "The Precursors of Ricci," p. 32.

34 Ibid., p. 36; Wright, *The Counter-Reformation*, p. 91; Parker, "The Papacy," p. 67. Even from China, Ricci remained in touch with Clavius.

35 See Peterson, "Western Natural Philosophy," p. 297. Sister Patricia Reif, "Textbooks in Natural Philosophy, 1600–1650," *Journal of the History of Ideas*, Vol. 30 (1969), p. 23.

36 See Harris, "The Mission of Matteo Ricci," pp. 7, 151.

37 Ricci, *Fonti Ricciane*, Vol. 1, p. 154, n. 207. Ricci is specific that he was learning what he called *mandarina*. See Harris, "The Mission of Matteo Ricci," pp. 38–39.

to learn to speak Mandarin (*guanhua*), and to read. With their teachers' help, they put the Ten Commandments, prayers, and a catechism into Chinese. Ricci worked out a map of the world with the place names represented in Chinese characters. Ruggieri traveled north to Shaoxing and also west into Guangxi and up into Hunan; he was looking for contacts rather than converts so as to expand the mission beyond Zhaoqing.[38] In 1588 Ruggieri was ordered by Valignano to return to Rome to persuade the authorities to commission a papal embassy to the Ming emperor. This had been Xavier's hope as the most effective means to secure permission to proselytize in China, and Valignano wanted to try it again. Ricci remained in the Zhaoqing residence with another Jesuit, Antonio de Almeida, who also began to study the Chinese language.[39]

Already in 1585 Ricci claimed, "I can now converse with everyone without an interpreter and can write and read fairly well."[40] In a letter in 1592 he recalled more modestly, "I diligently gave myself to the study of the language and in a year or two I could get along without an interpreter. I also studied the writing. This is more difficult, however, and although I have worked hard at it up to the present time, I am still unable to understand all books."[41] The previous year, Ricci had been told by Valignano to translate the Four Books into Latin, which immersed him in the key classical texts. In 1594 he started again with a tutor, after being without one for at least seven years.

Every day I have two lessons with my teacher and devote some time to composition. Taking courage to write by myself, I have begun a book presenting our faith according to natural reason. It is to be distributed throughout China when printed.[42]

Ricci was acquiring the skills that would enable him to reach his target audience, the literati, by using their language and "natural reason."

In the meantime, Ricci and Almeida had been expelled from Zhaoqing in 1589, but were allowed to take up residence in Shaozhou, several hundred *li* to the north in Guangdong. They still wore Buddhist-style

---

[38] Harris, "The Mission of Matteo Ricci," pp. 8–10, 40–41.
[39] Ibid., p. 10.
[40] As translated in Harris, "The Mission of Matteo Ricci," p. 41, from a letter Ricci sent to the general of the Society of Jesus, in Venturi, ed., *Opere Storiche*, Vol. 2, p. 60.
[41] As translated in Harris, "The Mission of Matteo Ricci," p. 43, from Venturi, ed., *Opere Storiche*, Vol. 2, p. 91.
[42] As translated in Harris, "The Mission of Matteo Ricci," p. 44, from Venturi, ed., *Opere Storiche*, Vol. 2, p. 122.

robes and shaved heads. Local men seem to have regarded their chapel and residence as a Buddhist temple (*si*). They would arrange to have
their own gatherings there, including banquets, as had been the practice at Zhaoqing. They were also attracted by the books, pictures, maps,
and curious mechanical instruments, including clocks and astrolabes.[43]
Ricci realized at Zhaoqing that officials could come because it was not a
private residence; it had a quasi-public status. When important people
were gathered there, "the street was filled with their palanquins and the
riverbank in front of our door was filled with the large, handsome boats
of the mandarins."[44]

One of the literati who called on them was Qu Rukui, a certified student (*shengyuan*) from Suzhou.[45] Qu went to Ricci for information about
silver and quicksilver (mercury), but it is not clear if his purpose was
alchemical or metallurgical. (New processes involving mercury or quicksilver for increasing the yield of silver extracted from ore had been developed in the sixteenth century and were being used with great effect in Peru
and Mexico.)[46] Regardless of Qu's intent, Ricci thought such requests
concerned making real silver (*vero argento*) from quicksilver (*argento
vivo*), and the missionaries could not help.[47] Nevertheless, Qu continued
to associate with Ricci over a two-year period. Apparently he was the
one who suggested Ricci and Almeida ought not to be (Buddhist) monks
(*seng*), but should let their hair grow and be called Confucians (*ru*).[48]

For such a change, Ricci had to receive permission from Valignano,
who arrived in Macao from Japan in the autumn of 1592. Another year
or more passed before Lazzaro Cattaneo, a newly arrived Jesuit, pressed
the question with Valignano. According to Ricci, Cattaneo urged that in
China the missionaries should let their hair and beards grow long and
should wear silk robes and ceremonial hats. The request was granted
by Valignano.[49] Cattaneo then went to Shaozhou to help Ricci in 1594.

---

[43] Harris, "The Mission of Matteo Ricci," pp. 86–87.

[44] Ricci, *Fonti Ricciane*, Vol. 1, p. 259, n. 312; slightly altered from the translation in Harris,
"The Mission of Matteo Ricci," p. 86.

[45] Ricci, *Fonti Ricciane*, Vol. 1, p. 295, n. 1.

[46] See the summary in Spence, *The Memory Palace of Matteo Ricci*, pp. 185–188. Also
Harris, "The Mission of Matteo Ricci," pp. 44, 124.

[47] Ricci, *Fonti Ricciane*, Vol. 1, p. 240, n. 295.

[48] According to Li Zhizao in his discussion of the Nestorian inscription from Tang times.
Li, "Du Jingjiao beishu hou," 13a, in Li Zhizao, ed., *Tianxue chu han*, Vol. 1, p. 85.
Presumably Li was told this by Ricci. Cf. George Harris, "The Mission of Matteo Ricci,"
p. 87, and Paul Rule, *K'ung-tzu or Confucius?* p. 18.

[49] Ricci, *Fonti Ricciane*, Vol. 1, pp. 335–337, n. 429. Partly translated in Harris, "The
Mission of Matteo Ricci," p. 89.

(Almeida had died of fever in Macao in 1591, as did his replacement.) They stopped shaving their heads and faces, but still wore Buddhist robes.

The next spring Ricci traveled north into Jiangxi. At Jishui, in Ji'an prefecture, he called on an official who had served in Shaozhou. For the first time in public, he wore his new clothes.[50] He described his robe in a letter written later in 1595:

The formal robe, worn by literati (*letterate*) and notables, is of dark purple silk with long, wide sleeves; the hem, which touches my feet, has a border of bright blue silk half a palm in width and the sleeves and collar, which drops to the waist, are trimmed in the same way. ... The Chinese wear this costume on the occasion of visits to persons with whom they are not well acquainted, formal banquets, and when calling on officials. Since persons receiving visitors dress, in accordance with their rank, in the same way, my prestige is greatly enhanced when I go visiting.[51]

By the end of the year, when he had established a residence at Nanchang, Ricci was also being carried in a chair and accompanied by a retinue of servants.[52] Ricci was quite explicit that he would not present himself as an official representative of a foreign power, whether the Spanish king or the pope, but as a peer to learned Chinese with cultivated relations to officials. Recalling this juncture, Ricci wrote, "Thus, it was better now to proceed confidently as though we were in fact men of China."[53] He had started writing a book the previous year, and now, from 1595, Ricci was embarked on his new role as a literatus or even Confucian from the West (*xi ru*). Although not a literatus (*shi*) in the sense of one who is skilled enough in the written language to produce passable examination-type essays, Ricci was acceptable as a peer of literati roughly to the degree that some Buddhist clergy or figures such as Wang Gen were.

### RICCI AS A LITERATUS

Wearing his new clothes, Ricci traveled down the Gan River to Nanchang, and then down the Yangzi to Nanjing, which he reached at

---

[50] Ricci, *Fonti Ricciane*, Vol. 1, pp. 346–347, n. 7.
[51] Slightly altered from the translation in Harris, "The Mission of Matteo Ricci," p. 90, from Venturi, ed., *Opere Storiche*, Vol. 2, pp. 199–200. See the Rubens drawing that appears as the frontispiece and opposite p. 177 in Dunne, *Generation of Giants*.
[52] Harris, "The Mission of Matteo Ricci," pp. 90–91.
[53] Ricci, *Fonti Ricciane*, Vol. 1, p. 378, n. 491. Altered from the translation in Harris, p. 70.

the end of May 1595. He called on various contacts he had made in Zhaoqing and Shaozhou, but within a couple of weeks he was forced to leave, although he vowed he would rather be imprisoned than leave the southern capital.[54] Ricci retreated to Nanchang, where, after some initial tribulations, he was able to reside for three years. He cultivated provincial officials and imperial princes, but mostly he engaged in extensive social and intellectual exchanges with the local literati.[55] As a direct outcome of these involvements, in 1595 Ricci wrote an essay in Chinese entitled *You lun* (On friendship) or, as he referred to it, *Amicitia* or *Amicizia*.[56] It circulated in manuscript and then in printed versions, although Ricci himself complained he could not publish it, as he could not secure the requisite permission from his superiors in the Society of Jesus.[57] Similarly, in response to the admiration expressed for his powers of memorization, which he was pleased to demonstrate at gatherings of literati, he completed another small treatise in 1596 in Chinese, *Ji fa* (The art of memory) or, as he referred to it, *Trattato della memoria locale* (A treatise on compartmentalized memory).[58] He was able to buy a house in Nanchang, but instead of having a chapel, as at Zhaoqing and Shaozhou, Ricci had a room or hall for discussions, or what the literati would call discourses on learning (*jiang xue*).[59] In addition to going out to visit, Ricci reported he was inundated by visitors in the autumn of 1597, when thousands of literati assembled in Nanchang for the Jiangxi provincial examination.[60] Thus two years after he put on robes to present himself as a literatus rather than as a cleric, Ricci was demonstrating in his conversations and writings, and in his conduct and environment, that he was one. The book he was drafting in these years, which was first printed in 1603 as the *True Meaning of the Lord of Heaven* (*Tianzhu shiyi*), was

---

[54] See the translation in Dunne, *Generation of Giants*, p. 39, from Venturi, ed., *Opere Storiche*, Vol. 2, p. 201.

[55] See Dunne, *Generation of Giants*, p. 41.

[56] Matteo Ricci, *On Friendship: One Hundred Maxims for a Chinese Prince*, trans. Timothy Billings (New York, 2010). A Wanli print of the treatise bears the title *You lun*; it later went under the title *Jiaoyou lun*.

[57] Dunne, *Generation of Giants*, p. 44, from Venturi, ed., *Opere Storiche*, Vol. 2, p. 248.

[58] Ricci, *Fonti Ricciane*, Vol. 1, pp. 359–360, 362–363, 376–377, nn. 469, 475, 490; Dunne, *Generation of Giants*, p. 40; Spence, *The Memory Palace of Matteo Ricci*, esp. pp. 135–142.

[59] Two letters written by Ricci in the autumn of 1596, quoted in Dunne, *Generation of Giants*, p. 46, from Venturi, *Opere Storiche*, ed., Vol. 2, pp. 215, 230. Also see Ricci, *Fonti Ricciani*, Vol. 2, p. 46, n. 536.

[60] Dunne, *Generation of Giants*, p. 47, referring to Venturi, ed., *Opere Storiche*, Vol. 2, p. 242.

structured as a dialogue between a Chinese literatus (*zhong shi*) and a literatus from the West (*xi shi*), referring to Ricci himself.

Ricci was persuaded that it was not practicable to try to reach Beijing as part of an embassy from a king or pope, but he still had Beijing as his goal. He had raised the possibility that one of the princes at Nanchang might make arrangements for him,[61] but a real opportunity presented itself when Cattaneo arrived from Shaozhou with the news that Wang Honghui (1542–1601?) was coming to see him in a few days. Wang, a 1565 *jinshi* from Guangdong, had passed through Shaozhou a few years earlier on his way home after retiring as minister of the Nanjing Ministry of Rites. In his conversations with Ricci, Wang raised the idea that Ricci might be able to contribute to the current discussions on the reform of the Ming calendar, which was under the supervision of the Ministry of Rites.[62] Now, in 1598, as Wang was traveling north in the hope of again receiving an appointment to office, he stopped at Shaozhou to offer to take Ricci with him. Thus, in June, Ricci and Cattaneo, accompanied by two Chinese Jesuit brothers (*fratelli*), Zhong Mingren and You Wenhui, embarked from Nanchang in the entourage of Wang Honghui. Wang was going to Nanjing and then on to Beijing to take part in the birthday congratulations for the emperor in the eighth lunar month.[63]

Ricci's first trip to Beijing did not go well. Wang went north from Nanjing separately from Ricci's group. Once in the capital Ricci found no way to present the gifts he had brought for the emperor, and his contacts all seemed wary of him. Ricci retreated south, first to Suzhou, where Qu Rukui cared for him while he was ill, and then, in the spring of 1599, to Nanjing. With Wang Honghui's encouragement, he managed to buy a house there and pursued the activities that had made him an attractive figure in Nanchang: interviews with the curious and influential, displays of his clocks, prisms, musical instruments, maps, pictures, and other exotic items, and discussions of his ideas. In the spring of 1600, he set out again for Beijing, accompanied by Zhong Mingren, You Wenhui (who had become skilled in Western-style painting), and the Jesuit Diego Pantoja (who knew how to tune, play, and teach the clavichord, which was being

---

[61] Ricci, *Fonti Ricciane*, Vol. 2, pp. 6–7, n. 503.
[62] The discussions were precipitated by a long memorial in 1596 proposing calendar reform. See Willard Peterson, "Calendar Reform Prior to the Arrival of Missionaries at the Ming Court," *Ming Studies*, Vol. 21 (1986), pp. 49–55.
[63] Ricci, *Fonti Ricciane*, Vol. 2, pp. 8–10, nn. 504–6; also Dunne, *Generation of Giants*, p. 50.

presented among the gifts intended for the emperor).[64] After various difficulties, attendant especially on the ambiguities over whether his was an embassy bearing tribute to the court and, if not, how he and the gifts were to be handled, Ricci, by the beginning of 1601, was ensconced at the capital for the remainder of his life.

As a literatus in Beijing, Ricci was an enormous success. There was a constant flow of visits to the Jesuits' residence, many of which Ricci had to repay. As Ricci acknowledged, he was a beneficiary of the large number of literati and officials who came to Beijing each year for examinations or government matters.

Among the thousands who thus flock here from all fifteen provinces, there are many who either already know the Fathers in Beijing or in other residences, or who have heard of us and our teachings, or have seen the books which we have published or which speak of us. As a consequence, we have to spend the entire day in the reception hall to receive visitors.... To all of them we speak of the things pertaining to our holy faith.[65]

Most callers were merely curious, but with some Ricci also was able to maintain serious intellectual relationships that lasted for years, and a few of those cases included their conversion to his "holy faith."

To be a literatus was not simply a matter of changing clothes. Ricci had committed himself to a mode of living that may or may not have been detrimental to the Christianizing mission that was the purpose of his being in China. The tactic of being more Chinese, initiated by Valignano, had no necessary stopping point. Learning to speak Chinese led to reading, which led to writing. Writing Chinese entailed using Chinese vocabulary to express non-Chinese concepts, and losing important distinctions in the translation. The boundary shifted. For example, after Ricci's death, the written version of the Latin formula used at baptism began to be translated rather than just transliterated.[66] For his part, Ricci was confident he was drawing his hosts' ideas closer to his own. "I make every effort to turn our way the leader of the literati sect, that is Confucius, by interpreting any ambiguities

[64] Harris, "The Mission of Matteo Ricci," p. 14; Dunne, *Generation of Giants*, pp. 53–60, 69–71. For a discussion of the gifts, see Spence, *The Memory Palace of Matteo Ricci*, esp. pp. 194–195, and the lists in Ricci, *Fonti Ricciane*, Vol. 2, pp. 123–124.

[65] Ricci, *Fonti Ricciane*, Vol. 2, pp. 353–354, n. 769, altered from the translation in Dunne, *Generation of Giants*, p. 92.

[66] See Dunne, *Generation of Giants*, p. 146, and Ricci, *Fonti Ricciane*, Vol. 1, p. 370.

in his writing in our favor."[67] However, describing the experience of the Chinese literati rather than reflecting on his own, Ricci observed, "This doctrine [of the literati] is not acquired by choice, but is imbibed with the study of the literature, and neither degree holder nor official leaves off professing it."[68] To some extent, then, by learning to read and write in Chinese, Ricci and the other missionaries were indoctrinating themselves as they prepared to disseminate the Learning from Heaven (*Tianxue*) they had brought with them. This tension between what was Western and what was Chinese, between the imported and the indigenous, and how much compromise was permissible were at the core of the debates among missionaries as well as among Catholics back in Europe over the policy of accommodation, over decisions of whether and how to translate key terms, and over the status of rituals that might continue to be performed by converts or adapted by missionaries.[69] From the way he conducted himself after 1595, it seems clear that Ricci had decided acting as a literatus did not jeopardize his Christian mission even as it diminished his foreignness.

## THE LEARNING FROM HEAVEN PRESENTED IN RICCI'S BOOKS

From Ricci's perspective, he was talking and writing about and for "our holy faith." He used ancillary parts of his cultural baggage the way he used curious nonreligious objects, such as clocks and prisms, and curiosity about himself to attract and hold men long enough for God to "soften their hearts."[70] Ricci knew he was leading them to the gospel, but it was not his starting point, either in his discussions or in his writings. The bulk of his literati audience probably never had access to the central doctrines of his holy faith. Leaving aside the relatively few who were baptized, most literati whose acquaintance with Ricci and his writings passed beyond satisfaction of their curiosity were confronted with a range of ideas that went by the broad but distinguishing label of the Learning from Heaven. While he was alive, and even after he died in 1610, Ricci and his writings were treated as a novel part of the literati intellectual milieu.

---

[67] Ricci, *Fonti Ricciane*, Vol. 2, p. 296, n. 709. Also translated in Rule, *K'ung-tzu or Confucius?* p. 1.

[68] Ricci, *Fonti Ricciane*, Vol. 1, p. 115, n. 176. Partly translated in Dunne, *Generation of Giants*, pp. 112–13. *Questa legge pigliano loro non per elettione, ma con lo studio delle lettere la bevono, e nessuno graduato nè magistrato lascia di professarla.*

[69] See Dunne, *Generation of Giants*, pp. 227–230. The debates are considered in Rule, *K'ung-tzu or Confucius?*, esp. pp. 43–50, 70–149.

[70] Dunne, *Generation of Giants*, p. 91, quoting from Ricci, *Opere storiche*, Tacchi Venturi, ed., Vol. 2, p. 376. *Ammollira i loro cuori.*

Much of Ricci's vocabulary and some of his ideas were shared by all literati, but part of the attraction was that some of the vocabulary and many of his ideas were new, or strange, or odd, or finally, foreign. There was a continuum. For example, Ricci introduced his collection of a hundred items on friendship with a perfectly apt allusion to *Analects* 16.8: he had traveled by sea from far to the west in order to show his respect for the cultural power (*wen de*) of the Son of Heaven of the great Ming.[71] Ricci demonstrated expectable willingness to be patronized when he explained that the impetus for his compilation came at a banquet in Nanchang when a prince took his hand and asked to hear of the way of friendship in his Western country.[72] Once the manuscript was circulating, his readers could not have been surprised by such observations as that one should be circumspect in making friends and steadfast in keeping them, or that merchants in pursuit of profits could not truly be friends. The idea and ideal of friendship, or fellowship (*you*), had been discussed among literati, especially those involved in discourses on learning, for several decades, so Ricci's contribution could be assimilated to that debate. His readers would notice that some of Ricci's examples named some hitherto unknown countries and persons as explicitly Western. (This was inevitable, as Ricci drew the mostly aphoristic comments of ancient authors from an anthology on friends compiled by André de Resende, 1498–1573.)[73] Most literati would have paused at reading that friends come in pairs, just as "[t]he Divinity on High (*shang di*) gave humans two eyes, ears, hands and feet."[74] They would not previously have seen the classical term *shang di* in such a sentence, and Ricci's book on friendship did not explain how he meant it. Similarly, his treatise on the art of memory, which describes techniques for mnemonic associations and for placing and finding images, particularly Chinese written words,[75]

---

[71] Ricci, "Jiao you lun," 1a, in Li, *Tianxue chu han*, p. 299. The passage is also translated in Fang Hao, "Notes on Matteo Ricci's *De Amicitia*," *Monumenta Serica*, Vol. 14 (1949–55), p. 574.

[72] Ricci, "Jiao you lun," 1b, p. 300.

[73] Spence, *The Memory Palace of Matteo Ricci*, pp. 142, 150. Spence infers that Ricci dredged the examples from what he remembered of de Resende's book. Cf. Pasquale M. D'Elia, "Further Notes on Matteo Ricci's *De Amicitia*," *Monumenta Serica*, Vol. 15 (1956), p. 366.

[74] Ricci, "Chiao yu lun," 6a, p. 309. In a note Ricci observed that in the seal style of writing, both words for "friend," *peng* and *you*, involve a pair of images.

[75] Spence, *The Memory Palace of Matteo Ricci*, is constructed on the basis of Ricci's second section, which explains how to use the technique. See Ricci, *Ji fa*, 4b–5b; reprinted in *Tianzhujiao dong chuan wenxian* (Taipei, 1965), pp. 16–18.

includes many unknown Western names in passing, and it begins with the proposition, "The spiritual soul bestowed on humans by the lord, maker of things (*zao wu zhu*), is the most intellective compared to the other ten thousand things."[76] Thus, in his writings that he began to circulate in the mid-1590s and that have a strong humanistic rather than religious orientation, Ricci interjected new names as well as a new, central concept he hoped to disseminate in China: the idea of a supreme deity as creator.

Ricci provided a more extensive, but not exhaustive explanation of his idea in his book entitled *The True Meaning of the Lord of Heaven* (*Tianzhu shiyi*). He had begun working on this at least by 1595, when he was in Nanchang as a literatus, and it was first printed in 1603 in Beijing.[77] Presented as dialogues between Chinese literati (*zhong shi*) and a literatus from the West (*xi shi*), it was based in part on actual conversations Ricci had.[78] Using the terms "Lord of Heaven," Divinity on High" (*shang di*), and "Divinity of Heaven" (*tian di*) interchangeably,[79] Ricci argued for his God's existence and that he was creator and ruler of heaven-and-earth, eternal and unfathomable, and the source of morality. Worshipping the Lord of Heaven was the only true means of moral self-cultivation, for man's immortal soul would be judged after death.[80] Ricci made extensive use of scholastic arguments to support his view and to refute erroneous ideas held by Buddhists, Taoists, and some mistaken Confucians (*ru*). Toward the end of the dialogues, Ricci brought up the subject of Jesus. "[The Lord of Heaven] thereupon acted with great compassion, descended to this world Himself to save it, and experienced everything [experienced by man]. One thousand six hundred and three years ago, on the third day after the winter solstice in the second year of the Yuanshou period of the Han emperor Ai, [the Lord of Heaven] chose as his mother a chaste woman who had never experienced sexual intercourse, and He became incarnate in her and was born. His name was Jesus [*Ye-su*], which

[76] Ricci, *Ji fa*, 1a, p. 9.

[77] See Matteo Ricci, *The True Meaning of the Lord of Heaven*, trans. Douglas Lancashire and Peter Kuo-chen Hu (St. Louis, 1985), p. 19. In addition to the translation, this volume includes an edited version of the Chinese text; another version in two *juan* that includes prefaces omitted by Lancashire and Hu is in Li Zhizao, ed., *Tianxue chu han*.

[78] Ricci, *The True Meaning of the Lord of Heaven*, p. 61; cf. pp. 16–17. There is some overlap between the dialogues in the *Tianzhu shiyi* and the dialogues in Ricci's *Jiren shi pian* (Ten chapters on the extraordinary man) of 1608, where mostly Ricci's interlocutors are named, and include Xu Guangqi and Li Zhizao.

[79] Ricci, *The True Meaning of the Lord of Heaven*, p. 56, n. 6. Ricci also explained that in Western countries the Lord of Heaven was called Dou-si, that is, Deus, p. 71.

[80] Ibid., pp. 337, 375, 383. Cf. Ricci's own description, translated in Dunne, *Generation of Giants*, pp. 96–97, from Ricci, *Fonti Ricciane*, Vol. 2, pp. 293–295, n. 709.

means 'saves the world.' He established his own teachings and taught in the Western lands. In his thirty-third year he reascended to Heaven. These were the true actions of the Lord of Heaven."[81] Except for this passage, Ricci did not "discuss in depth God's revelation of Himself in history."[82] Rather than arguing from the mysteries of faith, Ricci had the literatus from the West stress that he was responding on the basis of *li*, the crucial term (usually translated as "principle" or "coherence") in the Learning of the Way. Ricci intended *li* as approximate to *ratio*, his word for "reason."[83] To his Western audience, Ricci was quite explicit about what he was doing in his book in Chinese. "This does not treat of all the mysteries of our holy faith, which need be explained only to catechumens and Christians, but only of certain principles, especially such as can be proved with natural reason (*ragioni naturali*) and understood with the same natural light (*lume naturale*)."[84]

Ricci was not requiring that his broad literati audience first believe in his teachings in order to understand them. He was minimizing the differences by assimilating his teaching to theirs – at least, theirs before it went astray. He told them in his introduction to the *True Meaning of the Lord of Heaven* that, when he reached their country, "I thought that in China the people of Yao and Shun and the followers of the Duke of Zhou and Confucius certainly could not shift and sully the principle of heaven (*tian li*) and the Learning from Heaven (*tian xue*). But even here it was not avoided."[85] In such passages, Ricci's stance was that his ideas were not wholly new, but were precedented in China's antiquity if not in Zhu Xi's Learning of the Way. He was not being disingenuous; he was presuming there had been a pre-Christian natural theology. In a letter in 1609 to Pasio, he wrote that "in ancient times they followed the natural law as faithfully as in our countries. For fifteen hundred years they

---

[81] Slightly altered from the translation in Ricci, *The True Meaning of the Lord of Heaven*, p. 449.

[82] Ibid., p. 24. Lancashire and Hu, in the notes to their translation, are thus moved to describe Ricci's book as a "pre-evangelical dialogue."

[83] Ibid., p. 71.

[84] Altered from the translation in Dunne, *Generation of Giants*, p. 96, from Ricci, *Fonti Ricciane*, Vol. 2, pp. 292–293, n. 709. Also see John W. Witek, "Understanding the Chinese," p. 69, in Ronan and Oh, eds., *East Meets West*, and Witek, "Principles of Scholasticism in China: A Comparison of Giulio Aleni's Wanwu zhenyuan with Matteo Ricci's Tianzhu shiyi," in Tiziana Lippiello and Roman Malek, eds., *"Scholar from the West," Giulio Aleni, S.J. (1582–1649) and the Dialogue between Christianity and China* (Nettetal, 1977), pp. 273–290.

[85] Altered from Ricci, *The True Meaning of the Lord of Heaven*, p. 59.

hardly worshipped idols, and those they did were not as reprehensible as those of the Egyptians, Greeks and Romans.... In the most ancient authoritative books of the literati, only heaven and earth and the Lord of both is worshipped. When these books are examined, we discover little that is contrary to the light of reason and much that conforms to it, and their natural philosophies yield to none."[86] In his writings in Chinese, Ricci pointed to the many classical passages, particularly in the *Book of Documents* (*Shu jing*) and *Book of Poetry* (*Shi jing*), in which the terms *shang di* (Divinity on High) and *tian* (Heaven) appear in contexts that treat them as names of a deity (or deities) with extraordinary, nonhuman power that was responsive to human supplication.[87] For literati who were willing to start with that reading, even though it was not wholly warranted in the contexts of the classics, Ricci was prepared to proceed to the revelations and elaborations that had obtained since antiquity in the Western lands, but not in China.

On the other hand, some of the learning that Ricci introduced to literati in China was unambiguously new. Almost immediately after arriving in Guangdong, he realized he had an attractive curiosity in the map of the world as it then was known by European cartographers. From 1584, copies were made and circulated, sometimes without his approval.[88] Comments and annotations, some by Ricci, but others by appreciative viewers, accumulated in the margins and on the open spaces for oceans. Hemispheric views were placed in the corners. The map was printed several times, from wooden blocks. A version dated 1602 measures 4.1 by 1.8 meters.[89] With the Americas on the right and the Eurasian land mass spreading to Africa at the left margin, China, or Da Ming as it was labeled,

---

[86] Venturi, ed., *Opere Storiche*, Vol. 2, p. 386. Also translated in Jacques Gernet, *Chine et Christianisme. Action et reaction* (Paris, 1982), p. 39, trans. Janet Lloyd as *China and the Christian Impact: A Conflict of Cultures* (Cambridge, 1985), p. 25.

[87] See Benjamin I. Schwartz, *The World of Thought in Ancient China* (Cambridge, MA, 1985), pp. 50–53. Some twentieth-century commentators have implied Ricci was arguing that a fully developed idea of the Christian God was already present in the classical texts from early Chou. It seems to me Ricci was arguing that in the Ancient Theology there were glimmers or adumbrations of the idea of the True God. He was using antique vocabulary with some of the connotations he could assimilate, but he used scholastic arguments to establish the characteristics of the deity that are not apparent in the Chinese classics, particularly those of Creator of all things, omnipotence, and an ontological standing that separates it from our phenomenal world.

[88] Ricci, *Fonti Ricciane*, Vol. 1, pp. cxxvii, 207–212, nn. 262–263.

[89] Ibid., p. 207. At least eight versions are distinguished in Hong Weilian (William Hung), "Kao Li Madou de shijie ditu," *Yu gong*, Vol. 5, Nos. 3–4 (1936), p. 28; reprinted in Zhou Kangxie, ed., *Li Madou yanjiu lunji* (Hong Kong, 1971), p. 94.

was near the middle. It was clearly but a part of a much larger world than had previously been known in China. Ricci would give detailed accounts of how he had traveled, how long it had taken, and the names and wonders of new places.[90] There was more here than expanding geographical horizons. Ricci was teaching that the earth is a sphere.

To a literati audience that adhered to the view that the earth is essentially a flat square encompassed by a dome called heaven, Ricci presented clear accounts of the Aristotelian theory of an immobile, spherical earth located at the center of a series of concentric spherical orbs.[91] The first essay in the *Qian kun ti yi* (The structure of heaven and earth), a book in three *juan* printed in 1614 under Ricci's name, described the shape of the heaven and earth: "The lands and oceans are basically of a round shape and conjoined as a unitary globe. They are located at the center of the celestial globe, like the yellow of an egg in the white. As for the assertion that the earth is square, that is referring to the power [of the earth], to its quiescent and unshifting nature; it is not referring to its physical shape."[92] Ricci explained how, in coming to China (Zhongguo), he had to sail far south of the equator around Africa and thus was on the opposite of the globe from China. He assured his readers that there one sees the sky above his head, not below. "Therefore all but babies believe that the shape of the earth is round and it has circumference."[93] Ricci was similarly unaccommodating when he explained the dimensions and speeds of the eleven encompassing global or spherical heavens (*tian*) on which the planets and stars move inside the immobile, outermost sphere. He insisted that there are only four elements (*si yuan xing*), not five as most authors in China maintained, that their characteristics of hot, cold, dry, and damp were as he described them, and that the Creator had separated them from primal chaos in making the universe.[94]

---

[90] For a reproduction of the 1602 map, see *Li Madou kunyu wanguo quantu* (Beiping, 1936) and Pasqule M. D'Elia, *Il mappamondo cinese del P. Matteo Ricci, S.J.* (Vatican City, 1938). A convenient summary of the maps is in Kenneth Ch'en, "Matteo Ricci's Contribution to and Influence on Geographical Knowledge in China," *Journal of the American Oriental Society*, Vol. 59 (1939), pp. 325–359.

[91] See Peterson, "Western Natural Philosophy," p. 298. On Ricci's construction of the role of the "missionary mathematician" see Florence C. Hsia, *Sojourners in a Strange Land: Jesuits & Their Scientific Missions in Late Imperial China* (Chicago, 2009), Ch. 2.

[92] Matteo Ricci, *Qian kun tiyi* (1614); reprinted in *Siku quanshu zhenben*, 1a, *wu ji* (Taipei, 1974). This essay originally appeared on the maps.

[93] Ibid., pp. 2a–b.

[94] Ibid., pp. 5a–6b, 10a–13a.

Western mathematics was attractive as a powerful example of learning that seemed universally acceptable on the basis of "reason" and yet was then unknown in China.[95] Ricci had taught some arithmetic and geometry to Qu Rukui at Shaozhou in the early 1590s,[96] and it was a regular topic in his discussions at Beijing. Perhaps at the instigation of Xu Guangqi, in 1606–1607 Ricci and Xu worked on a translation of the first six books of Euclid's *Geometry* in a version arranged by Christopher Clavius, who had been Ricci's professor in Rome. Their procedure was for Xu to write as Ricci translated orally from Latin to Chinese. They went quickly, skipping some parts, and their work was printed in 1608 as the *Jihe yuan ben*.[97] Xu, in his preface, recorded that Ricci had told him that if Euclid was not translated, the other books (on astronomy in particular) could not be understood.[98] Other books involving mathematical learning also were translated and printed. There was a short treatise on the astrolabe in 1607. Ricci sometimes referred to it simply as *Sfera* (Sphere), but the Chinese title was *Hun gai tong xian tushuo* (Explanation of the comprehensive rules for the celestial dome). It was based on Clavius's 1593 book about using a model celestial sphere and an astrolabe for calculating the positions of celestial bodies.[99] A book on arithmetic, also based on one by Clavius, his *Arithmetica Pratica*, was translated with Li Zhizao and printed in 1613, after Ricci's death, as the *Tong wen suan zhi* (Guide to calculating in our shared language).[100]

---

[95] It should be noted that in his prefaces for the mathematics books Xu Guangqi, e.g, consistently referred to antique Chinese precedents to justify interest in and knowledge of the subjects of the books.

[96] Ricci, *Fonti Ricciani*, Vol. 1, pp. 297–298, n. 362.

[97] Ibid., Vol. 2, pp. 356–360, n. 772. In a note on pp. 358–359, D'Elia briefly indicates the contents of the six books as translated. A more detailed account, with translations of the prefatory material, is in Pasquale D'Elia, "Presentazione della Prima Traduzione Cinese di Euclide," *Monumenta Serica*, Vol. 15 (1956), pp. 161–202. For a brief indication of Ricci's mathematical training and Clavius's view of its importance for Jesuits, see Spence, *The Memory Palace of Matteo Ricci*, pp. 142–143. The best study of the *Jihe yuan ben,* including its sources in Europe and its reception in China, and translations of selected passages is Peter M. Engelfriet, *Euclid in China: The Genesis of the First Chinese Translation of Euclid's "Elements," Books I–VI (Jihe yuanben, Beijing, 1607) and Its Reception up to 1723* (Leiden, 1998).

[98] Xu Guangqi, "Xu," 2b, in Ricci, *Jihe yuanben*, in Li Zhizao, *Tianxue chu han*, Vol. 4, p. 1924. Cf. Ricci, *Fonti Ricciane*, Vol. 2, p. 356, n. 7.

[99] See Ricci, *Fonti Ricciane*, Vol. 1, p. cxxviii, Vol. 2, pp. 174–177, and Spence, *The Memory Palace of Matteo Ricci*, p. 148. The text is in Li Zhizao, ed., *Tianxue chu han*, Vol. 3.

[100] Ricci, *Fonti Ricciane*, Vol. 2, p. 175. The text is in Li Zhizao, ed., *Tianxue chu han*, Vol. 5. The "shared language" seems to have referred to reviving earlier Chinese mathematical vocabulary for the foreign content. See Ricci, *Fonti Ricciani*, Vol. 2, p. 175, n. 2.

It began by making reference to the use of calculating sticks and the abacus, and then explained how Westerners added columns of figures, multiplied, and so on. It used Chinese numbers, rather than the so-called Arabic numerals current in Europe. The third *juan* of the *Qian kun tiyi* explained plane and spherical geometry. Ricci was thus instrumental in making a solid introduction to the Western mathematical techniques for understanding and solving problems in astronomy available to readers of Chinese.

The implicit ideal was that as one learned geometry and trigonometry and applied the techniques to analyzing phenomena in the sky (heaven), one also learned that the cosmos (heaven-and-earth) was structured as taught by Ricci, and as one accepted thinking in terms of that structure, one also might accept the premise that it was made by a creator (the Lord of Heaven). These exact connections were made succinctly, and more explicitly than Ricci would have condoned, by one of his contemporaries. Strongly influenced by Neoplatonism, Johannes Kepler in 1610 wrote a letter to Galileo, whose book *Sidereus Nuncius* (Sidereal messenger) had just been published in Venice. Kepler declared, "Geometry is one and eternal, shining in the mind of God. That share in it accorded to men is one of the reasons that Man is the image of God."[101] If one accepted that there was a creator, one was beginning to understand one of the attributes of the Lord of Heaven, and Ricci was then ready to expound on other attributes of his God as well, including His being the ground of morality and salvation. This was further testimony to the motive for Ricci's being in Beijing, the basis for his confident knowledge of truth, and the source of his strength of character. The ideal was sometimes realized; both Qu Rukui and Li Zhizao were literati who were first attracted to "other" parts of Ricci's learning and went on to be baptized as Christians. The intellectual process was alluded to in 1601 in a preface written for the *Tianzhu shiyi* by Feng Yingjing (d. 1607), who did not become a Christian. "Ricci traveled 80,000 *li* [to China]. He measures the heights of the nine heavens and the depths of the nine oceans without the slightest error. He has already fathomed forms and figures [in the sky] which we never have. Having such reliable evidence in these matters, [his teachings about] divine principles (*shen li*) ought to contain no falsehoods."[102] Certainty

---

[101] J. Kepler, *Dissertatio cum Nuncio Sidereo*, trans. J. V. Field in "Astrology in Kepler's Cosmology," in Patrick Curry, ed., *Astrology, Science and Society*, (Woodbridge, 1987).

[102] Feng Yingjing, "Tianzhu shi yi xu," 3a–b, in Li Zhizao, ed., *Tianxue chu han*, Vol. 1, pp. 363–364. Cf. Ricci, *Fonti Ricciane*, Vol. 2, p. 167.

involving mathematics and astronomy, as aspects of the Learning from Heaven with no clear demarcation between what we might call science and religion, lent credence to Ricci's "holy faith."

For his part, Ricci was keenly aware that he was expediently using these other aspects of Western culture to establish his reputation as a man of learning, which was a means both to attract interest in his faith and to enhance the opportunities for him and his confreres to propagate it in Ming China. In a letter to Rome in the spring of 1605 he wrote, "Because of my world-maps, clocks, spheres, astrolabes, and the other things I do and teach, I have gained the reputation of being the greatest mathematician in the world, and without any astrology book (*libro di astrologia*), I am able to predict eclipses with the aid of some Portuguese ephemerides and catalogues more accurately than they [i.e., his Chinese hosts]."[103] (As noted earlier, his first fruitless trip to Beijing, in 1598, was facilitated by an official of the Ministry of Rites who thought Ricci could be useful in the reform of the calendar.) In the same letter, he said he had been making an unheeded request for several years.

Nothing could be more advantageous than to send some father or brother [of the Society of Jesus] who is a good astrologer (*astrologo*) to this court. I say astrologer because with regard to geometry, clocks, and astrolabes, I know them well enough and have enough books on them. But [the Chinese] do not make so much of these as they do of the course and actual place of the planets, the calculation of eclipses, and especially of one who is able to make ephemerides [i.e., tables from which solar, lunar and planetary positions through the year can be derived].... Therefore I say that if this mathematician (*matematico*) of whom I speak should come, we should be able to translate our tables into Chinese, which I do with facility, and undertaking the task of correcting the calendar (*anno*) would enhance our reputation, give us freer entry into China, and assure us of greater security and liberty.[104]

Although Ricci could foresee how the situation would develop, his request was not realized during his lifetime.

Matteo Ricci died in Beijing in the spring of 1610, reportedly worn out from the crush of activities in which he was involved, including receiving many candidates in the capital for the *jinshi* examination that year.[105]

---

[103] Ricci's letter to João Alvarez, in Venturi, ed., *Opere Storiche*, Vol. 2, p. 285, slightly altered from the translation in Dunne, *Generation of Giants*, p. 210.

[104] Venturi, ed., *Opere Storiche*, Vol. 2, pp. 284–285, slightly altered from the translation in Dunne, *Generation of Giants*, pp. 210–211.

[105] Ricci, *Fonti Ricciane*, Vol. 2, pp. 534–535, 542; Dunne, *Generation of Giants*, pp. 105–107.

He was at the height of his reputation as a literatus from the West. After memorials to the emperor by Li Zhizao and others, imperial permission was granted for a burial ground for Ricci.[106] The *Veritable Records* for the fourth month of the thirty-eighth year of the Wanli reign period simply states, "On the *renyin* day [the emperor] granted some empty ground for burial for Li Madou, the former adjunct minister (*pei chen*) from the Western Ocean country."[107] After some maneuvering, Jesuit missionaries took possession of a plot of land outside the city wall that had belonged to a eunuch. It was long and narrow, about twenty *mou* (or three acres), surrounded by walls, with most of the south half taken up by more than thirty rooms and halls, one of which became a chapel.[108] Ricci was buried there in 1611.

Of course, propagation of the Learning from Heaven did not end with Ricci. He had nominated Niccolo Longobardo (1559–1655) to be his successor as the mission's superior. At Ricci's death there were at least seven Jesuits from Europe in China. Diego Pantoja (1571–1618), who had been with Ricci in Beijing since 1601, and Sabatino DeUrsis (1575–1620) were in the capital; Alphonso Vagnone (1568–1640) was in Nanjing; Lazzaro Cattaneo (1560–1640) was in Shanghai; Gaspar Ferreira (1571–1649) and João da Rocha (1565–1623) were in Nanchang; and Longobardo was in Shaozhou.[109] There were eight Jesuit brothers who were Chinese, and an estimated 2,500 Chinese Catholics.[110] Most influentially, there were a handful of literati and officials who were sympathizers or converts to the Learning of the Way.

[106] Henri Bernard, *Aux origines du cimetière de Chala. Le don princier de la Chine au P. Ricci (1610–1611)* (Tianjin, 1934), summarizes the Western-language evidence on the events surrounding Ricci's death and burial. See also Nicolas Standaert, *The Interweaving of Rituals: Funerals in the Cultural Exchange between China and Europe* (Seattle, 2008), pp. 187–190.

[107] *Shenzong shilu, Ming shilu* (mid-seventeenth century; reprint, Taipei, 1966), Ch. 470, 8b (p. 8884). *Pei chen* was a term from the Zhou dynasty that referred to officials from other states who reached the court of the Zhou king and was sometimes used to refer to officers from a tributary state; the idea was that if their tributary rulers were ministers, they were ministers of ministers.

[108] Bernard, *Aux origines*, pp. 35–36.

[109] Dunne, *Generation of Giants*, pp. 120, 122, 126. Nicolas Trigault and Manoel Dias arrived in Macao in 1610. For the spelling of the Jesuits' names and their dates, I have followed Joseph Dehergne, *Répertoire des Jesuites de Chine de 1552 à 1800, Bibliotheca Instituti Historici S.I.* (Rome, 1973), Vol. 37.

[110] Ricci, *Fonti Ricciane*, Vol. 1, p. 289, n. 4. Also see Standaert, ed., *Handbook*, pp. 307, 382. The eight brothers are discussed in Harris, "The Mission of Matteo Ricci," pp. 147–151.

LITERATI WHO ASSOCIATED THEMSELVES WITH
THE LEARNING FROM HEAVEN: THE THREE PILLARS

From the beginning of Ricci's stay in Guangdong, literati manifested their
interest in different facets of the learning that he brought from the Far
West. In responding to their interests, Ricci was led to involvement with
some of them in a program of translating and printing books that continued after Ricci's death. Literati assisted with other Jesuits' books by
contributing to the translation and editing and to the printing, especially
in the form of prefaces endorsing the book but also in the form of money
toward publishing costs. Literati also wrote and printed their own books
on topics related to the Learning from Heaven, and theirs formed a corpus with those published in the missionaries' names that continued to
accumulate to the end of the Ming period.[111]

Xu Guangqi (1562–1633) was the most prominent literatus associated with the Learning from Heaven, both in the eyes of his contemporaries and in the view of later writers. Born in the then small
town of Shanghai to a father who was engaged in commerce and a
mother from a local literati family, Xu grew up in sometimes straitened
financial circumstances, due in part to the devastating piratical raids
on the coastal areas during his childhood years. He passed the prefectural examination in his twentieth year, but he failed in at least four
attempts at the Nanjing provincial examinations from 1582 to 1594,
just the years Ricci was establishing himself in Guangdong.[112] After his
mother died in 1592, Xu accepted employment as a teacher for the
sons of an official appointed as a prefect in Guangxi.[113] On the way
south from Jiangxi, Xu passed through Shaozhou, where he visited the
chapel established by Ricci, who by this time was on his way north in

---

[111] Nicolas Standaert, "Well-Known Individuals," in Standaert, ed., *Handbook*, pp. 404–428.

[112] Liang Jiamian, *Xu Guangqi nianpu* (Shanghai, 1981), pp. 33–53. Also see Wang
Zhongmin, *Xu Guangqi*, ed. He Zhaowu (Shanghai, 1981), pp. 5–8, 14–15. For a short
summary of Xu Guangqi's life, see the entry in Arthur W. Hummel, *Eminent Chinese
of the Ch'ing Period*, 2 vols. (Washington, DC, 1943–44), pp. 316–319. A more comprehensive introduction is provided in Monika Übelhör, *Hsü Kuang-ch'i (1562–1633)
und seine Einstellung zum Christentum. Ein Beitrag zur Geistesgeschichte der Späten
Ming-Zeit* (Hamburg, 1969). Several aspects of Xu Guangqi are studied in Catherine
Jami, Peter Engelfriet, and Gregory Blue, eds., *Statecraft and Intellectual Renewal
in Late Ming China: The Cross-Cultural Synthesis of Xu Guangqi (1562–1633)*
(Leiden, 2001).

[113] Wang Zhongmin, *Xu Guangqi*, pp. 16–17, 22–23; Liang Jiamian, *Xu Guangqi nianpu*,
pp. 57–58.

his literati robes. Xu chatted with the missionary at the chapel, Lazzaro Cattaneo, and was shown a picture of the Savior.[114] In 1597, still in the entourage of the official who had hired him to teach his sons, Xu went to Beijing, where that autumn he again tried the provincial examination. He passed with the top rank, and though he failed the metropolitan examination the following spring, he returned to Shanghai in 1598 as a *juren* of high repute and as a de facto follower of the chief examiner in 1597, Jiao Hong.[115] For twenty years, roughly 1582 to 1602, Xu prepared for the examinations and compiled dozens of conventional manuscripts of reading notes and comments on the classics and other texts.[116] As his friend pointed out in 1603, his efforts had been strongly oriented to the classics,[117] and he continued as an indefatigable writer and compiler. But Xu's life was about to take a turn.

Xu Guangqi had already heard of Ricci and his world map when they first met in the spring of 1600 in Nanjing.[118] Ricci recalled that as Xu was in a hurry he was able to hear only a little about serving "the Creator of heaven and earth and Author of all things," that is, the Lord of Heaven.[119] After their brief encounter, Ricci set off to Beijing for the second time. In the winter of 1603, Xu again traveled from Shanghai to Nanjing. He called on João da Rocha, who was in charge of the mission there, and pressed to be instructed in the faith. He read and memorized manuscript copies of Chinese translations of a catechism and *Christian Doctrine* (*Dottrina Cristiana*), which probably was a version of Ricci's *True Meaning of the Lord of Heaven* (*Tianzhu shiyi*). He discussed the doctrine with da Rocha, and within ten days Xu Guangqi was baptized as Paolo.[120] He returned to Shanghai for the New Year with his family, but then was back in Nanjing, where he lodged with da Rocha and heard mass every day.[121]

---

[114] Ricci, *Fonti Ricciane*, Vol. 2, p. 253, n. 681, which is the original source for the incident. Cf. Liang Jiamian, *Xu Guangqi nianpu*, p. 57, and Wang Zhongmin, *Xu Guangqi*, pp. 22–23.

[115] Liang Jiamian, *Xu Guangqi nianpu*, pp. 59–61.

[116] The titles, most of which are lost, are given in Liang Jiamian, *Xu Guangqi nianpu*, p. 69.

[117] See Wang Zhongmin, *Xu Guangqi*, p. 24.

[118] Xu Guangqi, "Ba Ershiwu yan," in Xu Guangqi, *Xu Guangqi ji*, ed. Wang Zhongmin (Shanghai, 1963), Vol. 1, p. 86.

[119] Ricci, *Fonti Ricciane*, Vol. 2, p. 253, n. 681. Also quoted in Willard Peterson, "Why Did They Become Christians?" p. 143.

[120] Ricci, *Fonti Ricciane*, Vol. 2, pp. 254–255, n. 682; Liang Jiamian, *Xu Guangqi nianpu*, p. 69; Wang Zhongmin, *Xu Guangqi*, p. 24.

[121] Ricci, *Fonti Ricciane*, Vol. 2, p. 255, n. 683. Also cited in Peterson, "Why Did They Become Christians?" p. 144.

In the spring of 1604 Xu proceeded to Beijing, where he found Ricci and received Communion. Going in again for the metropolitan examinations, he passed to become a *jinshi*. To start his official career he was appointed to the extremely prestigious Hanlin Academy, which afforded Xu ample opportunity to develop a working relation with Ricci.[122]

Almost immediately, Xu wrote a postscript for Ricci's soon to be published booklet entitled *Ershiwu yan* (Twenty-five discourses), which were selections drawn from the doctrines attributed in the *Encheiridion* to Epictetus, a second-century Stoic.[123] Xu recalled his first contacts with Ricci but did not directly mention his baptism at the end of the previous year. He wrote that Ricci's learning (*xue*), touching on every subject, had as its main doctrine the continuous and open service of the Divinity on High (*shang di*). All Ricci said and wrote was in accord with precepts of being loyal to one's ruler and filial to one's father, of improving the individual's mind and the society's well-being. Xu acknowledged that he had been skeptical at first, but as he came to comprehend the explanations, "I took it to heart and asked to serve."[124] Xu added that he had remarked to Ricci that more of the many books he had brought should be translated, and of course that is what Ricci already was of a mind to do. Xu himself became involved. In 1606 and 1607, after his duties at the Hanlin Academy, he spent many afternoon hours with Ricci, preparing the Chinese version of the *Geometry*.[125] In 1607 Xu also worked with Ricci to complete a little book on surveying, the *Celiang fayi* (Methods and interpretation of surveying), which Ricci had started ten years earlier.[126] Their direct collaboration ended when Xu's father, who had been baptized, died in the fifth month of 1607. Xu resigned his official appointment and returned to Shanghai.[127] Before Xu returned to the capital in 1610, Ricci himself was dead.

---

[122] Ricci, *Fonti Ricciane*, Vol. 2, p. 308, n. 714.

[123] See Christopher Spalatin, "Matteo Ricci's Use of Epictetus' *Encheiridion*," *Gregorianum*, Vol. 56, No. 3 (1975), pp. 551–557.

[124] Xu Guangqi, "Ba Ershiwu yan," *Xu Guangqi ji*, Vol. 1, p. 87. Also see Peterson, "Why Did They Become Christians?" pp. 145–146.

[125] Ricci, *Fonti Ricciane*, Vol. 2, p. 357, n. 772. Cf. Liang Jiamian, *Xu Guangqi nianpu*, p. 81.

[126] Xu Guangqi, "Ti Celiang fa yi," *Xu Guangqi ji*, Vol. 1, p. 82. If Ricci had discussed surveying methods with Xu when they met in Nanjing in 1600, it would undermine the claim by Wang Zhongmin that Xu was especially interested in applied mathematics before he was involved with Ricci, as the only evidence for his early interest is a set of explanations on surveying he apparently sent to the magistrate of Shanghai in 1603. See Wang Zhongmin, *Xu Guangqi*, pp. 22–23.

[127] Liang Jiamian, *Xu Guangqi nianpu*, pp. 85–86.

Xu Guangqi continued to be involved in the Learning from Heaven. While in mourning, he worked on the publication of the *Jihe yuanben* and the *Celiang fa yi*, and he wrote a treatise on triangles and another comparing Western methods of surveying and the earliest extant Chinese textual materials on surveying.[128] In 1608 he invited Cattaneo to move from Nanjing to Shanghai and had a chapel built near his own home.[129] Xu traveled to Macao to inspect the situation there.

When he reached Beijing in 1610, Xu was reappointed to the Hanlin Academy. He also began collaborating with Pantoja and DeUrsis on texts dealing with astronomical instruments and calendrical tables.[130] After a solar eclipse late in 1610 was inaccurately predicted by officials at the Directorate of Astronomy, the two Westerners were suggested for posts as calendar experts in response to a call from the Ministry of Rites, and at the beginning of 1612, a memorial from the ministry proposed that Xu Guangqi and Li Zhizao (who was serving in the Ministry of Works in Nanjing) be ordered along with Longobardo and DeUrsis to translate Western works relevant to calendars lest the errors become more egregious.[131] Nothing came of that proposal, but in 1612 Xu wrote down from DeUrsis's oral translation a collection of ideas and advice based on Western ideas on water technology. In his preface, Xu wrote that Ricci had instigated the project, and he had proposed to DeUrsis that they complete it.[132] When published, the *Taixi shui fa* (Western methods involving water) consisted of four *juan* of advice, some of it technical and some lore (e.g., how to site a well), one *juan* of answers to questions about water and solutions based on the Aristotelian four elements theory, and one *juan* of rudimentary illustrations of boilers, storage tanks, and water-moving devices. DeUrsis added an introductory essay on fundamentals that opened with the cardinal assumption, "The making of the ten thousand things of heaven and earth long ago by the Lord, Creator of Things, is like the use of tools in a master craftsman's making a palace." The tools and materials used by the Creator, it was argued, were the four elements (earth, water, air, and fire), and if one understands them, one understands how heaven and earth and all phenomenal things are put together.[133]

[128] Ibid., pp. 88, 92.
[129] Ibid., p. 89.
[130] Ibid., p. 97.
[131] Ibid., pp. 95, 98–99, quoting from the *Ming Shilu*.
[132] Xu Guangqi, "Taixi shui fa xu," *Xu Guangqi ji*, pp. 67–68. Two other prefaces also credit Ricci; see Liang Jiamian, *Xu Guangqi nianpu*, pp. 99–100.
[133] DeUrsis, "Shui fa ben lun," 1a, in *Taixi shui fa*, in Li Zhizao, *Tianxue chu han*, Vol. 3, p. 1549.

Again, the connection was being made between technology, natural philosophy, and the religious implications of a supreme, omnipotent deity.

In his own 1612 preface for the *Taixi shui fa*, Xu set the context from another perspective. "I have said that this religious doctrine (*jiao*) certainly can 'supplement Confucianism and replace Buddhism' (*bu ru yi fo*), and the remainder [of the teachings] moreover has a type of learning (*xue*) involving 'investigating things and fathoming their coherence' (*ge wu qiong li*), so that whether it is a question about within or outside of the realm of human society, whether about the coherence of the ten thousand [human] affairs or of the ten thousand things [in the realm of heaven and earth], they can endlessly respond with extremely detailed explanations. When one thinks them over, whether for months or years, one increasingly sees the necessity and immutability of their theories."[134] Xu was arguing for the incorporation of the theories being introduced by the Westerners into the learning of the literati.

Xu made the point in a different way in the preface he wrote in 1614 for the *Tong wen suan zhi* (Guide to calculating in our shared language). He used the same metaphor of the tools and materials of the craftsman building a palace as had DeUrsis (but without mentioning a creator) to show the practical importance of mathematics, which he called the art of calculating (*suan shu*). According to Xu, from the time of the sages of high antiquity until the Tang dynasty, mathematical learning had an important place, but it had particularly declined in the past few hundred years (i.e., since the Song dynasty). He gave two reasons for this. Confucian philosophers had come to denigrate the practical affairs of the world, and charlatans had claimed to predict the future by means of the mysteries of numbers (*shu*). Thus the constructive, useful mathematical techniques of antiquity atrophied, and the books transmitting them were mostly lost to the literati. But the numbers one to ten are shared by all countries, just as all humans have ten fingers and use them to count. Xu wrote that his friend Li Zhizao had searched for remnants of the ancient mathematics, and then at Beijing, he worked with Ricci and his confreres, whose calendrical and numerical learning was more refined and far more extensive than what remained from Han and Tang. After reading the manuscript Li prepared with Ricci, Xu joined with Li in comparing old Chinese techniques with the Western ones and found they were congruent. It was Li Zhizao who then combined the two traditions and

---

[134] Xu Guangqi, "Taixi shui fa," *Xu Guangqi ji*, p. 66. Also in Willard Peterson, "Why Did They Become Christians?" p. 147.

published the book entitled *Tong wen suan zhi* (Guide to calculating in our shared language).[135]

Li Zhizao (1565–1630) was another prominent literatus who became involved in the Learning of Heaven. He was from Hangzhou and passed the *jinshi* examination in 1598. He was serving in the Ministry of Works when, he recalled years later, "[i]n 1601, Ricci had come [to Beijing]. I went with several associates to call on him. Hanging on his wall was a map of the world with finely drawn lines of degree [of longitude and latitude]. Ricci said, 'This was my route from the West.'"[136] Ricci recorded that Li was attracted to the greatly expanded geography of the countries and continents on the map,[137] but it seems that Li was even more fascinated with the new model of the earth as a sphere. Li recalled that, after seeing the map, he did his own calculations to verify Ricci's claim for its size and spherical shape and for its location at the center of the spherical heavens.[138] As Ricci described it, "With his great intelligence he easily grasped the truths we taught about the extent and sphericity of the earth, its poles, the ten [concentric] heavens, the vastness of [the spheres of] the sun and stars compared with the earth, and other things that other men found so difficult to believe."[139]

Li helped prepare an enlarged version of the map, which was printed in 1602 with a long note by Li in which he reviewed Chinese precedents for the idea of a spherical earth divided into degrees, as was the sphere of the stellar heaven. He endorsed the ideas that the earth was much larger than previously thought and that spherical heavens encompassed it.[140] According to Ricci, "From this a close friendship developed between us, and when the duties of his office allowed it, he liked to learn more of this knowledge (*questa scientia*)."[141] Over the next few years Li learned from Ricci about Western mathematics and astronomy, including making

---

[135] Xu Guangqi, "Ke Tongwen suan zhi xu," *Xu Guangqi ji*, pp. 79–81.
[136] Li Zhizao, Preface dated 1623 to Aleni, *Zhifang wai ji*, 1a, in Li Zhizao, *Tianxue chu han*, Vol. 3, p. 1269. Also quoted in Peterson, "Why Did They Become Christians?" p. 137.
[137] Ricci, *Fonti Ricciane*, Vol. 2, p. 168, n. 628.
[138] Li Zhizao, Preface to *Zhifang waiji*, 1b-2a, in Li Zhizao, *Tianxue chu han*, Vol. 3, pp. 1270–1271.
[139] Ricci, *Fonti Ricciane*, Vol. 2, pp. 170–171, n. 628; also in Peterson, "Why Did They Become Christians?" p. 137.
[140] Li Zhizao's note in the mid-Pacific in [Li Zhizao?], *Li Madou kunyu wanguo quantu* (Beiping, 1936). Cf. Peterson, "Why Did They Become Christians?" p. 141. Also see Ricci's prefatory note on the 1602 map for Li Zhizao's role in producing the enlarged version.
[141] Ricci, *Fonti Ricciane*, Vol. 2, p. 171, n. 628.

and using gnomons, astrolabes, and celestial and terrestrial globes. They translated a treatise on the sphere and astrolabe in 1607, entitled the *Hun gai tong xian tushuo* (Explanation of the comprehensive rules for the celestial dome).[142] In his preface, Li Zhizao provided an extended argument for understanding that the earth is a relatively small sphere in the midst of the encompassing heavenly spheres.[143]

Li Zhizao wrote prefaces for Ricci's *Tianzhu shiyi* (True meaning of the Lord of Heaven) in 1607 and for his *Jiren shipian* (Ten essays on the extraordinary man) in 1608. In the latter, Li says that he had known Ricci for nearly a decade and now realizes that when he is going to do something and it accords with Ricci's words, he knows he should do it, and if it does not, he knows not to do it.[144] At about this same time Ricci wrote of Li, "He is very well instructed in matters of our Holy Faith and stood ready to be baptized if the Fathers had not discovered the impediment of polygamy, which he promises to rid from his house."[145] Presumably Li Zhizao had sent his concubine away by 1610, when he fell critically ill. Ricci attended to him day and night for several weeks, and he urged Li to declare his faith. Li agreed and was baptized as Leone. He also donated a hundred taels of silver for the church.[146] Li recovered, but Ricci died in the spring of that year. Li continued to be involved in the Learning from Heaven. He resigned from office in the spring of 1611 to be with his ailing father. Returning home to Hangzhou, he invited Cattaneo and Trigault to join him there. He seems to have entrusted them with "matters relating to the rites of death" after his father died,[147] and his reliance on them seems to have stimulated his friend Yang Tingyun to learn more about their religious faith.

Yang Tingyun (1557–1627) met Cattaneo and Trigault when they were in Hangzhou with Li Zhizao. A *jinshi* in 1592, he was appointed the district magistrate of Anfu in Ji'an prefecture, Jiangxi, which was still a center for discourses on learning (*jiang xue*) promoting Wang

---

[142] Ibid., pp. 173–178, n. 631.

[143] Li Chih-tsao, "Xu," in Li Zhizao, ed., *Tianxue chu han*, Vol. 3, pp. 1711–1722. Li did not include Ricci's name as an author, only his own.

[144] Li Zhizao, "Jiren shi pian xu," 1a–2a, in Li Zhizao, ed., *Tianxue chu han*, Vol. 1, pp. 101–103.

[145] Ricci, *Fonti Ricciane*, Vol. 2, p. 178, n. 632. Also in Peterson, "Why Did They Become Christians?" p. 139.

[146] Fang Hao, *Li Zhizao yanjiu* (Taipei, 1966), p. 29. Also see Peterson, "Why Did They Become Christians?" p. 139.

[147] See Peterson, "Why Did They Become Christians?" p. 139.

Yangming's teachings.[148] One of the leading figures there was Liu Yuanqing (1544–1609), a 1570 *juren* who supposedly failed his only attempt at the metropolitan examination because of his criticism of current politics. He returned to Anfu and taught at an academy (*shuyuan*) established there in 1572.[149] Liu held that "[d]iscourses on learning are nothing more than gathering colleagues to clarify moral relations" and that "[w]ithout discourses, learning cannot be made clear."[150] Yang Tingyun was acquainted with Liu Yuanqing and with Zou Yuanbiao (1551–1624), who was involved in discourses and academies at nearby Jishui.[151] While serving as a censor, Yang contributed money and writing toward the establishment of the Donglin Academy in 1603–1604, and he participated in meetings there in the next few years.[152] While an education intendant in Nanjing, he edited a new printing of Qiu Jun's (1418–1495) version of the *Jia li* (Family rituals) attributed to Zhu Xi. Yang's preface appears with others by officials in Jiangnan, including several affiliated with the Donglin Academy.[153] During the years Yang also became friendly with such artistic types as Chen Jiru (1558–1639) and Dong Qichang (1556–1636) in Songjiang, and Li Rihua in Jiaxing.[154]

When Yang resigned from office in 1609 on a plea of illness and returned to Hangzhou,[155] he became active there in discourses on learning. With the encouragement of the governor of Zhejiang, Yang organized a study group called the Truth Society (Zhen shi she) to propagate the Learning of the Way.[156] At the same time, Yang contributed money and other support to local Buddhist temples and lay societies.[157] Lay

---

[148] Nicolas Standaert, *Yang Tingyun, Confucian and Christian in Late Ming China: His Life and Thought* (Leiden, 1988), pp. 7–8. Standaert's is the most detailed account of the Chinese and Western language materials on Yang's life.

[149] Huang Zongxi, *Ming ru xue'an*, Ch. 21, p. 498. Cf. Standaert, *Yang Tingyun*, p. 9.

[150] Slightly altered from the translation in Standaert, *Yang Tingyun*, p. 10.

[151] See ibid., pp. 111–112.

[152] Ibid., p. 35.

[153] Ibid., pp. 46–47. One of the prefaces was by Fang Dazhen (1558–1631), son of Fang Xuejian and grandfather of Fang Yizhi.

[154] Ibid., pp. 26–31. Li Rihua was a *jinshi* in Yang's year, 1592, and remained out of office after 1604. See Goodrich and Fang, *Dictionary of Ming Biography*, Vol. 1, pp. 826–827.

[155] Standaert, *Yang Tingyun*, p. 12.

[156] Ding Zhilin, *Yang Qiyuan xiansheng chao xing shiji* (a late Ming print is in the Bibliotheque Nationale in Paris, Courant No. 3370), 1a–b. Ding wrote this account from the dictation of Aleni, who had known Yang. Also see Standaert, *Yang Tingyun*, p. 52.

[157] Ding Zhilin, *Yang Qiyuan xiansheng chao xing shiji*; also Standaert, *Yang Tingyun*, p. 40.

Buddhism was a flourishing movement in Hangzhou at this time, led by the monk Zhuhong (1535–1615).[158] In 1605 Gao Panlong had gone to Hangzhou to visit the West Lake; he remarked on the number of literati there who admired Zhuhong and his books, even though he attacked Zhu Xi and the established doctrines in order to promote that "other strand" (*yi duan*), Buddhism.[159] Yang seems to have been able to contribute both to Gao Panlong's efforts at restoring discipline to the Learning of the Way at the Donglin Academy and to Zhuhong's efforts at restoring discipline in Buddhism to clerics and lay adherents. A man with wide horizons, Yang had performed well as an official, had been involved in the most prominent intellectual, artistic, and religious circles of the day, and seemed to have access to ample wealth in one of the most attractive cities in the empire.[160] He was a successful literatus affiliated with organized religious pursuits when he met Cattaneo and Trigault in 1611.

Earlier, Yang had been friendly with Ricci in Beijing, but without being attracted to his teachings. He was attracted when he met the two missionaries in Hangzhou, and he engaged them in a series of discussions, even inviting them to be guests in his house. Gradually, Yang was persuaded that the Lord of Heaven is the Creator of heaven and earth, that He suffered when He descended to earth to live as a man to atone for the world's sins, and that to serve Him requires a commitment to the rules of morality and ritual that belief in the religion impose. After sending away his concubine, Yang was baptized as Michele in the sixth month of 1611, two months after he first met Cattaneo and Trigault. He was in his fifty-fifth year.[161] Yang is the primary example of a literatus who pursued the religious aspects of the Learning of Heaven and was relatively indifferent to the scientific ones. He wrote in a preface for the *Tong wen suan zhi* in 1614 that, unlike Xu Guangqi and Li Zhizao, he could not comprehend

---

[158] See Yü Chün-fang, *The Renewal of Buddhism in China: Chu-hung and the Late Ming Synthesis* (New York, 1981), pp. 76–87, and Yü Chün-fang, "Ming Buddhism," in Denis C. Twitchett and Frederick W. Mote, eds., *The Cambridge History of China*, Vol. 8: *The Ming Dynasty, 1368–1644, Part 2* (Cambridge, 1998) pp. 893–952.

[159] Gao Panlong, *Gaozi yishu* (late Ming Ed.; reprint. Taipei, 1983), 3.52a–b. Also cited in Gernet, *Chine et Christianisme*, p. 37 (in English translation, pp. 252–253).

[160] Cf. the summary in Standaert, *Yang Tingyun*, p. 225.

[161] This summary is drawn from the account in Ding Zhilin, *Yang Qiyuan xiansheng chao xing shiji*, 4a–5a. Cf. Peterson, "Why Did They Become Christians?" pp. 131–134, and Standaert, *Yang Tingyun*, p. 54. Dunne, *Generation of Giants*, p. 114, gives the date of Yang's baptism as 1613, but early that year Trigault was on his way to Europe to solicit books and astronomically trained Jesuits for the China mission.

the mathematics taught by Ricci.[162] Instead, he wrote on moral and religious questions, in effect continuing Ricci's strategy of accommodating the religious teachings from the West with selected aspects of the Chinese philosophical tradition.

A few years after his conversion, Yang corrected Pantoja's book called the *Qi ke* (Seven [sins] to overcome), which was finished in 1614. In his preface Yang reduced the Jesuits' message to two precepts: "To venerate the One Lord of Heaven above the myriad creatures, and to love all others as oneself."[163] He pointed to passages in the classical texts of "us Confucians" (*wu ru*) that convey the same ideas, as in "serving the Divinity on High" (*shi shang di*, in *Book of Poetry*, no. 236) or "offending Heaven (*zui yu tian*, in *Analects* 3.13). Yang assimilated Pantoja's moral exhortations to the established vocabulary of the Learning of the Way, notably Zhang Zai's "Western Inscription." In Yang's summary, "To overcome pride, to temper rage, to free oneself from desire, to oppose parsimony, to avoid jealousy, to be temperate in eating and drinking, and to be rid of idleness are seven overcomings [of sin] in order to do good. By overcoming the bad in one's mind, one can plant the seeds of virtue in one's mind. What provides love is purely the Mind of the Way (*dao xin*), and the Mind of the Way is purely the Mind of Heaven (*tian xin*)."[164] Yang was freely associating the vocabulary of discourses on morality with the new meaning for Heaven being promoted by the missionaries. He was evolving a means to incorporate the new ideas into his own.

Yang Tingyun, Li Zhizao, and Xu Guangqi later became known as the Three Pillars of Christianity in China. Their relatively recent commitment to the religion and the missionaries was put to a test in 1616–1617.

## ATTACK ON THE MISSIONARIES AT NANJING

Since 1611 the Nanjing mission had flourished. Shen Defu (1578–1642) observed that Chinese literati (*zhongtu shiren*) teaching the ideas from the Western Ocean were everywhere, and particularly in Nanjing.[165] Vagnoni was the superior there, and under him, a church was constructed along Western lines on a site purchased by Li Zhizao, lay societies were organized

---

[162] Yang Tingyun, Preface to Li Zhizao, ed., *Tongwen suanzhi*, 1b–2a, in *Tianxue chu han*, Vol. 5, pp. 2904–2905. Cf. Standaert, *Yang Tingyun*, p. 53.
[163] Slightly altered from the translation in Standaert, *Yang Tingyun*, p. 120.
[164] Altered from the translation in ibid., p. 121.
[165] Shen Defu, "Da Xiyang," in his *Wanli Yehuo bian* (1619; reprint, Beijing, 1980), Vol. 3, p. 784.

for charity and study, and the number of converts increased.[166] But the missionaries began to be squeezed from two directions. The provincial of Japan, Valentim Carvalho (1559–1630), moved to Macao in 1614 to evade the rigorous proscription of Christianity then under way in Japan. He had authority over the Jesuit missionaries in China, and in 1615 he instructed them to cease giving instruction in mathematics and to refuse to become involved with any official undertaking of calendar reform. (This was directed against DeUrsis and Pantoja in Beijing.) Instead, they were to concentrate on preaching.[167] Presumably in response to Carvalho's order, Vagnoni put more emphasis on preaching in the Nanjing church and on drawing more public attention to church activities as a means of attracting more converts.[168] At the same time, Shen Que (d. 1624) took up an appointment as vice-minister of rites at Nanjing in 1615.[169] Like Yang Tingyun, Shen was a 1592 *jinshi* from Hangzhou, and they must have been acquainted. Shen had served in the Hanlin Academy, and he was to return to Beijing to be a grand secretary in 1621–1622, perhaps in alliance with Wei Zhongxian. The year after his arrival in Nanjing, Shen began submitting a series of memorials in which he proposed the expulsion of the foreign missionaries, the punishment of their followers, and the suppression of the Learning from Heaven movement. It was the gravest crisis for the Christians since Ricci left Guangdong.

In the summer of 1616, Shen Que submitted his first memorial denouncing, by name, Vagnoni and Diaz in Nanjing, and Pantoja and DeUrsis in Beijing.[170] He stressed that they were foreign barbarians whose presence had no legal or other basis and should no longer be condoned. They may claim that they have come and been transformed (i.e., become Chinese), but they call their country Great West Ocean (Da Xiyang), which rivals our Great Ming (Da Ming), and they call their doctrine the Teaching of the Lord of Heaven (*Tianzhu jiao*), which conflicts with the imperial

---

[166] Dunne, *Generation of Giants*, p. 121.

[167] Ibid., p. 123.

[168] Ibid., p. 125.

[169] For a summary of Shen Que's career, see Goodrich and Fang, *Dictionary of Ming Biography*, Vol. 2, pp. 1177–1178. See also Ad Dudink, "Opponents," in Standaert, ed., *Handbook*, pp. 503–533.

[170] Shen Que's memorial is translated in Edward Thomas Kelly, *The Anti-Christian Persecution of 1616–1617 in Nanking* (Ph.D. dissertation, Columbia University, 1971), pp. 277–282. Kelly's study, the most detailed account of the affair, judiciously draws on Chinese and Western sources. He includes the Chinese text of Shen's memorials, as they appeared in Xu Changzhi, ed., *Poxie ji*, originally compiled in 1639, but preserved only in Japan, where it was reprinted in 1855.

implications of such terms as heaven's king (*tian wang*) and the Son of Heaven (*tianzi*), who rules all under heaven (*tianxia*). Although he had been aware of the presence of Ricci and other missionaries in Beijing, Shen said that when he arrived in Nanjing he discovered the barbarians had attracted a crowd of adherents among the commoners and that even some learned literati believed their theories. Shen charged that the barbarians misled the common people to turn away from ritual veneration of their ancestors in order to worship the Lord of Heaven instead. (It is ironic that critics of Ricci's strategy among the Christian community in China and elsewhere faulted it for condoning the continued worship of ancestors by converts.)[171] They induced the poor with charity and money rewards to join them, and Shen insinuated that there must be rebellious intentions behind their organizing efforts. There was the same insinuation in Shen's dwelling at length on the Western barbarians' knowledge of calendars and celestial phenomena, which normally was the prerogative of the emperor's agents. Acknowledging that they had been recommended by the Ministry of Rites in 1611 to assist in correcting the astronomical basis for calculating the imperial calendar, Shen stressed that their knowledge was different, and dangerous. He sought to display his own knowledge of the tradition of calendar making. He pointed out in particular that the barbarians' claim that the sun, moon, and five planets each had its own heaven (*tian*) moving at different speeds and at different distances from the center of the earth was contrary both to what had been known about the patterns of heaven since antiquity in China (*zhongguo*) and to the analogous political idea of one ruler on earth.

His first memorial having received no response from the emperor, Shen sent in another early in the autumn of 1616 in which he added that the foreign barbarians held regular clandestine meetings with their adherents in Nanjing and that they maintained a residence near the tomb of the Hongwu emperor, again insinuating some antidynastic purpose. He expressed his concern that some literati and officials were sympathetic to them and their teachings, including their numerical arts.[172] Although Shen Que's motives for attacking the missionaries remain a subject of speculation,[173] the rationale offered in his and in memorials by others aligned with him has three main aspects: they are foreign barbarians

---

[171] See Rule, *K'ung-tzu or Confucius?* pp. 74–76, and Gernet, *Chine et Christianisme*, pp. 247–252 (in English translation, pp. 181–185).
[172] Kelly, "The Anti-Christian Persecution of 1616–1617," pp. 282–286.
[173] Ibid., pp. 108–123, reviews the evidence and some of the speculations.

whose presence is unwarranted and potentially dangerous to China; they are organizing poor commoners, which is socially disruptive and potentially antidynastic; and they have admirers among the literati, which is divisive and apparently antitraditional.[174]

Although the literati associated with the Learning from Heaven were not named in Shen Que's memorial, they knew they were being attacked as well. Xu Guangqi returned to his post in the Hanlin Academy in the seventh month of 1616 after recuperating from an illness,[175] and the next month he wrote a letter to his family in Shanghai to tell them the gentlemen from the West (*xiyang xiansheng*) had been impeached in memorials from the Ministry of Rites. Xu said he did not know why, nor did he know why Shen Que had suddenly turned against them. He could not understand why the issue of spying had come up after the missionaries had been living in the capital for seventeen years, but he had assurances from a eunuch that the emperor understood the situation. Xu told his family to ready the western hall in their residence for the Nanjing missionaries in case they reached Shanghai.[176]

Xu Guangqi, whose rank as a corrector in the Hanlin Academy was lower than Shen Que's, submitted his own long memorial to the emperor.[177] Shen's first memorial, a summary, had appeared in the Capital Report (*Di bao*), which Xu referred to explicitly in his memorial. Xu said he was familiar with the learning of the men from far away. (He avoided using any term with the implication of barbarian.) He had discussed their teachings with them and been involved in the writing and printing of their books. He also had investigated their method of calendar making and had memorialized on their behalf. Thus he was one of those officials who believed in them, as alluded to in Shen Que's memorial. If the "adjunct

---

[174] In his discussion of Shen Que's arguments, E. Zürcher also discerned three main ones: the missionaries were promoting "immoral activities," "suspect political activities and affiliations," and "subversive activities among the people." See E. Zürcher, "The First Anti-Christian Movement in China (Nanjing, 1616–1621)," in P. W. Pestman, ed., *Acta Orientalia Neerlandica, Proceedings of the Congress of the Dutch Oriental Society* (Leiden, 1971), p. 191. Zürcher pointed out that Shen was critical of the missionaries' influence among both commoners and literati.

[175] Liang Jiamian, *Xu Guangqi nianpu*, p. 113.

[176] Xu Guangqi, Eleventh letter, *Xu Guangqi ji*, Vol. 2, p. 492.

[177] Xu's memorial, which exists in several versions, is in *Xu Guangqi ji*, Vol. 2, pp. 431–437. It is translated in Kelly, "The Anti-Christian Persecution of 1616–1617," pp. 294–302, and in E. G. Bridgman, "Paul Su's Apology, addressed to the emperor Wanlih of the Ming dynasty, in behalf of the Jesuit missionaries, Pantoja and others, who had been impeached by the Board of Rites in a Report dated the 44th year, 7th month of his reign (A.D. 1617 [sic])," *The Chinese Repository* (Canton, 1850), Vol. 19, pp. 118–126.

ministers" (*pei chen*, which was the term in the Wanli emperor's decree allowing Ricci to be buried at the capital) ought to be punished, how, Xu asked rhetorically, could he avoid being punished? He pointed out that there were many historical precedents for foreigners residing in China; he particularly cited the Hongwu emperor's employing Muslims (Huihui dashi) to translate books from Arabic on calendar making. Xu did not add that a Muslim office continued to be staffed at the Directorate of Astronomy; he did note, however, that temples (mosques) for worship according to the Islamic religion were everywhere, but its canonical texts had not been translated into Chinese to be checked (for immoral or seditious doctrines).

Xu stressed that every aspect of the teachings and conduct of the "adjunct ministers" was impeccably correct and wholly compatible with the Way of the sages. Their learning could be used to serve Confucianism and salvage Buddhism. Rather than being socially disruptive or morally corrupting, Xu claimed, they encouraged all men to do good with their idea of serving Heaven and loving all humans. Evidence for this, Xu argued, was the harmony that had prevailed for centuries among the Western countries. He proposed that, instead of sending the "adjunct ministers" away, the emperor should summon them to the capital to be examined, to translate their books, to debate the Taoists or Buddhists who would slander them, and then to be judged by competent officials. They should be allowed to spread their teachings to literati and commoners, to rich and poor wherever they reside, and to be required to report periodically on their followers' and their own conduct. If they ever were to do any wrong, of course they should be sent away. Near the end of his memorial Xu mentioned in passing that the matter of reforming the calendar was hardly relevant (which might be an oblique response to the views of some that proposals to involve missionaries in calculating the imperial calendars were at the heart of the affair).[178] Xu was compelled by Shen's attack to do what missionaries since Ricci had wanted; he was requesting formal permission from the emperor for the propagation of the Christian religion by foreigners. Just a year before, in 1615, Vagnoni had urged that such permission be sought from the emperor, but he had been dissuaded by Xu Guangqi and others on the grounds that such a request was still not expedient.[179]

[178] Xu Guangqi, "Bian xue zhangshu," *Xu Guangqi ji*, Vol. 2, pp. 431–436.
[179] Kelly, "The Anti-Christian Persecution of 1616–1617," pp. 31–32; cf. Dunne, *Generation of Giants*, pp. 120–121.

Yang Tingyun was living in retirement in Hangzhou when he learned of Shen Que's first memorial. According to Jesuits' accounts, he wrote letters on their behalf to his friends in Beijing, and he invited missionaries into his residence. Soon Cattaneo, Longobardo, Aleni, Sambiasi, and Pierre van Spiere (1584–1628) were sheltered by him.[180] Perhaps at this time, Yang wrote an essay particularly addressed to the idea that the religion of the Lord of Heaven (*tianzhu jiao*) from the Western countries was clearly not to be regarded as an evil or heretical religion (*xie jiao*) such as the White Lotus heretical religion. He listed fourteen points on which they were different, but they all seemed to derive from his first point, that heretical religions induced men to do evil but the Western religion only induced men to do good.[181] Yang proposed that the doctrines of the Western religion be carefully reviewed for any traces that might encourage men to do evil, and that a couple of men be ordered to infiltrate both the Western religion and the White Lotus to learn about them and their fundamental differences. Yang pointed to the reputation for integrity the Westerners had established over thirty years of contact with literati and commoners as proof against the unfounded charges of their critics.[182]

Before the elaborate processes of discovery that Xu and Yang recommended could be discussed at court, much less implemented, Shen Que received authorization to arrest the missionaries from Fang Congzhe, the minister of rites at Beijing, who shortly was to become the leading grand secretary. Warned, Longobardo and Aleni were able to leave Nanjing before Shen sent officers to the Jesuits' residence to take away Vagnoni. The other Jesuit, Alvaro Semedo (1586–1658), was ill and remained under house arrest temporarily. No Chinese were arrested at first, but

---

[180] Kelly, "The Anti-Christian Persecution of 1616–1617," pp. 39, 191–192, from Jesuit sources.

[181] Yang Tingyun, "Xiao luan bu bing ming shuo." A manuscript copy held in the Vatican Library is reproduced in *Tianzhujiao dong chuan wenxian xu bian* (Taipei, 1966), Vol. 1, p. 39. Yang's essay is translated in Kelly, "The Anti-Christian Persecution of 1616–1617," pp. 303–307.

[182] Yang Tingyun, "Xiao luan bu bing ming shuo." Yang's proposal that one or two men be ordered to enter the White Lotus religion (4a, p. 45) persuades me that his essay, which replies to one of Shen Que's main insinuations, was written in 1616–1617, and not in 1622, as Standaert, *Yang Tingyun*, p. 93, infers, i.e., during or immediately after the major White Lotus uprising in Shantung. It would have been foolish in 1622 to claim the government needed to ascertain whether the White Lotus represented a danger. It is quite possible that in a letter in 1622, as Semedo later recorded, Xu Guangqi set forth (Yang's) fourteen points on the differences between the religion of the Lord of Heaven and the White Lotus religion. Standaert wonders if Semedo was mistaken about the attribution to Xu instead of Yang in 1622.

gradually lay brothers, the mission's servants, and local Christians who called at the residence were taken into custody.[183] In Beijing, DeUrsis and Pantoja, although named in Shen Que's first memorial, were not arrested. Pantoja drafted a pamphlet defending the religion of the Lord of Heaven and its adherents, and he sent it to Nanjing to be printed, which may have exacerbated the situation.[184] Printing blocks were cut and about a hundred copies were printed, but before they could be distributed all involved were arrested.[185]

Everyone had to endure months of jail, interrogations, and beatings, until at the end of 1616 (or early in 1617 by the Western calendar), an edict was prepared and later issued ordering that Vagnoni, Pantoja, and their accomplices be taken to Guangzhou and sent back to their own countries.[186] The rationale given in the edict was that, as foreigners, they were a threat to the security of the state and that Vagnoni in particular had been involved in establishing a religion to mislead commoners. The only allusion to their involvement with literati was a reference to the earlier recommendation that Pantoja assist in calendrical calculations.[187] Shen Defu, who had met and admired Ricci, commented on the affair in 1618 or 1619. He summarized the main point in the memorials by Shen Que and the others as follows: "In Nanjing the religion of the Lord of Heaven is inflaming ignorant commoners, and the believers are numerous," but he also noted that the Ministry of Rites had requested that Pantoja and others with knowledge of calendrical methods be allowed to participate in the investigation of the sun, moon, and planets. The barbarians were expelled, and Shen Defu added that "[t]hey were quite mistaken if they thought they could take advantage of our turmoil to penetrate China (Zhonghua)."[188]

Pantoja and DeUrsis left Beijing under escort for Guangzhou in the spring of 1617. Sambiasi and Longobardo, who had not been specifically named in any of the memorials, went to stay with Yang Tingyun in Hangzhou.[189] In Nanjing, Vagnoni and Semedo were taken to a hearing to verify their identities as foreigners, and then, after being allowed

---

[183] Kelly, "The Anti-Christian Persecution of 1616–1617," pp. 45–51.

[184] Ibid., pp. 54, 59–60.

[185] Ibid., pp. 60–64.

[186] *Shenzong shilu*, Ch. 552, 1a–2a (Vol. 121, pp. 10425–10426). The edict is translated in Kelly, "The Anti-Christian Persecution of 1616–1617," pp. 85–86.

[187] Kelly, "The Anti-Christian Persecution of 1616–1617," pp. 85–86.

[188] Shen Defu, *Wanli Yehuo bian*, Vol. 3, p. 748. Shen's report is a shortened version of the material that also appears in the *Shilu*.

[189] Kelly, "The Anti-Christian Persecution of 1616–1617," p. 88.

to dispose of some personal effects that had not been confiscated, they were placed in wooden cages and carried to Guangzhou.[190] The twenty or so Chinese who had been arrested with them had trials and received sentences ranging from forced labor service to being sent home after a final beating.[191] Vagnoni, Semedo, Pantoja, and DeUrsis were confined in Guangzhou until 1618, when they were taken to Macao, supposedly to await a ship to carry them away. Pantoja soon died there, as did DeUrsis in 1620. Vagnoni and Semedo remained in Macao until they could reenter the Ming realm as missionaries in 1622. From 1617 to 1620 missionary activity was at a near standstill, with no new books printed and no overt attempts to engage the literati.

REESTABLISHING THE LEARNING FROM HEAVEN

After the Nanjing incident faded, the renewed dissemination of the Learning from Heaven through publications and public roles for the missionaries was effected under the leadership of Xu Guangqi, Li Zhizao, and Yang Tingyun. In the last few years of the Wanli reign (1573–1619) Xu was increasingly active in military affairs, particularly military preparedness near the capital and defense policy in the northeast against the growing Manchu menace. In collaboration with Yang, who was still in retirement in Hangzhou, and with Li, who was still serving as an official of the Ministry of Works at Gaoyou on the Grand Canal north of Yangzhou, Xu, in 1619–1620, arranged for four cannons to be brought from Macao to bolster Ming defenses.[192] The implication was that Jesuits would follow the cannons north to aid in their deployment and give instruction on their use. From 1620 the missionaries were moving away from Yang's residence in Hangzhou. Aleni went to Shanxi. Cattaneo and then Sambiasi went to Shanghai and nearby Jiading, where a new church was opened. Semedo left Macao in 1620 for Hangzhou, the younger Manoel Diaz reached Beijing in 1621, and a few years later, Vagnoni, with a new Chinese name, went to the mission in Shanxi.[193] The leading foe of the Jesuits, Shen Que, was appointed a

---

[190] Ibid., pp. 91–94.
[191] Ibid., pp. 99–103.
[192] Liang Jiamian, *Xu Guangqi nianpu*, pp. 132–133, 138; Fang Hao, *Li Zhizao yanjiu*, pp. 157–167.
[193] Fang Hao, *Li Zhizao yanjiu*, pp. 167–171; Goodrich and Fang, *Dictionary of Ming Biography*, s.v. Aleni, Cattaneo, Sambiasi, Semedo, and Vagnoni; Dunne, *Generation of Giants*, p. 187.

grand secretary in 1621, and a major White Lotus uprising occurred in Shandong in 1622, which brought renewed protests against the presence of the foreigners, but they returned to the capital after Shen left office in 1622. Two new Jesuits arrived in Macao in 1619, Johann Adam Schall von Bell (1592–1666) and Johann Terrenz (or Schreck, 1576–1630). Both were especially knowledgeable in astronomy and other Western sciences, and were sent to Beijing with Longobardo in 1623.[194] Another newly arrived missionary, Francisco Furtado (1587–1653), went first to Jiading and then remained in Hangzhou in association with Li Zhizao, who resigned from office in 1623.[195]

Yang Tingyun took the lead in renewing publications. In 1621 he printed his two-*juan* book entitled *Dai yi pian* (In place of doubt). It was cast as responses by Mi-ge (i.e., Michael, referring to Yang himself) to twenty-four sets of questions put by a Confucian (*ru*) expressing doubt about certain ideas brought by the literati from the West (*xi shi*).[196] Yang rehearsed the Aristotelian model of a spherical earth inhabited on all sides by humans and in the middle of concentric spheres carrying the visible celestial bodies. He dismissed Buddhist concepts of multilayered heavens as contrary to the pattern of the heavens (*tian wen*) that was made by the one Lord of Heaven.[197] The Lord of Heaven was the Creator of all things, and Yang contested the theory of Zhang Zai that everything is constituted from unitary *qi* (particles, or material force) and the Cheng-Zhu theory that the coherence (*li*) in the particular clusters of *qi* is what makes things as they are. He disputed the claim of Zhu Xi that there is no need to think there is something, in particular a ruler (*zhuzai*), that "made" the phenomenal world, as all things come into being "of themselves" (*ziran*) without the intentionality of any external agent.[198] The evidence of our senses should persuade us, Yang argued, that the physical world is not accidental but can only be the result of the omnipotence of the Lord of Heaven, who made heaven and earth in seven days.[199] The position taken on whether the cosmos was created by an exterior something, or was generated autonomously,

---

[194] Goodrich and Fang, *Dictionary of Ming Biography*, s.v. Schall and Terrenz.
[195] Ibid., s.v. Furtado; Fang Hao, *Li Zhizao yanjiu*, p. 205.
[196] Yang Tingyun, "Zong lun," 1a, *Dai yi pian*; reprinted in *Tianzhujiao dong chuan wenxian*, p. 495.
[197] Yang Tingyun, "Zong lun," 1.12a–15a (pp. 546–551).
[198] Yang Tingyun, "Zong lun," 1.1a (p. 503). Parts of this first response are translated in Standaert, *Yang Tingyun*, pp. 111–112.
[199] Yang Tingyun, "Zong lun," 1.2a–3a (pp. 506–507).

marked a fundamental difference between the Learning from Heaven of the missionaries and the Learning of the Way transmitted from the Sung philosophers.

Yang also explained the concept of the omnipresent Lord of Heaven, called Deus (Dou-si) in the Western countries, where, in the temples of worship in antiquity, he was represented by a canonical text, not by a form or shape.[200] He described how the Lord of Heaven took pity on humans, who earlier had innate moral knowledge (*liang zhi*) but had lost it; the Lord descended to earth and assumed a human identity, called Jesus (Ye-su), or savior of the world.[201] Yang told of how Mary was the mother, of the crucifixion and the meaning of the cross, and of the Trinity.[202] Yang pointed out that knowledge of these is not contained in the Five Classics or the Four Books, although they do contain the ideas of Heaven's power and the worship of Heaven. He stressed that rather than being either wholly inborn or a product of one's culture, knowledge of morality and the capacity to be moral come to each person by the grace or gift of the Lord of Heaven.[203] This idea of Heaven's grace had precedents in the classics, too, but there were important differences, as Yang tried to show. Finally, Yang devoted several of his responses in the book to allaying doubts about the origins, motives, conduct, and learning of the literati from the West, all the while sharply distinguishing their teachings from Buddhism.

All the efforts to assimilate or accommodate the Learning from Heaven to Chinese vocabulary and precedents notwithstanding, Yang was making some of the differences plain. In a work that was published posthumously, he was explicit and succinct. "The teaching of veneration of Heaven and service to Heaven is similar [in the canonical texts of the West and China], but to point to material substance as heaven and to recognize coherence (*li*) and particles (*qi*) as constituting heaven, [which was taught by Zhu Xi,] is different from saying that heaven must have a Lord. The theory that the Lord is without voice or smell and surpasses the human's sense of hearing, seeing, and thinking is similar, but the great Lord's coming down to redeem and save the world, [the distinct stages of] the teaching by the Word, the teaching by His person, and the teaching by grace, and morality prospering more after the teaching by grace than in

---

[200] Ibid., 2.1a–b (pp. 583–584).
[201] Ibid., 2.2a (p. 585). This passage is translated in Standaert, *Yang Tingyun*, pp. 129–130.
[202] Yang Tingyun, "Zong lun," 2.3b–11b.
[203] Ibid., 2.16b (p. 614). Standaert, *Yang Tingyun*, pp. 150–151, 207, provides other examples on this point from Yang's writings.

ancient times are all differences from the concept that people now are not as good as those of ancient times."[204] In the introduction to his *In Place of Doubt* (*Dai yi pian*), Yang explicitly addressed the question of why, given the similarities, "we Confucians" (*wu ru*) should be concerned with these ideas instead of dismissing them as "other strands" (*yi duan*), as in Chan Buddhism, or the speculative philosophizing of the third century.[205] His book was an attempt to elucidate an answer that would persuade his literati readers.

Yang's writings were not limited to religious doctrine, although it was the aspect of the Learning from Heaven that most concerned him. After he returned to Beijing in 1622 to accept official appointment again, he wrote a preface for Aleni's treatise on the system of education in the Western countries called the *Xi xue fan* (General account of study in the West). Giving their names in transliteration, Aleni described the six disciplines in universities as rhetoric, (natural) philosophy, including physics and mathematics, medicine, law, canon law, and theology, in ascending order of importance. He explained what was covered in each course of study and when they were studied in the student's career.[206] In his preface Yang stressed that the Learning from Heaven published in Chinese had behind it an enormous body of knowledge not exhausted by what had been translated or even by the seven thousand works recently brought by ship and that this knowledge had long been absent in China.[207] Yang also wrote a preface for another book Aleni published in 1623 with Yang's editorial assistance, the *Zhifang wai ji* (Record of countries not listed in the Records Office). The five *juan* of this book described Asia, Europe, Africa, America, and the Four Oceans, with maps, and named the countries and some of their attributes.[208] In his preface Yang returned repeatedly to the theme that when we confront this immense world and all that is in it, we must ask who or what causes it to be so. Each time Yang answered his own question: the Great Ruler,

[204] Yang Tingyun, *Dai yi xu pian*, 1.2a, altered from the translation in Standaert, *Yang Tingyun*, p. 207.

[205] Yang Tingyun, "Zong lun," esp. 1a (p. 495). Cf. the beginning of *Dai yi xu pian*, translated in Standaert, *Yang Tingyun*, p. 206, for the same question, but more sharply posed.

[206] Aleni, *Xixue fan*, in Li Zhizao, *Tianxue chu han*, pp. 27–59. Notice that Li put this text first in the collection.

[207] Aleni, *Xixue fan*, esp. 1a–b, 4b–5a (pp. 9–10, 16–17).

[208] A more detailed account is in Bernard Hung-kay Luk, "A Study of Giulio Aleni's *Chih-fang wai chi*," *Bulletin of the School of Oriental and African Studies*, Vol. 40, No. 1 (1977), pp. 58–84. Also see Peterson, "Western Natural Philosophy," pp. 306–307.

the Master Craftsman, the omnipotent Lord of Creation. According to Yang the literati from the West were drawing men to a more profound respect for the Divinity in Heaven (*tian di*).[209] Of course, ambiguities remained. Yang's longtime acquaintance Chen Jiru wrote in a commemoration of him that when Yang resigned from office in 1625, he returned to Hangzhou to "discourse on learning and discuss the Way."[210] Such formulations obscured Yang's repeated assertion that new ideas were being propagated.

Ye Xianggao (1562–1627) is an example of a literatus who was sympathetic but never became a convinced adherent of the Learning from Heaven. From Fuzhou prefecture, Ye achieved his *jinshi* degree at a young age, in 1583. He served in the Hanlin Academy and then at the Imperial College (Guozijian) in Nanjing,[211] where he met Ricci, probably in 1599. Nine years later he went to Beijing as minister of rites and grand secretary, and from 1608 to 1614 he was the leading, and sometimes the only, grand secretary. Called out of retirement to be a grand secretary to his former pupil, who had become the Taichang emperor in 1620, Ye served from 1621 to 1624, when he resigned as the conflicts between Wei Zhongxian and Donglin partisans were becoming more vicious. On his way back to Fuzhou, Ye met Aleni in Hangzhou and invited him to Fujian. Aleni went and, partly with Ye's backing, started the first mission in Fujian in 1625 and made hundreds of converts. He remained there until his death in 1649.[212]

After leaving Beijing in 1624, Ye Xianggao wrote a sympathetic preface for Yang Tingyun's booklet, never published, on the Ten Commandments.[213] He commented on how learned the men from the Great West were, and how they set an example in venerating Heaven. While noting Yang's sincerity in pursuing their doctrines, Ye also observed

---

[209] Yang Tingyun, Preface, esp. 5b (p. 1296), in Giulio Aleni, *Zhifang waiji*, in Li Zhizao, *Tianxue chu han*, Vol. 3.

[210] Chen Jiru, Quoted in Liang Jiamian, *Xu Guangqi nianpu*, p. 153.

[211] See Goodrich and Fang, *Dictionary of Ming Biography*, s.v. Yeh Hsiang-kao [Ye Xianggao].

[212] See ibid., pp. 2–6; Dunne, *Generation of Giants*, pp. 189–192, 259–261; Eugenio Menegon, *Un Solo Cielo: Giulio Aleni S.J. (1582–1649). Geografia, Arte, Scienza, Religione dall'Europa alla Cina* (Brescia, 1994); and Li Jiubiao, *Kouduo Richao: Li Jiubiao's Diary of Oral Admonitions – A Late Ming Christian Journal*, trans., ed., and annotated Erik Zuercher, Monumenta Serica Monograph Series, No. 56 (Sankt Augustin, 2007).

[213] The preface by Ye is translated in Bernard Luk, "A Serious Matter of Life and Death: Learned Conversations at Foochow in 1627," in Ronan and Oh, eds., *East Meets West*, pp. 201–202.

that aspects of their learning might seem fanciful to some, even when they were an improvement on Buddhism. In Ye's view, "Many literati and officials have studied with them, but relatively few admire them so profoundly and believe them so wholeheartedly as to think they have truly found out about human nature and solved the questions of life and death."[214] In the spring of 1627 Ye Xianggao made a visit to Fuzhou from his home in a nearby district. Aleni called on him, and the next day Ye in turn called on Aleni, who subsequently published a record of their conversations over the two days on the Learning from Heaven.[215] Aleni, of course, was concerned with distinguishing his doctrine from Buddhism and arguing for a single creator, the Lord of Heaven. Since he was the one who published it, the account is designed to convey his answers to questions or responses to objections, as was Yang Tingyun's *Dai yi pian*. Ye's questions seem to be his own but also represent what other literati might ask.[216]

After listening to Aleni's theory that "there is a Lord of Heaven who made the ten thousand things of heaven and earth and rules over them," Ye wondered how there could be a Lord of Heaven before there was a heaven and earth of which to be lord.[217] Aleni argued that what makes it so (*suo yi ran*) must be prior to that which is its consequence (*qi gu ran*).[218] The issue was whether the cosmos had to be created by something external to it or was generated from spontaneous processes within it. When Ye Xianggao pointed to the Song idea of a Supreme Ultimate (*tai ji*) being prior and responsible for the separation of the physical heaven from the earth, Aleni insisted, quite correctly, that the idea of the Supreme Ultimate did not go beyond the concepts of *li* (coherence) and *qi* (particles) and that they could not of themselves have the consciousness to make something.[219] Ye asked Aleni if this external Creator made the bad as well as the good, a problem he seemed to find troubling.[220] When

---

[214] Slightly altered from the translation in ibid., p. 201.
[215] Giulio Aleni, *Sanshan lun xue ji* (1847 ed.); reprinted in *Tianzhujiao dong chuan wenxian xu pian*, Vol. 1, pp. 419–493. Aleni described the two meetings, 1a, p. 435, and 7b, p. 448. The conversations are the subject in Luk, "A Serious Matter," pp. 173–206.
[216] Luk, "A Serious Matter," p. 176.
[217] Aleni, *Sanshan lun xue ji*, 4b, p. 442; Luk, "A Serious Matter," p. 187.
[218] Aleni, *Sanshan lun xue ji*, 4b, p. 442; Luk, "A Serious Matter," p.187.
[219] Aleni, *Sanshan lun xue ji*, 5b, p. 444; Luk, "A Serious Matter," p. 187.
[220] Aleni, *Sanshan lun xue ji*, 6a, p. 445; Luk, "A Serious Matter," p. 188. Even without assuming there was a creator, the proponents of the Learning of the Way had struggled, too, with the problem of the presence of evil or disorder in a world they held was characterized by coherence (*li*).

Ye resumed the questioning on the second day, he returned repeatedly to the problem of evil. If the omnipotent Lord of Heaven created everything for the benefit of humans, Ye asked, why did he create fanged and poisonous things that are not only useless but harmful to humans?[221] Why do good men suffer harm? Aleni answered that "[t]he way of the Creator is unfathomable and the understanding of humans is limited."[222] Why are good men harmed while bad men escape? Or why are there so many bad people and so few good ones?[223] (Ye was asking these questions when Wei Zhongxian was at the height his influence and causing the deaths of men affiliated with the Donglin Academy with whom Ye was aligned.) Ye asked other versions of these questions about evil without appearing to be convinced by Aleni's answers that the Lord of Heaven has his purposes. Ye also questioned Aleni's expositions of the immortal soul, the existence of heaven and hell for souls after death, the coming of Jesus, the good effects of the teaching in the Western countries, and so on. Ye's position at the end seemed still to be one of distanced, but polite curiosity, although Aleni records at the end that Ye was expressing his continued interest in the teachings that were new and strange.[224] Aleni did not have a chance to pursue these ideas with Ye, who died before the year was out.

The next year, 1628, another literatus published a small book on the doctrine of the Lord of Heaven (*tianzhu zhi jiao*) while he was serving as a prefectural judge in Yangzhou.[225] Wang Zheng (1571–1644) was from Shaanxi, not from Jiangnan.[226] After passing the provincial examination in 1594, he seems to have failed nine times in the metropolitan examinations before he passed in 1622. Wang became aware of the missionaries on his trips to Beijing. He told of reading Pantoja's *Qi ke* (Seven [sins] to overcome), which was printed in 1614. Wang was so moved that he abandoned his interest in Buddhism and Taoism, which he had been pursuing for twenty years. He had many discussions on the new doctrine with Pantoja, who was forced to leave Beijing in 1617.[227] It is not clear when Wang Zheng was baptized, but it may have been while he was in

[221] Aleni, *Sanshan lun xue ji*, 7b–8a, pp. 448–449; Luk, "A Serious Matter," p. 189.
[222] Aleni, *Sanshan lun xue ji*, 9b–10a, pp. 452–453; Luk, "A Serious Matter," p. 190.
[223] Aleni, *Sanshan lun xue ji*, 11a, 12b, pp. 455, 458; Luk, "A Serious Matter," pp. 191–192.
[224] Aleni, *Sanshan lun xue ji*, 30a, p. 493; Luk, "A Serious Matter," p. 196.
[225] Fang Hao, "Wang Zheng zhi shiji ji qi shuru xiyang xueshu zhi gongxian," *Wen Shi Zhe xuebao*, Vol. 13 (1964), pp. 39–40.
[226] For a summary of his life, see Hummel, *Eminent Chinese*, s.v. Wang Cheng.
[227] Wang Zheng, *Wei Tian ai ren ji lun* (1628); (a copy is preserved in Paris at the Bibliotheque Nationale, Courant No. 3368), 3b–5b.

contact with Pantoja; Wang later wrote that when he was baptized he made a vow not to take a concubine, but he submitted to his father's demands after passing the *jinshi* examination in 1622.[228]

In any case, Wang publicly expressed his commitment to the Lord of Heaven in a preface he wrote in 1621 for Yang Tingyun's book, *Dai yi pian* (In place of doubt). Elaborating on the theme of faith (*xin*), Wang wrote that in his book Michael (i.e., Yang Tingyun) provided evidence for believing what had been brought by the literati from the West.[229] Probably while he was in mourning in 1625, Wang briefly studied Latin with Nicolas Trigault (1577–1628) in Xi'an, Shaanxi. Together they worked on a booklet showing the systematic use of Roman letters to record the pronunciation of Chinese characters without recourse to other characters. The printed version in 1626 was called *Xi ru er mu zi* (Western Confucians' aids for the ear and eye [in reading characters]).[230] While he was in Beijing awaiting reappointment to office in 1626, Wang met the Jesuits Longobardo, Schall, and Terrenz. Based on discussions with Terrenz, Wang translated and published another book in 1627 called *Yuan Xi qi qi tushuo lu zui* (Epitome of illustrated explanations of exotic devices from the Far West), which included wood-block prints of machines and tools. Both books intentionally presented material that had not been previously known in China.[231]

The issue of new ideas was raised explicitly in Wang's own exposition of the new faith, which was printed in 1628 as the *Wei Tian ai ren ji lun* (Exemplary discussion of [the doctrine of] fearing Heaven and loving mankind). The question posed was why, given the rich and various literature transmitted from antiquity that Wang had studied for more than twenty years, would he reject it to "firmly believe what the Confucians from the West call the doctrine of the Lord of Heaven?"[232] Put in other words, "Why do you simply dismiss what you have already learned and believe what you have not? Why do you dismiss traditional learning and believe the new learning, dismiss the learning from close at hand and believe the learning from far away?" This was a strange doctrine that the

[228] See Albert Chan, "Late Ming Society and the Jesuit Missionaries," in Ronan and Oh, eds., *East Meets West*, pp. 171–172.
[229] Wang Zheng, "Xu," 2a–b, in Yang Tingyun, *Dai yi pian*; reprinted in *Tianzhujiao dong chuan wenxian*, pp. 485–486. Cf. Fang Hao, "Wang Zheng," p. 40–41.
[230] Luo Changpei, "Yesu hui shi tsai yinyunxue shang de gongxian," *Guoli Zhongyang yanjiu yuan lishi yuyan yanjiu suo jikan*, Vol. 1, No. 3 (1930), pp. 274–275.
[231] As pointed out in Wang Zheng, *Wei Tian ai ren ji shuo*, 2b.
[232] Wang Zheng, *Wei Tian ai ren ji shuo*, 1b–2a.

sages of antiquity did not have,[233] although they, and we Chinese now, he contended, knew the ideas of fearing Heaven and loving other humans.[234] To answer these (rhetorical) questions, Wang reviewed his discussions with Pantoja, and then explained in his own words the attributes of Deus, or the Lord of Heaven, as omnipotent, omniscient Creator who must be venerated by his creation, humans. To save their enduring souls, humans must do good and eschew evil; thus they might enter heaven (*tian tang*) and avoid hell (*di yu*).

Wang made no mention of Jesus, either as man or savior, nor did he refer to the concept of the Holy Spirit. His message was one of moral rectification set in a framework provided by the Lord of Heaven. In explaining the Ten Commandments, he reduced them to two themes: fear Heaven and love your fellow humans.[235] This seems to have been the core teaching that Wang promoted when he went back to Shaanxi after being impeached and exiled because troops in his jurisdiction in the northeast rebelled in 1631. Wang's book was addressed to a wider audience and was more like Ricci's *Tianzhu shi yi* than Yang Tingyun's *Dai yi pian*. It followed the strategy of arguing on the basis of a "natural religion" that had precedents to be found in the Five Classics, but not presenting in detail some of the core doctrines of the revealed religion. Wang's book offered an elaborate new rationale for persuading oneself and others of the need to be moral. This was part of Wang's motive when he founded a benevolent society (*ren hui*) in 1634 to do good works in Shaanxi a few years after he had helped Giacomo Rho (1593–1638) build a church.[236]

The more important publishing event in 1628 was the completion of a collectanea edited by Li Zhizao. Entitled *Tianxue chuhan* (First collection on the Learning from Heaven), it included most of the important works on the Learning from Heaven up to that time.[237] Li divided the collection into two parts, labeled "general principles" (*li*) and "concrete phenomena" (*qi*), each containing ten titles. Under the "general principles" heading, Li placed Ricci's books on friendship, the *Twenty-five Discourses*, the

[233] Ibid., 2a.
[234] Ibid., 3a.
[235] Ibid., 43b–44a.
[236] Ibid., 43, 46.
[237] Fang Hao pointed out that if they had not been collected and reprinted by Li, some of the twenty works he included would have been lost, as their earlier versions are not extant. See Fang Hao, "Li Zhizao ji ke Tianxue chu han kao," introducing Li Zhizao, ed., *Tianxue chu han*, p. 1. Liang Jiamian, in *Xu Guangqi nianpu*, p. 180, argued that *Tianxue chu han* was printed in 1629 or 1630, not 1628, the date of the preface.

*Ten Essays on the Extraordinary Man*, and *Bian xue yi du* (Posthumous documents of [Ricci's] *Debates on Learning*), which assembled a few of his polemical written and oral exchanges with critics. Also included were Pantoja's *Seven [Sins] to Overcome*, a book by Francesco Sambiasi (1582–1649) on the soul, which was translated by Xu Guangqi with his preface in 1624, and Aleni's two books on the education system in Europe and on the geography of the world. Li Zhizao also included a short treatise on the recent discovery of a stele in Xi'an that recorded the presence of (Nestorian) Christianity at the Tang capital in the eighth century.[238] The second part of the collection comprised the book on water technology by DeUrsis and Xu Guangqi and eight works on mathematics and astronomy. These involved various degrees of authorship, editing, and preface writing by Ricci, DeUrsis, Xu Guangqi, and Li Zhizao on geometry, arithmetic, trigonometry, surveying, and the new instruments for measuring celestial phenomena. The tenth title in the second part was a little book, first printed in 1615 by Manoel Diaz (1574–1659), called *Tian wen lue* (Catechism on the heavens). Diaz provided a summary of the Aristotelian cosmos and added a report on the recent discovery, through the use of a telescope (by Galileo), of the moons of Jupiter, Saturn's ring, sun spots, and numerous stars that could not be seen by the unaided eye.[239] (A small book by Schall on the telescope, printed in 1626, was not included by Li.)[240]

Li Zhizao's selection of titles, although seemingly biased toward works with which he was involved, represents the breadth of the Learning from Heaven as it was represented to the literate audience over a thirty-year period in late Ming. From cosmology to technology, geometry to geography, ethics to eschatology, the parts were interrelated and mutually sustaining. They were all connected, even if ambiguously, by the new meanings imputed to the word *tian*, heaven. Li Zhizao explained in his preface that the collection made the writings easily available; they conveyed "what is called the most primary, the truest, and broadest doctrine, which the sage [i.e., Confucius] would not change if he came back."[241] It was this broad doctrine, the Learning from Heaven rather than the

---

[238] Michael Keevak, *The Story of a Stele: China's Nestorian Monument and Its Reception in the West, 1625–1916* (Hong Kong, 2008), pp. 5–13.

[239] Manoel Diaz, *Tianwen lue*, 43a–b, in Li Zhizao, *Tianxue chu han*, Vol. 5, pp. 2717–2718. Cf. Benjamin A. Elman, *On Their Own Terms: Science in China, 1550–1900* (Cambridge, MA, 2005), Ch. 2.; Pasquale M. D'Elia, *Galileo in China*, trans. Rufus Suter and Mathew Sciascia (Cambridge, MA, 1960), p. 8, and Peterson, "Western Natural Philosophy," p. 298.

[240] See D'Elia, *Galileo in China*, pp. 33–41.

[241] Li Zhizao, "Ti ci," 1b, in *Tianxue chu han*, p. 2.

Catholic doctrines that were the missionaries' main concern, that represented an intellectual alternative for literati. Appearing at the beginning of the Chongzhen reign (1628–1644), the *Tianxue chu han* represented the Learning from Heaven as a coherent, practicable set of teachings.

## THE LEARNING FROM HEAVEN IN THE EMPEROR'S SERVICE

The accession of a new emperor in 1627 allowed a new political climate in which it was possible to enhance the legitimacy of the Learning from Heaven. Xu Guangqi, who had been living in retirement since resigning on a plea of illness in 1621, returned to office in the Ministry of Rites in the first month of 1628.[242] An opportunity presented itself in the fifth month of 1629, when there was a solar eclipse visible in north China. Xu Guangqi submitted a prediction of the time the eclipse would be witnessed at Beijing that turned out to be more accurate than the prediction made by the Directorate of Astronomy.[243] Putting a negative interpretation on the fact that the system for computing astronomical and thus calendrical events had not been adjusted for 260 years, the Ministry of Rites proposed that an office for calendar reform be established and that Xu Guangqi, Li Zhizao, Xing Yunlu, Fan Shouyi (all four of whom had been similarly nominated in 1611–1612), and others with relevant expertise be appointed to staff the new office. It was noted that Pantoja and DeUrsis, who also had been nominated twenty years earlier, were now dead, and Longobardo and Terrenz were named instead as the foreigners from the West who could participate.[244] The proposal was accepted, and before the year was out the order had been issued for a calendrical (reform) office (*li ju*) to be built on the site of the Shoushan Academy, which had been demolished in 1622.[245] Li Zhizao, though ill, was recalled from retirement in Hangzhou, and artisans were hired to make the instruments needed for accurate observation of celestial phenomena.[246] In a memorial

---

[242] Liang Jiamian, *Xu Guangqi nianpu*, pp. 142, 158.

[243] See Xu's memorial in Xu Guangqi, *Xu Guangqi ji*, pp. 319–322. The times calculated for the beginning, maximum, and end of the eclipse according to the Datong, the Muslim, and the new method are given in a note, pp. 323–324.

[244] Liang Jiamian, *Xu Guangqi nianpu*, pp. 163–164; also *Ming shi*, 31, p. 529. The most complete account in a Western language of the Jesuits' participation in efforts at calendar reform is in Henri Bernard, "L'Encyclopédie astronomique du Père Schall (Tch'ongtcheng li-chou, 1629, et Si-yang sin-fa li-chou, 1645). La réforme du calendrier chinois sous l'influence de Clavius, de Galilée et de Kepler," *Monumenta Serica*, Vol. 3 (1938), pp. 35–77, 441–527.

[245] See Liang Jiamian, *Xu Guangqi nianpu*, p. 147.

[246] Liang Jiamian, *Xu Guangqi nianpu*, pp. 164, 166.

detailing ten factors in the calendar system that had to be revised and ten instruments to be built, Xu Guangqi stressed the need to combine correct theory and accurately measured observation.[247] He also argued that the reforms would bring supplemental benefits, including more accurate surveying, accounting, construction, mapping, timekeeping, and even medical practice (because doctors who understood the relation between astral conditions and their patients' health could adjust medicines and acupuncture treatment with more precision).[248]

Terrenz was well trained in mathematics and astronomy. He had studied with Galileo in Padua and was accepted as one of the Lincei in Rome in 1611; later that year he joined the Society of Jesus. Terrenz had been recruited for the China mission during Trigault's travels in Europe from 1614 to 1618 to gather money, books, and experts in anticipation of such a project as was approved in 1629. Terrenz reached Macao in 1619, Jiading in 1622, and had been in Beijing since 1625. He continued to send letters from China asking Kepler for advice on predicting eclipses and adjusting European ephemerides to Beijing's longitude.[249] However, Terrenz as well as Li Zhizao died in 1630, before much work could be done.[250] Xu Guangqi then recommended that Giacomo Rho (1593–1638) and Johann Adam Schall von Bell (1592–1666) be called to the capital.[251] Rho came from Shanxi and Schall from Shaanxi, where each had worked with Wang Zheng.[252] Both spent the remainder of their lives in Beijing as foreign experts on calendrical and astronomical matters.

As it became known that foreigners with no examination degrees were being appointed to government offices and receiving stipends for their knowledge of calendar making, others sought to compete with them. In 1630 a certified student from Sichuan was recommended by a censor as an expert who could correct many of the accumulated errors in the old system for computing the calendar. Xu Guangqi sought to thwart him by exposing the deficiencies in his method, including misunderstandings of the old system, and the inaccuracies of his predictions.[253] The next year, 1631, a commoner named Wei Wenkui, who had been influenced by the

---

[247] Xu Guangqi, "Tiao yi lifa xiuzheng suicha shu," in *Xu Guangqi ji*, pp. 332–338. Cf. Liang Jiamian, *Xu Guangqi nianpu*, pp. 164–165. Xu's points are also abstracted in *Ming shi*, 31: 530.

[248] Xu Guangqi, "Tiao yi lifa xiuzheng suicha shu," pp. 337–338.

[249] See Goodrich and Fang, *Dictionary of Ming Biography*, s.v. Terrenz.

[250] Liang Jiamian, *Xu Guangqi nianpu*, pp. 172, 174.

[251] Ibid., p. 173. See Xu Guangqi, *Xu Guangqi ji*, pp. 345–346.

[252] Liang Jiamian, *Xu Guangqi nianpu*, p. 183.

[253] Xu's memorial is in Xu Guangqi, *Xu Guangqi ji*, pp. 359–361. Cf. Liang Jiamian, *Xu Guangqi nianpu*, p. 176, and *Ming shi*, 31:531.

attempts by Xing Yunlu twenty years earlier to reform the calendar,[254] had two works he had written submitted to the court for examination of his claims for improving the accuracy of the calendar. Xu Guangqi again wrote a critique, contrasting Wei's proposals with the new method's results for times of eclipses and for calculating the time of the winter solstice, which was the crucial moment in the Ming calendar.[255] Commoner Wei's claims had little chance against the authority of Xu, who was a grand secretary and an examiner for the metropolitan examinations that spring.[256] For three years, Xu submitted a series of detailed memorials, some with diagrams, explaining eclipses and eclipse prediction and arguing over and over for the superiority of the new methods and the new tabulated data, all in an apparent effort to educate the emperor and the court on the merits of the new ideas and the Western experts associated with the Learning from Heaven. By 1632 Schall and Rho and their Chinese collaborators, basing their work, in part, on the theories of Tycho Brahe, had prepared and presented to the emperor more than seventy *juan* of explanations of theories, methods, and instruments, as well as the more accurate tables to be used in reckoning the positions of the sun and moon (for solstices and eclipses). They also presented star tables and charts and ephemerides for the five planets.[257]

Xu Guangqi died in 1633, but even after the loss of their most vigorous advocate and the last of the so-called Three Pillars, Jesuits continued to benefit from their involvement with an imperially sponsored project. The calendar office was taken over by Li Tianjing, a provincial official nominated by Xu just before he died.[258] Li was not a Christian, and he was criticized by Schall for not being a forceful advocate for the office.[259]

---

[254] Liang Jiamian, *Xu Guangqi nianpu*, p. 190, n. 17.

[255] *Ming shi*, 31:532–534; Liang Jiamian, *Xu Guangqi nianpu*, pp. 185–186.

[256] Liang Jiamian, *Xu Guangqi nianpu*, p. 185.

[257] See Xu's memorials on the presentations, in *Xu Guangqi ji*, pp. 371–372, 385–386. The titles are also listed in Bernard, "L'Encyclopédie astronomique," App. 5, pp. 443–444. The presentation of tables and essays continued at least until 1636. A detailed discussion of the sections on cosmologies, the telescope, and other observational instruments in the calendar writings is in Hashimoto Keizō, "Chongzhen li shu ni miru kagaku kakumei no ikkatei," in *Science and Skills in Asia: A Festschrift for Prof. Yabuuti Kiyoshi* (Kyoto, 1982), pp. 370–390; also see Hashimoto Keizō, "Chongzhen kaireki to Xu Guangqi no yakuwari," in *Explorations in the History of Science and Technology in China: Compiled in Honour of the Eightieth Birthday of Dr. Joseph Needham* (Shanghai, 1982), esp. pp. 192–198.

[258] Xu's memorial is in *Xu Guangqi ji*, pp. 424–426. Cf. Dunne, *Generation of Giants*, p. 222.

[259] See Bernard, "L'Encyclopédie astronomique," p. 453, and Dunne, *Generation of Giants*, p. 309.

In 1634, with Xu Quangqi gone, Wei Wenkui memorialized again on his proposals for the calendar system. This time he was summoned to the capital and a calendar office was established for him on the east side of the city to balance the Jesuit-dominated office on the west. Both offices continued in competition with the regular calendar office and the Muslim office in the Directorate of Astronomy.[260] In the first month of 1636, for example, the four sets of competitors gathered one night to correlate the accuracy of their predictions for the times of a lunar eclipse. Li Tianjing was there with Rho and Schall, along with Wei Wenkui and officials from the Directorate of Astronomy and the Ministry of Rites. It was determined that Li's figures for the times of the eclipse were the best.[261] The superiority of the Western method of predicting planetary positions was repeatedly demonstrated, and Li Tianjing continued to supervise the production of tables and other writings by the western office. Although not all of them were printed in their entirety, the texts, tables, and charts totaled about 137 *juan* by 1636. They were known collectively as the *Chongzhen li shu* (Writings on the calendar from the Chongzhen reign), a name changed under the Manchus to the *Xiyang xin fa li shu* (Writings on the calendar according to the new method from the West). During the Chongzhen reign the calendar was refined but never reformulated on the basis of Western methods.[262] Schall closed the western calendar office in 1642 rather than have it absorbed into the Directorate of Astronomy, but in 1644 he accepted the patronage of the Manchus. Appointed as the head of the directorate, he and the new method were unrivaled for twenty years.[263]

During the 1630s the Jesuits enjoyed relative security to promote the Learning from Heaven. In 1637 there were sixteen missions. There were thousands of converts throughout the empire, but none so prominent as Xu, Li, and Yang had been.[264] In Fujian, Aleni produced a book on natural philosophy called the *Xing xue cu shu* (A general account of the study of the natures of living things) that was based on Galen's distinctions of the natural, vital, and animal (i.e., having to do with anima or soul) spirits.[265] Aleni also wrote another short introduction to European

[260] *Ming shi*, 31:536. Some Jesuits suspected Li Tianjing had studied with Wei and was sympathetic to him; see Dunne, *Generation of Giants*, p. 309.
[261] *Ming shi*, 31:541.
[262] See *Ming shi*, 31:543.
[263] See Goodrich and Fang, *Dictionary of Ming Biography*, p. 1154.
[264] Dunne, *Generation of Giants*, p. 309.
[265] See Peterson, "Western Natural Philosophy," pp. 308–309.

culture called *Xifang da wen* (Answers to questions about the West).[266] In Shanxi, Vagnoni published a version of the Aristotelian cosmos that he called *Huanyu shimo* (Comprehensive account of the universe). About the same time (1636–1637), Schall published another elaborate argument for a creator in a book called *Zhu zhi qun zheng* (A host of evidence that the Lord rules).[267] But these were overshadowed by the work on the calendar at the capital as the foundation of the missionaries' continuing presence in China. Symbolic of this was the emperor's bestowing an inscription in his own hand on Rho and Schall in 1638; the inscription was four words, *Qin bao tian xue*, or "Imperial Praise on the Learning from Heaven."[268] This inscription may have been a reference only to their knowledge of celestial phenomena, but its recipients must have been willing to construe it to apply to all that they had been teaching in China for more than forty years.

The corpus of writings that represented the Learning from Heaven had at least three main, interrelated aspects with implications for literati in late Ming.

First, it presented knowledge of another cultural tradition that was geographically removed and previously unknown in China. The foreignness and newness were obvious to its admirers and seized upon by its opponents, but in late Ming it was generally tolerated and not simply dismissed out of hand. It is noteworthy that at the time and over the next two centuries, the opponents and their writings did not fare as well in the estimation of the literati audience as did the writings of the proponents of the Learning from Heaven. Although in Qing times literati were less interested in knowing about the foreign culture, many of the new ideas, particularly about astronomy and other technical knowledge, were incorporated into their writings as well as imperially sponsored compilations. The missionaries did not always convey the newest European ideas (e.g., post-Copernican cosmology in particular, which had not yet been widely recognized in Europe),[269] but they published what was, in effect, a

---

[266] See J. L. Mish, "Creating an Image of Europe for China: Aleni's *Hsi-fang ta wen*," *Monumenta Serica*, Vol. 23 (1964), pp. 1–87.

[267] Schall's book is reprinted in *Tianzhujiao dong chuan wenxian xu bian*, Vol. 2, pp. 495–615.

[268] Dunne, *Generation of Giants*, p. 310.

[269] See the summary of the cosmology presented in some of the Jesuits' writings in Ming in Sivin, "Copernicus in China," pp. 76–82. For a thoughtful reflection on the slowly changing state of knowledge in Europe as a standard for judging what was introduced to Chinese readers, see Roger A. Blondeau, "Did the Jesuits and Ferdinand Verbiest

comprehensive sampling of the current teaching in universities of the late sixteenth and early seventeenth centuries.[270] It was new enough to be an alternative to inherited learning on these subjects in China.

Second, at the same time that the corpus revealed similarities in moral precepts in its teachings and in Chinese traditions, it presented broad philosophical propositions that were at variance with prevailing ideas. The propositions had Chinese analogues and were not therefore unimaginable to the readers. For example, proposals that the cosmos we perceive must have been caused by a creator or maker external to the processes of heaven and earth had appeared in various forms in the Chinese tradition, even if they were usually dismissed. The notion that the foundation of moral good was not simply inherent in all humans, waiting only to be discovered, also found proponents in the tradition as well even in late Ming times, so even though the missionaries' teaching of morality based on grace ran counter to Mencian assumptions, it was not inconceivable that an external power was the basis of the morality to be shared by all humans. Thus it seems unwarranted to conclude that on the plane of the "big ideas," or what might be called universal principles, Chinese and European concepts were incompatible or even mutually incomprehensible on some a priori grounds.[271] One may not want to allow the possibility (which may have emboldened Ricci) that a "natural theology" existed in pre-Christian and even non-Christian thinkers, but it is instructive to see an Enlightenment philosopher such as Leibniz having no trouble construing a theist's sense of a divinity in Zhu Xi's concept of *li* (coherence).[272]

Third, the corpus included ideas that required faith before they could be accepted and that tended to be culturally specific rather than appearing to be universal. Examples are the idea of the incarnation of the divinity as a historical person in a remote place (from the Chinese

---

Import Outdated Science into China?" in John W. Witek, ed., *Ferdinand Verbiest (1623–1688): Jesuit Missionary, Scientist, Engineer and Diplomat* (Nettetal, 1994), pp. 47–54.

[270] See Peterson, "Western Natural Philosophy," esp. pp. 315–316. For a summary of Western ideas and knowledge available to a Chinese scholar at the very end of the Ming see Dominic Sachsenmaier, *Die Aufnahme europäischer Inhalt in die chinesische Kultur durch Zhu Zongyuan (ca. 1616–1660)* (Zhu Zongyuan's integration of Western elements into Chinese culture), Monumenta Serica Monograph Series, Vol. 46 (Nettetal, 2002).

[271] Jacques Gernet comes to this conclusion in an eloquently argued study. See his *Chine et Christianisme*. Gernet provides the best overview of the attacks on the Jesuits in late Ming, which he sees as no different from the situation in Qing.

[272] See the example cited in ibid., pp. 279–280 (in the English translation, p. 206).

perspective), the idea of eternal salvation after death, or the idea of giving precedence to a classical text from the West over the classics transmitted from Confucius.

Literati were sensitive to various degrees to these three aspects, but they were aware of them all in reading the texts of the Learning of Heaven. A scholar named Sun Lan had gone to Schall to learn about heaven and earth and had a rather typical response. In his judgment, "It is always said that the classicists from the West (*xi ru*) have the religious doctrine of overcoming the seven [sins], similar to the Confucians' (Kong men) teaching that 'controlling oneself and adhering to the rites [is righteousness].'"[273] Moreover, when one meets them and listens to their theories, the theories are quite detailed with regard to calendars and numbers, and are well suited for exposing the main principles of technologies and celestial phenomena, but when they prostrate themselves before a heavenly divinity (*tian shen*) and speak extravagantly about a celestial palace and a [sub] terrestrial prison, then [the theories] are an 'other religion' (*yi jiao*), and not to be incorporated."[274] More generally, early on Li Zhi, whom no one would charge with being a narrow-minded partisan of cultural conservatism, had expressed his astonishment that Ricci's aim might be to displace the learning stemming from the duke of Zhou and Confucius.[275] Yet that was, of course, what the Western proponents of the Learning from Heaven hoped to do. They wanted the Learning from Heaven to be the main doctrine, not just "another strand" (*yi duan*).

---

[273] From *Analects*, 12:1.

[274] Sun Lan, "Liu ting yu di yu shuo," quoted in Xie Guozhen, *Ming mo Qing chu de xuefeng*, (Beijing, 1982), p. 6.

[275] Li Zhi, "Yu you ren shu," *Xu Fen shu*, p. 36. Also see Shen Defu, *Yehuo bian*, p. 783.

# 3

# Catholic Missions and the Expansion of Christianity, 1644–1800

John W. Witek, S.J.[†]

## AMID THE TERRORS OF WAR

When Li Zicheng passed through the gates of Beijing in 1644, the only Westerner in the capital was the Jesuit priest Johann Adam Schall von Bell (1592–1666). A few years earlier the Chongzhen emperor, the last of the Ming dynasty to rule in Beijing, ordered him to make cannons for the defense of the city. Having heard the news of the advance of Li's forces, the emperor tried to flee, but the eunuchs thwarted his efforts and fired on him the same cannon he had ordered Schall to cast. Later that same day the emperor rode past the Jesuit residence on his way to Coal Hill (Meishan) and eventual suicide. Schall had served the Chongzhen emperor for nearly two decades and declared that as a ruler he was "almost the greatest in the world and second to none in the goodness of his character," but "with no companion and abandoned by all, through his imprudence [he] perished by an unworthy death at the age of thirty-six." The Ming Empire, which had lasted 276 years, was now extinct, but Schall added:

Although the emperor, to my sorrow, did not follow me when I showed him the way of salvation, yet he merits a deep lament because he not only sustained Christianity, which had been maintained in China and in the court by his grandfather [Wanli emperor, r. 1572–1620], but he also praised and fostered it, to the maximum advantage of his subjects. He would have done even more had he not died such a violent and untimely death.[1]

[1] Johann Adam Schall von Bell, S.J., *Lettres et mémoires d'Adam Schall, S.J. Relation historique. Text latin avec traduction française du P. Paul Bornet, S.J.*, ed. Henri Bernard (Tientsin, 1942), p. 109; see also John W. Witek, S.J., "Johann Adam Schall von Bell

With such a noteworthy expression of sympathy for the last Ming monarch, Schall alluded to the uncertain fate of Christianity under a new regime.

During several days of terror in Beijing, Schall stood guard over the Christian community. In late May, as Wu Sangui and the Manchus forced Li to abandon the city, Schall again witnessed the burning of several houses and palaces. The conquerors ordered the Chinese to leave the newly designated Manchu or Tartar area of Beijing, but within two days Schall successfully petitioned the new regime to allow the Jesuit residence to remain there. It was his first major step in cultivating friendship with the Manchus. In September the Prince Regent Dorgon (1612–1650) appointed him director of the Bureau of Astronomy (Qintianjian zheng). This act ensured the continuation of Christianity in China, at least in the territory under Qing control.

In the early years of the Qing consolidation, there were about 100,000 Christians throughout China. The Jesuits in Beijing developed more contacts with the Qing court, but some of their confreres in the provinces maintained connections with Southern Ming loyalist courts. The commitment to the Yongli emperor (1623–1662) of such Chinese Christians as Qu Shisi (1590–1651) and Pang Tianshou (1588–1657) enabled the Jesuits Michał Boym (1612–1659) and Andreas Koffler (1612–1652) to baptize a significant number of the imperial Ming family. As the Qing forces were taking control of Canton in November 1650, the grand empress dowager (d. 1651), baptized with the name of Helena, wrote to Pope Innocent X (1574–1655) and to the Jesuit Father General Francesco Piccolomini (1582–1651) to send more missionaries to China. Boym, accompanied by a Christian convert, Zheng Andeluo, personally delivered these messages in Rome, then returned to Guangxi via Tonkin (northern Annam, or Vietnam) by 1658, only to discover that the Southern Ming cause was hopeless. Unable to reenter Tonkin and seriously ill, he died the following year and was buried near the border.[2]

and the Transition from the Ming to the Qing Dynasty," in Roman Malek, ed., *Western Learning and Christianity in China: The Contribution and Impact of Johann Adam Schall von Bell, S.J. (1592–1666)*, 2 vols., Monumenta Serica Monograph Series, No. 35 (Nettetal, 1998), pp. 109–124.

[2] Lynn A. Struve, ed. and trans., *Voices from the Ming–Qing Cataclysm: China in Tiger's Jaws* (New Haven, CT, 1993), pp. 235–238; on Boym and Koffler, see Goodrich, L. Carrington and Chaoying Fang, eds., *Dictionary of Ming Biography*, 2 vols. (New York, 1976), pp. 20–22, 722–724; see also the biography of Boym by Edward Kajdanski, *Michal Boym Ostatni Wyslannik Dynastii Ming* (Warsaw, 1988); on the Ming loyalists, see Lynn A. Struve, "The Southern Ming, 1644–1662," in Frederick H. Mote and Denis Twitchett, eds., *The Cambridge History of China*, Vol. 7: *The Ming Dynasty, 1369–1644,*

During these same years, Schall's stature in the capital continued to rise. In 1650 the emperor granted him a large plot of land to build a church. The Nantang (South Church), as it was later called, was erected in the form of a Latin cross, with a beautiful high altar and four side chapels. The inscriptions on the interior walls explained the Decalogue, the Eight Beatitudes, and the articles of the Catholic faith. Besides presenting an inscription of four characters in gold for the interior of the church, the emperor ordered the carving of a stele granting imperial authorization for the construction of the church. The stone stele is presently imbedded in the interior side of the east wall of the compound enclosing the Nantang.[3] In his essay *Zeng Tianzhu xintang ji* (In honor of the new Catholic Church), Liu Zhaoguo (*jinshi*, 1643), a member of the Hongwen yuan (Palace Academy for the Advancement of Literature), related his conversation with Schall not only about his plans to build the church, but also about Schall's replies to his questions concerning the calculation of the stars and the planets. Liu pointed out that Schall told him that the bishop wanted the church large enough to accommodate the Christian community in Beijing.[4]

After Dorgon's death in December 1650, the young Shunzhi emperor abolished the regency and assumed control over the state. His personal relationship with Schall "was indeed more that of grandfather and grandson than that of emperor and subject."[5] Two years after ascending the

*Part 1* (Cambridge, 1998), pp. 641–725, and Struve, *The Southern Ming, 1644–1662* (New Haven, CT, 1984).

[3] Manuscript versions of the Chinese text of the stele are in Munich, Bayerische Staatsbibliothek, Fernostsammlung, 4 L. sin. C 136, and Munich, Universitätsbibliothek, 2 P. or. 20; see also Huang Bolu, *Zhengjiao fengbao*, 3rd ed. (Shanghai, 1904), pp. 25a–b. A French translation is in W. A. Grootaers, "Les deux stèles de l'église du Nan-t'ang à Pékin," *Neue Zeitschrift für Missionswissenschaft*, Vol. 6 (1950), pp. 248–251.

[4] Liu Zhaoguo (*zi* Mingong, *hao* Ruanxian) was a native of Qianjiang in Hubei province. See Yang Tingfu and Yang Tongfu, eds., *Qingren shi mingbie cheng zihao suoyin*, 2 vols. (Shanghai, 1988), Vol. 2, p. 2641; his *jinshi* examination see *Ming Qing jinshi timing beilu suoyin*, 3 vols. (Taipei, 1982), Vol. 3, pp. 2010, 2622; for his essay, see Archivum Historicum Societatis Iesu, *Japonica et Sinica*, III, 24 (intorno V), 3a–6b. In 1650 no bishop resided in Beijing. Presumably the reference is to the bishop of Macao.

[5] George H. Dunne, *Generation of Giants: The Story of the Jesuits in China in the Last Decades of the Ming Dynasty* (Notre Dame, IN, 1962), p. 347. On this special relationship, see Alfons Väth, *Johann Adam Schall von Bell, S.J. Missionar in China, kaiserlicher Astronom und Ratgeber am Hofe von Peking, 1592–1666. Ein Lebens- und Zeitbild.* 2d ed. Monumenta Serica Monograph Series, No. 25 (Nettetal, 1991), pp. 171–211; Li Lanqin, *Tang Ruowang* (Beijing, 1995), pp. 93–114. For the relations of the missionaries with successive Qing emperors see Erik Zürcher, "Emperors," in Nicolas Standaert, ed., *Handbook of Christianity in China: Volume One: 635–1800*, Handbook of Oriental Studies, Section Four, China, 15/1 (Leiden, 2001), pp. 492–502.

throne, the emperor wrote a special decree conferring on Schall the title *tongxuan jiaoshi* (religious teacher who comprehends the mysterious). Underlining the significance of publishing a calendar for the advancement of a dynasty, the decree pointed out that Xu Guangqi (1562–1633) had first recommended Schall as a reformer of the calendar. The emperor stated that when Schall's name had been recently presented to him, he already knew that Schall conducted himself perfectly in the Bureau of Astronomy and faithfully fulfilled his duties. The bestowal of the title was, in the eyes of the emperor, truly deserved. Because of this special relationship between them, Schall explained at length the tenets of Christianity in the hope of converting the emperor, but by 1658 the latter had turned to Chan Buddhism. Nonetheless, six months before his death, he sent Schall an apologetic note, declaring, "Your law [i.e., Christianity] is already widely spread. Through your exertions the science of astronomy has become known."[6]

The Kangxi emperor (1654–1722) succeeded to the throne in 1661 and a regency dominated by Oboi (d. 1669) was in place. Christian communities existed in all of the provinces of China, except Yunnan and Guizhou, although the turmoil at the fall of the Ming had taken its toll. A number of church buildings, such as those at Taiyuan (Shanxi), Wuchang (Huguang), Nanchang and Ganzhou (Jiangxi), and Fuzhou (Fujian), were destroyed by fire. When the Qing government ordered those living on the coasts of Shandong, Jiangsu, Zhejiang, Fujian, and Guangdong to move thirty or more *li* (about fifteen kilometers, or ten miles) inland as a countermeasure to the piratical raids of Zheng Chenggong (1624–1662, known in the West as Koxinga), the churches and residences in Fujian were razed as part of a "scorched earth" policy. Such property losses, however, were offset by the continuing growth in the number of converts. According to an official report, there were 114,000 Christians in 1663, thanks to the efforts of no more than two dozen missionaries, mostly Jesuits along with some Dominicans and Franciscans.[7] Despite the confusion in a country still caught up in civil disturbances, the prospects for the spread of Christianity appeared hopeful.

The famous "three principal scholars," Gu Yanwu, Huang Zongxi, and Wang Fuzhi,[8] during the transition from the late Ming to the early Qing

---

[6] Dunne, *Generation of Giants*, p. 353.

[7] Ibid., pp. 359–360. On the disputed issue of the number of Christians in China during the late Ming and early Qing, see the statistics in Standaert, ed. *Handbook*, pp. 380–382.

[8] The three were Gu Yanwu (1613–1682), Huang Zongxi (1610–1695), and Wang Fuzhi (1619–1692). See John E. Wills, Jr., "Brief Intersection: Changing Contexts and

era refused to have any relations with the new imperial court or with any other foreigners. Convinced that a principal cause of the Ming collapse was that its intellectual leaders lacked a sense of reality, they earnestly strove to return to it by advocating practical statesmanship contained in the principles of the Chinese classics. The more they studied such works, the more they encountered difficulties in understanding them. Toward the end of the seventeenth century and the beginning of the next, this movement would lead to the school of empirical research with its emphasis on textual criticism, bibliography, and epigraphy. There were, however, literati developing new studies on the reconciliation of Confucian and Christian principles, perhaps most strikingly found in the work of Zhang Xingyao (1633–1715+) of Hangzhou.[9] Even when remaining sympathetic to Christianity, the Jiangnan literati no longer had the type of powerful network they had developed in the late Ming period. As the Qing widened its control over more Chinese provinces, Schall's position at the court influenced the attitudes of provincial officials toward the missionaries and the converts, but his role was always subject to scrutiny and the possibility of dramatic change.

## SCHALL'S ENCOUNTER WITH YANG GUANGXIAN

The involvement of the Jesuits with the court in Beijing was vital to the continuation of Christianity in China. Because of their service in astronomical calculations, they were implicitly assured that the new regime would allow their confreres and other missionaries to preach. By the same token, if the accuracy of their astronomical work were to be seriously challenged, the spread of Christianity would be endangered. In 1660 Yang Guangxian (1597–1669) led a movement to discredit Schall and his foreign system of astronomy. At first the imperial officials in the last days of the Shunzhi reign and the first years of the Kangxi era paid no heed to his views. But in a memorial of September 15, 1664, Yang charged Schall with several errors in astronomical calculations and declared that Christianity

Prospects of the Christian Chinese Encounter," in John W. Witek, ed., *Ferdinand Verbiest (1623–1688): Jesuit Missionary, Scientist, Engineer and Diplomat*, Monumenta Serica Monograph Series, No. 30 (Nettetal, 1994), pp. 383–394.

9  David E. Mungello, *The Forgotten Christians of Hangzhou* (Honolulu, 1994), pp. 12–39; for the direct contacts of Schall with Huang Zongxi, see Xu Haisong, "Xixue dong jian yu Qingdai Zhedong xuepai" (The Eastward spread of Western learning and the Eastern Zhejiang school in the Qing dynasty), in Xiaoxin Wu, ed., *Encounters and Dialogues: Changing Perspectives on Chinese–Western Exchanges from the Sixteenth to Eighteenth Centuries* (Sankt Augustin, 2005), pp. 141–160.

filled the people with false ideas. Quoting from the *Tianxue quangai* (A survey on the propagation of heavenly learning) by the Christian convert Li Zubo (d. 1665), a court astronomer working under the guidance of Schall, Yang decried Li's suggestion that the Chinese were descendants of the Hebrews, an alien race. In contrast to Li's view that 3,701 years after the first man, the Lord of Heaven gave the Ten Commandments to Moses on Mount Sinai, Yang exaggerated Chinese chronology in claiming, "From the *jiazi* of the establishment of the world ... till now, there have been 19,379,496 years in all. If Jesus is the Lord of Heaven, all the periods before the emperor Ai of the Han dynasty lacked the Heaven [of God]."[10] Along with his memorial Yang forwarded an essay blaming Schall for choosing an inauspicious day for the burial of an infant prince. This charge caught the attention of the Manchu officials, who started an investigation. In his tract, *Budeyi* (I could not do otherwise), Yang further developed his views on the absurdity of Christianity. He frequently demonstrated a very limited understanding of basic Christian teachings, such as the incarnation and redemption. From Yang's perspective Matteo Ricci's use of the Chinese classics to uphold Christianity was an affront against Confucian principles. Despite the arguments of missionaries and distinguished Chinese Christian intellectuals who supported Ricci, Yang and some literati still perceived a wide chasm between the organic cosmology of Cheng-Zhu Neo-Confucianism and the fundamentals of the Christian worldview.[11]

Although Li's work contained a preface by an imperial censor, and the Jesuit Ludovico Buglio (1606–1682) tried to answer Yang's charges by his *Budeyi bian* (I cannot do otherwise – refuted), these were insufficient to prevent Oboi, the regent, from taking sides with Yang. In November 1664 Schall, already stricken with paralysis, was imprisoned, along with his confreres, Ferdinand Verbiest (1623–1688), Gabriel de Magalhães

[10] Quoted in John W. Witek, S.J., "Chinese Chronology: A Source of Sino-European Widening Horizons in the Eighteenth Century," in *Appréciation par l'Europe de la tradition chinoise à partir du XVIIe siècle*, Colloque international de sinologie, 1980 (Paris, 1983), pp. 234–235. For detailed analyses of Yang's opposition to Christianity, see John D. Young, *Confucianism and Christianity: The First Encounter* (Hong Kong, 1983), pp. 77–96; Eugenio Menegon, "Yang Guangxian's Opposition to Johann Adam Schall: Christianity and Western Science in His Work *Budeyi*," and Zhang Dawei, "The 'Calendar Case' in the Early Qing Dynasty Re-examined," in Malek, ed., *Western Learning and Christianity in China*, pp. 311–337, 475–495, respectively.

[11] Young, *Confucianism and Christianity*, pp. 76–77; on the earlier encounter of such ideas, see Chapter 2, this volume. On Ming and Qing opponents see also Ad Dudink, "Opponents," in Standaert, ed., *Handbook*, pp. 503–533.

(1610–1677), and Buglio. By April 30, 1665, the emperor had received the decision of the Board of Rites (Libu), which condemned Schall and seven others in the Bureau of Astronomy to death by *lingchi*, that is, slicing or dismemberment of the living body. The emperor spared their lives and told the board to deliberate again on the penalty to be meted out to them. Its decision was to flog, imprison, and banish them. But on May 17 the emperor rejected the board's order and allowed Schall and the others to be set free. This action was taken against the backdrop of an earthquake that struck Beijing and a fire that broke out in one of the palaces thirteen days later, which in the eyes of several court officials were signs of Heaven's displeasure. However, five of Schall's Christian converts, including Li Zubo, who worked with him at the bureau, were executed. With the exception of three Dominicans in Fujian, who remained hidden for some time, all the other missionaries – twenty-five Jesuits, four Dominicans, and one Franciscan – were brought to Beijing and then banished to detention in Canton. Not one church in China was open.[12]

Before Schall died in 1666, his archrival Yang headed the Bureau of Astronomy, despite his own protests that he had almost no astronomical knowledge. His ineptitude was uncovered through the efforts of the Kangxi emperor, who took charge of the government in August 1667, but was still involved in a continuing struggle against Oboi. In December 1668 the emperor summoned the Jesuits and ordered investigations of the defects in Yang's calendar for 1669. Yang's incompetence was exposed.[13] Several months later an imperial commission reported that the Western system was accurate, and the emperor declared that in the future all calendars were to follow these new methods. Verbiest replaced Yang, who, dismissed from office and condemned to death, received an imperial commutation of the sentence and was allowed to return home

---

[12] In his writings to religious superiors, Magalhães objected to Schall's taking official posts in the court, but later changed his opinion. See Irene Pih, *Le père Gabriel de Magalhães. Un Jésuite portugais en Chine*, Cultura Medieval et Moderna, No. 14. (Paris, 1979), pp. 236–239; Ludovico Buglio, S.J., *Budeyi bian* in *Tianzhujiao dongchuan wenxian* (Collectanea of Catholic essays), ed. Wu Xiangxiang, Zhongguo shixue congshu, No. 24. (Taipei, 1965), pp. 225–332; Goodrich and Fang, *Dictionary of Ming Biography*, pp. 1153–1157 (on Schall), esp. p. 1155; Dunne, *Generation of Giants*, p. 363.

[13] John E. Wills, Jr., *Embassies and Illusions: Dutch and Portuguese Envoys to K'anghsi, 1666–1687*, Harvard East Asian Monographs, No. 113 (Cambridge, MA., 1984), pp. 110–111; *Da Qing lichao shilu*, Kangxi reign, 28:6a–b, 31:4–5; Lo-shu Fu, *A Documentary Chronicle of Sino-Western Relations (1644–1820)* (Tucson, 1966), pp. 44–46, 453, n. 72; see also Benjamin A. Elman, *On Their Own Terms: Science in China, 1550–1900* (Cambridge, MA, 2005), pp. 133–149.

because of his age. An imperial edict on September 5, 1669, restored Schall's titles and ranks and allowed the Jesuits then in Beijing to practice their religion.

In 1668–1670 the extensive conversations concerning astronomy, mathematics, and European culture that the young emperor conducted with the Jesuits at the capital were a basis for hope among the missionaries in Canton and outside China that the status of Christianity could still change. The Jesuits spoke to the emperor about the critical situation in Macao that began in 1662 with the regents' prohibition of all maritime trade and orders to all Chinese to evacuate the city. These talks contributed to the court's positive attitude toward the embassy of Manoel de Saldanha, which arrived in Macao in 1667. Saldanha entered Beijing in June 1670. En route from Canton his Jesuit chaplain visited a number of Christian communities that had lacked the services of a priest for five years because of the forced exile of all missionaries to Canton. The emperor granted many favors to the ambassador and his retinue as a sign of his increasingly positive attitude toward the Jesuits and the transition to his personal rule.[14] In March 1671 the Jesuits learned that the missionaries in Canton would be allowed to return to their stations in the interior. Not until September of that year were they able to do so.

### THE CANTON CONFERENCE

The exile of the missionaries at Canton had at least one positive result, since enforced confinement gave them an opportunity to discuss missiological questions. With their Dominican and Franciscan counterparts, the Jesuits deliberated over the Ricci method of inculturation, especially concerning the Chinese rites issue, in a conference from mid-December 1667 to late January 1668.[15] Despite discussions that at times were quite polemical, the participants finalized a series of resolutions that guided future mission policies.

With his extensive knowledge of Chinese literature, Matteo Ricci (1552–1610), the founder of the Catholic missions in China in the modern era, sought a common ground for Christianity and Chinese civilization. Seven

---

[14] Wills, *Embassies and Illusions*, pp. 82–126, 193–236.
[15] On the term "inculturation" and its significance for the missions in China, see Nicolas Standaert, "L'inculturation et la mission en Chine au XVIIe siècle," *Église et Mission*, Vol. 240 (December 1985), pp. 2–24. Biographical data on the participants of this conference at Canton are in Josef Metzler, *Die Synoden in China, Japan und Korea, 1570–1931* (Paderborn, 1980), pp. 23–24.

years before his death, he issued a directive that accepted the literati's periodic honors to Confucius as academic, not religious, and that declared that the common veneration of ancestors was not superstitious. Since some external signs associated with the ceremonies might be so construed, some months later he qualified this last point by noting that such veneration was perhaps not superstitious. Moreover, he affirmed that, besides "Tianzhu" (Lord of Heaven), the two expressions "Tian" (Heaven) and "Shang Di" (Lord on High) could designate the Christian concept of God.[16] Such views and practices, which form the core of the Chinese Rites Controversy, alarmed the Dominican Juan Bautista de Morales (1597–1669) and the Franciscan Antonio de Santa Maria Caballero (1602–1669) upon their entry into China in 1633. The Dominicans and Franciscans as well as the Jesuits sought to achieve unanimity on these difficult questions. Discussions with the principal Chinese converts and exchanges of letters in China led to some understanding of the differences involved.[17] The Jesuits and their converts increasingly accepted the principles of Ricci. But the nature of the discussion changed significantly when it was moved from China, where all concerned were aware of the difficulties in interpreting Chinese practices and the nuances of the Chinese language, to Rome, where such awareness could not be expected. Reluctant to support the views of Ricci, the Dominicans brought the matter to the attention of the Congregation for the Propagation of the Faith (Congregatio de Propaganda Fide, commonly called Propaganda). Its 1645 condemnation of the ceremonies was endorsed by Pope Innocent X (1641–1655). To offset this viewpoint, the Jesuits sent Martino Martini (1614–1661) to Rome to present their case. By a decree of March 1656, the Holy Office approved the ceremonies. Because of the discrepancies between the two Roman documents and the ensuing confusion in the mission, the Holy Office in 1669 ruled that both decrees were binding according to the questions and circumstances that caused them to be issued (*juxta exposita*).

Just one year before the decision was reached in Rome, the exiled missionaries in Canton, for more than forty days, both orally and in writing, at times strenuously argued about pastoral practices such as administering the sacraments, the role of the catechists, the propriety of

---

[16] Matteo Ricci, *Fonti Ricciane*, 3 vols., ed. Pasquale M. d'Elia, S.J. (Rome, 1942–1949), Vol. 1, pp. 118–120; Vol. 2, pp. 72–80, 289–301.

[17] Metzler, *Die Synoden in China*, pp. 11–21; see also Erik Zürcher, "Jesuit Accommodation and the Chinese Cultural Imperative," in David E. Mungello, ed., *The Chinese Rites Controversy: Its History and Meaning*, Monumenta Serica Monograph Series, No. 33 (Nettetal, 1994), pp. 42–57.

the priest at mass having his head covered, the practice of some converts inscribing the names of Jesus, Mary, or the saints on the doorposts of their houses, and so on. The next to last of the resulting forty-two articles declared, "As to the ceremonies by which the Chinese honor their master Confucius and the dead," the 1656 position of the Holy Office was to be followed "absolutely." The reason was that the contents of the latter decree was based on "a very probable opinion, to which it is impossible to offset any evidence to the contrary."[18] This attempt to reach an accord among the religious orders was short-lived. Later that year Caballero wrote a learned essay against the policy statement in reply to a letter from the Jesuit visitor for the Vice-Province of China and the Province of Japan, Luis da Gama (1610–1672). The Dominican Domingo Navarrete (1618–1686) signed the conference minutes but slipped out of Canton in December 1669. In Rome he was not successful in obtaining a formal reconsideration of the earlier decisions, yet his writings there and elsewhere in Europe raised doubts in the minds of some Catholic intellectuals about the Ricci policies of inculturation.[19]

### THE KANGXI EMPEROR AND VERBIEST

After the missionaries left Canton and reopened their churches, they encountered a better reception among the Chinese. In 1675 the Kangxi emperor visited the Nantang (South Church) in Beijing and presented the inscription *Jing Tian* (Honor Heaven) to the Jesuits. With imperial permission this was recopied for installation in all the Jesuit churches in China to manifest to everyone, but especially to the provincial and lesser officials, the attitude of the emperor toward Christianity. The Jesuits understood "Tian" to be a possible alternative name for "Tianzhu," or God, but some of the other missionaries held that it was a materialist or idolatrous meaning, so that the inscription should not be allowed in a Christian church. Over the next few decades this dispute became a major element in the Chinese Rites Controversy.[20] Yet most of the missionaries

---

[18] Quoted in Joseph Brucker, "Ricci, Matteo," *Catholic Encyclopedia*, 13:38; for the forty-two articles, see Metzler, *Die Synoden in China*, pp. 24–28.

[19] Metzler, *Die Synoden in China*, pp. 28–35; Goodrich and Fang, *Dictionary of Ming Biography*, pp. 24–31, S.V. Caballero; J. S. Cummins, ed., *The Travels and Controversies of Friar Domingo Navarrete, 1618–1686*, 2 vols. (Cambridge, 1962), Vol. 2, pp. 413–24; Cummins, *A Question of Rites: Friar Domingo Navarrete and the Jesuits in China* (Aldershot, 1993), pp. 191–192.

[20] Claudia von Collani, "*Jing tian* – The Kangxi Emperor's Gift to Ferdinand Verbiest in the Rites Controversy," in Witek, ed., *Ferdinand Verbiest*, pp. 453–470.

understood that the imperial inscription itself was a means of protecting the churches from destruction, since removing such an imperial epigraph could incur serious political risks.

Serving as director of the Bureau of Astronomy and on good terms with the emperor, Verbiest continued Schall's practice of informing himself about the new governors and other officials who were to be sent to the provinces. He called on those who visited Beijing and recommended to them the Christians and the missionaries. Honored by this attention from an influential person at court, the officials gained a better understanding of the foreign religion and not infrequently assisted the missionaries on the local scene.

The closer the relationship of Verbiest to the emperor, the more responsibility was placed on the priest-astronomer's shoulders. Since the Western methods of astronomical observation proved more accurate than those of the Chinese, Verbiest was asked to make quite a number of instruments for the imperial observatory. In 1678 he published the *Kangxi yongnian lifa* (Perpetual astronomy of the Kangxi era), a work that included calculations of seven planets, solar and lunar eclipses for two thousand years, and other pertinent calendrical data. Besides undertaking such research, Verbiest received imperial orders similar to those given to Schall that he was to manufacture cannons that were needed to protect the empire against the Rebellion of the Three Feudatories. Despite his protest against such a directive, Verbiest developed the foundries for the cannons and the calculations for testing them.[21] Moreover, he expanded the knowledge of the Chinese view of the world by his *Kunyu quantu* (Complete map of the terrestrial globe) with the zero meridian drawn through Beijing. Cartographic data presented descriptions of animals unknown to the Chinese and located as close as possible to the countries they inhabited. Additional details included the distances of the various kingdoms from China and the form of government in each of them.[22] In addition, he composed a Latin grammar of the

---

[21] See Giovanni Stary, "The 'Manchu Cannons' Cast by Ferdinand Verbiest and the Hitherto Unknown Title of His Instructions," and Shu Liguang, "Ferdinand Verbiest and the Casting of Cannons in the Qing Dynasty," in Witek, ed., *Ferdinand Verbiest*, pp. 215–225 and 227–244, respectively.

[22] Lin Tong-yang, "Aperçu sur la Mappemonde de Ferdinand Verbiest. Le *K'un-yü ch'üan-t'u*," and Christine Vertente, "Nan Huai-Jen's Maps of the World," in Edward Malatesta and Yves Raguin, eds., *Succès et échecs de la rencontre Chine et Occident du XVIe au XXe siècle. Varietés Sinologiques*, New Ser. 74. (San Francisco, 1993), pp. 145–173 and 257–263, respectively; Song Gang and Paola Demattè, "Mapping an Acentric World: Ferdinand Verbiest's *Kunyu Quantu*," in Marcia Reed and Paola Demattè, eds., *China on Paper: European and Chinese Works from the Late Sixteenth to the Early Nineteenth Century* (Los Angeles, 2007), pp. 71–87.

Manchu language and a translation into Manchu of the first six books of Euclid, which Ricci had first translated into Chinese. Above all, he was the author of several important treatises on Christian doctrine in Chinese that were reprinted as recently as seven decades ago.[23] It is noteworthy that his writings on astronomy[24] and especially his map attracted the attention of the Japanese in the late seventeenth and early eighteenth centuries, despite the Tokugawa government's general ban on the importation of books associated with Christianity.[25]

For the amusement of the emperor Verbiest made various mechanical toys. Of all of them, perhaps the most significant was "the first, documented, automotive machine," which he built, successfully ran, and later described in his *Astronomia Europaea*.[26] His confrere Claudio Filippo Grimaldi (1638–1712) constructed hydraulic machines, including a clock. To fulfill the emperor's desire to learn Western music, Tomas

---

[23] The fifth edition of *Jiaoyao xulun* (An introduction to doctrinal essentials) appeared in Shanghai in 1935. See Witek, "Presenting Christian Doctrine to the Chinese: Reflections on the *Jiaoyao xulun* of Ferdinand Verbiest," in Witek, ed., *Ferdinand Verbiest*, pp. 437–452, esp. p. 451. For further studies about some of Verbiest's philosophical and religious ideas in this same collection, see Nicolas Standaert, "The Investigation of Things and the Fathoming of Principles (*Gewu Qiongli*) in the Seventeenth-Century Contact between Jesuits and Chinese Scholars," and Joseph Hsing-san Shih, "The Religious Writings of Father Ferdinand Verbiest," pp. 395–420 and 421–436, respectively. See also John W. Witek, S.J., "Explaining the Sacrament of Penance in Seventeenth-Century China: An Essay of Ferdinand Verbiest (1623–1688)," in Noel Golvers, ed., *The Christian Mission in China in the Verbiest Era: Some Aspects of the Missionary Approach*, Louvain Chinese Studies, No. 6 (Leuven, 1999), pp. 55–71. On the extensive project of translating European philosophical texts into Chinese, see Adrian Dudink and Nicolas Standaert, "Ferdinand Verbiest's *Qiongli Xue* (1683)," and Noel Golvers, "Verbiest's Introduction of *Aristoteles Latinus* (Coimbra) in China: New Western Evidence," in Golvers, ed., *The Christian Mission in China in the Verbiest Era*, pp. 11–31 and 33–53, respectively.

[24] Lists of Verbiest's Chinese and Manchu works are in Louis Pfister, S.J., *Notices biographiques et bibliographiques sur les Jésuites de l'ancienne mission de la Chine, 1552–1773* (Shanghai, 1932; reprint, San Francisco, 1976), pp. 352–362; Xu Zongze, *Ming Qing jian Yesu huishi yizhu tiyao* (Taipei: Zhonghua shuju, 1958; reprint, Beijing: Zhonghua shuju, 1989), pp. 390–392, and in the Vatican Library, Yu Dong, *Catalogo delle opere cinesi missionarie della Biblioteca Apostolica Vaticana (XVI–XVIII sec)*, Studi e Testi, No. 366 (Vatican City, 1996), pp. 104–107.

[25] Minako Debergh, "Les cartes astronomiques des missionnaires Jésuites en Chine. De Johann Adam Schall von Bell à Ignace Kögler et leur influence en Corée et au Japon," in Malek, ed., *Western Learning and Christianity in China*, pp. 543–554, esp. pp. 548–549.

[26] J. Ditlev Scheel, "Beijing Precursor," in Witek, ed., *Ferdinand Verbiest*, pp. 245–270; Ferdinand Verbiest, S.J., *The Astronomia Europaea of Ferdinand Verbiest, S.J. (Dillingen, 1687): Text, Translation Notes and Commentaries*, trans and commentaries Noel Golvers, Monumenta Serica Monograph Series, No. 28 (Nettetal, 1993), pp. 120–124, 430–436, 496–497.

Pereira (1645–1708) regularly conducted lessons and made an organ and other musical instruments for the palace.

If the mission was to perdure, Verbiest realized, more men were needed. Hitherto all missionaries entered China via Macao and the system of the *padroado*, that is, the papal grant to the Portuguese Crown of all the rights and duties of the missions in Asia, except the Philippines. This included financial support from the Portuguese king, but the increased number of Jesuits could no longer be maintained by such a fixed stipend. The entry of the Dominicans and the Franciscans by way of the Philippines created tensions not only among religious orders but also among their sponsors, Spain and Portugal. Since its beginning in 1622, Propaganda continued to seek control of all the missions. The Portuguese *padroado* with its claim over China through the bishop of Macao and the choice of Jesuits alone to labor in *padroado* territory were obstacles to Propaganda's goal. It was not clear in the first decades of Propaganda's existence that its challenge concerning such jurisdictional matters would also lead to opposition against the Ricci policy of inculturation. Yet even in 1659 Propaganda had declared that missionaries were

> not to seek for any reason to persuade peoples to change their customs, as long as they are not openly contrary to religion and morality. Indeed, what could be more absurd than to transplant France, Spain, Italy or some other part of Europe to China? It is not that which you are to import, but the Faith, which neither repulses nor scorns the usages and customs of any people, as long as they are not perverse, but which desires that they be guarded with all the respect which is their due.[27]

If this statement, originally addressed to the vicars apostolic sent to China, Tonkin, and Cochin China (the northern and central parts of modern Vietnam), had been heeded, the controversy over the Chinese rites might have taken a different turn.

Aware of the financial and personnel needs of the mission, Verbiest wrote an open letter to his confreres in Europe. This appeal of August 1678 asked for Jesuits well versed in philosophy and theology and ready

---

[27] Raphaélis de Martinis, ed., *Juris Pontificii de Propaganda Fide*, 8 vols. (Rome, 1888–1901), Vol 8, p. 115; translated in Joseph R. Levenson, *Confucian China and Its Modern Fate: A Trilogy* (Berkeley, 1968), Vol. 1, p. 118. For another translation see Ray Noll, ed., *100 Documents Concerning the Chinese Rites Controversy (1645–1941)* (San Francisco, 1992), pp. 6–7, with its further relevant statement: "Do not disdain Chinese ways, because they are different from European ways. Rather, do everything you can to get used to them."

to adapt to Chinese customs.[28] On that same day he also wrote to the
visitor, Sebastian d' Almeida (1622–1682), in reply to his request for
Verbiest's views about a native Chinese clergy. This issue had been discussed by several missionaries of different religious orders in China, but
no uniform policy had been reached. Verbiest indicated that in China
Western missionaries had no stable foundation for preaching the Christian
religion. In fact, it was much less firm than in other countries where a
missionary apostolate was also being carried out. From the remote past
until the present, this was due to the singular aversion of the Chinese
to other nations. Their laws did not allow foreigners to cross their bor-
ders. The Manchus imitated the Chinese and were daily acceding more
closely to their customs. Those missionaries who returned from exile in
Canton were only tolerated and would not be able to get replacements.
Verbiest emphasized that the Christian mission was bound with European
astronomy and depended on the will of the monarch, but this root was
extremely uncertain.[29] Over the years the Chinese had become adept at
calendar making according to Western methods and could do so independently. Whether his successor would be a European or a Chinese was
even more uncertain. Verbiest hoped that in the future there would be
two or three Western astronomy experts to work at court and thus aid in
getting missionary personnel into the provinces. He warned that if there
were none at court or if they were all expelled from the court, it would be
impossible for any missionary to hide or even to exist in the provinces for
a long time. These, then, were some of the premises he used to build his
arguments for the development of a native Chinese clergy to be trained
in China, not elsewhere. Verbiest did not live to see his plan for a native
clergy become fully operational. Less than a year after his death, a major
step had been achieved when three Jesuits (Wu Li [1632–1718], Liu Wende
[1628–1707], and Wan Qiyuan [1631–1700]) were ordained in Nanjing
in August 1688 by the Dominican bishop Luo Wenzao (1615–1691). As
Verbiest in other correspondence turned to France for new missionaries,
he added to the already existing religious jurisdictional issues in China.

## FRENCH JESUITS IN CHINA

In the late seventeenth century France sought to expand its influence in
Asia but had no established commercial networks comparable to those

---

[28] Ferdinand Verbiest, S.J., *Correspondance de Ferdinand Verbiest de la Compagnie de
Jésus (1623–1688)*, ed. H. Josson and L. Willaert (Brussels, 1938), pp. 230–53.
[29] Verbiest wrote, "Haec radix est valde incerta." See ibid., pp. 208–225, esp. p. 211.

of Portugal, Holland, and England. The first successful French voyage to China was not until 1698. Even science became part of the search for approaches to Asia, as French astronomers began to discuss the need of comparative astronomical data from the Near East and from China. When Philippe Couplet (1623–1693), who had known Verbiest since their days as Jesuit novices in Belgium, visited Louis XIV in 1684, the French had more concrete plans for such astronomical investigation. The Sun King decided to send several Jesuits to China on the ships that would take his envoy back to Siam. After their arrival there, they were to sail to China by any means available. Lisbon refused Versailles' request for passports for these royal mathematicians but did not object to their entering Macao. In Rome the Jesuit general accepted the plan on condition that the Jesuits fulfill the directives of Propaganda when they acted as missionaries in places controlled by the vicars apostolic. When he notified Propaganda about the imminent departure, the cardinals wrote to Paris to stop the trip, but it was too late.

In early 1685 the Jesuits Joachim Bouvet (1656–1730), Jean de Fontaney (1643–1710), Jean-François Gerbillon (1654–1707), Louis Le Comte (1655–1728), and Claude de Visdelou (1656–1737) left France and arrived in Beijing on February 7, 1688, just ten days after Verbiest's death. The royal mathematicians of Louis XIV were to make astronomical observations and to study Chinese literature. Some of them were expected to return to Paris, where they would translate Chinese books for the royal library.[30] From the five Jesuits, the Kangxi emperor chose Bouvet and Gerbillon for service at court; the others were allowed to live anywhere in China. Bouvet was soon occupied in translating books on geometry, philosophy, and Western medicine. Gerbillon accompanied Pereira to Nerchinsk, where both were interpreters and negotiators of the first treaty that China ever signed on the basis of the law of nations.[31]

---

[30] On the background of the French Jesuit mission, see John W. Witek, S.J., *Controversial Ideas in China and in Europe: A Biography of Jean-François Foucquet, 1665–1741*, Bibliotheca Instituti Historici Societatis Jesu, Vol. 43 (Rome, 1982), pp. 13–48; two other relevant biographies are Claudia von Collani, *P. Joachim Bouvet, S.J. Sein Leben und Sein Werk*, Monumenta Serica Monograph Series, No. 17 (Nettetal, 1985), and Yves de Thomaz de Bossierre, *Jean-François Gerbillon, S.J. (1654–1707). Un des cinq des missionnaires envoyés en Chine par Louis XIV*, Louvain Chinese Studies, No. 2 (Leuven, 1994). On the relations of the French missionaries and the Paris Académie des Sciences see Florence C. Hsia, *Sojourners in a Strange Land: Jesuits & Their Scientific Missions in Late Imperial China* (Chicago, 2009), Chs. 3–7.

[31] Joseph S. Sebes, *The Jesuits and the Sino-Russian Treaty of Nerchinsk (1689): The Diary of Thomas Pereira, S.J.*, Bibliotheca Instituti Historici Societatis Jesu, No. 18 (Rome, 1961), pp. 103–122.

In 1676 Verbiest had assisted the Chinese in their discussion with the Russians in Beijing and was later instrumental in having Pereira named a member of the Chinese delegation. Verbiest's aim was to find an overland route to China through Siberia that would replace the sea route, which the Dutch increasingly controlled to the detriment of the travel of missionaries and the shipping of other European nations. Despite the successful conclusion of the negotiations at Nerchinsk, the missionaries never gained regular access to this route, although Russia maintained its commercial and diplomatic contacts with China.

From 1687 to 1692 attacks on Christianity by several officials in Zhejiang, especially in Hangzhou, transformed the somewhat tranquil status of the Catholic Church in China. In March 1687 the Beijing Jesuits received a book written by a military official in Zhejiang claiming in several sections that Christianity was one of those false and seditious sects against which an imperial decree, issued just the year before, had warned. The missionaries appealed to the emperor to have the sections excised and asked him to grant full toleration to Christianity. The emperor agreed to remove the sections but mentioned nothing about tolerating Christianity. Later that same year, on a southern tour of the provinces, he visited Hangzhou and summoned Prospero Intorcetta (1625–1696) to an audience. Seeing his advanced age, the emperor told Intorcetta that he need not follow the entourage, but could remain in his residence. Not long after this imperial favor, Zhang Pengge (1649–1725), the governor of Zhejiang and a friend of Yang Guangxian, decided to enforce the 1669 decree banishing Christianity. He ordered the local officials to change the church into a temple, to burn the wooden bookplates in Intorcetta's residence, and to denounce Christianity as heterodoxy against the state. It took several months before the emperor learned about Intorcetta's plea for help from his confreres in Beijing. After receiving the deliberations of the imperial bureaucracy, the emperor declared that since the Westerners admired Chinese civilization, helped with calendar making and with the negotiations with the Russians, and had committed no crimes or caused trouble by their religion, it was unjust that it be prohibited. The Edict of Toleration of March 22, 1692, promulgated in all the provinces, was a watershed for the missionary effort in China.[32] Before this, the missionaries

---

[32] For the Chinese text, see Huang, *Zhengjiao fengbao*, 115b–116a; Fu, *Documentary Chronicle*, pp. 104–106; John W. Witek, S.J., "Understanding the Chinese: A Comparison of Matteo Ricci and the French Jesuit Mathematicians Sent by Louis XIV," in Charles E. Ronan, S.J., and Bonnie B. C. Oh, *East Meets West: The Jesuits in China, 1582–1773* (Chicago, 1988), pp. 90–93.

could preach their faith; now the Chinese were at liberty to accept it. In 1670 the emperor had issued his well-known Sixteen Injunctions, which became the basis of many clan rules during the Qing dynasty. One of these injunctions urged the abjuration of heretical religions.[33] By the 1692 Edict of Toleration he notified the empire that Christianity was no longer to be placed in that category.

MAIGROT'S DIRECTIVE

By a complex series of efforts between 1680 and 1700, Propaganda began to establish an ecclesiastical hierarchy in China independent of the Portuguese *padroado*. Missionaries who were not Portuguese or Jesuits were named as either bishops or vicars apostolic. One of them, Charles Maigrot, of the Missions Étrangères de Paris (Paris Foreign Mission Society, 1652–1730), vicar apostolic of Fujian, reopened the Rites Controversy just one year after the Edict of Toleration. On March 23, 1693, he published a directive condemning the use of the terms "Tian" and "Shang Di" to designate God and prohibiting the Christians in the vicariate from participating in the rites honoring Confucius and one's ancestors. He also condemned as false and scandalous the propositions that Chinese philosophy, correctly understood, contained nothing contrary to the Christian law and that by the use of "Taiji" (the Supreme Ultimate) the ancient sages sought to define God as the first cause of all things.[34]

Maigrot was carrying out the papal assignment of inquiring about the rites issue, which was becoming an important topic of discussion in France. He was concerned that accommodation to native customs would not be appropriate for the increasing number of converts, because Catholicism might thereby lose its identity. His directive, although limited to Fujian alone, served to reopen the Chinese Rites Controversy both in Europe and in China. The Christians in Fujian were perplexed by his moves and at times openly voiced their opposition.

Before the full impact of this controversy was felt, the Catholic Church continued to grow in China. The 1696 accord between the *padroado* and

[33] Hui-chen Wang Liu, "An Analysis of Chinese Clan Rules: Confucian Theories in Action," in David S. Nivison and Arthur. F. Wright, eds., *Confucianism in Action* (Stanford, CA, 1959), p. 74.

[34] Francis A. Rouleau, "Chinese Rites Controversy," *New Catholic Encyclopedia*, Vol. 3, pp. 610–611; Claudia von Collani, "Charles Maigrot's Role in the Rites Controversy," in Mungello, ed., *The Chinese Rites Controversy*, pp. 149–184.

the Holy See created a better geographic distribution of missionary territories. Portugal received the privilege of designating titular bishops to the three dioceses of Macao, Nanjing, and Beijing. Beyond these, Pope Innocent XI reserved the right of creating vicariates apostolic. In 1701 there were 117 missionaries in twelve provinces of China: 59 Jesuits in charge of 70 residences and 208 churches; 29 Franciscans in charge of 21 residences and 19 churches; 18 Dominicans in charge of 8 residences and 6 churches; 6 Augustinians in charge of 6 residences and 4 churches, and 15 diocesan clergy (mostly members of the Missions Étrangères de Paris ) in charge of 9 residences and 7 churches.[35] In some instances several religious orders were in the same city, for example, Canton, Fuzhou, Jinan, Ningbo, but more frequently they were located in different municipalities. This was a remarkable growth in the thirty years since 1671, when the emperor allowed the small band of two dozen missionaries to return to their posts. The Kangxi emperor raised the status of Christianity still further in 1693 by permitting the French Jesuits to build a residence in Beijing. Completed in 1703, the Beitang (North Church), which was erected near the residence, added significantly to the presence of Christianity in the capital.

Some of the principal Christians in the early Qing era were members of families who had become converts in the Ming period. By her outstanding leadership Candida Xu (1607–1680), granddaughter of Xu Guangqi (1562–1633), the well-known scholar-official and friend of Matteo Ricci (1552–1610), arranged for the opening of 135 churches and chapels in and around Shanghai.[36] Widowed at an early age, she became such an important benefactress to the Jesuit missions that upon her death the Jesuit father general ordered that three masses were to be offered by all Jesuits for the repose of her soul. Her son, Basil Xu Zuanzeng (1627–1696?), received the *jinshi* degree in 1649 and became a provincial judge in Yunnan. He was later a censor at court and was implicated in the Yang Guangxian calendar controversy. Restored to his former status

---

[35] Henri Bernard-Maitre and E. Jarry, "Les missions de Chine après 1644," in Simon Delacroix, ed., *Histoire universelle des missions catholiques*, 4 vols. (Paris, 1957), Vol. 2, pp. 173–174; Dehergne, *Répertoire*, pp. 357–359; Anastasius van den Wyngaert, O. F. M., Fortunato Margiotti, O.F.M., et al., eds. *Sinica Franciscana*, 11 vols. (Quaracchi-Firenze, 1929–2006), Vol. 7: xxi–xliii. Another set of figures for that year lists 82 Jesuits, 12 Dominicans, 29 Franciscans, 6 Augustinians, 15 with unknown affiliations, and 9 Chinese, for a total of 153. Standaert wisely observes, "Calculating the number of missionaries in China is a complicated matter." *Handbook*, pp. 300, 307.

[36] Gail King, "Couplet's Biography of Madame Candida Xu (1607–1680)," *Sino-Western Cultural Relations Journal*, Vol. 18 (1996), pp. 41–56.

after Yang was ousted from office, Xu Zuanzeng became known for his poetry and for his essay *Yuyingtang quan shan wen* (Descriptions and advice on philanthropy for foundling hospitals).[37] In a precious reference to the charitable work of the missionaries, it notes that in Yunnan from 1675 to 1696 there were 5,480 unwanted children found on the roads and brought to a foundling institution.

In the latter half of the seventeenth century, several publications made Europeans more aware of Chinese civilization.[38] Many of their authors had temporarily left China as procurators for the missions and, after staying a year or more in Europe, departed for Canton or Macao. Having witnessed the rise of the Qing dynasty, Martini wrote a short description of it in his *De bello Tartarico in Sinis Historia*, first published in 1654, with many later editions and translations.[39] His *Novus Atlas Sinensis* was published by the famous Amsterdam cartographic house of Blaeu in 1655, presenting a general map of China and maps of each province.[40] Lists of ancient and modern names of towns and cities, population statistics, and descriptions of flora and fauna were included. His *Sinicae Historiae Decas Prima*, published in 1658, was for a long time the only history of China before the Christian era based on Chinese sources. Additional chronological data became available in Europe in 1688 in *Nouvelle relation de la Chine* by Gabriel de Magalhães, S.J., who never left China but continued to work with Schall and Verbiest. His study filled in some gaps in Europe's knowledge of the Middle Kingdom, by describing Chinese literature, social customs, public buildings, commerce, manufacturing, and navigation.[41] In 1687 Couplet, who had an audience with Louis XIV, dedicated his *Confucius Sinarum Philosophus* to the Sun King.[42] In discussing traditional Chinese thought, including the Four Books, Buddhism, and Taoism, he commented on Ricci's method of solving the difficulties that the missionaries had encountered in China.[43] In 1693 the Kangxi emperor

---

[37] Fang Hao, *Zhongguo Tianzhujiao shi renwu zhuan*, 3 vols. (Hong Kong, 1967–1973), Vol. 2, pp. 75–76.

[38] Donald F. Lach and Edwin J. Van Kley, *Asia in the Making of Europe*, Vol. 3, 4 books (Chicago, 1993), Book 4, Ch. 21; David E. Mungello, *Curious Land: Jesuit Accommodation and the Origins of Sinology*, Studia Leibnitiana Supplementa, No. 25 (Stuttgart, 1985; reprint, Honolulu, 1989), Chs. 3, 4, 7.

[39] Antwerp, B. Moret, 1654; reprinted in Martino Martini, S.J., *Opera Omnia*, 3 vols., ed. Franco Demarchi and Giuliano Bertuccioli (Trent, 1998–2002).

[40] Martino Martino, S.J., *Novus Atlas Sinensis* (Amsterdam, 1655; reprint, Trent, 1981).

[41] Gabriel de Magalhães, S.J., *Nouvelle relation de la Chine* (Paris, 1688).

[42] Philippe Couplet, S.J., ed., *Confucius Sinarum Philosophus* (Paris, 1687).

[43] Giorgio Melis, ed., *Martino Martini, geografo, cartografo, storico, teologo, Trento 1614–Hangzhou 1661* (Trent, 1983); Franco Demarchi and Riccardo Scartezzini, eds., *Martino*

sent Bouvet as his envoy to the court of Versailles in order to thank the French monarch for his assistance in starting the French Jesuit mission. Not long after his arrival in France in March 1697, Bouvet completed his *Portrait historique de l'empereur de la Chine* and *L'Estat présent de la Chine en figures*.[44] The first study sought to flatter the Sun King and arouse his support for the China mission by comparing the splendor of his court and his virtuous rule to that of the Kangxi emperor. The latter contained a series of engraved figures depicting life in China. The similarity of the two monarchs made an impression on Gottfried Wilhelm Leibniz, who translated the *Portrait* in his *Novissima Sinica*, published in 1697. Through correspondence with Bouvet he learned about the binary arithmetical system of the *Yi Jing* (Book of changes).[45]

On a different scale, Le Comte, who returned to France several years before Bouvet, published in 1696–1698 *Nouveaux mémoires sur l'état présent de la Chine*.[46] Essentially a collection of fourteen letters addressed to various nobles, it contained a wide range of substantive comments on China, from its government and antiquity, its books and morality, to the progress Christianity had already achieved. Further editions of many of these works and translations into the principal languages of Europe helped to disseminate knowledge of China. In the opening years of the eighteenth century, moreover, one series of volumes about missionary endeavors in the East Indies and China stirred the imagination of the reading public in Europe. The *Lettres édifiantes et curieuses* first appeared in 1702; by 1776 there were thirty-four volumes. Reprinted in several French editions even in the following century, the series was also translated, in whole or in part, into German, Italian, English, and Spanish.[47] Despite some flaws in editing

*Martini: A Humanist and Scientist in Seventeenth-Century China* (Trent, 1996); see also Martini, *Opera Omnia*. On Couplet, see Jerome Heyndrickx, ed., *Philippe Couplet, S.J. (1623–1693): The Man Who Brought China to Europe*, Monumenta Serica Monograph Series, No. 22 (Nettetal, 1990); on Couplet's book, see Mungello, *Curious Land*, pp. 247–299.

44  Joachim Bouvet, S.J., *L'Estat présent de la Chine en figures* (Paris, 1697), and Bouvet, *Portrait historique de l'empereur de la Chine* (Paris, 1697).

45  Rita Widmaier, ed., *Leibniz korrespondiert mit China. Der Briefwechsel mit den Jesuitenmissionaren (1689–1714)* (Frankfurt am Main, 1990), pp. 49–54, 58–79, 102–109, 132–145, 147–169, 173–177, 179–196, 205–207, 216–219, 236–242, 265–268; G. W. Leibniz, *The Writings on China*, ed. and trans. Daniel J. Cook and Henry Rosemont (La Salle, IL, 1994), a translation of four essays; David E. Mungello, *Leibniz and Confucianism: The Search for Accord* (Honolulu, 1977).

46  For the recent edition, see Louis Le Comte, S.J., *Un jésuite à Pékin. Nouveaux mémoires sur l'état présent de la Chine, 1687–1692*, ed. Frédérique Touboul-Bouyeure (Paris, 1990).

47  The editions and their contents are described in Henri Cordier, *Bibliotheca Sinica*, 5 vols. (Paris, 1904–1924), Vol. 2, pp. 926–952.

and perhaps at times an overly optimistic portrayal of China, these letters developed an image of China for such leaders of the Enlightenment as Voltaire, Diderot, and Montesquieu. Nor should it be forgotten that this European literature and a considerable collection of works in European languages were in the library of the Beitang in Beijing.[48]

## PAPAL LEGATIONS TO CHINA

In 1693 Maigrot, besides promulgating his directive against the Chinese rites, also sent a copy with an exposition of his views to Propaganda in order to institute a judicial process on the issue in Rome. For seven years (1697–1704) a special commission of cardinals pondered the conflicting interpretations presented by both sides. Once a digest of the material was completed, the cardinals and their consulters were expected to present their views. Then the Holy Office would make its decision. But this process took considerably longer than the spokesman for Maigrot, Nicholas Charmot, M.E.P. (1645–1714), anticipated, since other business kept qualified theologians from considering the case. Differences of opinion among lesser officials involved in the process led Charmot to influence the Holy Office in Maigrot's favor. After reading Le Comte's *Nouveaux mémoires*, Charmot observed that Le Comte had changed the traditional view of the Jesuits in China. Schall and Verbiest limited themselves to the same claim as Ricci, that is, that the rites were probably not superstitious. But in place of such a probability, Le Comte claimed, according to Maigrot's spokesman, it was certain that they never had an idolatrous or even a superstitious significance. To expedite the decision in Rome, Charmot asked the archbishop of Paris, Louis Noailles, to present Le Comte's views to the Sorbonne. Its prompt denunciation in 1700 contributed to some degree to the policy that Rome announced not many years thereafter.[49]

Later that same year, the Jesuits in Beijing, at the insistence of their confreres in Europe who alerted them to the debates taking place there,

---

[48] Hubert Verhaeren, *Catalogue de la Bibliothèque du Pé-t'ang* (Beijing, 1949; reprint, Paris, 1969).

[49] Antonio S. Rosso, *Apostolic Legations to China of the Eighteenth Century* (South Pasadena, CA, 1948), p. 136; George Minamiki, *The Chinese Rites Controversy from Its Beginnings to Modern Times* (Chicago, 1985), pp. 37–40. In the present essay the Chinese Rites Controversy is discussed in its Chinese contexts; it was, of course, also a major event in European intellectual history. For starting points see Nicolas Standaert, "Rites Controversy," in Standaert, ed., *Handbook*, pp. 680–688; Mungello, ed., *The Chinese Rites Controversy*; Noll, ed., *100 Documents*.

asked the emperor for a clarification of the rites issue. They wanted to know whether they were correct in stating that Confucius was honored as the master of all men but that no rank or happiness was sought from him, that ancestor veneration was intended as a sign of remembrance of the ancestors, and that the souls of the ancestors did not dwell in the tablets erected in their honor.[50] The emperor replied that their statement on these matters was accurate. Not all the missionaries, including some Jesuits, considered such a request to the emperor a prudent tactic. But the Jesuits at court realized that interpreting customs so integral to the Confucian state was an imperial prerogative alone. In their view the emperor was not called upon to decide a question in Christian theology, but to explain what certain Chinese customs signified in practice.

None of these arguments were found convincing in Rome, for in 1701 the initial decision against Ricci's method of inculturation was reached. Three years elapsed before a decree was made final in November 1704 accepting Maigrot's arguments and confirming his prohibitions. As a consequence of the initial decision, the papacy planned to send a legate to China to investigate all ecclesiastical issues and, above all, to enforce the decree on the Chinese rites that would follow. Charles Maillard de Tournon, a bishop and later a cardinal, left Rome in July 1702 and arrived in Canton in April 1705. During his visit to India on his way to China, he had already condemned the Malabar rites, that is, accommodations to south Indian culture somewhat analogous to the Ricci perspective of inculturation in China, and thus showed what might be in store for the China mission. Only thirty-four years of age, the legate was too young in Chinese eyes for such an important post. One of his first encounters with ecclesiastical affairs in Canton was his receipt of a manuscript in Chinese. Entitled *Tianxue benyi* (Essential meaning of the teaching of Heaven), this essay by Bouvet claimed that the Chinese, both old and new, had known the true God under the terms "Tian" and "Shang Di." Since the approval of the president of the Hanlin Academy, Han Tan, was placed where the episcopal imprimatur was normally found, Tournon refused to approve its publication.[51] He ordered the bishop of Beijing

[50] Joseph Dehergne, "L'Exposé des Jésuites de Pékin sur le culte des ancêtres présenté à l'empereur K'ang-Hi en novembre 1700," in Colloque international de sinologie, Chantilly, 1977, *Les Rapports entre la Chine et l'Europe* (Paris, 1980), pp. 201–204.

[51] The incident is described in a letter of Claudio Filippo Grimaldi, the Jesuit visitor of the Vice-Province of China and the Province of Japan, to Father General Tirso González, Beijing, October 18, 1705, Archivum Romanum Societatis Iesu, *Japonica et Sinica, 168,* ff. 342–344v; see also the biography of Han Tan (1637–1704) in Arthur Hummel, ed.,

to confiscate all the printed copies, and the Jesuits were to take an oath that no other copies existed. In fact, the study had never been published, although Tournon could not be convinced otherwise.

In a memorable audience with the emperor in late December, Tournon proposed the establishment of an apostolic nunciature in Beijing. As a delegate of the pope, the nuncio was expected to have the integrity and understanding needed to act as a liaison between the Holy See and the emperor. His secondary function would be to centralize all missionary activity in China.[52]

After the emperor rejected this proposal and failed to persuade the legate to discuss the rites issue, Tournon, already ailing in body and in spirit, left the capital in August 1706. On behalf of the legate, Maigrot, with limited command of the Chinese language and less of its literature, was involved in a discussion of the rites issue with the emperor at his summer estate in Chengde, the "Jehol" (Rehe) of the European sources.[53] He summarily dismissed Maigrot from his presence and notified Tournon about the proceedings.[54]

A few months later the emperor ordered all the missionaries to apply for a *piao* (certificate), which was to be issued only after the recipient promised to remain in China for life and to follow the practices of Ricci. The legate, then in Nanjing on his way to Canton, issued the Nanjing Decree of 1707, forbidding the missionaries to fulfill the imperial command. In so doing he knew he had the support of the 1704 papal decision against the Jesuit interpretation of the rites question, although he did not have the formal document. The hostility of the emperor, the challenge

---

*Eminent Chinese of the Ch'ing Period* (Washington, DC, 1943–1944; reprint, Taipei, 1967), pp. 275–276; Joseph Sebes, "China's Jesuit Century," *Wilson Quarterly*, Vol. 2 (1978), pp. 170–183.

[52] Francis A. Rouleau, "Maillard de Tournon, Papal Legate at the Court of Peking: The First Imperial Audience (31 December 1705)," *Archivum Historicum Societatis Iesu*, Vol. 31 (1962), pp. 271–75; Rosso, *Apostolic Legations*, pp. 149–186; Claudia von Collani, "Legations and Travelers," in Standaert, ed., *Handbook*, pp. 355–366.

[53] When the Kangxi emperor asked if he had read the Chinese works of Matteo Ricci, Maigrot replied that he had read some parts ("quelques endroits de ses livres"). Moreover, he was not able to read all four of the Chinese characters above the throne when the emperor made that request. See Maigrot's own admissions in *Opus R. D. Maigrot Episcopi. Cononensis apud Sinenses,* Bibliotheque Nationale, Paris, *Mss. Latin 17608*, ff. 337, 371. This codex of 902 pages divided into eighty-two chapters is on the Tournon legation in China.

[54] Translations of the basic documents are in Noll, *100 Documents*; *Kangxi yu Luoma shijie guanxi wenshu. Qianlong yingshi jinjian ji*, Zhongguo shixue congshu, xubian, 23 (Taipei, 1973), p. 21; and von Collani, "Charles Maigrot's Role in the Chinese Rites Controversy," pp. 149–184.

to the *padroado* implicit in his mission, and the discord that developed among the missionaries contributed to the detention of the legate in Macao, where he died in 1710. The Nanjing Decree forced the missionaries to choose between the legate and the emperor. Within a year, fifty-seven missionaries (Augustinians, Franciscans, and Jesuits) had requested the *piao* on the basis of an appeal to the pope against Tournon's decree. The others were allowed to leave China freely or were expelled. Realizing the gravity of the controversy and convinced that the pope would be persuaded by the reasonableness of his views, the emperor sent four Jesuits as his envoys to the pope. Regrettably, none ever returned to China (two drowned at sea near the Portuguese coast; one died in Spain after he left Rome; the last died at the Cape of Good Hope on his return trip to Canton). Just a few days before the emperor's death in 1722, a mausoleum was erected in Canton in honor of this last envoy, Antonio Provana (1662–1720).[55]

In the provinces some missionaries at times encountered profound ethnocentrism and cultural conservatism in response to their preaching. In Fuzhou a Jesuit missionary noted in 1703 that the disdain of the Chinese, even the common people, for all other nations was one of the greatest obstacles to their conversion. When they realized that Christianity was holy and sound, they still coldly replied that it was a foreign religion not found in Chinese books and asked, "Is there anything good outside of China and any truth that our learned men have not known?"[56]

To answer that type of question and also the inquiries that some Jesuits sent to them, several Christian literati, by carrying out extensive research in the Chinese classics and other sources, wrote a number of essays on the Rites Controversy. After the persecution of Christianity in connection with the Yang Guangxian controversy in Beijing, the Dominican Francisco Varo (1627–1687) arrived in Fujian in 1671 and some time later published *Bian Ji* (A debate on memorial rites). In this dialogue between

---

[55] Rouleau, "Maillard de Tournon," p. 268, n. 7; John W. Witek, S.J., "Sent to Lisbon, Paris and Rome: Jesuit Envoys of the Kangxi Emperor," in Michele Fatica and Francesco D'Arelli, eds., *La missione cattolica tra i secoli XVIII–XIX. Matteo Ripa e il collegio dei cinesi: atti del colloquio internazionale, Napoli, 11–12 febbraio 1997* (Naples, 1999), pp. 317–340. Elaborate funeral ceremonies for Provana funded by the emperor and conducted in the presence of Western merchants are described in Antonio Vasconcelos de Saldanha, *De Kangxi para o Papa, pela Via de Portugal*, 3 vols. (Lisbon, 2002), Vol. 1, pp. 418–420, with an illustration of the remnant of the tombstone.

[56] Emeric de Chavagnac (1670–1717) to Charles Le Gobien, Fuzhou, February 10, 1703, in M. L. Aimé-Martin, ed., *Lettres édifiantes et curieuses*, 4 vols. (Paris, 1838–1843), Vol. 3, pp. 77–78.

a missionary and a scholar from Fuan, Fujian (a center of Dominican mission activity), questions and answers were developed to understand the meaning of *ji* (memorial rites). In 1681 the Jesuit Simão Rodrigues (1645–1704) accidentally found a copy. In his opinion the book had merits but did not clarify the topic. He encouraged the Christian literati to read the work and to write their own critiques. The result was a number of essays on this significant theme in the Chinese Rites Controversy. Yan Mo, a native of Zhangzhou in Fujian, whose Christian name was Paul, composed several works, such as *Ji Zu Kao* (On memorial tablets), *Kao Yi* (Doubts), and *Bian Ji* (On memorial rites). In these essays Yan addressed two principal questions: Were the Chinese rites religious in nature? Was the practice of the rites intended to seek benefits and blessings? After tracing the original meaning and various uses that *ji* had accrued over time, Yan concluded that there never was a practice of any unusual rites that considered the ancestors to be gods and paid homage to them.[57] Moreover, the rites to ancestors were expressions of the recollection and love for the dead, not of seeking blessings from them. This argument he demonstrated in *Ji Zu Kao* as he drew upon his reading of the annotated editions of the early Chinese classics and his examination of the words used in the rituals since the Tang dynasty, which indicated to him that no family from the common people to the emperor used a word for blessing.[58] In his reply to Varo's essay entitled *Kao Yi*, Yan agreed that in the *Li Ji* (Book of rites) there was a passage about *ji* that included praying, rewarding, and punishments for the descendants. But this meant that one prayed to Shangdi and the other gods, not to the ancestors. He concluded that in the rites for ancestors there was no proof that petitions for blessings existed.

An allied question was whether the souls of the dead resided in the wooden tablets that the Chinese erected in their houses. These signified, the Christian literati argued, not that the souls actually were in the tablets, but that the latter were expressions of filial piety by which to serve the dead as one is expected to serve the living. Zhang Xingyao, mentioned earlier in connection with the inscriptions of the church in Hangzhou, indicated in his *Si Dian Shuo* (Discussion of sacrificial rites) that it was only in the Ming dynasty that the use of such tablets had been imposed.

---

[57] Yan Mo, "Bian Ji," Archivum Romanum Societatis Iesu, *Japonica et Sinica* I, 41, 6a, pp. 4–5, as discussed by Lin Jinshui, "Chinese Literati and the Rites Controversy," in Mungello, ed., *The Chinese Rites Controversy*, p. 68.

[58] *Ji Zu Kao*, Archivum Romanum Societatis Iesu, *Japonica et Sinica*, I, 41, 1a, p. 10, as discussed by Lin Jinshui, "Chinese Literati," p. 69.

The tablets were to express one's sincere love for the ancestors. Even if their souls were not present, a person could not change his mind about serving the dead and remembering them as if they were alive. Zhang stressed that if their souls were good, they would enter heaven; if not, hell was their destiny. He asked rhetorically whether it was so important that the souls be present.[59] Although many of these essays were composed in Fujian and Zhejiang, apparently few, if any, of the opponents of the Jesuit viewpoints cited them.[60]

Even though they did not become converts, there were other Chinese literati who held positive attitudes toward Christianity. In 1702–1703, the Jesuits compiled testimonials in favor of the Chinese rites with the Chinese texts and Latin translations that were forwarded to Rome. At least seventy-one literati from Nanjing, Suzhou, Ganzhou, and elsewhere signed separate documents in defense of the Jesuit view; about forty *jinshi* also joined them. Intended to show solidarity among the lay Christians for the Ricci method, these testimonials also contained the signatures of Kong Youqi, a descendant of Confucius, Wang Xi (1628–1703), Zhang Ying (1638–1708), and several other non-Christian leaders in Beijing.[61] It is very noteworthy that such scholars were willing to uphold in writing a non-Chinese teaching whose standing at court was becoming more uncertain even as elite culture was emphasizing its Confucian heritage. Such support from Christian and non-Christian scholars helped the further development of Christianity, despite the reduced number of missionaries after Tournon's visit.

What prompted Chinese scholars to view Christianity as acceptable to their society was not merely the 1692 Edict of Toleration, but Chinese essays explaining Christian principles. Of the many works available in the opening decades of the eighteenth century two remained most influential: *Tianzhu shiyi* (True meaning of the Lord of Heaven) by Ricci and

---

[59] *Si Dian Shuo*, Archivum Romanum Societatis Iesu, *Japonica et Sinica*, I, 40, 7a, pp. 44–45, as discussed by Lin Jinshui, "Chinese Literati," p. 73.

[60] For additional essays by Chinese Christians on the rites issue, see Huang Yinong, "Bei hulue di shengyin – Jieshao Zhongguo Tianzhujiao tu dui 'Liyi wen-ti' taidu di wenxian," *Qinghua Xuebao* (*Tsing Hua Journal of Chinese Studies*), Vol. 25, No. 2, New Ser. (June 1995), pp. 137–160. See also his *Liang toushe. Mingmo Qingchu de diyidai Tianzhu jiaotu* (Xinzhu, 2005), pp. 412–422; pp. 411–421 in the Shanghai edition of 2006.

[61] Van den Wyngaert, Margiotti, et al., eds., *Sinica Franciscana* (Rome, 1975), Vol. 8, pp. 751–152, n. 133. There were 182 documents collected; for further analysis about the Chinese literati and the Chinese Christian astronomers in this controversy, see Han Qi, "The Role of the Directorate of Astronomy in the Catholic Mission During the Qing Period," in Golvers, ed., *The Christian Mission in China in the Verbiest Era*, pp. 90–93.

*Wanwu zhenyuan* (True origin of all things) by Giulio Aleni (1582–1649).[62] Both discussed such topics as the existence of God and the immortality of the soul, and also showed how Christian thought differed on these points from several Chinese philosophical principles. Starting from the intellectual encounter of the Ming period, these works and others remained exemplars of the dialogue of Christianity with the Chinese.

## WESTERN MEDICINE AND MAPMAKING

The initial respect of the Kangxi emperor for the Western missionaries and their religion was based on their expertise in astronomy and mathematics. Throughout his reign, he called on them to participate in additional scientific projects. Toward the beginning of 1692 he asked Bouvet and Gerbillon about various illnesses in Europe and their cures. After getting their written report, he told them to set up a pharmaceutical laboratory in the palace and to write detailed analyses of their experiments. This scientific activity led to the composition of the *Manchu Anatomy*, a collection of illustrations accompanied by a translation from one of the best French works on the topic. This five-year project, completed by Dominique Parennin (1665–1741), never received imperial authorization for publication.[63] Although the emperor widely encouraged the dissemination of many kinds of knowledge, he allowed only very few scholars to consult the three manuscript copies of these medical essays (two in Beijing and one in Rehe). Consequently, this field of Western scientific inquiry had little effect on the development of Chinese medicine of that day. Nonetheless, when the emperor, suffering from bouts of fever in 1693, sought a remedy, he took some quinine that a few Jesuits through court officials offered him. His cure resulted in the high esteem he had

---

[62] Jean-François Foucquet to the Duc de La Force, Nanchang, November 26, 1702, in, Aimé-Martin, ed., *Lettres édifiantes*, Vol. 3, p. 59; John W. Witek, S.J., "Principles of Scholasticism in China: A Comparison of Giulio Aleni's *Wanwu zhenyuan* with Matteo Ricci's *Tianzhu shiyi*," in Tiziana Lippiello and Roman Malek, eds., *"Scholar from the West," Giulio Aleni, S.J. (1582–1649) and the Dialogue between Christianity and China*, Fondazione Civiltà Bresciana *Annali*, No. 9, and Monumenta Serica Monograph Series, No. 42 (Nettetal, 1997), pp. 273–289; see also Gianni Criveller, *Preaching Christ in Late Ming China: The Jesuits' Presentation of Christ from Matteo Ricci to Giulio Aleni* (Taipei, 1997), pp. 428–439.

[63] Pierre Huard and Ming Wong, *Chinese Medicine* (New York, 1972), pp. 118–123; T. Kue-hing Young, "French Jesuits and the 'Manchu Anatomy': How China Missed the Vesalian Revolution," *Canadian Medical Association Journal* Vol. 111 (September 21, 1974), pp. 565–568, with some incorrect statements on the background of the French Jesuits in China.

for Western knowledge of medicine, on which he relied a few more times during his reign.[64] Several Jesuit brothers were pharmacists whose dispensary was open to the public, so that in times of persecution they would see the patients and exhort those whom they knew as Christians to be steadfast in their faith.

Perhaps one of the most arduous tasks that the emperor assigned to the missionaries at court, and one of the most impressive demonstrations of his trust of them, was the compilation of an accurate map of the Chinese Empire. The initial steps in ascertaining the accuracy of the Western methods of combining astronomy and geography occurred as early as 1682 when Verbiest determined the longitude of Mukden in Manchuria. In 1686 imperial officials surveyed the border with Korea. For this newly assigned mapping project, which extended from 1708 to 1717, the emperor ordered Manchu and Chinese officials to assist the missionaries. Such imperial trust in the missionaries is all the more remarkable in light of the tendency of Chinese officials to consider all foreigners potential spies. The principal cartographers were Jean-Baptiste Régis (1663–1738) and Pierre Jartoux (1668–1720), who were joined by several Jesuit confreres and by an Augustinian, Guillaume Fabre-Bonjour (1669–1714). After calculating the exact position of the Great Wall and the surrounding areas, they sent the results to Beijing. The expedition went to Manchuria, then Shandong, Shanxi, and Shaanxi, and eventually the rest of the provinces, including Taiwan. Upon consulting the maps and gazetteers of each city and province, they interrogated the civil and military officials of the area. Unquestionably this experience gave the missionaries a clearer perspective of the complexity of the peoples, dialects, and customs of the empire. When possible, they preached to the Chinese and the non-Chinese in areas where no missionary had ever entered. There were two exceptions, for in Tibet, the lamas, trained by Manchus and Chinese, conducted the survey; in Korea, officials of that kingdom did so. Presented to the throne in 1719, the *Huangyu quanlan tu* (Complete survey map of the empire) was the product of an extensive geographical enterprise.[65] The emperor was highly pleased with the

---

[64] For a survey of medicine, including translations from the *Lettres édifiantes*, see Yazawa Toshihiko, ed., *Chūgoku no igaku to gijutsu. Yezusukaishi Chūgoku shokanshū* (Chinese medicine and techniques. Collection of Jesuit letters from China) (Tokyo, 1977), esp. i–xviii. See also Ursula Holler, "Medicine," in Standaert, ed., *Handbook*, pp. 786–802.

[65] Pfister, *Notices biographiques*, pp. 530–532; *Da Qing lichao shilu*, Kangxi reign, 283: 10–12b (Tokyo, 1937–1938; reprint, Taiwan, 1963), partially translated in Fu, *Documentary Chronicle*, pp. 127–128; Joseph Needham, *Science and Civilisation in China*, 7 vols. (Cambridge, 1959), Vol. 3, p. 585; the standard work on this map is Walter Fuchs,

results. Its printing in Paris from 1730 to 1734 created a keen appreciation in Europe, where no cartographer had ever undertaken such a feat until then.

In addition to such large and relatively public enterprises as the map project, the emperor was becoming interested in reviewing the traditional Chinese classics, especially the *Yi Jing*. After Bouvet, originally assigned to the map expedition, was forced to return to the capital because of injuries suffered in falling from a horse, the emperor began to inquire about his views on that classic. Ever since he had returned from Paris in 1698 and understood how enamored the emperor had become of Buddhism, Bouvet realized that his past expectation that the emperor would some day embrace Christianity was illusory. Indeed, this became abundantly clear after the abortive Tournon legation. But discussions of ancient Chinese literature with the emperor provided Bouvet with an opportunity to explain Christian philosophical principles that he found in the classics. Bouvet's methodology consisted of accepting Chinese philosophy as compatible with Christian principles and the *Yi Jing* as a synopsis of the best moral and physical doctrine of the Chinese. From his reading, Bouvet became convinced that the authors of the ancient classics and the ancient kings of China knew the mystery of the Trinity and thus adored the same God as the Christians. On these key concepts, he built a system later called figurism, that is, an attempt to find figures of the Old Testament in the Chinese classics. For Bouvet and the several Jesuits who espoused his cause, the truths of Christianity were hidden beneath the Chinese characters, whose veil had to be lifted in order that the Chinese might readily accept Christianity. Attracted to this movement were Jean-François Foucquet (1665–1741) and Joseph Henri de Prémare (1666–1736).The latter was one of the best Western scholars of Chinese language and literature.[66] Foucquet, a missionary in Jiangxi province, received an imperial summons in 1711 to work in Beijing with Bouvet on the *Yi Jing*. He remained in the capital until November 1720, when the Jesuit father general, learning about Foucquet's refusal to accept a confrere as a legitimately appointed superior, ordered Foucquet to return to France. Later he became a bishop at Propaganda in Rome. Foucquet's

---

*Der Jesuiten-Atlas der Kanghsi Zeit*, Monumenta Serica Monograph Series, No. 4 (Peiping, 1943); Theodore N. Foss, "Cartography," in Standaert, ed., *Handbook*, pp. 752–770.
[66] Prémare completed his *Notitia linguae sinicae* in Canton in 1728. It appeared in Malacca in 1831; reprint, Hong Kong, 1893. For his biography see Knud Lundbaek, *Joseph de Prémare (1666–1736), S.J.: Chinese Philology and Figurism* (Aarhus, 1991), pp. 109–140. On Bouvet, see von Collani, *P. Joachim Bouvet*, pp. 124–203.

desire to present figurism to the Holy See as a possible means of solving the Rites Controversy was never realized.[67] Figurism was not vain curiosity on the part of its very few Jesuit adherents but a serious and intellectually bold attempt to understand Chinese literature.[68]

## THE SECOND PAPAL LEGATION

In September 1710 Pope Clement XI (1700–1721) rejected the petitions of those who had appealed against the Nanjing Decree of Tournon. Delays in the mail for several years prevented authenticated copies from reaching the bishop of Beijing. Not until early 1715 did he attempt to promulgate the decision. A Lazarist missionary and skilled musician, Theodoric Pedrini (1670–1746), disclosed the contents of the papal decision to the emperor. After reading a Chinese translation, the emperor reiterated his past ordinances against those who would violate Chinese customs. Another apostolic constitution, *Ex Illa Die* (March 1715), reiterating Maigrot's views and strongly rejecting the Ricci approach to these issues, arrived in Beijing by late August the following year. The emperor again refused to accept such papal positions as final. In the Red Manifesto (*hong piao*) of October 1716, which was to be distributed to all ships leaving from Canton, and also to all those traveling overland with the Russian caravan then in Beijing, the emperor declared that only upon the return of the four imperial envoys whom he sent to Europe would he have a basis for accepting such papal pronouncements.[69] The emperor's appeal for information about the envoys proved fruitless, for, as noted earlier, they never returned to China.[70]

---

[67] See Witek, *Controversial Ideas*, pp. 125–283.

[68] For short overviews of figurism, see Paul A. Rule, *K'ung-tzu or Confucius? The Jesuit Interpretation of Confucianism* (Sydney, 1986), pp. 150–182, and Claudia von Collani, "Figurism," in Nicolas Standaert, ed., *Handbook of Christianity in China.*, pp. 668–679.

[69] The Red Manifesto was originally written in Manchu; Chinese and Latin versions were then added. Several original printed copies of this trilingual document are extant in libraries in Europe and in the United States. Excellent reproductions are in *Exotic Printing and the Expansion of Europe, 1492–1840* (Bloomington, IN, 1972), pp. 70–72, and Monique Cohen and Nathalie Monnet, *Impressions de Chine* (Paris, 1992), pp. 118–119.

[70] On his return trip to China, Antonio Provana, S.J. (1662–1720), died at sea near the Cape ofGood Hope. Fan Shouyi (1682–1753), who accompanied Provana to Europe and became a Jesuit there, was aboard the same ship. He insisted on bringing Provana's body to Canton, where imperial officials were required to report these events to the emperor and arranged for the proper burial. At an audience in Beijing, Fan gave the emperor an account of his journey to the West. See Paul A. Rule, "Louis Fan Shou-I: A Missing Link

During the last decade of the Kangxi reign, several signs of bureaucratic intrigue toward the Chinese Christians, missionaries, and other Europeans arose. An example is that of Fan Shaozuo, an imperial censor, who openly attacked Christianity and demanded that it be rooted out of the empire.[71] The role of the censors was to avert public disorder and to point out the faults of the magistrates, even those of the emperor, if they found something reprehensible. An event in his family Fan considered a symptom of social disorder. He had a grandson who was engaged to be married to a Christian neophyte. Fan's family had agreed to the marriage, even to the extent of assuring the bride that she would have freedom to practice her religion. After the wedding ceremony, she was conducted to a room with several well-adorned idols. Her mother-in-law and several other women insisted that she pay homage to the idols, but she steadfastly refused that day and several days later. At that point Fan, the grandfather of the bridegroom, wrote a memorial attacking Christianity and seeking to proscribe it in China. The emperor received the memorial on December 23, 1711, just as he was preparing to go on a hunting expedition. He ordered the Board of Ceremonies (Li Bu) to consider the matter and report to him. This caused consternation for the Jesuits and other missionaries at the court since the board was not considered to be a supporter of Christianity. No decision had been reached by January 14, 1712, when the Jesuits at court learned about another memorial that Fan had sent to the emperor, outlining his proposal of opening a canal in his native area. Technically such a project belonged to the Board of Works (Gong Bu) under the direct supervision of the emperor. His reply, which appeared in the *Jing Bao* (the imperial gazette sent to all the provinces), depicted Fan as an ignorant, inconsiderate person, who knew nothing about dikes and whose proposal was impracticable. As this was a separate issue from Fan's first memorial, this imperial reply contained no hint of whether the government would rule in his favor.

In his attack on Christianity, Fan claimed that the Christians followed a false and dangerous doctrine in stating that the Lord of Heaven had

---

in the Chinese Rites Controversy," in E. Malatesta, Yves Raguin, and A. Dudink, eds., *Échanges culturels et religieux entre la Chine et l'Occident*. Variétés sinologiques, New Ser. 83 (San Francisco, 1995), pp. 277–294.

[71] See François-Xavier Dentrecolles to Jean-Charles Etienne de Broissia, Raozhou, May 10, 1715, in Aimé-Martin, ed., *Lettres édifiantes*, Vol. 3, pp. 251–253. This French letter and the Chinese texts of Fan Shaozuo are reproduced in Matteo Ripa, *Giornale (1705–1724)*, 2 vols., ed. Michele Fatica (Naples, 1991–1996), Vol. 2, pp. 251–266. For a biography of Dentrecolles, see Yves de Thomaz de Bossierre, *François-Xavier Dentrecolles et l'apport de la Chine à l'Europe du XVIIIe siècle* (Paris, 1982).

given a soul to a man called Jesus, born in Judea of the Virgin Mary during the time of the Han dynasty. According to them Jesus suffered and died on a cross in expiation for the sins of everyone. In fact, Fan added, Christians referred to themselves as sinners. For the most part they were poor people or in a mediocre social position. By putting images of God in their houses, reciting their prayers, and putting crosses on their doors, Fan wondered if they were not trying to overthrow the government. Since there were a great number of Christians near the imperial court, Fan feared that the Christians would soon inundate the empire. His recommendation to the emperor was that none of them should put any sign of Christianity on their doors nor possess any images in their houses. Indeed, if such images were found, they were to be destroyed. Nor would the Christians be allowed to assemble day or night. Those transgressing these orders were to be punished according to the full severity of the laws and the leaders were to be executed.

Fan apparently expected the Board of Ceremonies to support his view, but instead he received a rejection. The board cited past imperial edicts that had allowed the preaching and exercise of Christianity. Since these edicts had not been issued lightly, they were not to be revoked without serious reasons. Above all the board pointed to the 1692 Edict of Toleration, which it had granted because of the conduct and service of the missionaries that were beyond reproach. The board ruled that Fan's memorial was unacceptable and should be considered null and void. This was its recommendation to the Kangxi emperor, who immediately on receipt of the document endorsed the board's action. In Fan's attempt to oust Christianity from China not only had he lost, but the emperor thoroughly rejected his second memorial about building dikes in his native place. Fan's status as a censor was weakened, even as the Board of Ceremonies and the emperor continued to support the 1692 Edict of Toleration in 1712, just six years after Tournon's abortive legation ended in Beijing.[72]

Another attempt to drive Christianity from China arose, but this time in Canton in 1717. The regional commander (*zongbing*), Chen Mao, charged that foreign merchants and missionaries threatened the security of China. In his view Canton was fast becoming another

[72] For additional aspects about Christians in the capital, see John W. Witek, S.J., "The Emergence of a Christian Community in Beijing during the Late Ming and Early Qing Period," in Xiaoxin Wu, ed., *Encounters and Dialogues: Changing Perspectives on Chinese–Western Exchanges from the Sixteenth to the Eighteenth Centuries* (Sankt Augustin, 2005), pp. 93–116.

Batavia, controlled by the Dutch, or another Manila, controlled by the Spanish, both of which he had recently visited. Chen urged the emperor to ban the spread of Christianity and to reinstitute past restrictions on trade. Ultimately the emperor decided that missionaries with the *piao* would be allowed to preach, at least for the time being. The trade of foreigners at Canton was to continue, but he forbade Chinese maritime trade to dangerous places like Manila and Batavia.[73] The emperor was confident that the state was formidable enough to control the foreigners at Canton, even as he trusted the missionaries to complete the sensitive mapping project. He still waited anxiously for a positive reply from Rome despite pressures from some court and provincial officials who wanted stringent repression of the missionaries and their Chinese converts.[74]

During these uneasy years, Pope Clement XI made a further attempt to resolve the Rites Controversy by naming Archbishop Carlo Ambrogio Mezzabarba (1685–1741) as his legate to Beijing. To announce the archbishop's mission, Pope Clement XI sent two envoys in advance with a letter addressed to the emperor. Mezzabarba's first solemn audience on December 31, 1720, and several later ones gave evidence of his tact and diplomatic finesse. Yet upon reading the 1715 papal constitution *Ex Illa Die*, the emperor was displeased with its contents. Further negotiation, which included the legate's granting of eight permissions to Chinese Christians that modified the constitution, led to an agreement that the status quo would be maintained until Mezzabarba's return from Rome with new instructions from the pope.[75] The permissions, later issued in the legate's pastoral letter from Macao in November 1721, allowed Christians to have in their houses ancestral tablets inscribed with the name of the dead, without the statement about the tablet as the "seat of the soul" but portraying relevant Catholic beliefs. A tablet probably made according to these norms is preserved in the Bibliothèque Nationale, Paris;

---

[73] *Da Qing lichao shilu*, Kangxi reign, 272:8, 277:20b–21b; translation in Fu, *Documentary Chronicle*, pp. 123–127; Jonathan Spence, *Emperor of China: Self-Portrait of K'ang-hsi* (New York, 1974), pp. 82–83; Witek, *Controversial Ideas*, pp. 228–229.

[74] Some scholarship has incorrectly claimed that the emperor banned Christianity in 1717; see e.g., Zhu Weizheng, *Coming Out of the Middle Ages: Comparative Reflections on China and the West* (Armonk, NY, 1990), p. 223. But the emperor, without news about the four envoys he sent to Europe, told the Chinese officials to wait several years for such a possible prohibition. *Da Qing lichao shilu*, Kangxi reign, 277: 20b–21b.

[75] Noll, *100 Documents*, p. 57; Giacomo di Fiore, *La Legazione Mezzabarba in Cina, 1720–1721* (Naples, 1989), p. 107.

it prominently displays the symbol of the cross and succinctly explains that the son or grandson sets up the tablet as a reminder of his debt to his forebears, not that their spirits might dwell in it.[76] This was a significant, nuanced integration of Chinese culture and Catholic belief for many ordinary converts. Moreover, the legate's letter authorized all those Chinese ceremonies concerning the dead that were not superstitious or suspect, but merely civil. Such measures breathed a spirit of inculturation but did not settle the controversy.

The Kangxi emperor's experiences with Mezzabarba were more positive than those he had had with the first papal legate, Tournon. At a formal banquet in February 1721 he asked Mezzabarba to present imperial gifts to the pope. He also announced the appointment of the Jesuit Antonio de Magalhães (1677–1735) as the imperial envoy bearing gifts for the king of Portugal.[77] Although the gifts for the pope and the king were lost in the fire and sinking of the *Rainha dos Anjos* off the coast of Rio de Janeiro, Brazil, the papal legate and the imperial envoy continued their journey to Lisbon.[78] After meeting the Portuguese monarch, Mezzabarba proceeded to Rome. Magalhães later returned to Beijing, where he had an audience with the Yongzheng emperor on November 24, 1726.

Arriving in Rome in May 1723, Mezzabarba learned that several missionaries of various religious orders believed that the permissions caused more confusion. Propaganda, unwilling to review the papal decisions on the rites that had already been issued, recommended to Pope Innocent XIII (1721–1724) that he write a letter to the emperor instead.[79] Several months after the pope's death in March 1724, news of the death of the Kangxi emperor in December 1722 reached Rome and negated any plans for the return of Mezzabarba to China. Benedict XIII (1724–1730), learning from several missionaries that the Yongzheng emperor was well disposed toward Christianity sent five priests to congratulate him on his ascent to the throne. Only two were allowed an audience in Beijing; afterward all of them left China.

---

[76] A reproduction is in Dunne, *Generation of Giants*, p. 293.

[77] João de Deus Ramos, *História das relações diplomaticas entre Portugal e a China. O Padre António de Magalhães, S.J., e a Embaixada de Kangxi a D. João V (1721–1725)* (Macao, 1991), pp. 105–176.

[78] A description of some of the gifts is in Emily Byrne Curtis, "Foucquet's List: Translation and Comments on the Color 'Blue Sky After Rain,' " *Journal of Glass Studies*, Vol. 41 (1999), pp. 147–152.

[79] Nicolas Kowalsky, "Mezzabarba, Carlo Ambrogio," *Enciclopedia Cattolica*, 8:924–925;Rosso, *Apostolic Legations*, pp. 216–220; di Fiore, *La Legazione Mezzabarba*, pp. 63–74.

## THE YONGZHENG EMPEROR AND CHRISTIANITY

The last two decades of the Kangxi period had not settled the question of imperial succession. Upon the death of the emperor in 1722, a struggle among several of his sons and their contending factions erupted. The Yongzheng emperor took control, but doubts about the legitimacy of his rule persisted. The bureaucracy was also suffering the consequences of decades of somewhat relaxed supervision. Under these circumstances the new emperor adopted a policy that led to tightening control over the officials, clear affirmation of his cultural orthodoxy, and severe repression of the princes and their supporters who opposed his rise to power.[80] In this environment those calling for harsher measures against the missionaries saw the possibility that their voices would be heard. The situation became much worse for the Christians in general, since several among them were prominent allies of the rival princes. These included the convert sons of Sunu, the prominent Manchu official, and the Jesuit priest João Mourão (1681–1726), who shared years of exile in Xining with the former prince, Yintang (1683–1726), and eventually was put to death.[81]

The new emperor had not considered Christianity in a favorable light before he came to power. One year after his autocratic rule began, he forced the missionaries, even those with the *piao*, to leave for Canton. For him, Christianity had seduced the people and was useless, so that in the future no Chinese would be allowed to accept such a teaching.[82] Missionaries in the provinces were quickly deported, despite the imperial decree granting up to a half-year for the move. About three hundred churches and residences were confiscated. Some missionaries tried to hide in the mountains or on small junks; some witnessed their churches being

---

[80] Silas H. L. Wu, *Passage to Power: K'ang-hsi and His Heir Apparent, 1661–1722* (Cambridge, 1979), p. 144; Pei Huang, *Autocracy at Work: A Study of the Yung-cheng Period, 1723–1735* (Bloomington, IN, 1974), pp. 48–50.

[81] Hummel, *Eminent Chinese*, pp. 692–694, 915–20, 927–929; John W. Witek, S.J., "Manchu Christians at the Court of Beijing in Early Eighteenth-Century China: A Preliminary Study," in Malatesta and Raguin, eds., *Succès et échecs*, pp. 265–279; Pasquale M. d'Elia, *Il Lontano Confino e la Tragica Morte del P. João Mourão S.I. Missionario in Cina (1681–1726) nella Storia e nella Legenda Secondo Documenti in Gran parte Inediti* (Lisbon, 1963), pp. 16–17, 83–95. On the conversions in the family of Sunu beyond the Yongzheng era, see Chen Yuan, "Yong Qian jian feng Tianzhujiao zhi zongshi (Conversions to Catholicism in the imperial family during the Yongzheng and Qianlong reigns)," in Wu Ze., ed., *Chen Yuan shixue lunzhu xuan* Zhongguo dangdai shixuejia congshu (Shanghai, 1981), pp. 306–343.

[82] *Da Qing lichao shilu*, Yongzheng reign 14:14a–b, 27:16a–b, translated in Fu, *Documentary Chronicle*, pp. 138–140.

changed into grain storehouses or academic halls. In Beijing the emperor continued to attack his erstwhile political opponents in the struggle for succession.

In an address on the occasion of the birthday of the Buddha and the arrival of the Portuguese ambassador Alexandre Metello de Sousa e Meneses in 1727, the Yongzheng emperor indicated that his objection to Christianity was its claim to be the sole truth against what Christian followers contended were the heterodoxies of Buddhism and Taoism. In China, he added, a foreign religion would be banned only if its adoption harmed the normal way of life. In his opinion this was precisely the result of many irrational features of Christianity. Since China and Europe had their respective religious traditions, the European religion need not be practiced in China. Yet because the Westerners were expert calendar makers and their king presented tribute, China would continue to employ their talents.[83]

How useful Europeans were at court, despite the proscription of their religion in the empire, can be seen in the lives of some Jesuits who labored there during the reigns of the Yongzheng and Qianlong emperors. Antoine Gaubil (1689–1759), who arrived in Beijing in April 1723, claimed not many years later that although the emperor looked askance at Christianity, he needed the missionaries for the Bureau of Astronomy, for the conduct of affairs with the Russians, and to operate scientific instruments coming from Europe. Gaubil, "the greatest European sinologue of the eighteenth century," according to Paul Demiéville, had been designated a royal mathematician by Louis XV.[84] He replaced Dominique Parennin as the director of an imperial academy to teach Latin to future Manchu and Chinese diplomatic interpreters. How long the academy lasted and whether any Manchu or Chinese officials became sufficiently proficient in Latin to act as negotiators in Chinese–Russian relations are questions that await further research. Instrumental in furnishing Chinese and Manchu books to the Imperial Academy in St. Petersburg, Gaubil was nominated one of its members. In 1751 the Royal Society of London honored him with membership for his efforts in obtaining scientific information about China. His comparative chronology of the Bible and Chinese history, which included

---

[83] Fu, *Documentary Chronicle*, pp. 155–156.
[84] See Demiéville's preface to Antoine Gaubil, *Correspondance de Pékin, 1722–1759* (Geneva, 1970), p. vii.

detailed analyses of astronomical data, broadened the discussion of these subjects among French savants.[85] This work provided a basis for the general European acceptance of Chinese chronology.

Some missionaries were influential as writers about the history of China. Joseph de Moyriac de Mailla (1669–1748), whose *Histoire générale de la Chine* was a translation of the *Tongjian gangmu* (Summary of the comprehensive mirror for aid in government), by the Song dynasty philosopher and historian Zhu Xi (1130–1200). Updated to include the early Qing era, it has influenced Western historiography about China. A successor of de Mailla was Jean-Joseph Amiot (1718–1793), who arrived at the court in 1750 and devoted his talents to studies of the Chinese people, their languages, and dialects as well as their history and arts. The result of his efforts appeared in the *Mémoires concernant l'histoire, les sciences, les arts, les usages, etc. des Chinois par les missionnaires de Pékin*.[86] Both of these publications were leading sources for the development of Western views on China during the nineteenth century.

A different, but significant role in the intercultural relations of China and the West was that of the missionary artist Lang Shining. The Chinese name of the Jesuit brother Giuseppe Castiglione (1688–1766) is so well known among educated Chinese today that his Western identity is at times forgotten.[87] During his early years of service for the Kangxi emperor, Castiglione concentrated on paintings of natural history. For the Yongzheng emperor, who never allowed him to present them in person, he completed several panoramic paintings of battles and ceremonies. The Qianlong emperor, however, visited Castiglione's studio to admire his outstanding talents. On several occasions, the Jesuit pleaded with the emperor to overturn the condemnation of Christianity and to allow all religious orders to preach in China.[88] Although the emperor was unwilling

---

[85] Witek, "Chinese Chronology," pp. 241–246.

[86] *Mémoires concernant les chinois*, 15 vols. (Paris, 1777–1791); Joseph Dehergne, "Une grand collection. Mémoires concernant les Chinois (1776–1814)," *Bulletin de l'École française de l'Extrême-Orient*, Vol. 72 (1983), pp. 267–298; Joseph de Moyriac de Mailla, S.J., *Histoire générale de la Chine ou annals de cet empire. Traduction du Tong-kien kang-mu*, 13 vols. (Paris, 1777–1785). According to Endymion Wilkinson, de Mailla's work is "still the largest general history of China available in a Western language and has been used by many later textbook writers." *The History of Imperial China: A Research Guide*, Harvard East Asian Monographs, No. 49 (Cambridge, MA, 1973), p. 70.

[87] The interest in Castigilione is reflected in a recent novel by Su Liqun, *Lang Shining Zhuan* (Beijing, 1998).

[88] Pfister, *Notices biographiques*, pp. 635–39; Dehergne, *Répertoire*, pp. 48–49; George R. Loehr, "The Sinicization of Missionary Artists and Their Work at the Manchu Court

to accede to these requests, Castiglione continued his work by painting the imperial conquests of the Ölöds and with the planning and construction of the summer palace (Yuanmingyuan).[89]

## THE MISSIONS AND THE QIANLONG EMPEROR

During the early years of the Qianlong period (1735–1795) the missionaries in Beijing hoped that the new emperor would take into his own hands the issue of the Christian presence in China and not delegate it to his ministers, who generally opposed Christianity as harmful to Chinese civilization. Adopting a policy similar to that of his predecessor, the emperor retained the missionaries in the capital, even allowing replacements to come, but continued to ban them from the provinces during his entire reign. In a society whose elite sought to defend orthodoxy against many internal and external challenges and wherein imperial edicts forbade missionary activity and conversion, Christianity could continue only by keeping a low profile. Yet incidents of discovery and repression, especially when the court intensely feared secret societies and rebellion, threatened that survival. A major persecution lasting several years developed when foreign missionaries were discovered ministering to Chinese Christians in Fuan, Fujian, in 1746. The governor of Fujian, Zhou Xuejian, reported on the foreign connections and financial subsidies and also the "magic tricks and mysterious conduct" prevalent among these groups.[90] The vicar apostolic of Fujian, Pedro Sanz, O.P. (1680–1747), was executed and four other Dominicans were slain in their prison cells.[91] The emperor ordered all

during the Eighteenth Century," *Cahiers d'histoire mondiale,* Vol. 7 (1963), pp. 795–815; Cécile Beurdeley and Michel Beurdeley, *Giuseppe Castiglione: A Jesuit Painter at the Court of the Chinese Emperors* (Rutland, VT, 1971), pp. 39–44; Michèle Pirazzoli-'t Serstevens, "Artistic Issues in the Eighteenth Century," in Standaert, ed., *Handbook,* pp. 823–839.

[89] Zhongguo diyi lishi dang'anguan, ed., *Yuanmingyuan,* 2 vols. in series *Qingdai dang'an shiliao* (Shanghai, 1991), containing more than one thousand documents. On the project to restore this area in recent times, see the periodical Zhongguo Yuanmingyuan Xuehui choubei weiyuanhui, ed., *Yuanmingyuan,* 4 vols. (1981–1986); see also Regine Thiriez, "The 'Mission Palais d'Été' and Its Study of the European Palaces of the Yüan-mingyüan," in Edward J. Malatesta and Yves Raguin, eds., *Images de la Chine. Le Contexte occidental de la sinologie naissante* (San Francisco,, 1995), pp. 139–148.

[90] Zhou Xuejian, a native of Xinjian in Jiangxi province, became a *jinshi* in the first year of the Yongzheng era. For his biography, see *Qing shi gao jiaozhu,* 16 vols. (Taipei, 1986–1991), Vol. 12, p. 9427.

[91] For reports on the 1746 persecution, see José Maria González, O.P., *Misiones Dominicanas en China (1700–1750),* 2 vols. (Madrid, 1952, 1958), Vol. 2, pp. 172–212, and his

local officials to investigate and take action against any Christian groups they found; some reported that they had done so. But local Christian communities survived in Fuan.[92]

Although not a supporter of Christianity, the Qianlong emperor did not always accept at face value what Zhou reported. In July and August he had done so, but the Grand Council said that Zhou should deport to Macao all the foreign missionaries who were arrested. Chinese converts who were most guilty and could not be reformed or reeducated were to be severely punished, but the ignorant people who had been misled were to be freed. The emperor agreed with this approach. However, when Zhou sent a long memorial in November 1746, the emperor said that Zhou had exaggerated his statements, but he was to sentence the guilty according to Chinese law.[93]

The last general persecution of Christianity in the Qianlong period occurred in 1784–1785, when the Qing government learned that four Franciscans, then in Hubei, had intended to travel to Gansu. Just a few days before, the emperor had approved the judicial sentences of several rebel leaders of the 1781 Muslim uprising in that province.[94] Suspecting a Muslim–Christian conspiracy, the officials moved swiftly by conducting trials of the missionaries and Chinese Christians. By late summer of 1785, despite its lengthy investigation, the government found no evidence of a conspiracy, but had uncovered clandestine missionary operations in the provinces. The removal from office, payment of fines, and loss of several grades in rank imposed on the lower officials of the areas where

*História de las Misiones Dominicanas de China*, 5 vols. (Madrid, 1964–1966),Vol. 2. pp. 313–420; see also an account by the Jesuit Jean-Gaspard Chanseaume (1711–1755) sent to Madame de Sauveterre de Saint-Hyacinthe, in Aimé-Martin, ed., *Lettres édifiantes*, Vol. 3. pp. 804–825. The five Dominicans were among the 120 persons canonized by Pope John Paul II in Vatican City on October 1, 2000.

92 Eugenio Menegon, *Ancestors, Virgins, and Friars: The Localization of Christianity in Late Imperial China* (Cambridge, MA, 2009).

93 For the principal Chinese documents on the 1746 persecution, see *Da Qing lichao shilu*, Qianlong reign, *juan* 267:24b–25, 269:24a–b, 271:2b–3a, 275:19–20b, 287:18b–19a, 310:3b–4, 315:8–9, ch. 320: 12b–14, 327:17–18. Translations with a few incorrect citations of the original *juan* numbers are in Fu, *Documentary Chronicle*, pp. 178–185; see also John E. Wills, Jr., "From Manila to Fuan," Asian Contexts of Dominican Mission Policy," in Mungello, ed., *The Chinese Rites Controversy*, pp. 111–127.

94 For the principal Chinese documents, see *Tianzhujiao liuzhuan Zhongguo shiliao* (Chinese historical materials on the transmission of Catholicism), in *Wenxian congbian* (Collectanea of historical documents, Qing dynasty). 2 vols. (Taipei, 1964), Vol. 1, pp. 443–465; see also Bernward H. Willeke, *Imperial Government and Catholic Missions in China During the Years 1784–1785*, Franciscan Institute, Missiology Series 1 (St. Bonaventure, 1948), pp. 46–49, 164–165.

missionaries had been arrested were counterproductive to the central government's concern. Thereafter, such officials overlooked the presence of missionaries.

Another factor that threatened Christianity's continuance in the Qianlong era and afterward was the apostolic constitution *Ex Quo Singulari* (1742) definitively condemning the Chinese rites and explicitly revoking Mezzabarba's "eight permissions." This papal injunction caused discontent among the Christians and the missionaries operating clandestinely in the provinces, because no uniformity in its interpretation and execution could be readily achieved. Even Rome realized that circumstances and customs varied greatly in China, and later instructed the bishops that the goal was to have the Chinese Christians gradually accept the rites of the Roman Church as their own.[95] Such a policy included the abolition of performing the *ketou* (kowtow) in all social and ceremonial settings, the prohibition of using even the Christian ancestral tablets, and the requirement that Christians absent themselves from the funerals of non-Christian relatives and exclude non-Christians from Christian funerals. These prescriptions caused serious problems for the Chinese Christians and the missionaries, especially the bishops, who were ordered to enforce them. Despite the unanimous agreement of the bishops that the kowtow was only a civil act, their petition to Rome was not heeded. In April 1777 the Holy Office declared that the kowtow was intrinsically superstitious and thus forbidden.

Throughout the eighteenth century and especially after the early years of the Yongzheng era, the question of the ordination of native Chinese to the priesthood was never fully resolved by the Jesuits, Propaganda, or any other group working in China. Luo Wenzao (1615–1691, Gregory Lopez), a Dominican, had been named a bishop in the late seventeenth century, and a number of Chinese, including Wu Li (1632–1718), the famous Qing painter, became priests.[96] Propaganda and the missionaries

---

[95] *Collectanea Sacrae Congregationis de Propaganda Fide*, 2 vols. (Rome, 1907), Vol. 1, pp. 130–141; Joseph Krahl, *China Missions in Crisis: Bishop Laimbeckhoven and His Times*, Analecta Gregoriana, No. 137 (Rome, 1964), pp. 176–185; Noll, ed., *100 Documents*, pp. 47–71.

[96] Luo Wenzao ordained Wu Li on August 1, 1688. For a standard biography, see José Maria González, O.P., *El primer obispo chino. Exc.mo Sr. D. Fray Gregorio Lo, o Lopez, O.P.* (Pamplona, 1966).; see also Jarvis Hao Sy, "The Chinese Indigenous Clergy: The Case of the Dominican Gregorio Lo Wen Tsao (1615–1691)," *Philippiniana Sacra*, Vol. 27 (1992), pp. 313–325. On Wu Li as a painter see Laurence C. Tam, *Six Masters of Early Qing and Wu Li* (Hong Kong, 1986), pp. 83–164; on his thought and poetry see Jonathan Chaves, *Singing of the Source: Nature and God in the Poetry of the Chinese Painter Wu Li* (Honolulu, 1993).

saw that the viability of their work would depend heavily on an indigenous clergy, especially during the periods of persecution. In 1725 and in 1785 Propaganda seriously discussed the issues, consulted with various former missionaries to China, and sought further views from the mission itself. Some believed that foreign leadership of the Chinese church was still needed, and when persecution in China abated, Propaganda dropped further discussion of the topic.[97] Chinese priests, albeit in small numbers, continued to serve their people. There were no other Chinese bishops, however, until Pope Pius XI consecrated five Chinese priests in a ceremony in Rome in 1926.

The suppression of the Society of Jesus in Europe adversely affected the China mission. In 1762 the Portuguese government ordered its officials in Macao to arrest all the Jesuits there and deport them to Europe. Soon Spain and France followed the Portuguese lead. In fact, the Bourbon kingdom pressured the papacy for a total suppression of the Jesuit Order, which occurred in July 1773. The former Jesuits were allowed to continue their pastoral work in China on condition that they accept the brief of suppression that was announced in Beijing in 1775. Propaganda administered the property of the former Jesuits and tried to send its own missionaries. But the new arrivals were imprisoned and then expelled from China. After prolonged negotiations in Europe, the Lazarists arrived in Beijing in 1785 and eventually took control of the Beitang.[98] Despite the great efforts of the survivors of the French Jesuit mission and of the newly arrived Lazarists and others in Beijing and elsewhere, the French Revolution and the Napoleonic Wars undermined the entire foreign missionary enterprise in China. Funds and personnel from Europe became scarce. When the Qianlong emperor died in 1799, the vitality of the Catholic mission in China was seriously impaired.

Such impairment never meant the total disappearance of Christianity in China. During the reign of the Jiaqing emperor (1796–1820), there were about 200,000 to 215,000 Christians in nearly all the provinces.[99] Despite the prohibition against foreign missionaries, several managed to circulate in the provinces, where there were never enough native clergy.

---

[97] The issue was also connected with the attempts to introduce literary Chinese into the Catholic liturgy. François Bontinck, *La lutte autour de la liturgie chinoise aux XVIIe et XVIIIe siècles*, (Louvain, 1962), pp. 389–400; see also Chaves, *Singing of the Source*, pp. 47–80.

[98] Lazarists were members of the Congrégation de la Mission, who were also known as Vincentians.

[99] Nicolas Standaert, "Chinese Christians: General Characteristics," in Standaert, ed., *Handbook*, p. 383.

The first areas adversely affected by these shortages were Hunan, Hubei, and the lower Yangzi valley. For example, after 1790 there was no bishop in Nanjing for fourteen years. The frequency of local rebellions during the Jiaqing period created chaotic conditions that left congregations much more on their own. Some persevered under local leadership, but others declined.

In 1805 the court learned that a missionary had sent Rome a map of parts of China. This led to an overall investigation of Catholic practices and institutions, especially in the Beijing area, and the imposition of severe sentences for Chinese and Manchu Catholics, but above all the converts among the bannermen. The new imperial policy of repression and eradication resulted in execution, not deportation, of missionaries discovered in the provinces. Converts were to abjure their faith; refusal meant execution or exile. Search and destroy operations of all Catholic publications, including the woodblocks, were also begun.[100]

These new policies were not uniformly effective in China. One of the most flourishing missions of that time was in Sichuan, where 1,848 adults and more than 2,000 children were baptized in 1807. The arrest of a Chinese priest in Shaanxi in 1811 set off a more general persecution. Several Christians were arrested in Chengdu, Sichuan, and exiled to Yili. This did not adversely affect the Christian presence in Sichuan, which remained substantial owing to the continuing efforts of the Missions Étrangères de Paris and the indigenous clergy.[101]

Events in Beijing in 1811, meanwhile, led to further repercussions against Christianity within an environment of serious concern about the initial signs of opium smoking in southern China. In June the governor-general of Guangdong and Guangxi notified the imperial court that Westerners were smuggling opium. He argued that they knew it was contraband but brought it to make a profit. To stop the use that was beginning to affect various parts of the country, the supply must be cut off, he told the court, a policy that his instructions to the Western merchants underscored. In July the emperor issued an edict in reply to

---

[100] *Da Qing lichao shilu*, Jiaqing reign, 142:20b–26b, 143:1–2, 144:9b, 145:1–2b, with selected translations in Fu, *Documentary Chronicle*, pp. 350–57. See also Lars Peter Laamann, *Christian Heretics In Late Imperial China: Christian Inculturation and State Control, 1720–1850* (London, 2006), pp. 35–36, 70–76.

[101] Robert Entenmann, "Chinese Catholic Clergy and Catechists in Eighteenth-Century Szechwan," in Malatesta and Raguin, eds., *Images de la Chine*, pp. 389–410; Entenmann, "Catholics and Society in Eighteenth-Century China," in Daniel H. Bays, ed., *Christianity in China: From the Eighteenth Century to the Present* (Stanford, CA, 1996), pp. 8–23.

a request from the Board of Punishment (Xingbu) for new regulations to punish Westerners preaching their religion. If they published religious books and promoted assemblies and if the bannermen accepted this teaching and referred to the preachers with the title of "Father," both were to be executed by strangulation without delay. If these preachers affected only a few persons but did not accept the title, they were to be imprisoned and to wait for strangulation after the autumn assizes. Those who followed Catholicism and did not know how to return to the true teaching were to become slaves in Heilongjiang. The emperor insisted that the Westerners at the Board of Astronomy calculate the calendars and not have any contact with the bannermen or the common people. Those not skilled in science or technology were not to stay in Beijing, but were subject to deportation to their own countries.[102] As a result of a long accumulation of negative experiences and decisions, the Beijing court had reached a turning point in its perspective toward the presence of Westerners in China.

CONCLUSION

In the late Ming dynasty, Matteo Ricci had developed a path for Christianity to reenter China by his openness to its ancient civilization, very much facilitated by Chinese leaders who entered into dialogue with him. His Jesuit confreres' continued presence in Beijing during the early Qing period aided other religious orders in establishing mission stations from which to evangelize the cities and rural areas. The number of those involved was never very large, even in the most significant period of growth before the outbreak of the Rites Controversy at the end of the seventeenth century. That the principles of inculturation divided, so harshly at times, those who preached the love of God to the Chinese perhaps is difficult to fathom centuries later. Indeed, the amount of printed eighteenth-century polemical literature on this issue is not slight, and the number of multilingual manuscripts in European libraries is vast. There is, moreover, documentary material in the Qing archives that still needs to be consulted. As a result there can be no

---

[102] See Fu, *Documentary Chronicle*, pp. 381–385. These measures differed from some of those of his father, the Qianlong emperor. In 1785 he freed twelve missionaries who were incarcerated for their clandestine preaching but then were allowed to stay in the churches in Beijing or return to their own countries. See Witek, "Emergence of a Christian Community in Beijing," pp. 114–115.

definitive presentation of the controversy, but only an outline of some major trends of that complex issue.[103]

The impact of the Catholic missions in the early Qing period was largely determined by the attitude of the various emperors. At the outset the missionaries received permission to preach, but the Chinese could not legally become followers of the foreign religion until the 1692 Edict of Toleration. No longer considered a heterodox sect, Christianity was given an open chance to attract Chinese and Manchus to new ideas of God and of humans. During the Yongzheng and Qianlong reigns, such openness no longer existed. But even then, in a curious anticipation of the *tiyong* ideas (Chinese learning for essence and Western learning for practice) of the late nineteenth century, the imperial court and the Chinese elite who rejected Catholicism were still willing to make use of astronomy and arts from the West. In this way they reflected the widespread conservative trend in Chinese culture. As early as 1700 Wang Yuan (1648–1704) in his *Ping Shu* (Comprehensive plan for the reform of government) listed Westerners along with Buddhist monks and nuns, Taoist priests, Muslims, prostitutes, and actors as totally undesirable in Chinese society. He proposed deporting all Westerners, who should then break all relations with China. Li Gong (1659–1733), a follower of the philosophy of Yan Yuan (1635–1704), later edited Wang's work and included the comments of a number of readers. He indicated that one could retain those missionaries "who have talents as mathematicians or technicians but their doctrine" was to be "banned."[104]

After the first years of persecution under the Yongzheng emperor, Chinese and Manchu reactions to Christianity, from those of the highest officials to those of the lowest classes, took various forms. The conversion of several Manchu princes led to that of their wives and the entire household. Such was the case of several sons of Sunu in the later part of the Kangxi period and during the early years of his successor; indeed, some of their descendants were found to be Christians and were exiled to Yili in the crackdown in 1805.[105] Other members of the ruling class in the

---

[103] The first full-length Chinese study of the Rites Controversy is by Li Tiangang, *Zhongguo liyi zhi zheng. Lishi wenxian he yiyi* (Shanghai, 1998). For the first book on the topic in Japanese, see Yazawa Toshihiko, *Chūgoku to Kirisutokyō – Tenrei mondai* (Tokyo, 1972).

[104] Jacques Gernet, *Chine et Christianisme. Action et Réaction* (Paris: Gallimard, 1982), trans. Janet Lloyd as *China and the Christian Impact: A Conflict of Cultures* (Cambridge, 1985), pp. 125–126.

[105] In 1805 two great-grandsons of Sunu refused to retract their belief in Catholicism. Their names were removed from the Manchu genealogy, and they were ordered to wear the

capital and elsewhere became converts, continued to serve the state, but kept the fact of their conversion secret. An example is Depei (1688–1752), who was baptized at the age of thirty and under the Qianlong emperor served as governor or governor-general in several provinces, for example, Anhui, Fujian, and Kiangsi. He supported the efforts of Chinese Christians to practice their faith and did not harass missionaries who had entered those areas clandestinely. In general, the Manchus, bilingual in Chinese and Manchu, relied on Christian writings in Chinese to develop their knowledge of the new religion, for only some of these works were translated into Manchu.[106] Relatively little scholarly attention has focused on the Manchu Christians and their impact in this era, although a number of them were directly related to the imperial clan, which had its own rules and deities different from those of the Chinese.

From the onset of the persecution under the Yongzheng emperor down to the Opium War, Christianity perdured in China. When the Kangxi emperor died in 1722, there were about 200,000 Christians from all walks of life. The Beijing court continued to seek the expert services of the missionaries in astronomy, music, horology, and other types of Western science and technology. Their presence at court meant that the churches in Beijing remained open for most of the rest of the century. Missionaries not directly engaged in court service were the pastors in these churches and were able to work in mission stations up to the Great Wall and in other parts of Zhili (modern Hebei). Knowledge of these activities in the capital area encouraged Chinese Christians elsewhere to continue their religious practices despite the lack of missionary personnel.

Well-trained male and female catechists were vital to the continued presence of Christianity in China. A missionary might be responsible for mission stations scattered over an entire province and might visit them once or twice a year, if at all. The catechists held sessions for those interested in becoming converts and were able to verify the conduct of such neophytes before the latter were baptized and formally entered

cangue for six months before leaving for exile in Yili. *Da Qing lichao shilu*, Jiaqing reign, 146:21b–22, translation in Fu, *Documentary Chronicle*, pp. 357–358.

[106] Witek, "Manchu Christians," pp. 265–267; for a biography of Depei, see Hummel, *Eminent Chinese*, pp. 714–715. In censoring Catholic publications in Chinese, e.g., Verbiest's *Jiaoyao xulun*, the Jiaqing emperor was especially indignant that Manchu bannermen had become Christians. He ordered them to study Manchu, read the books of the Chinese sages, and follow the doctrine of the Confucian classics. Since by no means were they to accept Buddhism or Taoism, it was questionable how they could believe in the Western religion. See *Da Qing lichao shilu*, 144:9b, translation in Fu, *Documentary Chronicle*, pp. 355–56.

the Catholic Church. Catechetical literature in Chinese composed by Dominicans, Franciscans, Jesuits, and others was fairly easily printed and reprinted with woodblocks stored in the local church compound. There are also examples of lay Christian writers who expounded on the reconciliation of Confucianism and Christianity in essays appearing in the late seventeenth and early eighteenth centuries. Among them were Zhang Xingyao, who described how Christianity completed Confucianism in his *Tianzhujiao Rujiao tongyi kao* (Similarities and differences between Christianity and Confucianism, 1705) and Yan Mo in his *Di tian kao* (Investigation of the terms "Lord" and "Heaven").[107] By 1730, however, there were only a handful of native Chinese priests and at times a few foreign missionaries who had secretly entered China to take care of so many Christians dispersed over a vast territory. It was the catechists who led the common prayer services by reading the Scriptures and the lives of the saints. They reminded the community about the observance of holy days and feast days of the church. Since the church buildings had been confiscated or at times were destroyed, services were conducted elsewhere. Peasants in the fields sang the litanies or chanted hymns as part of their liturgy. The children learned from their elders and thus continued such practices. In a number of instances, Chinese Christian women entered marriage and then converted their husbands and the entire family.[108] Nor can one overlook the Chinese from families in the interior of the country, not just from Macao, who studied for the priesthood at the College of the Holy Family set up by an Italian diocesan priest, Matteo Ripa (1682–1746), in Naples from the late 1720s or in the colleges of the Jesuits in France from about 1740.[109] Their influence upon their return to China has so far not been fully explored.

As this book goes to press, prospects for scholarly advance on these and related topics have never been better. Scholars in China are doing research

---

[107] On Zhang's study, see Mungello, *Forgotten Christians*, pp. 96–111; for a penetrating analysis of Yan Mo's essay, see Nicolas Standaert, *The Fascinating God: A Challenge to Modern Chinese Theology Presented by a Text on the Name of God Written by a 17th Century Chinese Student of Theology*, Working Papers on Living Faith and Cultures, No. 17 (Rome, 1995), esp. pp. 61–78. Additional comments on Yan Mo's essay are in Huang Yinong, "Bei hulue di shengyin," pp. 139–146.

[108] Aimé-Martin, ed., *Lettres édifiantes*, Vol. 3, p. 785; Vol. 4, p. 91.

[109] For a biography of Ripa, see Christophe Comentale, *Matteo Ripa, peintre-graveur-missionnaire à la cour de Chine. Mémoires traduits, présentés et annotés* (Taipei, 1983). The manuscripts of his journal have been published as *Giornale (1705–1724)*, ed. Michele Fatica (Naples, 1991–1996). About the two Jesuits Gao Ren (1732–1795) and Yang Dewang (1733–1798?), both from Beijing who went to Paris and returned to China, see Dehergne, *Répertoire*, pp. 133–134, 301.

that strives to be free of prejudice and is sophisticated in approach.[110] There are important new guides to research[111] and source publications; the most exciting of the latter are the Chinese works preserved in the Xujiahui Library in Shanghai and in the Jesuit Archives in Rome.[112] The tendency toward "indigenization" of the study of Christianity in China, toward seeing Christianity as a Chinese religion among other Chinese religions,[113] is interacting in powerful ways with the interest among Catholic intellectuals in "inculturation," in the opening of the gospel message to the symbols and practices of non-Western cultures.[114] The long-run result is sure to be a merging of the topics of this chapter in the mainstream of historical study of early modern China and the interconnected early modern world.

By offering Western science and mathematics to the Chinese and the Manchus, the Jesuits created a positive dialogue. In order to present Christianity, Matteo Ricci in the late Ming era and those who followed him through the early Qing period knew that they needed to convince the Chinese that the West was civilized even as they simultaneously sought to understand and appreciate Chinese civilization. Joseph Needham noted that if bringing the science and mathematics of Europe to China was for the Jesuits "a means to an end, it stands for all time nevertheless as an example of cultural relations at the highest level between two civilizations theretofore sundered."[115] The principles of inculturation of Christianity within Chinese civilization, though not totally accepted by all the missionaries and at times not well received by the Chinese, contributed to a more comprehensive view of the missionary endeavor. Such an appreciation of China stands in sharp contrast to the forced entry into Canton during the Opium War in the mid-nineteenth century. That event the Chinese continue to consider offensive, if not intolerable. The earlier missionary entry, however, merits attention even today in Beijing. On a

---

[110] An excellent example is Han Qi, *Zhongguo kexue jishu di xi chuan ji qi yingxiang* (Shijiazhuang, 1999).
[111] Standaert, ed., *Handbook.*
[112] Albert Chan, S.J., *Chinese Books and Documents in the Jesuit Archives in Rome: A Descriptive Catalogue: Japonica-Sinica I–IV* (Armonk, NY, 2001); Nicolas Standaert, Adrian Dudink, Huang Yinong, and Zhu Pingyi, eds., *Xujiahui cangshulou Ming Qing Tianzhujiao wenxian*, 5 vols. (Taipei, 1996; Nicolas Standaert and Adrian Dudink, eds., *Chinese Christian Texts from the Roman Archives of the Society of Jesus. Yesuhui Luoma dang'anguan Ming Qing Tianzhujiao wenxian*, 12 vols. (Taipei, 2002).
[113] The landmark collection is Bays, ed., *Christianity in China.*
[114] Standaert, *The Fascinating God.*
[115] Joseph Needham, *Chinese Astronomy and the Jesuit Mission: An Encounter of Cultures* (London, 1958), p. 9.

remaining rampart of the old city wall, the astronomical instruments that Schall, Verbiest, and their successors used still stand for all to see. A few miles away is the Li Madou mu (Matteo Ricci cemetery), where the monuments of more than sixty missionaries of the old China mission were recently restored.[116] The one site points to heaven, the other to earth. Together they are a coordination of opposites so integral to traditional Chinese thought and civilization.

[116] Edward Malatesta, S.J., and Gao Zhiyu, eds., *Departed, Yet Present: Zhalan, the Oldest Christian Cemetery in Beijing* (Macao, 1995). Moreover, tombstones of twenty French and four Chinese Jesuits of the early Qing period are now located on the grounds of the Five Towers Temple (Wuta si) in Beijing. Nearby are tombstones of nine European and six Chinese Vincentians (Lazarists). The final sentence of the Chinese and English stone marker entitled "Tombstones of the Jesuits" reads, "Visiting China during Ming and Qing dynasty, the Jesuits not only did missionary work, but also brought China the modern scientific knowledge and took the ancient Chinese civilizations and sciences to Europe." An illustration of the marker is in Thierry Meynard, *Following the Footsteps of the Jesuits in Beijing: A Guide to Sites of Jesuit Work and Influence in Beijing* (St. Louis, 2006), p. 71.

# 4

# Trade and Diplomacy with Maritime Europe, 1644–c. 1800

## John L. Cranmer-Byng† and John E. Wills, Jr.

The connections summarized in this chapter show the early and middle Qing Empire involved in global changes. Tea from China was one of the transoceanic consumer goods that helped to stimulate the steady growth of intercontinental maritime connections and the emergence in northwestern Europe of prosperous and dynamic bourgeois societies. Chinese porcelain was less important in trade-value terms but very important for European consumption patterns and *rêves chinois*.[1] The export of tea shaped several sectors of the south Chinese economy, provided a convenient flow of revenue for the imperial household, and drew an inflow of silver vital to the monetization of the Chinese economy. By 1780–1800 other waves of world-historical change were reaching Fujian and Guangdong: ships from the new United States, some of them bringing Pacific sea otter skins and Hawaiian sandalwood; and private traders from the emerging British Empire in India bringing opium. The Qing rulers viewed these maritime connections with trepidation, recalling the early Qing–Ming loyalist resistance along the coast and never sure of the loyalty of Chinese settled in Southeast Asian ports. The maritime Chinese returned the distrust; very little of their rich knowledge of European and Southeast Asian trading partners made its way into print or into the files of the Qing bureaucracy. Qing wariness of the cultural contamination brought by Roman Catholic missionaries sometimes affected their attitudes toward European traders, especially the Portuguese of Macao. The result was a China involved in

---

[1] John E. Wills, Jr., "European Consumption and Asian Production in the Seventeenth and Eighteenth Centuries," in John Brewer and Roy Porter, eds., *Consumption and the World of Goods* (London, 1993), pp. 133–147.

an interactive early modern world in a variety of ways but with a ruling elite largely in denial, especially about the maritime connections. In the great trade at Canton, the traders and the Qing got what they wanted with a minimum of exchange of opinion and information and almost no foreign travel within the empire. Europeans could and did trade without sending tribute embassies to Beijing.

## EARLY QING, 1644–1690

The patterns of relations with maritime Europeans in the 1690s were different from what they had been in the 1630s.[2] The changes in the intervening decades cannot be understood without attention to the stages of Qing conquest and dynastic consolidation, but some of the most striking changes, like the Zheng conquest of Taiwan, were peripheral to that process or, like the expulsion of the Portuguese from Japan, were completely unrelated to it. Macao survived the immense blow of the exclusion from Japan, strengthened its trading connections with the sandalwood islands of eastern Indonesia, and eventually emerged as an important center of the Indian Ocean–South China Sea "country trade" of the eighteenth century. However, it did not recover its earlier prosperity or its centrality in Sino-European relations.[3] The Dutch and Zheng Zhilong, sometimes competing and sometimes cooperating, were not slow to take advantage of the immense opportunity for trade with Japan presented to them by the collapse of the expulsion of the Portuguese. They already had begun to expand their trade to Nagasaki as the Portuguese position there disintegrated in the late 1630s and continued to do so in the early 1640s. Quantities of Sino-Japanese trade between 1644 and the reopening of Qing maritime trade in 1684 are difficult to sort out.[4]

During these decades of disturbance, the Qing court and bureaucracy took their first steps toward establishing policies to manage commercial and political relations with Europeans. The lack of thriving trades and vigorous commercial interests in these decades gave the new dynasty

---

[2] See Wills, Chapter 1, this volume.

[3] George Bryan Souza, *The Survival of Empire: Portuguese Trade and Society in China and the South China Sea, 1630–1754* (Cambridge, 1986); John E. Wills, Jr., *Embassies and Illusions: Dutch and Portuguese Envoys to K'ang-hsi, 1666–1687*, Harvard East Asian Monographs, No. 113 (Cambridge MA, 1984), Chs. 3 and 4.

[4] Iwao Seiichi, "Kinsei Nisshi bōeki ni kansuru sūryōteki kōsatsu," *Shigaku zasshi*, Vol. 62, No. 1 (1953), pp. 1–40; Robert L. Innes, *The Door Ajar: Japan's Foreign Trade in the Seventeenth Century* (Ph.D. dissertation, University of Michigan, 1980), pp. 407–432.

some breathing space to experiment and change policies numerous times before it began to consolidate its own coherent approach in the 1680s. As in many aspects of ruling China, the Qing took Ming precedents as starting points. However, these did not offer much guidance for dealing with maritime Europeans. In the early and middle Ming, all relations with other polities were supposed to be managed in the framework of the tribute system. All foreign rulers visiting the Ming court or sending ambassadors to it had to accept ceremonial and documentary forms that portrayed them as tributaries paying homage to the Son of Heaven. Trade by foreigners in Chinese ports, border towns, or the capital was allowed only in conjunction with tribute embassies, and no Chinese were legally permitted to travel outside Ming territory except on rare official missions. The frequency of embassies, the number of people in an embassy party, even the number of ships that brought them were carefully prescribed. This elaborate system presented a possible model for dealing with traders from maritime Europe, but it had never been successfully applied to relations with them. In 1517–1524 a Portuguese embassy had been rejected. Local authorities allowed the Portuguese to settle at Macao in 1557, but it probably was not until after 1600 that the court realized that the inhabitants of Macao were the same people who had been banned from the empire in the 1520s. By that time, Macao was firmly entrenched in a new order of coastal administration that did not so much violate the tribute system as ignore it, licensing a large-scale overseas trade in Chinese ships and taxing that trade and the trade of the Portuguese at Macao and Canton in order to supplement provincial revenues.[5]

This new order also made possible trade relations with other Europeans that left questions of diplomatic form in abeyance. In 1567, after much confusion and debate, the Ming permitted and established controls on maritime trade in Chinese vessels, especially from Haicheng near Zhangzhou. The Spanish settled at Manila in 1571, but Chinese traders went to them there, and nothing came of Spanish efforts to acquire a coastal entrepôt like Macao. The Dutch eruption into East Asian waters in the 1620s was one of several catalysts of major political changes in coastal China. The Dutch first appeared on the coast as marauders, were never legally welcome to trade in Chinese ports, and eventually were mollified and kept at a distance by the large-scale trade in Chinese ships to Casteel Zeelandia on Taiwan.

[5] See Wills, Chapter 1, this volume.

The Portuguese presence at Macao was confirmed by the Qing court as early as 1647, and reconfirmed in 1650, after the Qing lost and retook Canton. It was hoped that the taxes on their trade would help to pay the Qing armies. Despite flowery rhetoric about how the Portuguese had "scaled the mountains and navigated the seas before they had a chanced to look upon the brilliance of the Celestial Empire,"[6] they were not required to send a tribute embassy; there was no Ming precedent for their doing so. In these first years of Qing rule, Macao profited greatly from the special relations of Jesuit missionaries with the Shunzhi elite. The personal relations of the Shunzhi emperor with Johann Adam Schall von Bell are well known.[7] Equally important for Macao was the interest in Roman Catholicism of high officials in Canton. Tong Yangjia, who submitted the first memorial in favor of Macao in 1647, was a member of an immensely powerful Manchu–Chinese family that included important patrons and converts of the Jesuits.[8] The feudatory prince Shang Kexi and his son Zhixin also were on good terms with the missionaries, and commercial ties with them and their client-merchants were important for Macao in the 1650s.[9]

Portuguese and Jesuit ties with the ruling elite were one source of the difficulties the Dutch East India Company encountered when it tried to open relations with the Qing in the 1650s.[10] Ming precedents were another. In 1651–1652 Martin Martini, S.J., passing through Batavia on his way to Europe, remarked that the new Qing government seemed more hospitable to foreigners than the Ming had been. The ruling council of the company in the Netherlands already had been urging the Batavia authorities to consider an embassy to China, and trade profits on Taiwan seemed to be declining. In 1652, on instructions from Batavia, the Dutch on Taiwan sent an exploratory mission to Canton. Chinese officials recalled that the Dutch had never been welcome in Chinese ports, and the Macao authorities did all they could to oppose them, but the feudatory princes, Shang Kexi and Geng Jimao, allowed them to carry on a

---

[6] Lo-shu Fu, *A Documentary Chronicle of Sino-Western Relations (1644–1820)*, 2 vols. (Tucson, 1966), p. 9.

[7] See Witek, Chapter 3, this volume.

[8] Pamela Crossley, "The Tong in Two Worlds: Cultural Identities in Liaodong and Nurgan during the 13th–17th Centuries," *Ch'ing-shih wen-t'i*, Vol. 4, No. 9 (June 1983), pp. 21–46; John E. Wills, Jr., "Contingent Connections: Fujian, the Empire, and the Early Modern World," in Lynn A. Struve, ed., *The Qing Formation in World-Historical Time* (Cambridge, MA, 2004), pp. 188–191.

[9] Wills, *Embassies and Illusions*, pp. 84–86.

[10] On Dutch relations with the Qing in the 1650s see ibid., pp. 40–44.

trade in which the princes themselves were major investors and told them they could pick out a site for a permanent factory. But before they left in March 1653 they were told they should send an embassy to Beijing to request trading privileges. When the Dutch on Taiwan ignored this directive and sent another trading voyage to Canton in the summer of 1653, it was sent away without any trade. The change in attitudes at Canton from 1652 to 1653 probably resulted partly from the general recovery of the Qing government from near disintegration after the death of the powerful regent Dorgon and partly from a turning back toward Ming models of foreign relations after it was decided in the fall of 1652 that it would be inappropriate for the Son of Heaven to go out beyond the Great Wall to meet the Dalai Lama while he was on tour in Mongolia.

Batavia sent an embassy in 1655 under Pieter de Goyer and Jacob de Keyser.[11] After many delays the ambassadors were received in audience on October 2, 1656. They performed all tributary ceremonies without hesitation, thus making "Holland" the first European power to be received into the tribute system. "Holland" (Helan) referred to the Dutch East India Company and the "king of Holland" to its governor-general in Batavia; cognate terms were generally used throughout the Indian Ocean, and the Qing authorities rarely betrayed any understanding of the difference between Java and the Netherlands. The Dutch, for their part, only occasionally understood that in Qing eyes they were presenting tribute, and even then did not care. They reminded themselves that in reality Beijing received such embassies from many powerful and independent states. Dutch requests for coastal trading privileges were supported by the feudatory princes in Canton, to whom the Dutch had promised 35,000 taels if such privileges were granted and who also would profit from their own involvement in any trade permitted to the Dutch. The Dutch proposed that they send an embassy every five years and be allowed to trade every year, and recorded that some in Beijing, especially Manchus, had been ready to approve this. But the final decision was for an embassy every eight years and trade only in conjunction with embassies. This curious throwback to mid-Ming restrictiveness owed something to the efforts of Schall, doing all he could to protect Macao from Dutch competition, but

[11] Leonard Blussé, *Tribuut aan China: Vier Eeuwen Nederlands–Chinese Betrekkingen* (Amsterdam, 1989), pp. 61–62; for images of China that were published in Europe as a result of this embassy see Leonard Blussé and R. Falkenburg, *Johan Nieuhofs Beelden van een Chinareis, 1655–1657* (Middelburg, 1987). See also Henriette de Bruyn Kops, "Not Such an 'Unpromising Beginning': The First Dutch Trade Embassy to China, 1655–1657," *Modern Asian Studies*, Vol. 36, No. 3 (2002), pp. 535–578.

more to Qing policies of economic warfare against Zheng Chenggong, adopted in August 1656. To ward off attacks from the sea, coastal defenses were improved, the Zheng network of merchant contacts in China uprooted, and all maritime trade in Chinese vessels forbidden. As at several times under the Ming, restrictive policies toward Chinese trade also led to new barriers to foreign trade in Chinese harbors. In addition, the Qing authorities must have known that Zheng traded with the Dutch on Taiwan, and thus would have viewed Dutch trading privileges in their ports as a leak in their blockade.

Although in the eyes of the Qing court the Dutch had no more business on the China coast until 1664, they did manage to buy and sell small amounts of goods in the Canton delta in 1657 and 1658. In 1661–1662 their situation was transformed by Zheng Chenggong's conquest of Taiwan. Trading privileges in mainland ports were much more important to the Dutch now that they had lost their offshore entrepôt. In their eyes revenge against Zheng and his successors was morally and politically necessary. Already in 1661 Qing local authorities had expressed interest in obtaining Dutch naval help against the Zheng regime and had promised rewards for it.[12] If the rewards took the form of trading privileges, both Dutch goals would be achieved at once.

In 1662–1665 the Dutch East India Company sent three substantial fleets to the Fukien coast under Balthasar Bort to cooperate with Qing forces in attacking the Zheng regime.[13] A Dutch fleet made a large, though perhaps not indispensable, contribution to the expulsion of Zheng forces from Amoy and Quemoy (Jinmen) in November 1663. But the Qing found the Dutch difficult allies, rude, impatient, prone to unilateral action against the common enemy, and most important simply a dangerous presence because of the firepower of their ships. The Zheng forces fled their last coastal strongholds early in 1664, and in 1665 the Qing lost interest in an attack on Zheng-controlled Taiwan. Thereafter, the Qing government had little reason to conciliate the Dutch even if these dangerous allies had behaved themselves.

The Dutch found the loose alliance even less satisfactory. They never understood or accepted the inevitable delays of Qing bureaucratic decision making. Qing negotiations for the surrender of Zheng commanders, sensible in a civil war, seemed to them cowardly and treacherous acts of

---

[12] John E. Wills, Jr., *Pepper, Guns, and Parleys: The Dutch East India Company and China, 1662–1681* (Cambridge, MA, 1974), p. 26.

[13] Ibid., Chs. 2 and 3.

dealing with the enemy. And the Dutch got the trading privileges they were seeking only in very limited and insecure forms. They were allowed to sell the cargoes brought on the three fleets as special favors to facilitate military cooperation. As a reward for their aid, in November 1663 they were granted permission to trade every other year. The privilege was enjoyed just once, in 1665, the very year in which the Dutch unwittingly made themselves less welcome. They did not send an embassy, although one had been due in 1664. They sent ships in three groups to two different ports, making administrative and reporting difficulties for the officials. Worst of all, when two Dutch ships cruising off Zhejiang for Zheng ships anchored off the great Buddhist sanctuary island of Putuoshan, their crews plundered some temples there, and local authorities reported this to Beijing. When the Dutch left Fuzhou at the end of the year, they were told that orders had been sent to all coastal officials that no more Dutch ships were to be allowed in Chinese harbors until an embassy was sent.[14]

An embassy was sent in 1666, under Pieter van Hoorn, and was received in Beijing in June 1667.[15] But its arrival led to a review of recent difficulties with the Dutch, and after the fall from power of Sunahai, one of the leading shapers of coastal policy in the previous years, the Dutch biennial trading privilege was revoked. According to this decision, after the departure of the embassy there would be no legal Dutch trade in Chinese ports until 1674![16] In Beijing, Van Hoorn could not obtain any discussion or explanation of this decision or any other substantive issue. He was even forbidden to open within the empire routine replies sent to the governor-general at Batavia. The ships that came to fetch him in 1667 had to take away their entire cargoes unsold. Two ships sent to Canton in 1668 sold only a very small quantity of goods, and that illegally.[17]

In Chinese official sources, relations with the Dutch in this period are fitted into the style and categories inherited from the Ming tribute system. A new tributary ruler is enrolled and given a statutory interval and route for tribute embassies. He then sends military aid, and he and his commanders receive presents and edicts of praise; a biennial trading privilege is granted in addition to the usual trade in connection with embassies, and the privilege is later revoked; a second embassy comes, and its

[14] Ibid,, p. 133.
[15] Wills, *Embassies and Illusions*, Ch. 2.
[16] Ibid., pp. 76–77.
[17] Wills, *Pepper*, pp. 139–144.

tributary presents and the imperial gifts in return are recorded in detail. We see no reason to doubt that Qing statesmen thought of other sovereigns as inferior to the emperor and of all formal embassies to Beijing as tribute embassies, when they thought about such matters at all. There was no chance that an embassy would be received at Beijing without performing the tributary ceremonies; the rejection of the Russian embassy of F. I. Baykov in 1656 makes that clear.[18] The Dutch could not have obtained their initial permission to trade if they had not sent an embassy, but the limitation of trade to that in conjunction with embassies had not been in effect in the late Ming, and its revival at this time was largely the result of the temporary imperatives of economic warfare against the Zheng regime. Similarly, the revocation of their biennial trading privilege was less a principled reversion to the early Ming system than a response to particular changes in Qing politics and particular offenses by the Dutch, of which their failure to send an embassy on schedule was by no means the most important.

The Portuguese also sent an embassy to Beijing in the 1660s, but an account of Sino-Portuguese relations centered on it would be even more misleading than a "tribute system" account of relations with the Dutch.[19] The embassy was sent to save Macao, and the center of this story is the impact on Macao of coastal evacuation and changing relations with officials in Canton.[20] When the Guangdong coast was ordered evacuated in 1662, all Chinese were forced to leave Macao, and the food supply of the remaining Portuguese and Eurasians was sharply curtailed. Shang Kexi cooperated with the Jesuits in efforts to obtain from the court at least exemption of Macao's non-Chinese population from the coastal evacuation decrees and, if possible, permission for Macao to continue its maritime trade. They thought they had succeeded, but then the regents reversed the favorable recommendations of the boards and ordered that all foreigners be sent away from Macao and all fortifications there be razed. This reversal may have come at about the same time as the regents' rejection of proposed Dutch trading privileges early in 1664 and may also have been linked to fearful reactions to the Dutch demonstrations of European naval power. Finally the Jesuits and their allies secured permission for non-Chinese to stay in Macao, but not for their maritime trade.

---

[18] Mark Mancall, *Russia and China: Their Diplomatic Relations to 1728* (Cambridge MA, 1971), pp. 45–53.
[19] Wills, *Embassies and Illusions*, Ch. 3.
[20] Ibid., pp. 83–101.

The situation was further complicated by the arrest of all missionaries in 1665, depriving Macao of its most influential and capable allies. Macao barely survived, its trade almost entirely cut off.

Then in February 1667 orders arrived that all the people in Macao were to be moved inland. This reversal of the previous toleration of Macao seems to have come about the same time as the revocation of the Dutch biennial trading privilege, and some of the same political changes in Beijing probably contributed to it. But the Macao authorities promised 250,000 taels to the governor-general of Guangdong and Guangxi if he would not cut off their food supplies and would write to Beijing in their favor. This was sufficient to keep Macao alive until late August, when it was learned that the court had accepted the governor-general's recommendation and exempted Macao from coastal evacuation. Macao's future was further ensured when Shang Kexi, seeing an opportunity in the emperor's assumption of ruling powers, reported to the court on the governor-general's extortions, leading to the latter's imprisonment and suicide, and causing the emperor to see Macao as an unfortunate victim of official extortion.

The four-year-long black comedy of the embassy of Manoel de Saldanha illustrates the masterfulness of the Kangxi emperor, Jesuit finesse, and the incompetence and factiousness of colonial outposts. The arrival of the embassy in 1667 probably contributed to Macao's new lease on life. It stayed in Canton until January 1670, partly because of the ambassador's reluctance to turn over to the authorities there the royal letter to the emperor or to show the presents being taken to him. The Canton officials probably tolerated this delay because the presence of the embassy legalized their trade with Macao and because the political situation in Beijing made the prospects for a Jesuit-connected embassy very uncertain. These prospects improved markedly after the emperor's coup against Oboi in June 1669.

When the Saldanha embassy finally reached Beijing in June 1670, the emperor demonstrated his break with the policies of Oboi and his partiality to the Jesuits by ostentatious signs of favor to the embassy. These gestures probably helped to defend Macao against renewed proposals for its extinction, but could not protect it from official extortion or from the competition of foreign traders in the nearby islands in the 1670s. The embassy had obeyed, sometimes unwittingly or unwillingly, all the rules for a tribute embassy and had been recorded as such, but no fixed interval had been established for Portuguese embassies. The letter Saldanha brought in the name of the king of Portugal declared that he was sent to congratulate the new emperor upon his succession to the throne. In Canton the Jesuits had seized on this to secure the change of the characters on its banners from *jin gong*, "presenting tribute," to *jin he*, "presenting congratulations." The Jesuits were convinced that they had won an epochal victory over the pretensions of the tribute system, but in fact *jin he* had been altogether acceptable within the system for centuries.[21] The Portuguese and their Jesuit advisers made the same terminological distinction in the two eighteenth-century Portuguese embassies, thereby convincing themselves that their involvement in the tribute system in no way compromised the honor of the king of Portugal.

A second Portuguese embassy under Bento Pereira de Faria in 1678 brought the emperor a lion from Mozambique but was otherwise entirely organized in Macao.[22] Qing officials had been careful about documenting the authenticity of the Saldanha embassy, but do not seem to have raised any objections to the irregularities of this one. The emperor was fascinated by the lion and had some of his courtiers write poems about it. His personal attention again enhanced the prestige of the embassy. Pereira de Faria quite sensibly left substantive negotiations in the capable hands of the Jesuits, and soon inspectors were sent from Beijing to visit Macao. Late in 1679 Macao's land trade with Canton was fully legalized. According to Portuguese sources its maritime trade was legalized in the fall of 1680. It is clear that from then to 1684 the Qing authorities treated Macao's trade differently from that of its would-be Dutch, English, and Chinese competitors, but the Chinese sources do not confirm that its maritime trade was fully legalized.

In the years 1676–1680 the Qing court and officials in Fujian again showed interest in obtaining Dutch naval aid against the Zheng regime, then occupying parts of southern Fujian as well as Taiwan, and even sent low-ranking emissaries to Batavia in 1679–1680. The Dutch, convinced that they had been used and then betrayed in the 1660s, were not much interested, and the negotiations got nowhere. But in the meantime the Dutch were allowed to trade every year in Fuzhou, although they had not sent an embassy since 1666–1667. The tribute system was less and less the center of the Qing government's relations with Europeans.[23]

By 1690 the linkage between tribute and trade had disappeared for Europeans. From 1684 on, trade in Chinese ports was open to all

---

[21] Ibid., pp. 114–115.
[22] Ibid., Ch. 4.
[23] Wills, *Pepper*, Ch. 4.

foreigners, regardless of whether their rulers had ever been enrolled as tributaries, and maritime trade was taxed and controlled by special agents of the court. These were changes in political economy, not in the dynamics of trade. European demand for Chinese goods was weak. The market for tea was just beginning to grow, and cheaper Bengal raw silk was undercutting demand for the Chinese product. The great economic change of the decade was the great surge of Chinese shipping and emigration that followed the full legalization of Chinese maritime trade.[24]

Qing decision making was focused on the permission and taxation of Chinese trade and Chinese overseas voyages; the application of these basic decisions to foreign traders was an afterthought. The surrender of the Zheng regime in Taiwan to the Qing in 1683 eliminated the economic warfare rationale for trade restrictions. In the summer of 1684, the emperor permitted maritime trading and fishing voyages from Chinese ports and dispatched metropolitan officials to supervise the taxation of maritime trade for three years; on the basis of their receipts and recommendations, quotas then would be established for each province. At first it was thought that after three years maritime customs collection might revert to the regular provincial officials, but maritime customs superintendents, the "hoppo" of the later Canton trade, remained in control of the Fujian customs until 1729 and the Canton customs until 1842. The emperor was aware that full legalization and effective central control of maritime trade were not in the interests of the high officials of the coastal provinces, who for years had profited from illegal trade dominated by their client-merchants. The presence of the maritime customs superintendents in the port cities eventually undercut provincial officials' domination of trade and allowed more merchants to participate. From 1685 on, the superintendents were allowed to levy tolls only on maritime trade, and in 1686 separate guilds were established in Guangdong for internal and maritime trade; one firm might belong to both, but it had to maintain a separate establishment for each. Thus the fundamentals of specialized official supervision and a specialized mercantile body for foreign trade, the foundations of the eighteenth-century Canton system, were established for the control and taxation of Chinese merchants, whether they traded with foreigners in Chinese

---

[24] John E. Wills, Jr., "China's Farther shores: Continuities and Changes in the Destination Ports of China's Foreign Trade, 1680–1690," in Roderick Ptak and Dietmar Rothermund, eds., *Emporia, Commodities, and Entrepreneurs in Asian Maritime Trade, c. 1400–1750*, Beiträge zur Südasienforschung, Südasien-Institut, Universität Heidelberg, No. 141 (Stuttgart, 1992), pp. 53–77.

ports or sent their own ships abroad, with no explicit reference to the foreigners who might be involved.[25]

The Portuguese, the English, and the Dutch all played catalytic roles in fitting European trade in Chinese ports into this framework. In 1682 communications from Macao and its Jesuit allies to the court combined with the vigorous administration of a new governor of Guangdong to cut off the illegal trade of its Chinese and European competitors in the nearby islands. In 1683 the Canton officials showed some interest in making Macao the center of all foreign trade, but the Portuguese were opposed and the idea was dropped. Later the Jesuits reportedly supported throwing maritime trade open to all, hoping that if all paid tolls the fiscal burden on Macao would be reduced.

The English had traded with the Zheng regime on Taiwan and Amoy since 1670 and had sold it some arms. In 1684 an English ship arrived at Amoy with a cargo that included guns, gunpowder, and lead. The Qing authorities voiced well-founded suspicions that these had been intended for the Zheng regime and would not allow the English any trade until most of the munitions had been turned over as a gift to the emperor. In return for this they were permitted to trade toll free in 1684 and were told they might come again in 1685. As far as we can tell nothing was said about their sending a tribute embassy.[26]

When the Dutch also sought to trade at Amoy in 1684, the Ministries of War and Ceremonies recommended that they should not be allowed to trade until they sent an embassy. The emperor decided that the harbors of the empire should be open to all, apparently without reference to tributary status, but that the Dutch would not be allowed to trade again until they sent an embassy. They did so in 1685, with Vincent Paats as ambassador.[27] It accomplished nothing for the Dutch, and the Dutch were told that the emperor had complained of the expense and expressed his wish that no more embassies come. There would not be another maritime European embassy for commercial purposes for a

[25] Peng Zeyi, "Qingdai Guangdong yanghang zhidu qiyuan," *Lishi yanjiu*, 1 (1957), pp. 1–25. For a full account of these interrelated changes in the 1680s see John E. Wills, Jr., *Toward the Canton System: Maritime Trade and Qing Policy, 1680–1690*, in preparation. The term "hoppo" used by foreigners for the superintendent of maritime customs had its origin in the dispatch of ministers from the capital, most often the Ministry of Revenue (Hu Bu) to fill this post. In one case, when the local superintendent was from the Ministry of Works (Gong Bu), the Dutch called him "the kampo."

[26] H. B. Morse, *Chronicles of the East India Company Trading to China*, 5 Vols. (Oxford, 1926–1929; reprint, Taipei, 1966), vol. 1, pp. 52–57.

[27] Wills, *Embassies and Illusions*, Ch. 5.

century. This break with the tribute system pattern can also be seen in other diplomatic relations, especially in the relations with Russia and Inner Asia that were so much more vital to Qing statecraft than the maritime relations discussed here. The tribute pattern remained in place for the states culturally tied to China – Korea, Ryukyu, and Vietnam – and for mainland Southeast Asia, including Siam, which maintained an important maritime trade within the tribute framework.[28] The fundamentals of taxation and control of foreign trade in Chinese ports were quickly established, largely on precedents worked out for the trade at Haicheng, Fujian, in late Ming. Ships paid a "measurement" tax, and their import goods were taxed according to elaborate tables of unit taxes on various kinds of goods. Agents of the imperial court were dispatched as superintendents of maritime customs for the Jiangnan, Fujian, and Guangdong. Practices and policies were very similar to those for inland toll barriers. The astute Kangxi emperor viewed all this from a considerable distance, managing at the same time hazardous relations with the Mongols and a canny domestication of the scholar-official elite and their Neo-Confucian convictions and quarrels.[29]

In the late 1680s, Macao sent an embassy to revive its old connection with Siam[30] and enjoyed a modest prosperity in the shadow of the immense Chinese maritime trades.[31] After 1690 the Dutch sent no more ships to China, but depended on the growing Chinese trade to Batavia for supplies of Chinese goods.[32] The English, with no port of their own regularly visited by Chinese shipping, expanded their investment both in the trade of the English East India Company and in private trade from Madras in the late 1680s. Between 1690 and 1699, the effects of the conflict between the old and new companies and the many private trade voyages make it impossible to get from surviving sources more than a

---

[28] John E. Wills, Jr., "Functional, Not Fossilized: Qing Tribute Relations with Annam (Vietnam) and Siam (Thailand), 1700–1820," *T'oung Pao*, in press.

[29] Huang Guosheng, *Yapian zhanzheng qian de dongnan si sheng haiguan* (Fuzhou, 2000), pp. 21–46, 89–92, 219–259; Gang Zhao, "Geopolitical Integration and Domestic Harmony: Foreign Trade Policy in Qing China, 1684–1757" (typescript, 2009), Chs. 4, 5, 6; Wills, *Toward the Canton System*, Chs. 4, 5.

[30] Leonor de Seabra, *A Embaixada ao Sião de Pero Vaz de Siqueira (1684–1686)* (Macao, 2000); English translation by Custódio Cavaco Martins, Mário Pinharanda Nunes, and Alan Norman Baxter, *The Embassy of Pero Vaz de Siqueira to Siam (1684–1686)* (Macao, 2005).

[31] Wills, *Toward the Canton System*, Ch. 7.

[32] Ibid., Ch. 9. Leonard Blussé, "No Boats to China: The Dutch East India Company and the Changing Pattern of the China Sea Trade, 1635–1690.", *Modern Asian Studies* Vol. 30, No. 1 (1996), 51–76.

fragmentary picture of English trade to China. Scattered references show that by 1700 Thomas Pitt and other Madras-based private traders were regularly sending ships to Canton and Amoy, where there were many competing traders, Chinese and foreign, and profits were erratic.[33]

PEACEFUL EXPANSION, 1700–1740

By 1690 economic conditions in China were moving out of the "Kangxi depression." The expansion of trade and emigration in Chinese ships remained the most important phenomenon in maritime China in terms of the amount of shipping, value of trade, and effects on imperial policy. The most dynamic expansions were in voyages and emigration to Java, to Taiwan, and probably to Siam. Between 1700 and 1715 twelve to fifteen Chinese ships per year went to Batavia, and after 1723 more than twenty. Throughout this period they were joined annually by several Portuguese ships from Macao. In the 1730s the Chinese sold at Batavia more than 20,000 piculs of tea, as much as all Europeans bought in Chinese ports at that time. They also brought many Chinese to settle in Java as petty traders, workers in the sugar fields and sugar mills, traders and tax agents along the Java coast, and so on.[34] The growth of trade to Siam was stimulated by the growth of Chinese imports of Siamese rice as well as by emigration and other exchanges of goods.[35] The least well documented development, and possibly the most important to the economy of coastal China, was the beginning of steady emigration to Taiwan, relieving population pressure on the coast and providing another source

---

[33] Ibid., Ch. 10; Ian Bruce Watson, *Foundation for Empire: English Private Trade in India, 1659–1760* (New Delhi, 1980), pp. 124, 151, 306; Søren Mentz, *The English Gentleman Merchant at Work: Madras and the City of London, 1660–1740* (Copenhagen, 2005), pp. 200–206; Sir Cornelius Neale Dalton, *The Life of Thomas Pitt* (Cambridge, 1915), pp. 246–249.

[34] Kristof Glamann, *Dutch–Asiatic Trade, 1620–1740* (The Hague / Copenhagen, 1958), pp. 219 and 236; L. Dermigny, *La Chine et l'Occident. Le Commerce à Canton au XVIIe Siècle*, 3 vols. (Paris, 1964), p. 539; J. de Hullu, "Over den Chinaschen Handel der Oost-Indische Companie in de Eerste Dertig Jaar van de 18e Eeuw," *Bijdragen tot de taal-, Land- en Volkenkunde van Nederlandsch-Indië*, Vol. 73 (1917), pp. 32–151; Leonard Blussé, *Strange Company: Chinese Settlers, Mestizo Women and the Dutch in VOC Batavia* (Dordrecht, 1986), Chs. 5, 6; Luc Nagtegaal, *Riding the Dutch Tiger: The Dutch East Indies Company and the Northeast Coast of Java, 1680–1743* (Leiden, 1996), Ch. 5; Hendrik E. Niemeijer, *Batavia: Een Koloniale Samenleving in de 17de Eeuw* (Amsterdam, 2005).

[35] Sarasin Viraphol, *Tribute and Profit in Sino-Siamese Trade, 1652–1853*, Harvard East Asian Monographs, No. 76. Cambridge, MA, 1977), Ch. 5; Wills, "Functional, Not Fossilized."

of grain for the coastal garrisons.[36] Trade with Nagasaki and Manila was still important but was declining by 1740. The trade with Japan was limited by the Japanese authorities to a value of 600,000 taels – roughly equal to the volume of Chinese and Macao trade at Batavia or to the volume of European trade in Chinese ports in the 1730s. Late in the 1730s the trade with Japan was declining as China became somewhat less dependent on Japanese copper and Japan developed its own silk industry and stopped buying Chinese raw silk and silk goods. Chinese trade with Manila may have been about 1 million taels per year between 1696 and 1710, but this was only about half the volume of the early seventeenth century, and after 1710 the figures usually were lower still.[37]

All this coming and going of long-distance ships and a flourishing coastwise trade stimulated piracy. Moreover, Taiwan was a sometimes violent, rapidly expanding frontier society, with outbreaks of rebellion in a regularly administered territory of the empire. Instability in Taiwan and piracy along the coast formed parts of the background for major changes in policy toward Chinese and European maritime trade. Although our knowledge of the Chinese in Southeast Asia in this period is fragmentary, it is clear that there was much opposition to the Qing among them; in Melaka they used a non-Qing reign period, and many in Batavia had not adopted the queue. Remnants of the Zheng regime fleeing from Taiwan had settled on the coasts of Vietnam and Cambodia.[38] At the end of 1716 the emperor, noting reports of concentrations of rebels in such places as Manila and Batavia, said that on one of his southern tours he had learned that many of the oceangoing ships built in China were sold in Southeast Asian ports and did not return. He also had less reliable information that rice was being exported from China, possibly to those areas. Trade that aided rebellious Chinese could not be tolerated. All Chinese

---

[36] John R. Shepherd, *Statecraft and Political Economy on the Taiwan Frontier, 1600–1800* (Stanford, 1993), Chs. 5–8.
[37] Pierre Chaunu, *Les Philippines et le Pacifique des Ibériques (XVIᵉ, XVIIᵉ, XVIIIᵉ siècles).* *Introduction méthodologique et indices d'activité,* Ports–Routes–Trafics, no. 11. (Paris, 1960), pp. 208–213.
[38] John E. Wills, Jr., "Early Sino-European Relations: Problems, Opportunities, and Archives," *Ch'ing-shih wen-t'i,* Vol. 3, No. 2 (December 1974), pp. 50–76, esp. p. 61; "Relação da embaixada que ElRey Dom João V Mandou, no anno de 1725 ... ," in Julio Firmino Judice Biker, *Collecção de Tratados e Concertos do Pazes que o Estado da India Portugueza fez com os Reis e Senhores com quem Teve Relações nas Partes da Asia e Africa Oriental,* 14 vols. (Lisbon, 1881–1887), Vol. 6, pp. 60–172, esp. p. 69; Li Tana, *Nguyễn Cochinchina: Southern Vietnam in the Seventeenth and Eighteenth Centuries* (Ithaca, NY, 1998), p. 33.

trade to Southeast Asia (Nanyang) was to be forbidden, while that to Japan and the Ryukyus (Dongyang) might continue, and foreign ships might continue to come to trade in China. The emperor speculated that in a hundred or a thousand years the Europeans might cause trouble for the empire, but the Chinese rebels were an immediate danger; the Han Chinese were never of one mind, always hard to govern, and their rulers must never cease to be aware of this danger.[39]

This ban was fairly effectively enforced; from 1718 to 1722 no Chinese ships got through to Batavia, and trade to Manila was sharply reduced. Trade to the Nanyang was not formally reopened until 1727. In a separate decision in 1718, Macao was allowed to continue its maritime trade, and Chinese maritime trade to Annam was exempted from the ban.[40] In the absence of Chinese competition, Macao's maritime trade grew rapidly. The Macaenses bought ships in other Asian ports, expanding their merchant fleet from about ten ships in the 1680s to twenty-five in 1724; these were smaller craft than those used by the East India Companies, and later in the century there rarely were more than twelve. The Canton authorities, justifiably confident that they could control Macao, nevertheless were made uneasy by this expansion and ordered that all Macao's ships be registered and no further increase in their number allowed.[41] The organs of autonomous local power, the Macao Senate and Misericórdia, were largely in control of the little settlement until reform efforts in the 1780s, and the Misericórdia's provision of credit extended beyond Macao's own voyages into the Canton financial web.[42]

Not everyone agreed with the emperor's emphasis on the dangers of Chinese rebellion rather than on those of European encroachment or with his willingness to sacrifice Chinese overseas trade to the security of the dynasty. After all, in the last years of Kangxi there was increasingly sharp criticism of Roman Catholic missionaries, and not all European traders were behaving themselves. In 1704 an English private trader took a Chinese junk at Johore on the Malay Peninsula, and in 1715 the English country trader *Anne* captured a Chinese ship off Amoy in a trade dispute. A point of view opposed to that of the emperor can be seen in fragmentary references to the views of Chen Mao, a Guangdong general who had

---

[39] Fu, *Documentary Chronicle*, pp. 122–123.
[40] Ibid., p. 127.
[41] Ibid., p. 141.
[42] Isabel dos Guimarães Sá, "Charity, Ritual, and Business at the Edge of Empire: The Misericórdia of Macau," in Liam Matthew Brockey, ed., *Portuguese Colonial Cities in the Early Modern World* (Burlington, VT, 2008), pp. 149–173, esp. pp. 152, 167–168.

engaged in maritime trade as a young man and recently had been on a mission of investigation to Manila and Batavia. Chen was a product of a milieu where many lived by maritime trade and many had seen European bullying of Chinese in the ports of Southeast Asia and the key role of the church in Spanish domination of the Philippines. He protested that if the Nanyang trade was prohibited, in some coastal areas half the people would lose their livelihood. Moreover, the Southeast Asian countries did not depend on China for rice; sometimes rice was imported from them when harvests were bad along the Chinese coast. Chen's protests were ignored. His proposal for stricter measures against European encroachment fared only a little better. He called for strict enforcement of the old controls of foreign trading ships, such as removing their guns while they were in port. This was approved, but enforcement remained rather perfunctory. His plea for renewal of the old bans on Roman Catholicism was accepted, but then enforcement was suspended.[43]

Qing attitudes toward European trade in these years were those of watchfulness but general confidence in the ability to keep control. As far as we can tell from the English translation of its rules, control of potentially dangerous foreigners was not one of the avowed purposes of the abortive guild of 1720. In one memorial of 1724, Kong Yuxun, governor-general of Guangdong and Guangxi, pointed out that only a few merchants from each ship came to Canton to trade, the crews staying on the ships at Whampoa. Trade proceeded tranquilly and equitably, and all foreigners were sent away again when the winds were right. "Thus the customs receipts are increased, people from afar are duly impressed, and there is nothing that can give rise to further trouble."[44]

There was no contradiction between these pro-trade attitudes and the antimissionary policies of these years. The Kangxi emperor seems to have thought that the restrictions imposed after the Tournon legation had given him a tamed Catholic mission. The missionaries were not seen as threats to Chinese security. Traditional Chinese theories of foreign relations warned against allowing potentially dangerous foreigners to see too much of the empire. However, in the last years of the Kangxi reign, Jesuits were sent on imperially ordered mapping expeditions in many remote areas. The Yongzheng antimissionary policies were justified in terms of the Christian threat to cultural orthodoxy, and were in part caused by the involvement

---

[43] Fu, *Documentary Chronicle*, pp. 122–127.
[44] *Yongzheng zhupi yuzhi* (1738; reprint, Taipei, 1964), Kong Yuxun, shang, pp. 56–56b; Fu, *Documentary Chronicle*, p. 139.

of some priests in the politics of the succession, but the emperor's famous discourse on the defects of Christianity does not mention the danger of subversion of the empire by missionaries and their converts.[45] This perception changed in the 1740s, and with that change and others in that decade would come more security-conscious policies toward European trade. But for the time being the court concentrated on finding ways to tax the growing trade and to keep its tax collectors honest.

In the basic structure established in the 1680s, the superintendent of maritime trade was changed every year. Many of those appointed to this post were bondservants of the Imperial Household Department, but it is not clear that all were. The tolls were based on the pattern developed in the late Ming. Duties, which averaged about 5 to 6 percent ad valorem, were paid on all imports and exports according to elaborate schedules for every type of goods. Each ship paid a "measurement" fee in discrete levels – 1,250 taels, 1,500, 1,750 – based on its measurement between the masts and across the beam. In addition, everyone from the superintendent down to the clerks and soldiers demanded presents and fees. The tax quota was reduced to a mere 40,000 taels in 1699, and as the trade grew thereafter, the superintendent diverted much of the growing income into the private purse of the emperor, sometimes taking so much that even this modest public quota could not be filled.[46]

Steady growth of European trade, with documented annual visits, can be traced from the successful visit of the French *Amphitrite* and the frustrating one of the English *Macclesfield*, both in 1699.[47] Dermigny estimates that forty-three English ships and twenty-three French ones visited Chinese ports between 1698 and 1715. The English tried three ports: Zhoushan (Chusan in the English records), with merchants coming

---

[45] Fu, *Documentary Chronicle*, pp. 155–156.

[46] Liang Tingnan, ed., *Yuehaiguan Zhi* (n.d.; reprint, Taipei, 1968), *juan.* 8, p. 14; Chang Te-ch'ang, "The Economic Role of the Imperial Household in the Ch'ing Dynasty," *Journal of Asian Studies*, Vol. 31, No. 2 (1972), pp. 243–273, esp. p. 256.

[47] This basic summary of the Canton trade is based largely on the chronologically ordered summaries in Morse, *Chronicles*. The best guides to the many facets and multiarchival challenges of studying the trade are Dermigny, *La Chine et l'Occident*; Paul A. Van Dyke, *The Canton Trade: Life and Enterprise on the China Coast, 1700–1845* (Hong Kong, 2005); and Van Dyke, *Merchants of Canton and Macao* (Hong Kong, in press). Other important studies are Kuo-tung Anthony Chen, *The Insolvency of the Chinese Hong Merchants, 1760–1843*, Institute of Economics, Academia Sinica, Monograph Series, No. 45 (Taipei, 1990); Weng Eang Cheong, *Hong Merchants of Canton: Chinese Merchants in Sino-Western trade, 1684–1798*, Nordic Institute of Asian Studies, Monograph Ser., No. 70 (Richmond, 1997); and Liang Jiabin, *Guangdong shisan hang kao* (Shanghai, 1937; reprint, Taibei, 1960). These studies are developing energetically in China; for samples see Guangzhou Lishi Wenhua Mingcheng Hui et al., eds., *Guangzhou hisan hang*

out from Ningbo to trade with them; Amoy; and Canton. The French seem to have concentrated on Canton from the beginning. The English abandoned Zhoushan in 1703 and tried it only occasionally thereafter. They found there not only official extortion and unreliable mercantile practices, but delays while merchants and officials went back and forth to Ningbo, and a lack of unity among the officials, especially when the Zhoushan local officials tried to manage things in their own interest and exclude their Ningbo-based superiors.

Many English ships went to Amoy in these years, especially country traders from Madras, but it was never used consistently after the *Anne* incident of 1715. The Amoy mercantile community was oriented more to maritime trade in Chinese ships than to waiting for Europeans to come to it. Amoy people had some bitter memories of European marauding in the area and of oppression of Chinese in Manila and other European-ruled ports. Moreover, although southern Fujian was the home of many important foreign trade merchants, some of them seem to have had trouble maintaining their business there, possibly because of the difficulties of the trade routes from the tea- and silk-producing areas. In 1715, for example, two merchants got into debt difficulties trading with the English at Amoy, had their ship taken by the English as described earlier, but managed to trade at Zhoushan and finally settled at Canton.[48] With the unstable and evolving politics of control on the Qing side and the split between the old and new East India Companies among the English, stable relations were not to be expected. The improvisations of people at home in this confusion, like one Alexander Hamilton, occasionally could give both sides what they wanted. In 1700, when an English warship broke up in a botched repair at Amoy, Hamilton cooperated with the Qing authorities to make sure that none of the other English ships departed without taking along a share of the personnel of the lost ship.[49]

For the Europeans, too, it was clear by 1715 that Canton was the most satisfactory port. Several reasons for this can be suggested. It was farther from the centers of silk and tea production than Amoy or Ningbo, but the overland trade routes from Jiangxi and Hunan were highly developed and efficient. Unlike Amoy it had a large and rich hinterland of its own, which made supplies of goods for export more flexible

---

cangsang (Guangzhou, 2001), and Pan Gang'er et al., *Guangdong shisan hang zhi yi: Pan Tongwen (Fu) Hang* (Guangzhou, 2006)..

[48] Morse, *Chronicles*, Vol. 1, pp. 102, 105, 122, 124, 128, 134–135.

[49] Alexander Hamilton, introduction and notes by Sir William Foster, *A New Account of the East Indies*. 2 vols. (London, 1930; reprint, Amsterdam / New York, 1970), Vol. 2, pp. 136–142. Hamilton was a good eyewitness but a credulous listener. His account gives a vivid picture of the improvised lives of East India Company and country traders in these years.

and reliable; goods brought in from other areas for local consumption could be diverted into foreign trade when necessary. Later in the century there was local production, most of it not of high quality, of silk and porcelain for export. The large and prosperous trade with Siam, based mainly on Siamese investment and shipping, had its Chinese terminus in Canton.[50] This trade and the thriving hinterland contributed to the general prosperity and substantial capital resources of the Canton merchant community. Here also there was experience in dealing with Europeans and organizing large-scale sales of Chinese goods to them, a heritage from the great days of the Macao trade. Because Canton was a provincial capital, the governor and the superintendent of maritime customs maintained direct supervision of relations with foreigners, and the Chinese mercantile community was accustomed to maintaining close relations with the high officials. The Europeans did not always like the results of such close relations, but they provided a more stable and organizationally sophisticated framework for the growth of trade than had been available at either Zhoushan or Amoy.

At Canton in 1699, the English dealt with at least two merchants who had traded with foreigners in the 1680s or earlier, one of whom spoke Portuguese. Several of them, in the "client-merchant" mode that had so vexed the Dutch in the 1660s and the 1670s, claimed the protection of individual high officials and sometimes used their masters' influence to hamper each other's trade.[51] At all three ports in these first years, merchants sometimes sought to evade or renegotiate contracts. The Dutch had no trouble with such reneging earlier, and it diminished later in the eighteenth century as the trade grew and the two sides developed considerable mutual trust and understanding. Worse, the trade at all three ports in 1702–1704 was hindered by the appearance of so-called emperor's son's merchants, who claimed a monopoly on trade with foreigners and frightened off all competitors. Some had experience in foreign trade and had gone to the capital to obtain their monopoly privileges; none, however, had anything approaching an adequate stock of goods to sell. Most had obtained their monopoly privileges by gifts to the heir apparent, Yinreng, or his notoriously corrupt entourage, but one had "the same Authority from the Emperor's Fourth Son," so apparently the already powerful Yinzhen was also involved in these disruptive efforts to

[50] Viraphol, *Tribute*.
[51] Morse, *Chronicles*, Vol. 1, pp. 85–108.

squeeze foreign trade. At Canton in 1704 the superintendent of maritime trade finally intervened, and the emperor's son's merchant was persuaded to accept a payment of 5,000 taels and yield to a combine of merchants headed by the very able Leanqua and Anqua, who moved back and forth between Amoy and Canton.[52]

By 1717 European trade at Canton had grown from the two ships of 1699 to a total of twenty. The English and French had been joined by the "Ostend Company," chartered by the Holy Roman emperor, based in the port of Ostend in what is now Belgium, but almost entirely a creature of English investment, shipbuilding, and commercial staffing. Chinese officials usually wanted to avoid the difficulties that arose from foreigners dealing with unreliable or insubstantial merchants; Chinese merchants frequently sought to maintain their profit margins by agreeing among themselves on import and export prices. Thus in December 1720 sixteen leading firms formed a merchant guild with official backing. Only these firms would be allowed to sell foreigners any goods except small handicraft items and porcelain, and on porcelain sales a nonmember had to pay 30 percent of the sale price to the guild. No firm was allowed to transact more than half of the trade with any one foreign ship. But in 1721, with the advice and cooperation of several merchants, the English protested this restraint to the governor-general, who ordered the dissolution of the guild. One of the cooperating merchants, Suqua, then broke with the rest of the former guild members to offer tea at lower prices, and remained a leading merchant and a key ally of the English for at least a decade thereafter.[53] Thus in this case rivalry among the merchants and a change of mind by one high official were sufficient to break the guild. The officials had approved it partly to avoid trouble with foreigners but then had found that it produced trouble.

In this as in so many spheres, the Yongzheng years were marked by a struggle for fiscal regularization, through the transformation of informal and private fees into formal and public sources of revenue. The superintendent's office was abolished in 1723, and its duties entrusted to the governor, Yang Wenqian. Yang combined efforts to increase imperial revenues with efforts to make his own fortune. In return for a payment of 200,000 taels, he gave a monopoly on foreign trade to an "exclusive guild" (*zhuanhang*) of Suqua and five other leading merchants. This guild

---

[52] Ibid., pp. 109–145.
[53] Cheong, *Hong Merchants*, pp. 37–44.

was noticed by the Dutch in 1729. But by 1736 the Dutch reported that about twenty firms were involved in foreign trade;[54] the English sometimes were allowed to buy from other merchants, but under the name of one of the six and probably with a fee to that firm. It probably was during Yang's years in control that the presents and fees previously paid were made part of the public revenue and regularized into a single payment of 1,950 taels per ship. One English account of the late 1730s shows this sum being shared in an astonishingly regular and meticulous fashion, from 1,606.201 taels for the emperor down to 1.2 taels for the Nanhai county magistrate and for the military officer at Macao. Yang Wenqian also levied a tax of 10 percent on all of the silver imported by the foreigners, which constituted more than 80 percent of their cargoes' value at this period. As a result of these changes, in addition to collecting the full quota of 43,750 taels, he was able to transmit to the Imperial Household Department 48,000 taels. Yang reported that he had uncovered and transferred to the public revenue private fees totaling 38,000 taels for that year, for a total public revenue of almost three times the previous quota. In the course of these changes, individual connections between officials and merchants in the old "client-merchant" mode became impossible. Merchants depended on the hoppo's approval as one of a group licensed for the foreign trade.[55] These merchants from the beginning also functioned as "security merchants," standing security for the payment of tolls on each foreign ship and the good behavior of its merchants and sailors. Already in the 1720s tolls were more likely to be paid by the Chinese merchants than by the foreigners, and the merchants expressed fears of being "bambooed" if the foreigners did not obey the officials.[56] In the Dutch records of their first visit in 1729, it is clear that the merchants trading with them were obliged to pay their tolls.[57] The first known English reference to a security merchant as such is from 1736, but it seems to refer to an already well established institution.[58]

In the first two years of the Qianlong reign, when fiscal rationalization efforts again were widespread, there was talk of cancellation of

---

[54] de Hullu, "Over den Chinaschen Handel," p. 78; Christiaan J. A. Jörg, *Porcelain and the Dutch China Trade* (The Hague, 1982), p. 67.

[55] Sasaki Masaya, "Etsu kaikan no roki," *Tōyō Gakuhō*, Vol. 34 (1955), pp. 132–161; Cheong, *Hong Merchants*, pp. 197–200.

[56] Morse, *Chronicles*, Vol. 1, p. 189. Van Dyke, *The Canton Trade*, pp. 11–12, 24–25, makes it clear that the security merchant system evolved out of normal commercial practice and only later was brought under formal official supervision.

[57] De Hullu, "Over den Chinaschen Handel," p. 87.

[58] Morse, *Chronicles*, Vol. 1, p. 247.

the practice of collecting 1,950 taels and 10 percent of the silver. The Europeans declared themselves willing to make large payments to the officials and merchants, especially Tan Hunqua, if they could bring this to pass; some payments were made, but it is not clear that there was any long-run change.[59] The office of the superintendent of maritime customs, revived in 1729, was maintained with only brief interruptions to 1739, then abolished and its duties shuffled among various high officials, always in the hands of a Manchu, in the security-conscious 1740s. It reached definitive form in 1750 with the revival of the superintendency, which thereafter was always in the hands of a bondservant of the Imperial Household Department, with provisions for concurrent reporting of customs revenues by the governor-general. Total revenue in 1750 was 466,000 taels, and by the end of the century it was more than a million per year. The regular quota was raised slowly, but it seems that more than three-fourths of this revenue always went to the Imperial Household Department.[60] Another private surcharge on the rates on goods was transferred to the public revenue in 1757, but there was no end of the creation of new surcharges and private fees, which probably equaled the burden on the trade of the public revenue.[61]

In these conditions of increasingly regular and predictable official management, the trade continued to grow. The period 1715 to 1739 was also the longest period in the eighteenth century in which there was no general European war that could lead to conflicts among Europeans in Chinese ports or waters. The Ostend Company was a formidable competitor from 1715 until 1727, when English and Dutch diplomacy at the court of Vienna secured its dissolution. In 1728 the Dutch East India Company, dissatisfied with the quality of tea obtained from the junks coming to Batavia, began direct voyages from Amsterdam to Canton. From 1735 on, it again relied on voyages to China from Batavia, until 1757, when it resumed direct voyages from Amsterdam.[62] From 1731–1732 the Danish and Swedish East India Companies were also regular traders at Canton. Total annual exportation of tea in the 1740s was five times that of 1719–1725. Macao's trade continued to prosper, especially in the

---

[59] On many of these negotiations Van Dyke, *Merchants of Canton*, offers much detail, and I thank the author for his clarifications.

[60] Preston M. Torbert, *The Ch'ing Imperial Household Department: A Study of Its Organization and Principal Functions, 1662–1796* (Cambridge, MA, 1977), pp. 98–102.

[61] Chen Guodong, "Qingdai qianqi Yuehaiguan jiandu de paiqian," *Shiyuan*, Vol. 10 (October 1980), pp. 139–168; Chen, *Insolvency*, pp. 121–136.

[62] Jörg, *Porcelain*, Ch. 1.

transportation of tutenague (lead–zinc alloy, mined in Guangdong) to Goa for sale and use in the great Indian brass industry.[63]

It is worth noting that this growth was accompanied by very little policy discussion important enough to be recorded in the *Veritable Records* or other important documentary collections and by no formal diplomatic activity. In both respects the contrast to the complexities and sensitivities of Qing–Russian relations in these years is striking. There were four embassies from maritime European sovereigns between 1700 and 1740, but all were motivated by crisis in the Christian missions, not by commercial problems. The papal legations of Charles Maillard de Tournon and Mezzabarba were rarely if ever called tribute embassies, although kowtows by the legates and condescending favors from the emperor maintained the fundamentals of imperial ceremonial superiority. Their stays in Beijing were longer and their opportunities for negotiation with the emperor greater than they would have been within the embassy regimen. The third papal legation, of Plaskowitz and Ildefonso, was called a tribute embassy, recorded as one in the *Statutes and Precedents*, and handled largely according to embassy protocol.[64] The Portuguese embassy of Alexandre Metello de Sousa e Menezes, received in Beijing in 1727, was sent by the king of Portugal in an effort to persuade the Yongzheng emperor to modify or abandon his anti-Christian policies. Sent directly by a monarchy growing rich from Brazilian gold and diamonds, it was much better planned and more richly provided with presents than the shabby Portuguese embassies of 1670 and 1678. The Portuguese monarchy was especially prone to acts that would present it as the great supporter of the mission because of its struggle to maintain Portuguese patronage over Asian missions against the encroachments of France and the papacy. When the ambassador left Canton for Beijing, he was allowed to bring a suite of more than forty, and he received from the Qing authorities an advance of 1,000 taels toward his travel expenses, both departures from the precedents for earlier embassies but within the structure of the tribute embassy system. Imperial officials acknowledged, according to a Portuguese source, that the embassy could not be compared with "the common embassies of ordinary tribute-bearers." The ambassador objected to every instance in which he was referred to as "paying tribute" and insisted on being called an envoy "presenting congratulations," but

---

[63] Souza, *Survival*, Ch. 6.
[64] *Da Qing huidian shili* (1899), 503, p. 10b; 506, p.10b.

as we saw in relation to the 1670 embassy, this did not place this embassy outside the tribute tradition. In Beijing he insisted on being allowed to present his credentials in person to the emperor; this was granted and duly recorded in the regulations as a variation in embassy routine that could be allowed if the ambassador had orders from his sovereign to insist on it. He kowtowed repeatedly and without hesitation. Despite deviations from embassy routine and recognition of the special character of his embassy, from the Qing perspective it was much more firmly within the tribute tradition than the first two papal legations had been. On the advice of the Beijing Jesuits, the ambassador did not bring up the missionary problem in his meetings with the emperor, and left with nothing more than the faint hope that he had gained a little goodwill for his monarch and his faith.[65]

## THE PATTERN OF TRADE

By the 1720s maritime European trade with China clearly was dominated by the exchange of silver for tea, but many other commodities were involved, and we can trace the broad outlines of changes through the century in their quantities and their shares in the trade. In the following paragraphs we take up first the tea trade, then other European exports from China, then imports in European vessels from Europe and from Asian ports, and finally the general picture of the structure of the trade that emerges when these pieces are put together.

Tea was drunk in the coffeehouses of London from the 1660s on, but it was expensive and the quantities imported were small. After about 1700 it began to be sold by grocers and in tea shops frequented by ladies as well as gentlemen. By the 1720s bohea (*wuyi*; used generically for black tea at this time) had declined in price, and some green teas were even less expensive. These lower prices were maintained for the rest of the century, even amid the moderate inflation of the last decades, and along with the general economic growth of these years they facilitated a steady spread of the tea-drinking habit until it was thought to be nearly universal in England and Scotland. There is evidence that for some kinds of tea the eighteenth-century expansion of imports was accompanied by a decline of quality, which would help to account for the stability of prices. Very

---

[65] Judice Biker, *Colleção de Tratados e Concertos*, Vol. 6, pp. 37–55, 60–172; *Qinding libu zeli* (1841; reprint, Taipei, 1966), 180, p. 9b.

early the English began drinking their black tea with milk and sugar; most early tea services include both sugar bowls and milk jugs.[66] The general popularity of tea can be attributed not just to its flavor and its stimulating qualities, but also to its convenience as a means of taking a bit of quick warm nourishment, including sugar. Tea, along with West Indian sugar, Arabian and Javanese coffee, and Indian textiles, became one of the first important transoceanic imports to be consumed by a non-elite population in the history of the world.[67] Tea also became very popular in the Netherlands, but seems to have been much less commonly used elsewhere in Europe; the English and Scottish market remained the great magnet that shaped the trade.

This did not lead immediately to English domination of the export of tea from China. Great Britain taxed tea imports at 80 to more than100 percent of the sale price at the London auctions, making it extremely profitable to smuggle tea into the kingdom. It seems likely that at many times in the eighteenth century half of the tea consumed in Great Britain was illegally imported; even as the quantities consumed grew rapidly after 1763, the scope and sophistication of smuggling grew proportionately. The smugglers sometimes provided teas of better quality and in wider assortments than those legally sold by the East India Company, and contributed to the development of a genuinely national market by distributing their imports from all the coasts of Great Britain rather than just from London.[68]

The tea destined to be smuggled into Great Britain was bought in China by the agents of various European East companies and found its way into smuggling channels from their home ports, most important of which

---

[66] K. N. Chaudhuri, *The Trading World of Asia and the English East India Company* (Cambridge, 1978), pp. 385, 396–397, 408. Information and statistics in the "Pattern of Trade" section are based on Chaudhuri, Chs. 15, 17 and pp. 533–539, 546; Jörg, *Porcelain*, esp. pp. 74–93, 304–309; Dermigny, *La Chine et 1'Occident*, in his sections on various commodities; and Morse, *Chronicles*, under the specific years cited. On tea see also the excellent England-centered study by Hoh-cheung Mui and Lorna H. Mui, *The Management of Monopoly: A Study of the East India Company's Conduct of Its Tea Trade, 1784–1833* (Vancouver, 1984). The best summary of the place of tea trade and production in the eighteenth-century Chinese economy is Robert Gardella, *Harvesting the Mountains: Fujian and the China Tea Trade, 1757–1937* (Berkeley, CA, 1994), pp. 33–47.

[67] Wills, "European Consumption," pp. 133–147.

[68] Hoh-cheung Mui and Lorna H Mui, "Smuggling and the British Tea Trade before 1784," *American Historical Review*, Vol. 74, No. 1 (October 1968), pp. 44–73; and their "'Trends in Eighteenth Century Smuggling' Reconsidered," *Economic History Review*, 2d Ser., 2, Vol. 8, No. 1 (February 1975), pp. 28–43.

were Copenhagen, Amsterdam, Ostend, and the ports of Normandy and Brittany. Competition in Canton gave Chinese officials and merchants considerable leverage in dealing with each nationality, and occasionally forced prices up, especially when one competitor tried to corner the market in a particular variety. The competition also stimulated the competing companies to increase their purchases and to hold their sale prices down, all of which helped to increase the consumption of tea in Great Britain and Europe.

The tea exported to Europe came largely from the hilly areas of Fujian, Jiangxi, and Zhejiang. The growing export market tapped a vast and sophisticated system of production for domestic markets, with many varieties based on location, size, and type of leaf and mode of processing. Europeans in Canton normally checked samples of tea being offered by a particular merchant, then placed their orders. The teas were spot-checked during packing, and generally were found to be up to sample and remarkably consistent within a batch purchased. The Dutch and the French had resident tasters in Canton for much of the century, the English not until the 1790s. The hong merchants allowed the Europeans not only to refuse teas not up to sample, but to return for reimbursement any chests that had arrived in Europe in unsatisfactory condition.[69]

In the tea-producing areas the Canton interest maintained a substantial but not controlling presence. In the early nineteenth century the two greatest merchant houses, Poankeequa and Howqua, owned some tea plantations of excellent reputation; the Howqua (Wu) family was reported to have owned land in Wuyi, Fujian, before it came to Canton. The hong merchants also had agents in the market centers of the tea-producing areas, and they may have directly supervised some processors (*chazhuang*). Some processors owned their own tea plantations. But the bulk of the coordination of planting and picking, processing, and transportation to Canton for sale to foreigners was based on market mechanisms, not vertical organizational integration. The most important contribution of the Canton trade was the steady flow of silver advanced by foreigners to the Canton merchants and by the latter to upcountry merchants or direct to processors, a flow that did much to smooth out the inherent difficulties of coordination and credit in a trade involving such a large number of small independent operators. Typically tea was grown in small plots and harvested by the households of the owners, who might sell the leaves fresh or do some preliminary processing. The processors

---

[69] Mui and Mui, *Management of Monopoly*, pp. 41–42.

carried out additional steps of preparation, sorting, mixing, and packing for shipment. All of this required a great deal of hand labor, some of it highly skilled. As the trade grew, the local labor force was supplemented by immigrants from impoverished nearby regions, who became tenants, shopkeepers, and processors. Here and on the complicated transportation route to Canton, we find an unsettled society full of people willing to work for very low wages and seeking to supplement those wages by petty trading and smuggling. This, and the fact that these people lived largely outside the silver economy, helped make possible the low and steady sale prices in Canton even in the inflation of the late eighteenth and early nineteenth centuries.

The general picture of the growth of tea exports to Europe is reasonably clear, although much statistical refinement and careful use of all available European archives are still necessary. It seems safe to say that between 1720 and 1740 the total doubled from about 30,000 piculs to about 60,000, doubled again to about 120,000 by 1765, and again to 240,000 by 1795.[70] From the 1770s on there was a shift toward finer and more expensive kinds of tea, especially congou (*gongfu*), and away from bohea. It seems likely that the smugglers led this shift and the English East India Company lagged behind. The Continental companies that supplied the smugglers shifted earlier and more rapidly than the English Company.[71] The shift to finer varieties and a more selective European market may have strained the coordinating capacities of the old system of free commercial relations among producers, processors, and merchants and stimulated more direct intervention in the upcountry processes by the Canton merchant houses; it is not clear, however, how far this process had gone by 1800.

There was a special charm to pouring one's Chinese tea from a Chinese pot into a Chinese cup, even when one added milk and sugar in a fashion that would have mystified any Chinese, and even when one used porcelain pieces made to European order with shapes and decorations quite unlike those the Chinese made for themselves.[72] The most important type of porcelain exported by Europeans was the famous blue and white ware that had been one of the leading products of the great porcelain center

---

[70] Dermigny, *La Chine et l'Occident*, p. 539.

[71] Mui and Mui, *Management of Monopoly*, pp. 98–100.

[72] See Jörg, *Porcelain*, for an excellent integration of the histories of art, companies, and an industry and a trade in China. For longer time perspectives and global dimensions see Robert Finlay, *The Pilgrim Art: Cultures of Porcelain in World History* (Berkeley, CA, 2010).

at Jingdezhen in Jiangxi since the early Ming. Much smaller quantities of "blanc de Chine" made at Dehua in Fujian and of the products of other potteries were exported. Goods that were not as fine, bought for Southeast Asian markets and occasionally for European, were the products of many kilns, including some in the Canton area. Blue and white ware made for the Chinese market had been exported since the early days of Macao and Manila, and was widely admired in Europe. As Jingdezhen revived after the Ming–Qing transition, export merchants at Canton cooperated with the manufacturers in developing wares in shapes and sizes that made them useful as well as ornamental in European homes: cups with handles, pots for coffee or chocolate as well as tea, soup bowls and tureens, and plates and platters of various sizes. The Europeans supplied drawings and occasionally models of the shapes wanted, which were forwarded to the manufacturers in Jingdezhen. Another interesting example of the adaptation of Jingdezhen production to the export market was the production there of large quantities of polychrome pieces imitative of the Japanese Imari ware, which had become popular in Europe in the 1600s.[73]

Jingdezhen was also the main center for making figurines, huge vases, and other elaborate "Chine de Commande" pieces to order for the European market.[74] Chinese porcelain painters would decorate these and more conventional and utilitarian pieces with any design furnished by the European buyer. These designs included heraldry, Masonic emblems, Catholic motifs (despite the proscription of that religion in China), and figures and landscapes drawn from European "chinoiserie" images rather than Chinese portrayals of their own country and people. From the 1730s on, much porcelain was sent to Canton unpainted. Painting and final firing were done there by firms that specialized in decoration for export. Many shops near the foreign factories kept large quantities of porcelain on their shelves for foreign buyers. These shops supplied much of the porcelain exported by individual Europeans in their private trades. The companies bought from the shops and also made larger contract purchases from the hong firms. From the 1740s on, European buyers were especially interested in buying matched "services" – tea sets, chocolate sets, dinner sets, and so on. Some of these were on hand in the shops, but European definitions of what constituted a proper service changed almost year by year, making necessary an increasing amount of special ordering. To the degree that the shopkeepers' business had been a cash

---

[73] Ibid., p. 125.
[74] Michel Beurdeley, *Chinese Trade Porcelain* (Rutland, VT, 1962).

one, this probably stimulated an increased use of credit. In special orders, half of the price was advanced by the purchaser, who had the right to refuse the goods delivered and to insist that the order be made over. The Dutch were told that at Jingdezhen the individual items of services – pots, cups, saucers, plates – were ordered from different specialized kilns, making the coordination of sizes and the matching of decorations an astonishing triumph of the Chinese penchant for coordination through market mechanisms rather than through increasing the scale of organization.[75]

Both Chinese and Europeans found the porcelain trade full of difficulties. The Chinese merchants complained of high risks and low profits, especially on custom orders. Europeans found it difficult to keep up with the rapid changes in orders from Europe and information on changing European tastes. Dutch records show unstable relations with Chinese suppliers. The East India Company sometimes relied a good deal on the shopkeepers, who may have had a better specialized knowledge of porcelain, and sometimes gave all their business to a few hong merchants who had greater capital resources and sometimes were willing to carry out this difficult and not very profitable trade for the sake of good relations with the company. The new regulations of 1760, discussed later, did not put the shops out of business. The most important of them were required to move to a guarded street near the foreign factories, and they could sell to the companies only by paying fees to the hong merchants, but apparently the sale of porcelain to private parties was exempted from the hong monopoly.

Porcelain rarely constituted more than 5 percent of the value of the exports of a company. In the late eighteenth century, exports of it do not seem to have kept up with the general growth of the trade. Private traders had to take what they could find on the Canton market. The companies showed little interest in new initiatives to overcome the problems of coordination with European taste and demand. The quality of porcelain available for export may have been declining. The Chinese merchants complained increasingly of the exactions of the officials. These persistent difficulties mattered much more from the 1770s on, because in Europe ordinary Chinese blue and white ware had to compete with the growing production of English stoneware, including the elegant work of Wedgwood, and "Chine de Commande" had to compete with the fine porcelains of Meissen, Sèvres, Copenhagen, and many more, responding to European taste without time lags or cross-cultural distortions. Thus,

[75] Jörg, *Porcelain*, p. 124.

while tea remained exclusively a product of China until the nineteenth century, porcelain exports faced increasing competition, in which they were weakened by long distances, the complex structure of the trade in China, and the weight of official extortion in the late eighteenth century.

In exporting raw silk and silk fabrics, China engaged in a much more complex competition with other sources of supply.[76] It is possible that some of the Chinese merchants involved were aware of these competitive situations to some degree, but we have found no evidence of this. Europe had its own silk industry, largely in France and Italy, and also imported large quantities of Persian silk in the well-established Levant trade. In the seventeenth century the English and the Dutch East India Companies sought to establish a trade in raw silk direct from Persian ports to Europe, but they encountered many frustrations. Far more important for the companies' silk trade was the growth of their trade with Bengal from the 1650s on.[77] Bengal silk was purchased and sold for lower prices than Chinese silk, but the profit margins on it usually were better than those on Chinese, both in Japan and on the European market. The Europeans were also attracted by the relative stability of trade in Bengal in the decades when the Dutch had lost their entrepôt on Taiwan and both they and the English lacked stable connections in China and were struggling to maintain their trade in Tongking (northern Vietnam) as another source of silk.[78] There were short-lived booms for Chinese raw silk in the Netherlands in 1685 and around 1700, but in general raw silk exports played a very small part in the steady growth of European trade at Canton in the early eighteenth century.

The Bengal trade continued to grow, providing a cheaper raw material for less exacting manufactures; Chinese silk was comparable in quality and cost to the Italian product, but English weavers could make little use of it until the 1730s,.when they learned the Italian technique of twisting its very fine fibers into the "organsin" needed for the warp of very fine silk fabrics. But there were no substantial imports until after 1750, when the duties on Chinese raw silk were reduced to equal those on Italian.

---

[76] Glamann, *Dutch–Asiatic Trade*, Chs. 6, 7; and Chaudhuri, *The Trading World of Asia*, Ch. 15.

[77] Om Prakash, *The Dutch East India Company and the Economy of Bengal, 1630–1720* (Princeton, NJ, 1985).

[78] Hoang Anh Tuan, "From Japan to Manila and Back to Europe: The Abortive English Trade with Manila in the 1670s," *Itinerario*, Vol. 29, No. 3 (2005), pp. 73–92; Hoang, *Silk for Silver: Dutch–Vietnamese Relations, 1637–1700*, TANAP Monographs on the History of the Asian–European Interaction, Vol. 5 (Leiden, 2007).

Dutch imports became regular at the same time, suggesting that a substantial part of them were for reexport to England. There may have been restrictions on raw silk exports as early as the 1730s, with somewhat more regular limits of 80 or 100 piculs per ship from about 1763. From 1767 to about 1790, Great Britain imported 1,600 to 1,800 piculs of Chinese raw silk per year, representing an investment at Canton of up to 500,000 to 1,000,000 taels, a substantial share of its total exports. But these imports declined in the 1790s as those from Bengal, now securely under English control, continued to grow. Raw silk was much less important in the Dutch trade, and negligible for the French, Danes, and Swedes. The great hong merchant Poankeequa had a special source of stability in his business in the dispatch of a junk full of raw silk and silk goods to Manila every year.[79]

The causes of these late shifts are not at all clear. By 1790 the English Company was exporting "only the superior kind" of silk produced in Jiangnan, while the English country ships and those of other countries exported much of the "cheaper Canton silk."[80] In contrast to the tea trade, there seems to have been no end to the complaints of European merchants at Canton about deceptive packaging and uneven quality in the raw silk they purchased. This was an expensive and complexly graded commodity, requiring great care on the part of the purchaser, as the profits to Chinese merchants successful in passing off low-grade silk as high must have been considerable. It is possible that such practices became more prevalent among the hard-pressed Canton merchants of the 1780s, while at the same time the English in Bengal were devising better systems of quality control, helping to tip the balance of the raw silk trade from Canton to Calcutta.

The trade in silk goods involved problems of quality control and keeping up with changing tastes as complex as those in porcelain, and much harder to understand today. We do not even understand all the terminology and have very little of the kind of specialized scholarly literature that has grown up on export porcelain and Indian textiles. Moreover, fine silk fabrics, not breakable and taking up very little space in a chest, were ideally suited to the private trade of East India Company servants, making the figures we do have for company exports almost useless for estimating the real volume of the trade. Throughout the seventeenth and

---

[79] Paul Van Dyke, personal communication, 2010; Van Dyke, *Merchants of Canton*.
[80] Morse, *Chronicles*, Vol. 2, p. 180.

early eighteenth centuries there were networks of merchants and weavers specializing in export goods close to major ports: Macao and Canton to 1640 and the Fujian ports under Zheng control in the 1640s and 1650s. In the 1720s, the English were told that there were no more weavers in the Amoy area, since the English had stopped going there. Dutch records contain names of entrepreneurs in the Canton area who specialized in producing various kinds of silk goods for export, sometimes from patterns or samples supplied by the Dutch.[81]

In the seventeenth century, the Dutch Company had bought Chinese silk goods primarily for sale in Japan and other Asian markets. As European taste for Asian silks and cottons and for constant novelty in their decoration grew from the 1680s on, the Dutch made a few attempts to order such goods on their voyages to China or through traders coming to Batavia, but concentrated their efforts in Bengal, leaving purchases of Chinese silk goods to the English. English Company investment in these goods peaked very early, between 1712 and 1719. English efforts in the 1730s to overcome quality control problems and to obtain top-quality goods seem to have had little success. After about 1760 the English Company ceased dealing in Chinese silk goods, leaving them entirely to the private trade. The Dutch Company did buy them, but never for more than about 10 percent of their total investment.

European lists of exports from China contain many other items in relatively small quantities, including China root, rhubarb, cassia, ginger, alum, mercury, lacquer goods, wallpapers, and paintings on glass. Sugar and tutenague were important in the "country trade," especially for sale in India. "Nankeen" cotton cloth bulked large in a few cargoes in the 1780s and 1790s, and became more important after 1800. Finally, China was a substantial exporter of gold from the early Qing until the 1750s. Europeans had been profiting from the fact that the price of gold in terms of silver was lower in China than in Europe and in India, but this price rose in the eighteenth century, and Brazil emerged as an abundant new source of supply, so that the purchase of Chinese gold was no longer profitable for European traders. English investments in gold peaked in 1732, at almost 200,000 taels (silver). The Dutch continued to buy some gold until 1779, probably because of its importance for the purchase of Indian cottons for sale in Indonesia.[82]

---

[81] Jörg, *Porcelain*, p. 84.
[82] Glamann, *Dutch–Asiatic trade*, Ch. 3; and Dermigny, *La Chine et l'Occident*, pp. 416–433.

It is well known that for most of the eighteenth century European exports from China were financed primarily by the import of silver, there being no goods that the Europeans could sell to the Chinese in sufficient quantities to pay for the tea, silks, and porcelain they wanted to buy; that the English were anxious to sell their woolens in China but found they could make no profit from them; and that in their search for commodities to balance their trade with China the English finally developed the opium trade. All these points are true but, on all, important qualifications need to be made, and many puzzles remain.

Until 1750, goods had formed only 2 to 5 percent of the value of the English Company's cargoes from London to China. But in 1775 the sale of such goods accounted for 400,000 of the 1,000,000 taels of income available for investment. In 1789, with English Company investments running more than 4,000,000 taels, goods from Europe accounted for slightly more than 1,000,000.[83] Lead, brought in part as convenient ballast and used in China to make shot for firearms, sold steadily but did not contribute much to this growth. The large trade in English clocks, French mirrors, and so on was almost entirely a part of the private trade, is not included in the figures just given, and cannot be adequately measured. The growth was in the sale of woolens: 180,000 taels' worth in 1761; 340,000 in 1775; 1,000,000 in 1789; 2,000,000 in 1799; and 2,800,000 in British and American trade in 1828.[84] Other European companies were also importing smaller quantities of woolens.

The English were not happy with the prices they received for their woolens, which were not rising and barely equaled the costs of purchase and transportation; they were willing to sell at these prices to mollify agitation in England against the English East India Company as an exporter of bullion that did nothing to stimulate the export of English manufactures. The Chinese merchants sometimes complained that the increasing quantities imported were piling up unsold in their warehouses. But in the longer run the woolens were being sold in rapidly increasing amounts, and thus were contributing to the investment in tea and to the support of cloth industries in England and elsewhere in Europe. We do not know what made these increased sales possible. It is probable that the best markets for woolens were in the north. The English noted in 1794 that a flood in the Yellow River valley had reduced demand for

[83] Morse, *Chronicles*, Vol. 2, pp. 6–7, 172–173.
[84] Ibid., pp. 50, 179; Vol. 5, p. 159.

their woolens;[85] Charles de Constant said they went to the far ends of the empire.[86] The great distances of these areas from Canton may help to account for the sluggish movement of these goods on the Canton market, while the large scale of northern markets for warm cloth must have been a key to the large quantities that were eventually imported. The stable prices of the woolens may have improved the market for them at the expense of competing domestic products.

It also should be noted that these woolens were being exchanged for tea, which was also on a price plateau. The stability of the sale prices of woolens and tea when many prices were rising sharply in China and less sharply in England facilitated the expansion of sales of woolens in China and tea sales in England in the late eighteenth century, and thus was an important part of the dynamics of the immense expansion of the Canton trade.

Europeans trading at Canton also imported a variety of goods from Southeast Asia, the most important of which were the pepper of Java and Sumatra, sandalwood from eastern Indonesia, and tin from northern Sumatra and the Malay Peninsula. For the English Company, it does not seem that these imports ever provided more than 5 percent of their funding in Canton; they were able to bring larger amounts of pepper and tin in the late eighteenth century, but these increases did no more than keep pace with the rapid growth of the Canton trade as a whole. These imports were much more important for the Dutch Company, which had privileged access to sources of pepper and tin in island Southeast Asia.[87] The great Chinese merchants of Canton were also active participants in trade with Southeast Asia in their own shipping.[88]

The British began to import Indian cotton to China about 1785; by 1792 it reportedly was accounting for more than 1,500,000 taels of a British investment at Canton of greater than 4,000,000.[89] These imports, largely in the country trade, continued to grow in the nineteenth century.

[85] Ibid., p. 257.

[86] Charles de Constant, *Les memoires de Charles de Constant sur le commerce à la Chine*, ed. by Louis Dermigny (Paris, 1964), p. 359.

[87] Yong Liu, *The Dutch East India Company's Tea Trade with China, 1757–1781* (Leiden, 2007), pp. 44–48.

[88] Paul A. Van Dyke, "A Reassessment of the China Trade: The Canton Junk Trade as Revealed in the Dutch and Swedish Records of the 1750s to the 1770s," in Wang Gungwu and Ng Chin-keong, eds., *Maritime China in Transition 1750–1850* (Wiesbaden, 2004), pp. 151–167.

[89] Morse, *Chronicles*, Vol. 2, p. 201.

China's other major import from India in this period was opium. Opium had been known in China and elsewhere in Asia for centuries. Taken by mouth, it could ease fevers or stomach pains but did not produce narcotic euphoria or addiction. That was possible only after opium was combined with tobacco and smoked. In the early eighteenth century both this practice and the inhaling of something like a vaporized pure extract were reported to be widespread on the north coast of Java east of Batavia, with many Chinese involved in distribution and sales.[90] Dutch imports of opium from Bengal to the Indonesian Archipelago tripled between 1680 and 1720.[91]

It is not clear when opium first arrived on the China coast. The Dutch trading there in the 1680s recorded no hint of a demand for it. Early in the eighteenth century we find references to English Company ships selling opium in Sumatra, Java, and the Malay Peninsula, but not in China. English Company ships did not bring opium from India to China, but it was asserted in 1733 that for years it had been "a usual thing" for ships coming from Madras (almost entirely private ships in the country trade) to bring opium for sale in China.[92] Macao's trade with India may have been another channel for early opium imports, and of course Chinese returning from Java may have brought the drug as well as the habit with them. The first imperial prohibition of opium, dated 1729, was based on information about trade in coastal Guangdong and Fujian; there also is good evidence for opium smoking in Taiwan at this time. It has been estimated that imports by Europeans at this time were only about 200 chests per year. In the 1760s imports ran about 1,000 chests a year, and it was asserted that almost every country vessel brought some. In 1780 more than 1,300 chests were imported, in 1786 about 2,000, and in 1800 an estimated 3,000. The rapid growth after 1780 was a result of changing circumstances both in India and in China. In Bengal the East India Company had asserted a monopoly on opium production and sale in 1773, and was systematizing production and distribution and encouraging export. In China the affluence and demoralization of the Heshen years gave many Chinese the means and the motive to acquire the opium habit. General official corruption made the illegal trade possible.

---

[90] Nagtegaal, *Riding the Dutch Tiger*, pp. 143–7; Zheng Yangwen, *The Social Life of Opium in China* (Cambridge, 2005), p. 45; John E. Wills, Jr., "The First Inhalers: A World-Historical Problem" (paper presented to the World History Association, 2009).

[91] Prakash, *The Dutch East India Company*, pp. 150–1.

[92] Morse, *Chronicles*, Vol. 1, p. 215.

The English Company sold its opium at auction in Calcutta and kept its distance from the trade carried on thereafter by private merchants. In the 1770s and 1780s much was sold along the coasts of the Malay Peninsula and Sumatra, some of it perhaps to Chinese, but soon China itself became the most important destination. There too the trade was kept separate from the legal trade at Canton, being channeled through Macao or through various coastal anchorages. Macao also carried on a vigorous opium trade of its own, tapping Portuguese-connected sources of supply in India and buying at the English Company auctions in Calcutta.[93] With a few marginal exceptions involving Portuguese and Armenian intermediaries, the Canton hong merchants had nothing to do with it, and when the company experimented in 1782 with sending opium on its own account through the Canton legal channel, it found the hong merchants very reluctant to stand security for the ship and had to accept a below-market price for the opium.

But there were strong financial connections between these ostensibly separate channels. The opium traders always insisted on immediate payment in silver, since they would have no legal recourse if cheated on a credit transaction. Their investment in Chinese goods at Canton did not absorb all the silver they earned, and they paid large quantities of it into the company's treasury in Canton in return for bills payable by the company in London. In 1787 more than 1,500,000 taels were paid into the company's Canton treasury in this way. We have only a few hints of the Canton merchants' involvement in the opium trade. One of the new merchants of 1782, Sinqua, had been in the opium trade before that. In 1786 two Chinese merchants asked the company to pay them for goods they delivered in bills on Calcutta, presumably so that they or others could use these bills to pay for opium without moving large quantities of silver.[94]

The figures presented in the preceding paragraphs must be taken only as rough indicators of trends. Much work remains to be done in several archives before available statistical material can be fully assembled and assessed. The same caution must be exercised in relation to estimates of silver imports and their effects on the Chinese economy. One study estimates that total European exports from China were less than 1,000,000 taels per year in the 1720s, about 3,500,000 in the 1760s, 4,400,000

[93] Ângela Guimarães, *Uma Relação Especial. Macau e as Relações Luso-Chinesas (1780–1840)* (Lisbon, 1996), pp. 200–215.
[94] Morse, *Chronicles*, Vol. 2, pp. 121, 137.

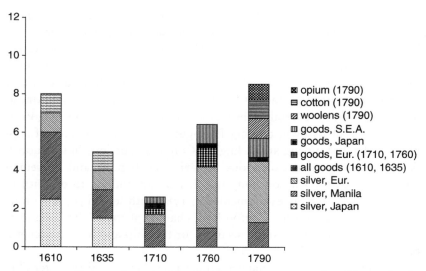

FIGURE 4.1. Estimated composition of imports, 1610–1790, in millions of taels.

around 1780, and 6,400,000 in the 1790s.[95] Down to the 1760s, 80 to 90 percent of these exports were paid for by imports of silver – perhaps 800,000 taels in the 1720s and 3,000,000 in the 1760s. In the 1790s China was buying more than a million taels' worth of woolens and perhaps an equal amount of Indian cotton from the British, and was buying from all foreigners at least 2,000 chests of opium at about 250 taels per chest, for another 500,000 taels. Adding another 500,000 taels for imports of other goods and by other nations, it seems that about 3,000,000 taels, almost half of the 6,400,000 in exports, was being covered by imports and that China's net import of silver had hardly risen since the 1760s. All of these figures are subject to revision as detailed work continues; the dramatic changes in the composition of imports since the late Ming can be best seen in graphic form (Figure 4.1).

There are many difficulties with the analysis of import prices. It is not surprising that our sources on foreign trade show steady inflation of some prices in the port where the impact of these silver flows was most direct. The pepper price series is the most reliable, presenting fewer difficulties of varying quality or alloy. Price changes for one important import and two exports are summarized in Table 4.1 and Figure 4.2.[96]

---

[95] Dermigny, *La Chine et l'Occident*, Vol. 1, p. 537.
[96] The 1680s prices are from John E. Wills, Jr., *Ch'ing Relations with the Dutch, 1662–1690*(Ph.D. dissertation, Harvard University, 1967), pp. 593–596, and Wills, *Toward the*

TABLE 4.1 *Prices at Canton (in Taels) and Percent Gains*

| Commodity | A<br>1680–1730<br>Prices | B<br>1760s<br>Prices | C<br>B/A | D<br>1790s<br>Prices | E<br>D/A |
|---|---|---|---|---|---|
| Raw silk, first grade, per picul | 155 | 265 | 176 | 290 | 193 |
| Gold, per tael | 11 | 15.7 | 143 | 17.5 | 159 |
| Pepper, per picul | 7.5 | 13 | 173 | 15 | 200 |

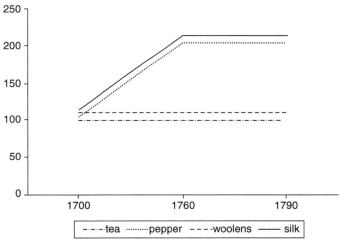

FIGURE 4.2. Estimated trends of import and export prices, 1700–1790 (prices c. 1700 = 100%).

There is a striking contrast between the series shown in the table and the low and stable prices of imports of woolens and exports of tea noted in earlier paragraphs, again best seen graphically. (Figure 4.2)

In this growing trade, then, the Europeans obtained tea, silk, and porcelain; the Chinese received, in addition to silver, some pepper, other Southeast Asian goods, Indian cotton, and woolens. They also bought opium, a shift in use patterns that was not as general as the English shift

*Canton System*, Apps.; see also Chaudhuri, *The Trading World of Asia*, p. 181; Morse, *Chronicles*, Vol. 1, p. 203; Vol. 2, pp. 41, 201–203; Vol. 5, pp. 116, 123–125, 131, 149; Paul Van Dyke, *Port Canton and the Pearl River Delta, 1690–1845* (Ph.D. dissertation, University of Southern California, 2002), tables; and Earl H. Pritchard, *The Crucial Years of Early Anglo-Chinese Relations, 1750–1800* (New York, 1970), pp. 142–198, 391–402.

from ale to tea and of tragically contrasting character. European luxurious tastes and *rêves chinois* involved Chinese silks and porcelains; many Qing officials may have owned English clocks, but these and other European imports had a smaller impact on Chinese culture. Silver imports, by increasing the quantity of silver in circulation, may have postponed the effects of the debasement of copper coinage on the copper–silver ratio, at least in regions where the silver economy was strongest. But silver imports had little direct effect on those not involved in the silver economy. Partly because they lived in the copper cash economy, partly because many were ready to work for subsistence wages or less, the number of people involved in tea production increased, but their remuneration did not rise.[97] It is plausible to see in China's maritime trade involvements by about 1800 a sort of paradigm of the situation of the commodity producer in the present era of global capitalism: the prices of the most important commodity exports do not rise, and even if the country has a positive balance of trade, that is of little benefit to the producers or many of its ordinary people. Meanwhile, the low prices of its exports contribute to the spread of their consumption in the importing countries. In the Chinese case we can see this pattern developing before the efficiencies of modern industrial production had an impact, and without colonial or even semicolonial political domination. In fact, Chinese control of foreign trade was in most respects tighter and more defensive in the 1780s than it had been a half-century before.

THE TURN TO RESTRICTION, 1740–1800

The Qing Empire in the mid-eighteenth century was an enormously energetic society with considerable cultural and social diversity. The rulers were capable of complex and stable differentiations among aspects of complex situations. Management of the Canton trade and other relations with maritime Europeans generally were differentiated and stable in this way. But the sheer growth of the trade led to strains, especially as the Canton merchants, overspecialized and burdened with quasi-bureaucratic responsibilities, could not find the financial resources to manage the growing trade. On two occasions a crucial differentiation broke down, and worries about missionaries affected policy toward the

---

[97] Richard Von Glahn, "Money Use in China and Changing Patterns of Trade in Monetary Metals, 1500–1800," in Dennis O. Flynn, Arturo Giraldez, and Richard Von Glahn, eds., *Global Connections and Monetary History, 1470–1800* (Aldershot, 2003), pp. 187–205.

Canton trade. Although we must avoid looking at these years in the light of the great crisis of the next century, it seems clear that after 1780 the Qing Empire and maritime Europeans, including some new types fresh from the plunder of Bengal, were increasingly on a collision course.[98]

In the early 1740s, Sino-European trade was touched by global changes. The War of Jenkins' Ear (1739), merging into the War of the Austrian Succession (1740–1748), brought English and French warships to Chinese waters. Commodore George Anson, after raiding the coasts of Chile and Peru and crossing the Pacific, refitted his ship near Macao and later returned with a captured Manila galleon and its cargo of almost a million taels of silver.[99] These were mere hints of an Anglo-French struggle for worldwide maritime dominance that would push the English into building an empire in India and thereby transform their relations with China, and sixty years later would lead to the English occupation of Macao. The Qing authorities were quite capable of the adaptations these beginnings required. Anson was allowed to hire carpenters and smiths to repair his ship. When he insisted that his warship was exempt from the tolls paid by trading ships and sailed past the Bogue forts without a customs pass, the officials who had failed to stop him were dismissed, but a precedent for the exemption of warships was established and generally honored thereafter.[100]

Major changes in Chinese trade and settlement in Southeast Asia can also be seen from about 1740. The Chinese concentrated less on such major centers as Manila, Batavia, and Bangkok, and spread out into many small ports and rural areas, frequently becoming partly assimilated to the local culture. In one of these centers this process was accelerated by an upheaval that was noticed even in Beijing. At Batavia, in 1740, an ill-conceived plan to deport illegal Chinese immigrants to Ceylon (Sri Lanka) led to a Chinese uprising; ten thousand Chinese were killed in its suppression and in the massacres that followed. To the east of Batavia along the north coast of Java, a tension-filled political system in which powerful Chinese allied with the Dutch exploited both Javanese and poorer Chinese dissolved in civil war and the massacre of

---

[98] The chronological sections that follow draw on Morse, *Chronicles*; Dermigny, *La Chine et l'Occident*; and Jörg, *Porcelain*, Ch. 1, all of which are chronologically organized.

[99] Chaplain Richard Walter, *Anson's Voyage Around the World in the Years 1740–44* (London, 1928; reprint, New York, 1974), pp. 333–348, 365–393; Glyn Williams, *The Prize of All the Oceans: Commodore Anson's Daring Voyage and Triumphant Capture of the Spanish Treasure Galleon* (New York, 2000), Ch. 7.

[100] Lo-shu Fu, *Documentary Chronicle*, pp. 175–176.

more Chinese.[101] The Qing coastal officials discussed the advisability of prohibiting Chinese trade with Java, but finally the emperor decided not to do so, stating that since many people in coastal areas depended on trade for their livelihood, it would be hard to prohibit trade with one country without prohibiting trade with all, and that the Chinese who had been killed "were born in Java, and thus are not different from the native barbarians."[102] Attitudes toward émigrés in Southeast Asia were nuanced and sometimes inconsistent; the Qing officials seem not to have objected to men with Chinese names coming to Canton in charge of Siamese tribute embassies, and occasionally sought information from émigrés about affairs in their countries of residence.[103]

The arrangements settled on around 1730, whereby most of the management of relations with Europeans was delegated to a few trusted merchants, seem to have worked well down through the 1740s. There were a few signs of tighter enforcement of old rules, and the security merchant system was formalized with imperial approval in 1745.[104] If there already was something of a turn toward stricter enforcement, it was accelerated by the effects of a quite separate crisis. This had its beginning in efforts to suppress the Catholic communities that were under the guidance of Manila-based Dominicans in Fuan, Fujian.[105] This repression began like many other local campaigns. Then the officials saw that these were well-organized communities with many churches and lay sodalities, and that communication was kept up with Manila and lists of converts were sent there. There were many literati converts. Thousands of people followed as five missionaries were taken away as prisoners in 1746. One of the five was executed in April 1747. The officials' alarm increased when a Spanish ship came to Amoy with a request for the release of the other missionaries. Two key converts fled on it, and an unrelated rebellion broke out in nearby Jianning. The other four missionaries were executed late in 1748.[106] Catholicism was now seen to be capable of local organization involving both the elite

[101] Johannes T. Vermeulen, *De Chinezen te Batavia en de Troebelen van 1740* (Leiden, 1938); Nagtegaal, *Riding the Dutch Tiger*, Ch. 12; Willem Remmelink, *The Chinese War and the Collapse of the Javanese State, 1725–1743* (Leiden, 1994).

[102] Lo-shu Fu, *Documentary Chronicle*, p. 174.

[103] Wills, "Functional, Not Fossilized."

[104] Cheong, *Hong Merchants of Canton*, pp. 93, 204; Van Dyke, *Canton Trade*, pp. 11–12.

[105] John E. Wills, Jr., "From Manila to Fuan: Asian Contexts of Dominican Mission Policy," in D. E. Mungello, ed., *The Chinese Rites Controversy: Its History and Meaning* (Nettetal, 1994), pp. 111–127.

[106] For the basic Spanish documentation on this episode see José Maria González, O.P., *Misiones Dominicanas en China (1700–1750)* (Madrid, 1952, 1958); for the Chinese

and commoners, with strong organizational ties with a foreign power, so that both Catholicism and foreign trade in Chinese ports were perceived as political threats more than before. As a result, the emperor ordered a thorough investigation throughout the empire to uncover and break up Catholic communities.[107]

The governor of Fujian had reported that the captive missionaries and their Chinese aides also confessed to having received assistance from Macao. According to the report, each church at Macao received funds from abroad and used them to support church activities in one province of China. The churches in China made lists of the foreign names of their converts and sent them to a foreign king, who donated funds in proportion to the number of converts.[108] These lists seemed especially menacing in their subversive potential. Who could tell what the real motives of the foreign preachers in China might be? The magistrate of Xiangshan county, where Macao was located, was ordered to investigate, and did so late in 1746 and early in 1747. He was especially alarmed to find that there was a special establishment in Macao, the Seminario de Nossa Senhora do Amparo, with a staff of Chinese Christians, devoted to converting Chinese to the forbidden faith. In addition to the Chinese Christian population in Macao there were communities in nearby counties, and every year many believers came from them and even from other provinces to worship in Macao during the Lenten and Christmas seasons. It was clear that the Seminario, a center of cultural and potentially of political subversion, must be closed at once, and the Macao authorities were so informed. They protested, but eventually acquiesced. The Qing authorities went on to work out a comprehensive set of regulations for Macao that settled some local difficulties as well as the original problem. These regulations were carved in both Chinese and Portuguese on stone tablets that were set up in Macao in 1749, supplementing the principles similarly engraved on stone in 1614–1617. All efforts to convert Chinese to Christianity were forbidden. Macaenses were forbidden to go hunting in nearby areas, to buy Chinese children, or to harbor Chinese criminals in their homes. Portuguese jurisdiction in Macao was severely limited; for all punishment of Chinese, or for punishment of Europeans for crimes punishable

contexts see Eugenio Menegon, *Ancestors, Virgins, and Friars: The Localization of Christianity in Late Imperial China* (Cambridge, MA, 2009).

[107] Lo-shu Fu, *Documentary Chronicle*, pp. 178–185.

[108] Ibid., pp. 179–180.

by death or banishment under the Qing code, the Portuguese courts and the Chinese local magistrates were to have joint jurisdiction.[109] The general repression of Roman Catholicism and especially the new impositions on Macao stimulated another embassy from the king of Portugal. The ambassador, Francisco de Assis Pacheco de Sampaio, arrived at Macao in 1752. He reported that he had received assurances that he was not being received as a tributary ambassador. Since it was a first embassy to the Qianlong emperor, it probably was labeled an "embassy presenting congratulations" as its predecessor had been. In Beijing in May and June 1753, the emperor received the ambassador at the Qianqing Gate in the palace, received the royal letter from his hands, later was present at one of the banquets for him, had the ambassador's portrait painted by Castiglione and came to see it, gave the ambassador another audience at which he gave him a jade *ru yi*, and invited him to enjoy the dragon boat races at the summer palace. These were extraordinary gestures of favor, but they were largely personal gestures of the emperor, not precedent setting, not elements of a formal bureaucratic system. The ambassador performed "the customary ceremonies" on all occasions. Neither this embassy nor any other European embassy between Paats in 1685 and Titsingh in 1794 was received before the full capital bureaucracy at an ordinary audience or other occasion prescribed by the regulations. Pacheco de Sampaio, like his predecessor, decided not to mention the missions to the emperor. The powerful Fuheng, grand secretary, trusted general, and imperial in-law, was very cordial and seemed inclined to disavow the previous policy of repression of Catholicism, but this seems not to have led to any policy changes. For the Europeans, embassies still offered no opportunities for negotiation and formal agreement. For the Qing emperors and officials, European embassies were oddities, managed in ad hoc fashion, scarcely part of a system that could guide policy.[110]

European trade at Canton expanded in the brief interval of peace among the European powers, 1749–1756. Anglo-French antagonism remained high and led to fights among sailors at Whampoa. A petition presented by

---

[109] *Xiangshan xianzhi* (Qianlong Ed.), 8, pp. 26b–46; and *Instrução para o Bispo de Pequim, e Outros Documentos para a Historia de Macau* (Lisbon,1943), pp. 33–39.
[110] "Relatorio de Francisco de Assis Pacheco de Sampaio a El-Rey D. Jose I dando conta de Embaixada ao Imperador de China, no anno de 1752," in Judice Biker, *Colleçao de Tratados e Concertos*, Vol. 7, pp. 52–106; J. S. de Neuvialle, S.J., "Relação da jornada ... e summaria noticia da embaixada," in E. Brazão, ed., *A Politica Europeia no Extremo Oriente no Seculo XIX e as Nossas Relações Diplomaticas com a China* (Porto, 1938), pp. 60–84.

the supercargoes of the English East India Company in August 1753 gives the impression that tensions and grievances were accumulating rapidly at Canton. They complained about slow unloading of ships, stealing from boats on the river, and the petty exactions of customs officials, constant themes of European merchants in Chinese harbors from the 1660s to the 1860s. They also complained of "very unhandsome Chops [proclamations] which have lately been affixed in public parts of the City and Suburbs accusing us of Crimes, the mention of which, is horrible to us: to them we attribute the frequent Insults we meet in the Streets."[111] This is the first sign we know of suggesting the popular antiforeignism in the Canton area that was to be a constant factor in Sino-foreign relations for a century or more. No doubt it was stimulated by the growing number and constant belligerence of the sailors at Whampoa. Perhaps it was reinforced by the official repression of Catholicism and control measures at Macao, which may have given new courage to local commoners and gentry who resented their Chinese Christian neighbors and tended to link all foreigners with them.

The first point in the 1753 petition was as follows: "We desire we may not be troubled with Securities for our Ships, and that whoever we purchase Goods of, or sell Goods to, they be answerable to the Government for the Duties to be paid on them. Those Merchants who are Securities for our Ships, are so distressed on account of Duties, which they are made answerable for, altho' they are neither the Purchasers or Sellers of the Goods, on which the Duties are due, that our Trade greatly suffers thereby." This is an excellent summary of one aspect of the security merchant problem. In the 1750s it was also reported that many small and unreliable merchants were buying goods from foreigners on credit and then paying their debts in inferior goods or not at all. Since this was described as resulting in burdens on the security merchants, apparently they were expected to guarantee payment of debts to the foreigners as well as duties to the government. All these burdens probably increased after 1750 as the trade grew and more of it was not with the security merchants.

That was only one side of the difficulties of the security merchants. The other involved the import of clocks and other fine European mechanical contrivances and craft goods in what was known as the "singsong trade." This importation was largely through the permitted private trade of servants of the English Company. The purchase of such rarities was the

---

[111] Morse, *Chronicles*, Vol. 5, p. 9.

prerogative of the imperial court, which reportedly allotted 30,000 taels per year for the purpose. The superintendent of maritime customs required the security merchants to purchase them when the ships arrived; the foreigners, being aware of this, demanded high prices. The superintendent then bought them from the security merchants, frequently for less than they had had to pay. Because it was English ships that provided this trade, it was especially burdensome to be a security merchant for such a ship, and in 1754 the English found it extremely difficult to find a merchant who would be willing to stand security for any of their ships.[112]

In 1755 these difficulties pushed the two parties in opposite directions, the English trying to break out of the restrictions and frustrations at Canton, the Qing authorities working to strengthen and systematize the controls there. The new Qing regulations made the English even more anxious to break out, which made the Qing even more determined to control them. By 1760 the Qing had won. In 1755 the English Company sent one ship to investigate the possibility of trade in the Ningbo area. The Zhejiang superintendent of maritime customs welcomed it and promised the English good trading conditions there, but we do not know how much trade was carried on. The Qing court was aware of this voyage, and noted a report that some of the Chinese servants on the ship did not have queues, but did not immediately forbid English trade there. When the English returned to Ningbo in 1756, they did some trade but encountered many difficulties, which they attributed to dissension among the officials and the intrigues of Canton officials and merchants, who hoped to make it impossible for them to trade anywhere but at Canton. The duties, which had been lower than those at Canton, were raised to the Canton rates, and the governor-general advised the English to trade at Canton in the future.[113] The court was already worried about the possibility of growth of foreign trade at Ningbo and hoped the increased duties would be enough to discourage it.

A Spanish ship was allowed to trade at Amoy in 1756, but it too may have increased the court's uneasiness about spreading foreign contact.[114] So may the discovery of Catholic missionaries and convert communities in Jiangnan. When the English came again to Ningbo in 1757, there was much delay and confusion, but finally they were not allowed to trade at all and were told that they must never come again. The English were

---

[112] Ibid., pp. 10–14.
[113] Ibid., pp. 49–53.
[114] Fu, *Documentary Chronicle*, pp. 197–198.

convinced that this represented the final victory of the Canton interest. No doubt this was an important factor, but Chinese documents make it clear that others were involved. In one document the fear is expressed that if many foreign ships come and go to Zhejiang, "they will come to know our border areas very well" – a revival of traditional fear of foreign spying that we have suggested was somewhat weaker earlier in the century. Another document states that they must be kept away so that Chinese "rascals will not lure and invite the foreigners and so cause trouble," echoing the traditional account of the Wako disasters in that area in the 1550s. An edict of 1757 is especially striking; if many foreign ships come to Ningbo, "in the future foreign ships will gather like clouds, and [foreigners] will remain there for longer and longer times, so that it will become another Macao. This is of great importance for an important part of our coastal frontier and for the customs of our scholars and people."[115]

In 1754 six of the most powerful hongs, including Poankeequa, worked out an arrangement to control the shares of imports going to each of them and to the other firms. For the Qing authorities, these moves by the merchants seemed to present an opportunity to solve some of the financial problems of the security merchants by giving them a monopoly on foreign trade, and to strengthen control of the foreigners by making it the clear and complete responsibility of the same merchants.[116] There were ten hongs or firms that were qualified to serve as security merchants. The smaller "shopkeeper" merchants managed to secure a modification of this monopoly by which they would form themselves into guarantee groups of five under the supervision of a security merchant and could participate in the trade with his approval. But the trade in tea and raw silk was strictly limited to the security merchants, as was the singsong trade. The interpreters also were brought more completely under the control of the security merchants, and the security merchants and the interpreters were made clearly responsible for the good conduct of the foreigners.

In 1759 the English at Canton sought to present their grievances directly to the imperial court without the interference of the "Canton interest," which seemed to be encircling them. James Flint, who had been left in China as a boy in 1736 to learn the language, was sent north on a small ship. Finding all access barred in the Ningbo area, he went on

[115] Liang Tingnan, *Yue haiguan zhi, juan.* 8, pp. 18, 21; Fu, *Documentary Chronicle,* pp. 200–202.
[116] Van Dyke, *Merchants of Canton.*

to Tianjin, where the presentation of his petition brought about, in less than a week, the dismissal of the Guangdong superintendent of maritime customs and the dispatch of imperial commissioners to investigate the situation in Canton. By sending a foreigner who knew Chinese by sea to the vicinity of the capital, the English had unwittingly reinforced the growing Qing concern about spies and set off another round of restrictive measures. When the commissioners reached Canton, they summoned the supercargoes of the foreign companies and informed them that the superintendent of maritime customs had been dismissed and that under his successor all abuses would be corrected. They also ordered an intensive search for the Chinese who had helped Flint write the petition, spurred by repeated references in imperial edicts to "treacherous people in the interior" who must have helped Flint. It turned out that Flint had been helped by his Chinese teacher, who was beheaded. Flint was imprisoned for three years.[117]

Having dealt with the scapegoat superintendent, the foreign spy, and his treacherous adviser, the court and the Canton authorities turned in the spring of 1760 to the elaboration of a new set of regulations, which would set the pattern for trade at Canton until the Opium War. Their basic provisions and subsequent developments can be summarized as follows:

1. Foreigners were forbidden to stay in the factories in Canton after their ships left. Chinese merchants were to settle accounts with them promptly so that they would have no excuse to delay their departure. Foreigners always went to Macao for the winter, but up to 1760 and again from about 1763 onward some of them remained for a few weeks to wind up business after the ships left.

2. The hong merchants were responsible for the conduct of the foreigners to whom they rented living and warehouse space; thus the authorities hoped to limit access to them and keep track of their comings and goings. The area of the foreign "factories" along the river front became an isolation zone, with no access to the walled city and allowance for only occasional outings to a temple on an island across the river.

3. Chinese were forbidden to borrow from foreigners. The court had understood this to be among the grievances presented by Flint.

---

[117] Morse, *Chronicles*, Vol. 5, pp. 68–84; Fu, *Documentary Chronicle*, pp. 215–229.

Also, the foreigners in Canton were not allowed to hire Chinese servants. Both prohibitions, however, were consistently violated.

4. Foreigners were not allowed to send letters into the interior without official permission. The authorities seemed to be especially concerned about communication between Macao and the Jesuit astronomers in Beijing.

5. More troops were to be stationed at Whampoa to maintain order among the large number of sailors there. This was the last in a series of steps to control violence in that area. From 1754 on, French sailors were allowed ashore only on French Island and English sailors on Danes Island, while others could use both. The shops on the islands were not supposed to sell strong drink, but frequently did so.[118]

The restrictive trend also made the authorities open to other proposals. The short-lived prohibition of raw silk exports and the later quota system were one example of this. Also, the English reported in 1760 that the hong merchants were trying to obtain official approval for a scheme in which they would abandon independent trading with foreigners and contribute fixed shares of capital to a "public guild" (*gong hang*, usually referred to by the Cantonese pronunciation "co-hong"), which would have as a single unit the same monopoly on foreign trade they had enjoyed previously as competing firms. Poankeequa saw his chance in the officials' desire to have everything under tight control and now would be a major participant. The proposal was approved, despite the protests of the foreign merchants. The governor-general, echoing a theme much more common in the state papers of these years than it had been earlier, told them, "If you can not get a tolerable profit upon your goods, you must not in future bring any, as it is of very small consequence to this country."[119] They also sought to split the combine by offering advantageous terms to any merchant who would make a separate contract, but to no avail. The cohong obviously was advantageous to all the Chinese merchants, except possibly the strongest, since they could virtually dictate import and export prices. The officials thought in terms of "fair prices" rather than competitive price setting, and at this time probably were receptive to any proposal that seemed to offer greater control of Chinese and foreign merchants and fewer opportunities for particular alliances between them. They surely understood that the cohong arrangement would make it

---

[118] Morse, *Chronicles*, Vol. 5, pp. 85–98.
[119] Ibid., p. 93.

easier for all the merchants to share the burden of the singsong trade, which continued to make them unwilling to stand security for English ships and was causing the English supercargoes to do all they could to discourage the import of clocks and other curiosities.

The "factory" buildings along the waterfront provided ample and flexible space for warehousing goods and for the residential and public spaces of the foreign companies. They were modifications of local building designs, and it was not until changes were made in the nineteenth century that they gave a strong impression of being a foreign enclave.[120] The daily routine of trade involved a good deal of arguing, some of it about the quality of tea samples, but generally went smoothly.[121] There was not much cultural interchange, but much friendly coming and going. In 1761 the English invited other Europeans and Chinese merchants to celebrate the accession of George III, with lanterns, fireworks, and an average of one and a half bottles of claret per person. William Hickey recorded a succession of dinner parties at Poankeequa's country estate in 1769; on the first evening the Europeans laughed while the Chinese attempted to eat European food with knife and fork, while on the following evening it was the turn of the Chinese to laugh at the foreigners trying to eat Chinese food with chopsticks. The highlight of the first dinner was a Chinese opera in which an actor appeared doing his impression of an English naval officer, bounding on stage shouting, "Maskee can do! God Damn!" whereupon the Chinese shouted, "Truly have muchee like Englishman." At Whampoa each of the ships had an excellent band, and they all played at sunrise and sunset every day, the music coming from various directions across the water making a delightful effect.[122]

The strongest hong merchants in this period were Poan (Pan) Keequa, frequently in conflict with a powerful combination of Tan (Chen) Chetqua, Chai (Cai) Hunqua, and Sweetia (surname Yan). The English continued their efforts to break the cohong, and in 1768 Tan Chetqua switched to

---

[120] Johnathan A. Farris, "Thirteen Factories of Canton: An Architecture of Sino-Western Collaboration and Confrontation," *Buildings & Landscapes: Journal of the Vernacular Architecture Forum*, Vol. 14 (2007), pp. 66–83; Patrick Conner, *The Hongs of Canton: Western Merchants in South China, 1700–1900, as Seen in Chinese Export Paintings* (London, 2009).

[121] The best picture of these routine interactions now available is in Paul A. Van Dyke, trans. and annotated, Cynthia Viallé, corrections, *The Canton–Macao Dagregisters, 1762, 1763, 1764* (Macao, 2006, 2008, 2009, respectively).

[122] William Hickey, *Memoirs*, ed. Alfred Spencer, 4 vols. (London, 1913–1925), Vol. 1, pp. 196–232; see also the abridged edition, ed. Peter Quennell (New York, 1962), which includes some passages on China omitted from the earlier edition.

a temporary alliance with Poankeequa. The two of them made a separate contract with the English, taking all their woolens and getting a favored position in their silk purchases in return. By 1771 two of Poankeequa's three opponents were dead and their firms in less capable hands. The cohong was moribund, and strenuous efforts to dissolve it no longer were necessary. Poankeequa did not explain this to the foreigners. He accepted 50,000 taels from the English – there is no evidence that the other foreigners were even asked to contribute – and took credit for the formal dissolution of the cohong.[123] He remained by far the wealthiest and most influential of the hong merchants until his death in 1778, and his son was an important figure until after 1800.[124]

After 1771 the hong merchants still had their monopoly of the silk and tea trades, but now they were free to make their own contracts and settle their prices individually. Competitive bidding and adjustments of supply and demand were important, but there was also a year-by-year negotiated trade in which the hong merchants agreed to take certain shares of the English imports of woolens in return for the right to supply the same fractions of their tea exports. Only about two-fifths of the English tea exports were apportioned in this way, and we do not know how important this system was for the other nationalities. Although the London directors were not happy about the negotiated trade, it was a sensible response to circumstances and was advantageous to both parties. The hong merchants' once-ample capital resources were strained by the growth of the trade. For necessary advances to their suppliers they depended on importers' supplies to them of silver or readily salable commodities. The English had to sell woolens to placate domestic opposition

---

[123] Van Dyke, *Merchants of Canton*; Van Dyke, "Cai and Qiu Enterprises: Merchants of Canton 1730–1784," *Review of Culture*, Int. Ed., No. 15 (July 2005), pp. 60–101; Van Dyke, "The Yan Family: Merchants of Canton, 1734–1780s," *Review of Culture*, Int. Ed., No. 9 (January 2004), pp. 30–85, also translated and published in Chinese as "Yanshi Jiazu: Guangzhou Shangren (1734–1780)," *Review of Culture*, Chinese Ed., No. 57 (Winter 2005), pp. 1–52. I am grateful to Paul Van Dyke for further discussion of these tangles.

[124] The best studies of the hongs based on Western and Chinese sources now are Van Dyke, *The Canton Trade*, and Van Dyke, *Merchants of Canton*. Important earlier studies are Chen Kuo-tung, *Insolvency*; Wing Eang Cheong, *Hong merchants of Canton*; and Ann White, *The Hong Merchants of Canton* (Ph.D. dissertation, University of Pennsylvania, 1976). Also fundamental are H. Cordier, "Les marchands hanistes de Canton," *T'oung Pao*, 2d Ser., Vol. 3 (1901–1902), pp. 281–315, and Liang Jiabin, *Guangdong shisan hang kao* (Shanghai, 1937; reprint, Taipei, 1960). The term "cohong" (Mandarin *gong hang*) has been retained for the highly unified monopoly guild of 1760–1771, but we find it misleading to apply it to other, looser combinations later in the century.

to the English East India Company and needed every possible source of funds for their growing purchases of tea. Woolens were salable in China, but not *readily* salable, partly because the largest markets were far from Canton. Thus the Chinese merchant would be much more willing to take his share of the woolens if he was assured that he would have a similar share in the profits of the tea trade.

From the early 1770s on, European trade at Canton was supported by large amounts of silver from India. English private fortunes amassed in the unbridled exploitation of Bengal were invested in Danish and Swedish trade with China, the earnings then being used to buy bills on London. English private traders based in India steadily expanded their trade with the hong merchants in Canton and also loaned money to them. Silver earned by the private traders was paid into the English Company's treasury in Canton in return for bills drawn on the company in London. But the normal hazards of trade involving huge cash advances to suppliers were increased by the politics of this period. We can see in the English records a growing number of cases of blatant extortion by officials after the rise of Heshen in 1775–1776.[125] This contributed to the hong merchants' difficulties in repaying their debts. Later debt cases resulted not from European loans but from the unwise trading practices of some of the less well established hong merchants and the ruthless price manipulations of the private traders. In all debt cases the hong merchants and the Canton authorities made conscientious efforts to arrange for the repayment of the debts by arranging long schedules of payment and contributions by the other merchants. All this was much harder to arrange because the creditors were contentious and hard-to-please individuals, not the great companies with their stake in the continuity of the trade.

The continued health of the Chinese merchant community required a stable source of common funds to repay the debts of bankrupts and to take some of the official "squeeze" off individual merchants by making presents to the officials on behalf of the whole guild. This was accomplished by the levying of small extra duties on imports for a "guild hall" (*gong suo/consoo*) fund. Hints of this can be found in English sources as early as 1755, and the "Consoo Fund" was clearly established by 1780.[126] With this important merchant-managed levy and the frequency of woolens-and-tea share agreements, aspects of European trade at

---

[125] Morse, *Chronicles*, Vol. 2, pp. 13–22.
[126] Van Dyke, *Canton Trade*, p. 100.

Canton functioned as a single unit almost as much as they had in the cohong of the 1760s.[127]

In 1782 five new firms were admitted to the maritime trade guild and made to stand security for each other. Morse writes of the reestablishment of the cohong in 1775 and in 1782, but it does not seem that there ever was a return to the complete amalgamation of capital and comprehensive price fixing of the early 1760s. The firms were assigned to stand security for foreign ships in strict rotation. Sometimes the assignments and rotations were virtually dictated by the foreigners. This seems to have worked well at first, but by 1786 the naming of security merchants was again a source of controversy between the English traders and the Canton authorities. In the 1780s and 1790s separate deals by individual merchants were common in trade with the companies, and were the general rule in the country trade and in the private trade of English Company servants. Many merchants not part of the guild also got a share in the country and private trade. A guild merchant might guarantee such a transaction, but if something went wrong with it an aggrieved foreigner had no recourse to the authorities. Nor were the measures of coordination sufficient to save the guild merchants from bankruptcy. Pressure on them to contribute to military campaign funds, to special gifts for the emperor, and so on was unremitting, as was the general "squeeze" by provincial officials and superintendents of maritime customs. Several of the new guild firms of 1782 were in serious trouble by 1792, and six more were added in that year.[128]

The Europeans deplored each restriction and extra charge in this system, but within the general context of Chinese restriction on foreign contact and late Qianlong corruption it is remarkable how well it served the interests of the merchants on both sides. A huge trade was smoothly coordinated, exacting quality control was maintained, and large transactions were agreed to and carried out on the simple word of individuals.

## NEW DIRECTIONS, 1780–1800

The basic pattern of official control and merchant monopoly at Canton and of life in the factories persisted well past 1800, in some ways right down to the Opium War. But this apparent continuity masked basic changes that already could be seen before 1800. The coasts of the Pacific

---

[127] Morse, *Chronicles*, Vol. 2, p. 82.
[128] Ibid., p.197.

were being linked to Canton by Western ships. The *Resolution* and the *Discovery* refitted in the Canton area in 1779, after Captain James Cook's death in Hawaii, and La Perouse's ships called at Macao in 1787 after their exploration of the North Pacific. Three ships called from Botany Bay, the first English settlement in Australia, in 1788, the year of its founding.[129] Manila was opened to foreign trade and rapidly became enmeshed in the growing English country trade network.[130] Ships bringing furs from the northwest coast of North America began coming to Canton in the 1780s. Some Chinese sailors and artisans even signed on for one voyage to North America.[131] Some of these ships were American, part of one of the most striking trends of the 1790s. The first American ship to trade at Canton arrived in 1784. By 1800 American trade constituted 15 to 20 percent of the total Western trade at Canton.[132] This rise was matched by a sharp decline in continental European trade. The Dutch East India Company was moribund by 1790 and finally was abolished in 1799. French trade at Canton was badly managed and unprofitable even before it was virtually eliminated by the events of the French Revolution and the wars with England.

The English dominated Canton trade after 1780, not just by default of their competitors, but also by their own growing wealth and power at home and in India and by one long overdue policy change. In the wars of 1776–1783 the English lost part of an empire in North America but extended their power in India and the Indian Ocean, making a revival of French power impossible. In 1784 Pitt pushed through the Commutation Act, reducing the duties on tea from more than 100 percent to 12.5 percent, which destroyed at a stroke the business of smuggling tea into Great Britain that had been so important to the Continental companies trading at Canton. In 1792 Continental trade at Canton measured in either tonnage of shipping or tea exports was less than half that of 1783. In the years 1799–1806 total tea exports averaged more than 280,000 piculs per year, of which almost 50,000 were American, less than 30,000 Continental, and about 200,000 English.[133] These English exports were

---

[129] Ibid., p. 151.

[130] W.E. [Wing Eang] Cheong, "Changing the Rules of the Game (The India–Manila Trade, 1785–1809)," *Journal of Southeast Asian Studies*, Vol. 1, No. 2 (1970), pp. 1–19.

[131] Morse, *Chronicles*, Vol. 2, p. 135; Dermigny, *La Chine et l'Occident*, pp. 1129–1198.

[132] Dermigny, *La Chine et l'Occident*, pp. 1129–1198; Jonathan Goldstein, *Philadelphia and the China Trade, 1682–1846* (University Park, PA, 1978); Philip Chadwick Foster Smith, *The Empress of China* (Philadelphia, 1984); James R. Fichter, *So Great a Profit: How the East Indies Trade Transformed Anglo-American Capitalism* (Cambridge, MA, 2010).

[133] Dermigny, *La Chine et l'Occident*, pp. 539, 1055.

between three and four times English exports in the 1780s. This pace of growth would have been impossible without the immense growth of the country trade from Calcutta and other Indian ports in opium, cotton, and other commodities. In 1792–1793 bills drawn on London by country traders provided 34 to 37 percent of the English Company's investment in exports from Canton.[134]

Free trade as an ideology had little effect on European relations with the Qing Empire before the 1830s, but free trade as a fact, as a source of dynamism and trouble, can be seen from the 1760s on. Even when country traders traded legally at Canton, they traded with individual merchants inside and outside the guild, subverting its control. Conversely, the Qing officials expected the European companies to control the private merchants of their own countries, but they were never able to do so. The opium trade was completely beyond the control of the Canton system. The two networks of uncontrolled private trade, European and Chinese, met in Southeast Asia, especially along the Straits of Melaka (Malacca in older books).[135] Trade with Chinese in that area had been an important early focus of English country trade from Calcutta in the 1770s. The English settlement of Penang in 1786 gave this contact a secure center that soon began to attract Chinese emigrants, some of then recruited by the English Company at Canton.

While its existing institutions of control at Canton were being subverted and outgrown in the 1780s, the Qing state was moving toward ever tighter and more detailed enforcement of them. Some of the reasons for this were endogenous to the Canton system. Superintendents of maritime customs sought to maximize revenue from the trade in order to make their own fortunes (one was supposed to have amassed more than a million taels in his one year in office),[136] to send large presents to court notables, and to send up to a million taels a year to the Imperial Household Department for the emperor's use. In 1792, at the height of the extortions of the Heshen regime, a superintendent told the Macao authorities he was under great pressure to send at least a million taels a year to the court.[137] Separate records on trade and its taxation were kept by the superintendents and the provincial officials and then compared at the end of each

[134] Morse, *Chronicles*, Vol. 2, p. 201.
[135] Nordin Hussin, *Trade and Society in the Straits of Melaka: Dutch Melaka and English Penang* (Copenhagen/Singapore, 2007).
[136] Jörg, *Porcelain*, p. 68.
[137] Jin Guoping and Wu Zhiliang, eds., *Correspondência Oficial Trocada Entre as Autoridades de Cantão e os Procuradores do Senado: Fundo das Chapas Sinicas em Português (1749–1847)*, 6 vols. (Macao, 2000), Vol. 1, p. 428.

year. The result was an increase in incidents of undisguised extortion and of petty enforcement of rules. Hong merchants had to pay large sums in order to be allowed to continue in the business of a deceased father or uncle. In contrast to the early hong merchants, who came with wide experience in business, some of it in Southeast Asia, and who retained multiple sources of funds, the late-eighteenth-century hong merchants were tightly focused on the trade with Europeans and were so burdened with the associated costs and troubles that soon it was hard to find anyone who would take over the assets and responsibilities of such a position.[138]

Foreigners had other grievances. Ships arriving or departing without cargo were frequently subject to delays and obstruction because empty ships yielded no duties and reports of them might lead to questions from Beijing. Trade might be stopped before the Chinese New Year so that the hoppo could close his books without reporting too great an increase in revenue.[139] Another cause of the restrictive trend was violence at Whampoa, where thousands of European sailors spent the trading season on their ships. Brawls were especially frequent in the 1790s, a decade of continual Anglo-French war and of mutinies in the English fleets at home. These incidents do not seem to have led to any new institutions or practices, but they contributed to the perception of the Europeans as dangerous and needing strict control.

This restrictive trend can also be traced to sources that had little or no direct connection to the European trade at Canton. The rulers and elite of the Qing Empire in 1780 were competent, cautious, and conservative, aware of the limits of their control and of the effects of corruption. The coast again was a danger zone with a major rebellion on Taiwan in 1786–1788 and large-scale piracy, much of it based in northern Vietnam, in the 1790s.[140] Correspondence between the Portuguese authorities in Macao and the Canton bureaucracy in the 1790s suggests a situation always almost out of control, with a large number of people moving around and engaging in petty crime, and pirates and opium ships lurking in the outer islands.[141] As we saw in our discussion of the late

---

[138] Chen, *Insolvency*, Chs. 3, 4. Some of these suggestions on the sources of the hong merchants' difficulties are drawn from Cheong, *Hong Merchants*.

[139] Paul Van Dyke, personal communication, 2010.

[140] Dian H. Murray, *Pirates of the South China coast, 1790–1810* (Stanford, CA, 1987); Guimarães, *Uma Relação Especial*, pp. 108–168; Robert J. Antony, *Like Froth Floating on the Sea: The World of Pirates and Seafarers in Late Imperial China* (Berkeley, CA, 2003).

[141] Jin Guoping and Wu Zhiliang, eds., *Correspondência Oficial*, Vol. 1, p. 137; Vol. 2, pp. 12–20; Zhongguo diyi lishi danganguan, Aomen jijinhui, and Jinan daxue guji

Kangxi policies, seaborne threats to the security of the empire did not always lead to restrictive policies against European trade, but the court of the 1780s had little of the self-confidence and breadth of vision that Kangxi had shown in 1716 in distinguishing immediate problems from those of a hundred or a thousand years hence. Moreover, in the 1780s there was a renewal of the worries about subversion by missionaries and Catholic converts that had catalyzed the turn toward restriction in the 1740s. In 1784–1785 four Italian Franciscans were discovered not far from a rebellious area in Shaanxi and, being accused of serving as cannoneers for the rebels, were thrown into prison.[142] The result was a revival of the fear of links between Catholicism and rebellion, a fear that had never entirely died out since the 1740s. The court groped for an understanding of how there could still be Chinese Catholics moving around the empire, maintaining their churches, aiding clandestine European priests.[143] A new repression of Catholic communities all over the empire was ordered. When one Chinese priest managed to take refuge in Macao, the Portuguese refused to give him up and the Canton authorities rather inexplicably backed down.[144]

In addition to contributing to the general perception of Europeans as dangerous and requiring special control, this incident led directly to the Europeans' most important new grievance in these decades, namely their treatment within the Qing legal system. There had been two previous cases of murder, the handling of which had aroused European apprehensions. In the first, in 1772–1773, a British sailor was accused of killing a Chinese. The Portuguese court of Macao found him innocent, but the Qing authorities insisted that he be turned over to them. The Portuguese complied, and he was executed.[145] In the second, in 1780, there seems to have been no doubt that the right man was found guilty of a murder, but the Europeans were disturbed by the fact that a Qing law court had tried and executed a European for the murder of another European.[146] In

---

yanjiusuo, eds., *Ming Qing shiqi Aomen wenti dangan wenxian huibian* (Beijing, 1999), Vol. 1, pp. 416–421; Liu Fang and Zhang Wenqin, eds., *Qingdai Aomen Zhongwen Dangan Huibian* (Macao, 1999), pp. 2–48.

[142] Fu, *Documentary Chronicle*, pp. 299–300.

[143] Zhongguo diyi lishi danganguan et al., *Ming Qing shiqi Aomen wenti*, Vol. 1, pp. 421–497.

[144] Morse, *Chronicles*, Vol. 2, p. 107.

[145] Ibid., pp. 182–185. A. M. Martins do Vale, *Os Portugueses em Macau (1750–1800)* (Macao, 1997), pp. 79–85, lists this case among ten homicides in Macao, 1766–1793, that led to negotiations with the Qing authorities. Preliminary checking shows that six of these cases can be traced in Qing archival documentation.

[146] Morse, *Chronicles*, Vol. 2, pp. 59–60.

some earlier cases of this kind, the authorities had allowed the Europeans involved to settle the matter and punish the guilty party themselves. In neither case was there any doubt that the execution was a legitimate penalty under Qing law.

In 1784 two Chinese in a boat were killed accidentally by the discharge of a salute from the country ship *Lady Hughes*. The gunner who had fired the salute feared for his safety and went into hiding. The Canton authorities, acting on their own principle of group responsibility, seized the supercargo of the ship and stopped the trade of the English Company in order to force the surrender of the gunner. Eventually he was surrendered to the Qing authorities and executed.[147] According to the Qing code, an accidental killing was nominally punishable by death, but commutation to a fine of 12.42 taels was mandatory. In previous cases, starting with a Dutch one in 1665,[148] such a fine and a payment to the family of the victim had always been sufficient. This kind of settlement was accepted again in 1807.[149] In the *Lady Hughes* case, however, although the Canton officials pointed out that the gunner had not intended to kill anyone and asked if he could be released and sent away, the emperor explicitly described it as a case of killing in a brawl (*dou ou*), which made the death penalty legally possible, and decreed that the loss of life must be atoned for. This drastic departure from norms and precedents becomes somewhat comprehensible when we note that the *Lady Hughes* incident took place about a month after the above-mentioned excitement about a Chinese priest fleeing to Macao. The edict ordering the execution also discussed the court's concern about communication between foreigners in Canton and Macao and the priest-astronomers in Beijing, about the dangers of foreigners causing trouble and plotting with local people in Guangdong, and about missionaries sneaking into the interior. After ordering the execution, it went on to explain that the offender could not be pardoned, "particularly during this critical time when we are detecting and investigating the Europeans [the missionaries] who have secretly penetrated into various provinces."[150]

The pressure to hand over a culprit, the principle of group responsibility, and the lack of any evidence of a fair trial convinced the English Company's council in Canton that Englishmen would never be safe in

[147] Ibid., pp. 99–109; Fu, *Documentary Chronicle*, pp. 297–298.
[148] Wills, *Pepper*, pp. 118–119.
[149] Morse, *Chronicles*, Vol. 3, pp. 40–46.
[150] Fu, *Documentary Chronicle*, p. 297.

China until they were exempted from Chinese jurisdiction.[151] One partial form of such exemption, which would also free them from many restraints on their trade, would be an island or other territory under English control. Already in 1781 the English had speculated that if Macao should ever "fall into the hands of an enterprising People, who knew how to extend all its advantages; we think it would rise to a State of Splendor, never yet equalled by any Port in the East."[152] Similarly, in the 1780s the French expressed some interest in obtaining a settlement in Taiwan or in taking over Macao.[153] Thus with the *Lady Hughes* case as a catalyst, the whole package of European demands for freedom of trade, extraterritoriality, and territorial concessions began to come together, and the English government became involved in pursuing these demands.

The East India Companies were at once mercantile and quasi-governmental. So was the Chinese maritime trade guild. At Canton both retained their key roles until well into the nineteenth century. But on the European side the two elements were present separately as well as in their company amalgam; along with the growth of private trade came direct intervention by Western governments in the relations of their peoples with the Chinese. There were only modest changes at Canton. In 1779 Admiral Vernon intervened on behalf of the private merchant debtors, over the strenuous objections of the company's servants to this infringement of their authority, and his efforts gave new impetus to Qing official efforts to settle a debtor case.[154]

The presence of a French consul from 1777 and an American consul from 1786 was necessary because these countries had no company monopolies in the China trade. The Prussian consulship of Daniel Beale from 1787 was simply an English private merchant's convenient guarantee of immunity from East India Company control. Before 1800 others would claim to represent Denmark, Genoa, and even Poland, and this type of consulship became more common after 1800.[155] In 1787 the French naval officer d'Entrecasteaux visited Canton at the end of a voyage of reconnaissance east of the Philippines, with instructions to seek to counter the growing English domination and to discuss with the Qing officials the difficulties the French had with the hong merchants over debts and other issues. In a curious throwback to Balthasar Bort in the 1660s,

[151] Morse, *Chronicles*, Vol. 2, pp. 106–107.
[152] Ibid., p. 68.
[153] Charles de Constant, ed. Louis Dermigny, *Memoires*, pp. 432–446.
[154] Morse, *Chronicles*, Vol. 2, pp. 47–49; Fu, *Documentary Chronicle*, pp. 291–292.
[155] Morse, *Chronicles*, Vol. 2, pp. 150, 206–207.

d'Entrecasteaux even offered the Qing officials the aid of French ships against the rebels on Taiwan, but apparently he accomplished nothing.[156] Finally, it is interesting to note that in these years Lisbon was seeking to bring Macao under more direct control. Instructions were sent in 1783 to give the governor greater authority, which included a veto over the decisions of the Senate and the establishment of a royal customs house.

Far more important was a general revival of European interest in formal diplomacy at Beijing that would include not only ambassadorial visits, but the establishment of resident envoys. This was the appropriate form of intergovernmental diplomacy within the European international order, and interest in it was bound to increase with direct involvement of European states. The interest in formal diplomacy also was a corollary to the European hostility to the "Canton interest." It was thought that no justice or honest response to their grievances was to be expected from the officials at Canton, but something might be accomplished if grievances, including those about the Canton officials, could be presented directly to the imperial court in Beijing. This line of reasoning, already to be found in the instructions for the Dutch embassies in the late seventeenth century, ignored the extent to which the Qing polity was based on balance and mutual dependence between court and provincial officials. The court depended on provincial officials for information about provincial conditions and for enforcement of its edicts, and rarely would act on provincial affairs except on the advice of the officials concerned.

The first effort to establish a Western-style diplomatic presence in the capital was the attempt of the Portuguese government to make a newly consecrated bishop of Beijing, Alexandre de Gouvea, a de facto resident envoy and an advocate of Portuguese interests in Beijing. He was dispatched in 1783 with instructions to carry out major changes in the government of Macao and to seek from the imperial court comprehensive improvements in its status, including the revocation of some of the limits of Portuguese jurisdiction there that were embodied in the decisions of 1749. De Gouvea remained in Beijing for more than twenty years in the emperor's service, but it is not known if he managed to accomplish anything for Macao.[157] The second attempt was an embassy from the Spanish viceroy of Mexico that arrived at Canton via Manila in 1787, hoping to go to Beijing and obtain permission to export Chinese mercury

---

[156] Dermigny, *La Chine et l'Occident*, pp. 1106–1111.
[157] *Instrução para o Bispo de Pequim*, esp. pp. 1–67; Vale, *Os Portugueses em Macau*, pp. 98–113.

for use in the Mexican silver industry. But the ambassador was to finance his embassy with the sale of two thousand fur pelts, and when these sold poorly he was forced to give up.[158]

Much more ambitious and important revivals of formal diplomatic activity were the English and Dutch embassies of the 1790s, which expressed the European frustrations, proclaimed some of their new ambitions, stimulated Qing defensiveness, and revived Qing illusions about the relevance of the tributary order in structuring relations with Europeans. In 1787 the London government sent Lieutenant-Colonel Charles Cathcart as ambassador to China, with instructions to complain about the vexations the English had suffered under the officials and merchants at Canton, "in contravention of the Orders and Intentions of the Imperial Courts," and propose the cession of a depot for English trade, where Chinese might remain under Qing jurisdiction but where Englishmen would be subject to their own laws and courts. Cathcart, however, died on the voyage out.[159]

In 1792 an experienced and able diplomat, George Lord Macartney, was named ambassador, and eventually a large and imposing embassy of ninety-five persons set sail in September of that year.[160] Macartney was instructed to seek changes in trade conditions and the cession of a trading depot. But his embassy had other goals, which amounted to nothing less than the presentation to the Qing elite of the new world of science, industry, and the order of nation-states. Permission to establish a resident minister in Beijing was to be sought. Prompted by the new manufacturing interests, the government sent samples of their products with the embassy

---

[158] Dermigny, *La Chine et l'Occident*, pp. 1158–1159.

[159] Morse, *Chronicles*, Vol. 2, pp. 154–171.

[160] The recent literature on the Macartney embassy is extensive. James L. Hevia, *Cherishing Men from Afar: Qing Guest Ritual and the Macartney Embassy of 1793* (Durham, NC, 1994), offers a rich and intellectually ambitious reinterpretation. Alain Peyrefitte, *The Immobile Empire*, trans. Jon Rothschild (New York, 1992), offers a well-documented and intelligent treatment of the English and other European sources but is obtuse in its interpretation of China. A full collection of the documents found by Chinese investigators cooperating with Peyrefitte have been published in Zhongguo diyi lishi danganguan, ed. *Yingshi Magaerni fang Hua dangan shiliao huibian* (Beijing, 1996; hereafter cited as *Yingshi Magaerni*), and a selection in French translation in Alain Peyrefitte, *Un Choc des Cultures. La Vision des Chinois* (Paris, 1991). For a basic text and full commentary see George Macartney, *An Embassy to China: Being the Journal Kept by Lord Macartney During His Embassy to the Emperor Ch'ien-lung, 1793–1794*, ed., annotated, and introduced J. L. Cranmer-Byng (London, 1962; reprint, St. Clair Shores, MI, 1972). See also Robert A. Bickers, ed., *Ritual and Diplomacy: The Macartney Mission to China, 1792–1794* (London, 1993).

in the hope of opening new markets for them. In order to impress the court with English science and technology, the presents included a planetarium, an orrery (clockwork model of the planetary system), a great burning glass, ornate clocks, and (singular gifts to the lord of Jingdezhen) Staffordshire vases and figures by Josiah Wedgwood. Other items sent for public display included a diving bell, an air balloon, an air pump, and apparatus for demonstrating experiments in electricity, mechanics, and so on.[161]

The ambassador, his deputy ambassador, Sir George Leonard Staunton, and their suite arrived by warship in the Gulf of Zhili at the end of July 1793. Other European tribute embassies had regularly come to Beijing by the inland route from Canton. The English knew this but deliberately sent their embassy as close to the capital by sea as possible, and when they informed the officials at Canton it was too late for any counterinstructions to be issued. As a result, permission was received from Beijing for the embassy to enter China by way of Tianjin. As long as the embassy conformed to the general rules for tribute embassies, it would be extremely satisfying for the emperor to enroll as a tributary the English, who had been trading at Canton for a century without "coming to be transformed." Moreover, the English were among the more troublesome foreigners at Canton, and the embassy would provide a good opportunity to show them the Qing Empire's superior culture, good order, prosperity, and military strength and, by kind treatment, to draw the English into the reciprocities of human feelings (*ren qing*).

At first all went well; the pennants on the boats taking the embassy up to Tongzhou near Beijing proclaimed it to be an English embassy bringing tribute, but Macartney turned a blind eye to them. There was some difficulty about the presents. The emperor was at the summer retreat and hunting park in Rehe (modern Chengde), and normally the presents should have been taken there. But some of the scientific instruments were much too delicate for that difficult journey, and Macartney insisted that they remain in Beijing. Finally they were set up in the Yuanmingyuan, the summer palace northwest of Beijing. According to Dr. Dinwiddie, the "mechanic" in the embassy, the officials of Beijing were uninterested in seeing any experiments demonstrated and viewed the planetarium and other presents "with careless indifference." The Qing had already adopted in their own calendrical calculations the superior Western astronomical

---

[161] J. L. Cranmer-Byng, "China, 1792–94," in Peter Roebuck, ed., *Macartney of Lisanoure, 1737–1806: Essays in Biography* (Belfast, 1983), pp. 216–243.

methods. Macartney eventually realized that the court officials were not impressed with elaborate clockwork because they already had so much of it, the results of the endless stream of "singsong trade" items that hoppos and other high Canton officials bought and then presented at court: "[O]ur presents must shrink from the comparison and 'hide their diminished heads.'"[162]

Even before Macartney reached Beijing, the accompanying officials insistently explained to him the ceremonies of the audience and urged him to practice the kowtow. This is odd; there was a place for such practice in the ordinary routine of an embassy, after it was well settled in the capital, when its presents were delivered to the Board of Ceremonies. Perhaps the officials already saw in the arrival of this unexpected and inexplicable embassy, or in the demeanor of the ambassador and his suite, signs that these foreigners might not bend easily to Qing ceremonial conventions. It is also clear that the Qianlong court at this particular moment was extremely sensitive to issues of ceremonial manifestations of its superiority, as a result of the whole anxious aftermath of its botched invasion of Annam in 1788, its subsequent recognition of the ruler it had sought to overthrow, Nguyễn Huệ, and its ostentatious reception of an Annamese embassy headed by a "double" taking the role of Nguyễn Huệ himself.[163] The kowtow was the issue that would turn an exercise in mutual bafflement into a conflict that embittered attitudes on both sides and has dominated Western historiography on the embassy. It seems very likely that all previous European ambassadors to Beijing had performed the kowtow. To Macartney, an experienced and able senior diplomat in the European tradition, ceremonial issues had to be properly handled in order to place his sovereign hierarchically as the full equal of all other sovereigns and inferior to none. But protocol was essentially preliminary to the negotiations that were the real business of an embassy. For the Qianlong emperor and his ministers, ceremony was the core of the business of an embassy. The superiority of the Son of Heaven was a basic principle of the tribute embassy routine. In relations with Inner Asian peoples, it was supplemented by efforts to build strong personal connections with other sovereigns; it seems likely that the Qianlong court's success in this more personalized diplomacy contributed to its anxious efforts to present a pleasant face to the English and to divine if the English were sincerely impressed and friendly in return. The court's efforts were doomed

---

[162] Macartney, *An Embassy*, p. 125
[163] Wills, "Functional, Not Fossilized."

to failure. In their anxious and abstract efforts to be neither too lenient nor too strict, they had no fund of prior knowledge or experience with European diplomats on which to build. Conversely, European experience with the embassy institution provided little foundation for English hopes for substantial negotiations in the capital. There was no reason to expect that a form of ceremonies could be arrived at that would really satisfy both sides. The English were plunging into a milieu about which they understood very little, while expecting that reason and progress would carry all before them.

On the kowtow question Macartney had little guidance from his instructions, which merely ordered him to conform to all ceremonials of the Qing court "which may not commit the honor of your sovereign or lessen your own dignity, so as to endanger the success of your negotiation."[164] Qing officials soon became aware that the English would create many difficulties concerning ceremonial forms and were ready to be patiently persuasive with them, recognizing that this was their first visit to the Celestial Court.[165] As a compromise Macartney suggested that he would be willing to perform before the emperor any ceremony that a Qing official of equivalent rank would be willing to perform before a portrait of George III that he had brought along. This was not an altogether implausible suggestion. Qing envoys had performed the kowtow in person before Russian sovereigns in 1729 and 1731. But the Qing officials rejected it and instead permitted the ambassador to perform the same ceremony before the emperor as he would before the king of England, simply kneeling on one knee. Since it was not proper to kiss the emperor's hand, as he would have his sovereign's, this was omitted. According to his journal and the accounts of several members of his suite, this was the ceremony that was performed at his audience. It is likely that the moment at which nonconformity was most noticeable was that of the emperor's entrance into the audience tent, when the English party knelt and lowered their heads repeatedly, conspicuously higher than the surrounding rows of officials prostrating themselves.[166] Like the Portuguese ambassadors, Macartney was allowed to deliver the king's letter into the emperor's own hands. The ceremony took place on September 14 in a large circular tent in the vast grounds of the summer park at Rehe. To the officials it must have seemed preferable to allow the modified ceremony rather than admit defeat and send the embassy away. Although it was not

[164] Morse, *Chronicles*, Vol. 2, p. 217.
[165] *Yingshi Magaerni*, pp. 13, 149, docs. 36, 205.
[166] Peyrefitte, *Immobile Empire*, pp. 219–226.

in Beijing, and not before the assembled metropolitan bureaucracy in the great courtyard before the Taihedian, it is clear that news of it did reach the capital and that in later dealings with English and Russian envoys the Qing officials hardened their stance and did not countenance any deviation from court ceremony. The account of the event in the Qing *Veritable Records* gives no hint that anything unusual had taken place.[167] No hint of later resentment of these difficulties can be found in the full collection of Qing documents, 783 of them.[168]

Macartney and his party were received by the Qianlong emperor twice more: at the entertainments to celebrate his eighty-third birthday, when they may have once again stuck out above a prostrating throng,[169] and before making a tour of Rehe, when they were shown the imperial hunting park, the lake, and the Buddhist temples and lamaseries. These sights made a great impression on Macartney, as his journal indicates.[170] Reading of all this splendor and considering how strongly the temples and palaces of Rehe echoed the Qing triumphs in Inner Asia, it is not hard to understand how the emperor and his court could take such a remote view of Canton and the people who traded there, seeing them as a source of trouble but also, of course, of revenue and graft. Rehe had been the scene of some of the empire's greatest successes in drawing foreigners into a web of human feelings and mutual obligations, and they could expect similar efforts to prevail with the English. Macartney also had conversations with Heshen and Fukang'an.[171] The latter, who had just returned from commanding the Qing expedition into Nepal, was openly hostile, perhaps because he knew something of the English conquest in India and efforts to develop relations with Nepal and Tibet. Heshen was more cordial, but neither in Rehe nor back in Beijing later was he willing to respond to any of the ambassador's efforts to discuss business with him. A note delivered to Heshen on October 3, however, did elicit an imperial edict giving somewhat more detailed explanations as to why the English requests were being refused.[172] The embassy left Beijing on October 7. It was not allowed to leave the way it arrived, traveled south by the river and canal route, and arrived in Canton on December 19.[173]

---

[167] Fu, *Documentary Chronicle*, pp. 325–326.
[168] *Yingshi Magaerni.*
[169] Peyrefitte, *Immobile Empire*, p. 247.
[170] Macartney, *An Embassy*, pp. 124–126.
[171] Ibid., pp. 120–129.
[172] Peyrefitte, *Un Choc des Cultures*, pp. 296–299.
[173] Peyrefitte, *Immobile Empire*, pp. 297–438.

The court's response to the embassy had been apparent in instructions to the Canton officials before it left Beijing: "Perhaps they intend to spy; this definitely cannot be allowed.... After the tribute envoy arrived he made many entreaties and repeatedly pestered us. It seems that these foreigners after all are ignorant ... perhaps they may conspire to stir up trouble in Macao, and we must be prepared to guard against it." "We now realize that England is the most powerful country of the Western Ocean states. Moreover, we have heard that they have been used to plundering the merchant ships of other Western Ocean countries on the high seas. Therefore, in the regions near the Western Ocean the foreigners fear their bullying."[174]

None of this annoyance or unease was allowed to show in the famous edict to George III, which, in the light of the other documents concerning the embassy, seems less self-assured and more defensive in its assertion of traditional ideas. The request to have an English envoy resident at the capital was rejected on the grounds that it did not conform to the Celestial Empire's fundamental system (*tizhi*). Many communications to the governors of coastal provinces focused on the rejection of this proposal and the prevention of any nonroutine contact.[175] The new governor-general at Canton, who had accompanied Macartney on part of his journey south, made some effort to understand and deal with English grievances at Canton, but to no permanent effect. The English tried to keep up the contact with the imperial court. At the end of 1795 further presents from George III were received at Canton and eventually transmitted to Beijing. But in connection with this transaction it was noted that by a recent edict the officials at various places along the coast were ordered to determine the contents of any letter brought by European embassies, or by other methods, and, before forwarding it to Beijing, to refuse to accept it if it contained a request for an extension of privileges or other changes "contrary to the Established Customs and Laws of the Empire."[176]

The Qing officials had managed to maintain most of the appearances of the tribute embassy and were more determined than ever to defend the entire institution as the obligatory form of dealing with an envoy from any country that came to the imperial court. Even the fact that an embassy had come, albeit a troublesome one bearing impossible requests,

[174] J. L. Cranmer-Byng, "Lord Macartney's Embassy to Beijing from Official Chinese Documents," *Journal of Oriental Studies*, Vol. 4, No. 1–2 (1957–1958), pp. 117–183, esp. 167–173.

[175] *Yingshi Magaerni*, pp. 161–176, docs. 222–237.

[176] Cranmer-Byng, "Official Chinese Documents," esp. pp. 173–183.

seemed to stimulate a renewed focus on the tribute system in relation to dealings with Europeans. Much attention was devoted to the Macartney embassy, for example, in the writings of Liang Tingnan, the nineteenth-century historian of foreign trade institutions at Canton.[177] The impression of relevance was strengthened in 1794 by the return to Beijing of the first European tributaries to the Qing, the Dutch.

This last Dutch embassy was sent by the commissioners general who were in charge of the financially and organizationally moribund Dutch East India Company, but the initiative came from a typically ambitious and restless son of the new age, A. E. van Braam Houckgeest, who had served the Dutch in Canton, then emigrated to America, then rejoined the Dutch Company as head of its Canton establishment. After the embassy he again settled in America and dedicated his account of the embassy to George Washington.[178] After the Macartney embassy, the officials at Canton seem to have been worried about the complaints about them that the embassy had carried and anxious to find some other group of foreigners that would send a less troublesome embassy. They told Van Braam that the Portuguese and the English were planning to send embassies to congratulate the emperor on the sixtieth anniversary of his reign, and surely the Dutch would not want to be left out of this important occasion. Van Braam promptly reported this to Batavia, urging that an embassy be sent. Although it is not clear what they hoped to accomplish given the decrepitude of the Dutch Company and its China trade, the Batavia authorities sent the distinguished Isaac Titsingh as ambassador, naming Van Braam as his second.

Arriving in Canton in September 1794, Titsingh found that Van Braam's recommendations had been based primarily on his own ambition and gullibility. None of the other Europeans had sent embassies, and there had been only the vaguest possibility that they would do so. The Canton officials then made sure that the embassy would be beneficial to them and useless to the Dutch by demanding a promise from Titsingh that he would not make any requests or complaints in Beijing, but was going simply to congratulate the emperor. Titsingh, fearing that otherwise his embassy would not be allowed to go at all, gave the promise.

---

[177] Liang Tingnan, *Yue haiguan zhi*, and Liang Tingnan, *Yuehdao gongguo shuo* (n.d.; reprint, Taipei, 1968).

[178] J. J. L. Duyvendaak, "The Last Dutch Embassy to the Chinese Court (1794–1795)," *T'oung Pao*, Vol. 34 (1938), pp. 1–137, 223–2277; Vol. 35 (1940), pp. 329–353; Isaac Titsingh, *Isaac Titsingh in China (1794–1796): Het Onuitgegeven Journaal van Zijn Ambassade naar Beijing*, ed. Frank Lequin (Alphen aan den Rijn, 2005).

The great celebration of the emperor's sixtieth jubilee would be around the Chinese New Year, which fell on January 21, 1795. The Dutch embassy would be even more advantageous to the reputations of the Canton authorities if it participated in the great occasion. Titsingh told the Canton governor-general he would cooperate if the emperor wished them to be present, thinking that this would be impossible because of the great distance. But the emperor approved the suggestion, and the embassy party was sent off on a cold, miserable, exhausting journey that reached Beijing in only forty-nine days. In Beijing they were treated with many signs of imperial favor, including an invitation to a theatrical performance within the palace. Some officials expressed sympathy for the miseries they had endured on their rapid trip north. They saw the emperor on several occasions, including a splendid entertainment at the summer palace with brilliant illuminations of the buildings. They performed the kowtow whenever they were told to do so. They were present at the New Year's banquet for tributary envoys in the Baohedian, a formal occasion primarily for Inner Asian and Korean tributaries in which no previous European envoy seems to have participated. The presence of tribute envoys at a New Year banquet was one of the longest continuities in the history of Chinese foreign relations, stretching back to the early years of the later Han. Titsingh and Van Braam made no requests and accomplished nothing for their masters. For their hosts their presence had been profoundly reassuring and deluding.[179]

After 1800 the basic continuity of the Canton trade and the lack of other forms of legal contact were punctuated by moments of conflict. The worry about ambassadors who might not perform the kowtow led to the rejection of the Russian ambassador Golovkin in 1806 and the fiasco of the Amherst embassy in 1816. In 1808 Qing fears about English aggression along the coast became reality when an English force occupied Macao to prevent a possible French occupation. The court sent vehement edicts ordering the foreigners to leave and the Canton officials to deal firmly with them. The Canton officials suspended English trade, and after three months the occupiers withdrew. This appeared to be another success for basic Qing policies of taming foreigners by controlling their trade. The court demoted several officials for not having expelled the foreigners immediately, but in fact the Canton authorities had no forces that would have been effective against the English.

---

[179] Fu, *Documentary Chronicle*, pp. 369–377. Blussé, *Visible Cities*, pp. 85–90.

We began by noting the need not to read the entire history of eighteenth-century relations with Europeans as a prelude to the Opium War, but the growth of trade, foreigners' grievances, and the Qing government's defensiveness – all these ingredients of the Opium War situation were present in 1800. All were far more conspicuous in that year than they had been twenty years before.

## SOME CONCLUSIONS

No European ambassador believed that he was presenting tribute on behalf of his monarch to the Son of Heaven, but that is what all the embassies discussed in this chapter were recorded as doing in Qing documents, and we know of no evidence that anyone in the Qing elite conceived of them differently. The Europeans knew they were involved in a system that generally implied paying tribute, but they convinced themselves in several ways that their own status was not tributary. The Dutch did not care about ceremonies and forms as long as they saw that in fact the Qing received embassies from powerful and independent monarchs. The Portuguese conformed with ceremonies but insisted on a change in nomenclature ("embassy presenting congratulations"), which they wrongly believed put them outside the tribute conventions. Macartney, conversely, turned a blind eye to "tributary" banners but was intransigent on the kowtow. All sustained a Qing illusion; all except possibly the Dutch operated under their own illusion that they were not doing so. All went to Beijing with some measure of hope that they were circumventing the obstructions of provincial officials and were about to do business with the real center of decision making. But the tribute embassy was a ceremonial institution, not a medium for negotiation and binding commitment. The only effective negotiations resulting from a tribute embassy were those carried on by the Beijing Jesuits after the departure of the Portuguese embassy of 1678.

In Qing bureaucratic compilations, European embassies were fitted into a pattern of regulation so that they seemed parts of a system. Many of the rules were real enough to the ambassadors who confronted them. There were only ten recorded European tribute embassies in the first 156 years of Qing rule in Beijing, and there were two spans of forty years when none were received. Only the four Dutch embassies were to any degree results of prompting by the Qing side.[180] European motives were

---

[180] This count omits the first and second papal legations. The forty-year gaps were 1686–1727 and 1753–1793.

varied and unsystematic. In the early Qing, the Dutch sought trading privileges and the Portuguese looked to the survival of Macao. The eighteenth-century Portuguese embassies presented the Portuguese monarchs as protectors of Asian missions, while Macartney brought to Beijing the vigor and self-assurance of the new national-commercial-industrial order.

The Dutch had to send embassies to the early Qing court if they wanted to trade in Chinese ports, and for a few years the old Ming system was applied to them. Their trade was limited to that carried on in connection with tribute embassies or permitted on a case-by-case basis closely tied to the embassy institution. This was less a principled reversion to the Ming system than a by-product of restrictions on maritime trade directed against the Cheng regime. From the 1680s on, European trade in Chinese ports was tacitly disassociated from the rules for tribute embassies. The turn toward more restrictive policies regarding maritime trade after 1750 brought, before Macartney, no European diplomatic efforts that would confront and perhaps challenge Qing practices. It is possible, indeed likely, that the precedents of the Ming tribute system and its brief revival in the early Qing helped to make such restrictions seem right and natural to Qing officials. These same precedents and the fortuitous revival of embassy activity in the 1790s may have enhanced the tendency of nineteenth-century statesmen and statecraft scholars to draw on earlier Chinese ideas about foreign relations in their efforts to deal with radically new challenges. But these are at best fragments of an explanation of the story of European relations with the Qing government before 1800.

How, then, can these fragments be fitted back into some more comprehensive view? The handling of traders, the management of embassies, and the changing policies toward missionaries and converts can be seen as a set of *defensive* policies that were loosely linked but were oriented against different threats: threats of disorder along the coast, challenges to the ceremonial supremacy of the emperor, threats to the integrity of Confucian culture, and the danger of subversive organization by the agents of a foreign religion. The causal links among these types of defensiveness were contingent and changed through time. Qing statesmen were quite capable of distinguishing between desirable and dangerous aspects of foreign relations. Only in the case of Macartney was there even a suggestion of challenge to the ceremonial supremacy of the emperor. This was an important reason for the court's strong negative reaction to this embassy, but it came at the very end of the period discussed here. The increasing worry about Christian corruption of cultural orthodoxy in the 1720s did not lead immediately to restrictive policies toward foreign trade. The strongest links were between perceptions of Catholicism as a source of political subversion and turns toward trade restriction in the 1750s and 1780s. In both periods the growth in the number of foreign ships and sailors in Canton increased security preoccupations.

This growth of trade must also be studied in relation to the impressive gains of commerce and productivity in the Qing Empire in these decades, on which there is a constantly growing literature in Chinese, Japanese, English, and other languages. Foreign trade was a stimulus to economic growth, through the import of silver and the very considerable economic benefits of the large exports of tea. The organization of the trade at Canton and its linkages to the areas where tea, silk, and porcelain were produced also offer abundant evidence of the sophistication of Chinese producers and merchants and their ability to increase the scale of their enterprises.

The Canton system became a less adequate framework for trade late in the eighteenth century partly because the volume of trade outgrew it and partly because of changes in political economy that involved both Beijing and Calcutta. Credit in the form of advances from the foreign purchaser to the Canton merchant to the upcountry supplier was increasingly necessary. Silver and readily marketable imports were supplied increasingly by the growth of private trade from Bengal, which also was destructive of the stability of the Canton system. Some of this trade was in opium, which circumvented the system entirely, while the private traders' demands for debt collection drew the hong merchants into political difficulties. Both the hong merchants' need for money and their political difficulties were exacerbated by the exactions of Heshen and his henchmen from the late 1770s on.

Students of European expansion in maritime Asia have emphasized the dynamism of the country trade and its contribution to the growth of European influence even in the early eighteenth century, when the great East India Companies still seemed to dominate the situation. Another set of "country traders," the Chinese overseas merchants, were an important part of the picture of Chinese maritime trade and of the Qing court's policy decisions about European trade. After 1740 an increasing number of European private traders arrived in Canton. There was a new pattern of Chinese emigration dispersing into many areas rather than concentrating on a few major ports, and the connections between overseas Chinese and private European traders in Southeast Asia had many ramifications. These trends were beyond the control of European companies or governments as well as beyond the direct control of the Qing government. The growth of these connections, and the spread of the opium trade by their means in Southeast Asia and onto the China coast, were given new impetus by the growth of English power in Bengal. This new empire, restless, rapacious, optimistic, intolerant of settled forms and commercial restrictions, and ultimately bringing state power in its wake, set maritime Europe on a collision course with the Qing Empire.

# Bibliography

## Archives

Munich. Bayerische Statsbibliothek.
Munich. Universitätsbibliothek.
Paris. Bibliothèque Nationale.
Rome. Archivum Romanum Societatis Iesu. Archives of the Japan–China Province.

## Printed Sources and Studies

Abella, Domingo. "Koxinga Nearly Ended Spanish Rule in the Philippines in 1662." *Philippine Historical Review*, Vol. 2, No. 1 (1969), pp. 295–347.

Aduarte, Fray Diego, O.P., *Historia de la Provincia del Santo Rosario de la Orden de Predicadores en Filipinas, Japon, y China*. 2 vols. Madrid: Consejo Superior de Investigaciones Cientificas, Departamento de Misionologia Española, 1962.

Aimé-Martin, M. L., ed. *Lettres édifiantes et curieuses*. 4 vols. Paris: Desrez, 1838–1843.

Andrade, Tonio. *How Taiwan Became Chinese: Dutch, Spanish, and Han Colonization in the Seventeenth Century*. New York: Columbia University Press / Gutenberg-e, 2007.

Antony, Robert J. *Like Froth Floating on the Sea: The World of Pirates and Seafarers in Late Imperial China*. Berkeley: Institute of East Asian Studies, University of California, 2003.

Arquivo Nacional da Torre do Tombo, ed. *As Gavetas da Torre do Tombo*. 12 vols. Lisbon: Centro de Estudos Históriocos Ultramarinos, 1960–1977.

Atwell, William S. "International Bullion Flows and the Chinese Economy circa 1530–1650." *Past and Present*, No. 95 (1982), pp. 68–90.

"Ming China and the Emerging World Economy, c. 1470–1650." In Twitchett and Mote, eds., *The Cambridge History of China*, Vol. 8: *The Ming Dynasty, 1368–1644, Part 2*, pp. 376–416.

"The T'ai-ch'ang, T'ien-ch'i, and Ch'ung-chen Reigns, 1620–1644." In Mote and Twitchett, eds., *The Cambridge History of China*, Vol. 7: *The Ming Dynasty, 1368–1644, Part 1*, pp. 590–640.

Bailey, Gauvin Alexander. *Art on the Jesuit Missions in Asia and Latin America, 1542–1773*. Toronto: University of Toronto Press, 1999.

Barros, João de, and Diogo de Couto. *Da Asia de João de Barros e Diogo de Couto*. 24 vols. Lisbon: 1777–1778; reprint, Lisbon: Livraria Sam Carlos, 1973–1975.

Bayly, C. A. *Indian Society and the Making of the British Empire*. In *The New Cambridge History of India*, Vol. 2, Part 1. Cambridge: Cambridge University Press, 1988.

Bays, Daniel H., ed. *Christianity in China: From the Eighteenth Century to the Present*. Stanford, CA: Stanford University Press, 1996.

Bernard, Henri. *Aux origines du cimetière de Chala. Le don princier de la Chine au P. Ricci (1610–1611)*. Tianjin: Hautes Études, 1934.

"L'Encyclopédie astronomique du Père Schall (Tch'ong-tcheng li-chou, 1629, et Si-yang sin-fa li-chou, 1645): La réforme du calendrier chinois sous l'influence de Clavius, de Galilée et de Kepler." *Monumenta Serica*, Vol. 3 (1938), pp. 35–77, 441–527.

Bernard-Maitre, Henri, and E. Jarry. "Les missions de Chine après 1644." In S. Delacroix, ed., *Histoire universelle des missions catholiques*. 4 vols. Paris: Grund, 1957.

Bethencourt, Francisco, and Diogo Ramada Curto, eds. *Portuguese Oceanic Expansion, 1400–1800*. Cambridge: Cambridge University Press, 2007.

Beurdeley, Cécile, and Michel Beurdeley. *Giuseppe Castiglione: A Jesuit Painter at the Court of the Chinese Emperors*. Rutland, VT: Tuttle, 1971.

Beurdeley, Michel. *Chinese Trade Porcelain*. Rutland, VT: Tuttle, 1962.

Bickers, Robert A., ed. *Ritual & Diplomacy: The Macartney Mission to China, 1792–1794*. London: British Association for Chinese Studies and Wellsweep Press, 1993.

Blair, Emma H., and James A. Robertson, ed. *The Philippine Islands, 1493–1803*. 55 vols. Cleveland, OH: A. H. Clark, 1903–1909.

Blondeau, Roger A. "Did the Jesuits and Ferdinand Verbiest Import Outdated Science into China?" In Witek, ed., *Ferdinand Verbiest*, pp. 47–54.

Blussé, Leonard. "The Dutch Occupation of the Pescadores (1622–1624)." *Transactions of the International Conference of Orientalists in Japan*, No. 18 (1973), pp. 28–43.

"Dutch Protestant Missionaries as Protagonists of the Territorial Expansion of the VOC on Formosa." In D. Kooijman, ed., *Conversion, Competition and Conflict: Essays on the Role of Religion in Asia*. Amsterdam: Free University Press, 1984, pp. 1–28.

"Minnan-jen or Cosmopolitan? The Rise of Cheng Chih-lung Alias Nicholas Iquan." In E. B. Vermeer, ed., *Development and Decline of Fukien Province in the 17th and 18th Centuries*, Sinica Leidensa, Vol. 22. Leiden: Brill, 1990, pp. 245–264.

"No Boats to China: The Dutch East India Company and the Changing Pattern of the China Sea Trade, 1635–1690." *Modern Asian Studies* Vol. 30, No. 1 (1996), 51–76.

"Retribution and Remorse: The Interaction Between the Administration and the Protestant Mission in Early Colonial Formosa." In Gyan Prakash, ed., *After Colonialism: Imperial Histories and Postcolonial Displacements.* Princeton, NJ: Princeton University Press, 1995, pp. 153–182.

*Strange Company: Chinese Settlers, Mestizo Women and the Dutch in VOC Batavia.* Dordrecht: Foris, 1986.

*Tribuut aan China: Vier Eeuwen Nederlands-Chinese Betrekkingen.* Amsterdam: Cramwinckel, 1989.

*Visible Cities: Canton, Nagasaki, and Batavia and the Coming of the Americans.* Cambridge MA and London: Harvard University Press, 2008.

"The V.O.C. as Sorcerer's Apprentice: Stereotypes and Social Engineering on the China Coast." In W.L. Idema, ed., *Leyden Studies in Sinology.* Leiden: Leiden University Press, 1981, pp. 87–105.

Blussé, Leonard, and R. Falkenburgh. *Johan Nieuhofs Beelden van een Chinareis, 1655–1657.* Middelburg: Stichting VOC Publicaties, 1987.

Blussé, [J.] L., and F. Gaastra, eds. *Companies and Trade: Essays on Overseas Trading Companies during the Ancien Régime.* Leiden: Leiden University Press, 1981.

*On the Eighteenth Century as a Category of Asian History: Van Leur in Retrospect.* Aldershot: Ashgate, 1998.

Blussé, J. L., M. E. van Opstall, and Ts'ao Yung-ho, eds. *De Dagregisters van het Kasteel Zeelandia, Taiwan.* 4 vols. Rijks Geschiedkundige Publicatien, Grote Ser. 195, 229, 233, 241. The Hague: M. Nijhoff, 1986–2000.

Bontinck, François. *La lutte autour de la liturgie chinoise aux XVIIe et XVIIIe siècles.* Louvain: Nauwelaerts, 1962.

Borao Mateo, José Antonio, et al. *Spaniards in Taiwan: Documents.* 2 vols. Taipei: SMC Publishing, 2001–2002.

Bouvet, Joachim, S. J. *L'Estat présent de la Chine en figures.* Paris: Pierre Giffart, 1697.

*Portrait historique de l'empereur de la Chine.* Paris: Michallet, 1697.

Bowen, H. V. *The Business of Empire: The East India Company and Imperial Britain, 1756–1833.* Cambridge: Cambridge University Press, 2006.

Boxer, C. R. *The Christian Century in Japan: 1540–1650.* Berkeley: University of California Press and Cambridge: Cambridge University Press, 1951.

*Fidalgos in the Far East.* 1948; reprint, Oxford: Oxford University Press, 1968.

*The Great Ship from Amacon: Annals of Macao and the Old Japan Trade, 1555–1640.* Lisbon: Centro de Estudos Historicos Ultramarinos, 1959; reprint, Macau: Instituto Cultural de Macau, 1988.

"Portuguese Military Expeditions in Aid of the Mings Against the Manchus, 1621–1647." *T'ien-hsia Monthly,* Vol. 7, No.1 (August 1938), pp. 24–50.

*Portuguese Society in the Tropics: The Municipal Councils of Goa, Macao, Bahia, and Luanda, 1510–1800.* Madison: University of Wisconsin Press, 1965.

"The Rise and Fall of Nicholas Iquan." *T'ien-hsia Monthly,* Vol. 11, No. 5 (April–May 1939), pp. 401–439.

"The Siege of Fort Zeelandia and the Capture of Formosa from the Dutch, 1661–1662." *Transactions of the Japan Society of London,* Vol. 24 (1927), pp. 15–48.

ed. and trans. *South China in the Sixteenth Century, Being the Narratives of Galeote Pereira, Fr. Gaspar da Cruz, O.P., Fr. Martin de Rada, O.E.S.A.* Hakluyt Society, Ser. 2, No. 106. London, 1953.

Braga, J. M. *China Landfall, 1513: Jorge Alvares' Voyage to China.* Hong Kong: K. Weiss, 1956.

*The Western Pioneers and Their Discovery of Macao.* Macao: Imprensa Nacional, 1949.

Bridgman, E. G. "Paul Su's Apology, addressed to the emperor Wanlih of the Ming dynasty, in behalf of the Jesuit missionaries, Pantoja and others, who had been impeached by the Board of Rites in a Report dated the 44th year, 7th month of his reign (A.D. 1617 [sic])." *The Chinese Repository.* Canton (1850) Vol. 19, pp. 118–126.

Brockey, Liam Matthew. *Journey to the East: The Jesuit Mission to China, 1579–1724.* Cambridge, MA: Belknap Press, 2007.

Brook, Timothy. "Communications and Commerce." In Twitchett and. Mote, eds., *The Cambridge History of China*, Vol. 8: *The Ming Dynasty, 1368–1644, Part 2,* (1998) pp. 579–707.

*The Confusions of Pleasure: Commerce and Culture in Ming China.* Berkeley, CA: University of California Press, 1998.

*Praying for Power: Buddhism and the Formation of Gentry Society in Late-Ming China.* Cambridge, MA: Council on East Asian Studies, Harvard University, and Harvard-Yenching Institute, 1993.

*The Troubled Empire: China in the Yuan and Ming Dynasties.* Cambridge, MA: Belknap Press, 2010.

Brucker, Joseph. "Ricci, Matteo." *Catholic Encyclopedia*, 13:38.

Buglio, Ludovico, S. J. *Budeyi bian* in *Tianzhujiao dongchuan wenxian.* Edited by Wu Xiangxiang. Zhongguo shixue congshu, No. 24. (Taipei, 1965), pp. 225–332.

Campbell, William. *Formosa under the Dutch.* London: K. Paul, Trench, Trubner, 1903; reprint, Taipei, n.d.

Cao Yonghe. *Taiwan zaoqi lishi yanjiu.* Taipei: Lianjing, 1979.

Cardim, Antonio Francisco, S.J. *Batalhas da Companhia de Jesus na sua Gloriosa Provincia do Japão.* Edited by Luciano Cordeiro. Lisbon: Imprensa Nacional, 1894.

*Cartas que os Padres e Irmãos da Companhia de Iesus escreverão dos Reynos de Iapao & China.* 2 vols. Evora, 1598; reprint, Tenri, Japan, 1972.

Chan, Albert, S.J. *Chinese Books and Documents in the Jesuit Archives in Rome: A Descriptive Catalogue: Japonica-Sinica I–IV.* Armonk, NY: Sharpe, 2002.

"Late Ming Society and the Jesuit Missionaries." In Ronan and Oh, eds., *East Meets West*, pp. 153–172.

Chan, Hok-lam. "The Chien-wen, Yung-lo, Hung-hsi, and Hsüan-te Reigns, 1399–1435." In Mote and Twitchett, eds., *The Cambridge History of China*, Vol. 7: *The Ming Dynasty, 1368–1644, Part 1*, pp. 182–304.

Chang Pin-ts'un [Zhang Bincun]. *Chinese Maritime Trade: The Case of Sixteenth-Century Fu-chien (Fukien).* Ph.D. dissertation, Princeton University, 1983.

"The First Chinese Diaspora in Southeast Asia in the Fifteenth Century." In Roderick Ptak and Dietmar Rothermund, eds., *Emporia, Commodities and Entrepreneurs in Asian Maritime Trade, c. 1400–1750*. Beiträge zur Südasienforschung, Südasien-Institut, Universität Heidelberg, No. 141. Stuttgart, 1992, pp. 13–28.

Chang, Stephen Tseng-hsin [Zhang Zengxin] . *From Malabar to Macau: The Portuguese in China during the Sixteenth Century*. Ph.D. dissertation, University of Reading, 2002.

Chang Te-ch'ang. "The Economic Role of the Imperial Household in the Ch'ing Dynasty." *Journal of Asian Studies*, Vol. 31, No. 2 (1972), pp. 243–273.

Chang T'ien-tse. *Sino-Portuguese Trade from 1514 to 1644*. Leiden: Brill, 1933; reprint, Brill, 1969.

Chaudhuri, K. N. *The Trading World of Asia and the English East India Company*. Cambridge: Cambridge University Press, 1978.

Chaunu, Pierre. *Les Philippines et le Pacifique des Ibériques (XVI$^e$, XVII$^e$, XVIII$^e$ siècles). Introduction méthodologique et indices d'activité*. Ports–Routes–Trafics, No. 11. Paris: SEVPEN, 1960.

Chaves, Jonathan. *Singing of the Source: Nature and God in the Poetry of the Chinese Painter Wu Li*. Honolulu: University of Hawaii Press, 1993.

Ch'en, Kenneth. "Matteo Ricci's Contribution to and Influence on Geographical Knowledge in China." *Journal of the American Oriental Society*, Vol. 59 (1939), pp. 325–359.

Chen, Kuo-tung Anthony [Chen Guodong]. *The Insolvency of the Chinese Hong Merchants, 1760–1843*. Institute of Economics, Academia Sinica, Monograph Ser., No. 45. Taipei, 1990.

Chen Guodong, "Qingdai qianqi Yuehaiguan jiandu de paiqian." *Shiyuan*, Vol. 10 (October 1980), pp. 139–168.

Chen Yuan. "Yong Qian jian feng Tianzhujiao zhi zongshi." In Wu Ze., ed., *Chen Yuan shixue lunzhu xuan*. Zhongguo dangdai shixuejia congshu. Shanghai: Renmin chuban, 1981, pp. 306–343.

Cheong, W. E. [Wing Eang]. "Changing the Rules of the Game (The India–Manila Trade, 1785–1809)." *Journal of Southeast Asian Studies*, Vol. 1, No. 2 (1970), pp. 1–19.

*Hong Merchants of Canton: Chinese Merchants in Sino-Western Trade, 1684–1798*. Nordic Institute of Asian Studies, Monograph Ser., No. 70. Richmond: Curzon, 1997.

Cohen, Monique, and Nathalie Monnet. *Impressions de Chine*. Paris: Bibliothèque Nationale, 1992.

Cohen, Paul A. "Christian Missions and Their Impact to 1900." In Fairbank, ed., *The Cambridge History of China*, Vol. 10: *Late Ch'ing, Part 1*, pp. 543–590.

Colín, Francisco, S.J. *Labor Evangélica de los Obreros de la Compañia de Jesús en las Islas Filipinas*. 3 vols. New Ed., edited and annotated by Pablo Pastells, S.J. Barcelona: Henrich, 1900.

*Collectanea Sacrae Congregationis de Propaganda Fide*. 2 vols. Rome: Typographia Polyglottta, 1907.

Colloque international de sinologie, Chantilly, 1977. *Les Rapports entre la Chine et l'Europe*. Paris: Belles Lettres, 1980.

Colloque international de sinologie, Chantilly, 1980. *Appréciation par l'Europe de la tradition chinoise*. Paris: Belles Lettres, 1983.

Comentale, Christophe. *Matteo Ripa, peintre–graveur–missionnaire à la cour de Chine. Mémoires traduits, présentés et annotés.* Taipei: Victor Chen, 1983.

Conner, Patrick. *The Hongs of Canton: Western Merchants in South China, 1700–1900, as Seen in Chinese Export Paintings.* London: English Art Books, 2009.

Constant, Charles de. *Les Memoires de Charles de Constant sur le Commerce à la Chine.* Edited by Louis Dermigny. Paris: SEVPEN, 1964.

Coolhaas, W. Ph., ed. *Generale Missiven van Gouverneurs-Generaal en Raden aan Heren XVII der Verenigde Oost-Indische Compagnie.* Rijks Gescheidkundige Publicatien, Grote Se., Vol. 104 et seq. The Hague: Nijhoff, 1960 et seq.

Cordier, Henri. *Bibliotheca Sinica.* 5 vols. Paris: Guilmoto, 1904–1924.

*Histoire générale de la Chine et de ses relations avec les pays étrangers depuis les temps les plus anciens jusqu'à la chute de la dynastie mandchoue.* 4 vols. Paris: P. Geuthner, 1920.

"Les marchands hanistes de Canton." *T'oung Pao,* 2d Ser., Vol. 3 (1901–1902), pp. 281–315.

Couplet, Philippe, ed. *Confucius Sinarum Philosophus.* Paris: D. Horthemels, 1687.

Cranmer-Byng, J. L. "China, 1792–94." In Peter Roebuck, ed., *Macartney of Lisanoure, 1737–1806: Essays in Biography.* Belfast: Ulster Historical Foundation, 1983, pp. 216–43.

"Lord Macartney's Embassy to Peking from Official Chinese Documents." *Journal of Oriental Studies,* Vol. 4, No. 1–2 (1957–1958), pp. 117–183.

Cremer, R. D. *Macau: City of Commerce and Culture.* Hong Kong: UEA Press, 1987.

Criveller, Gianni. *Preaching Christ in Late Ming China: The Jesuits' Presentation of Christ from Matteo Ricci to Giulio Aleni.* Taipei: Ricci Institute, 1997.

Cronin, Vincent. *The Wise Man from the West.* New York: E. P. Dutton, 1955.

Crossley, Pamela. "The Tong in Two Worlds: Cultural Identities in Liaodong and Nurgan during the 13th–17th Centuries." *Ch'ing-shih wen-t'i,* Vol. 4, No. 9 (June 1983), pp. 21–46.

Cummins, J. S. *A Question of Rites: Friar Domingo Navarrete and the Jesuits in China.* London: Scolar Press, 1993.

*The Travels and Controversies of Friar Domingo Navarrete.* Hakluyt Society, New Ser., Vols. 118, 119. Cambridge: Cambridge University Press, 1962.

Cunningham, Charles H. *The Audiencia in the Spanish Colonies, as Illustrated by the Audiencia of Manila (1583–1800).* Berkeley: University of California Press, 1919.

Curtis, Emily Byrne. "Foucquet's List: Translation and Comments on the Color 'Blue Sky After Rain.' " *Journal of Glass Studies,* Vol. 41 (1999), pp. 147–152.

*Dagh-Register gehouden in't Casteel Batavia, 1628–1682.* 31 vols. Batavia; Landsdrukkerij, 1887–1931.

Dai Yixuan. *Mingshi Folangji zhuan jianzheng.* Beijing: Zhongguo shehui kexue chubanshe, 1984.

Dalton, Sir Cornelius Neale. *The Life of Thomas Pitt.* Cambridge: Cambridge University Press, 1915.

*Da Qing huidian shili.* 1899.

*Da Qing lichao shilu.* Tokyo, 1937–1938; reprint, Taiwan, 1963.

D'Elia, Pasquale M., S.J. "Further Notes on Matteo Ricci's De Amicitia," *Monumenta Serica*, Vol. 15 (1956), pp. 356–377.

*Galileo in China.* Translated by Rufus Suter and Mathew Sciascia. Cambridge, MA: Harvard University Press, 1960.

*Il Lontano confino e la tragica morte del P João Mourão, S.I. Missionario in Cina (1681–1726) nella Storia e nella Legenda Secondo Documenti in Gran Parte Inediti.* Lisbon: Agência Geral do Ultramar, 1963.

*Il mappamondo cinese del P. Matteo Ricci, S.J.* Vatican City: Biblioteca Apostolica Vaticana, 1938.

"Presentazione della Prima Traduzione Cinese di Euclide." *Monumenta Serica*, Vol. 15 (1956), pp. 161–202.

De Bruyn Kops, Henriette, "Not Such an 'Unpromising Beginning': The First Dutch Trade Embassy to China, 1655–1657." *Modern Asian Studies*, Vol. 36, No. 3 (2002), pp. 535–578.

De Hullu, J. "Over den Chinaschen Handel der Oost-Indische Companie in de Eerste Dertig Jaar van de 18e Eeuw." *Bijdragen tot de Taal -, Land- en Volkenkunde van Nederlandsch-Indië*, Vol. 73 (1917), pp. 32–151.

De la Costa, H., S.J., *The Jesuits in the Philippines, 1581–1768.* Cambridge, MA: Harvard University Press, 1961.

De Mailla, Joseph de Moyriac, S.J. *Histoire générale de la Chine. Traduction du Tong-kien kang-mu.* 13 vols. Paris: Ph. D. Pieres et Clousier, 1777–1785.

De Marchi, Franco, and Riccardo Scartezzini, eds. *Martino Martini: A Humanist and Scientist in Seventeenth Century China.* Trent: Università degli Studi di Trento, 1996.

De Martinis, Raphaélis, ed. *Juris Pontificii de Propaganda Fide.* 8 vols. Rome: Typografia Polyglotta, 1888–1901.

Debergh, Minako. "Les cartes astronomiques des missionnaires Jésuites en Chine. De Johann Adam Schall von Bell à Ignace Kögler et leur influence en Corée et au Japon." In Roman Malek, ed., *Western Learning and Christianity in China: The Contribution and Impact of Johann Adam Schall von Bell, S.J. (1592–1666 ).* 2 vols. Monumenta Serica Monograph Series, No. 35 (Nettetal: Steyler Verlag, 1998), pp. 543–554.

Dehergne, Joseph, S.J. *Répertoire des Jésuites de Chine de 1552 à 1800.* Rome: Institutum Historicum Societatis Iesu and Paris: Letouzey and Ané, 1973.

"L'Exposé des Jésuites de Pékin sur le culte des ancêtres présenté à l'empereur K'ang-Hi en novembre 1700." In *Les Rapports entre la Chine et l'Europe*, Colloque international de sinologie, Chantilly, 1977. Paris: Belles Lettres, 1980, pp. 185–229.

"Une grande collection. Mémoires concernant les Chinois (1776–1814)." *Bulletin de l'École française de l'Extrême-Orient*, Vol. 72 (1983), 267–298.

Dennerline, Jerry. "The Shun-chih Reign." In Peterson, ed., *The Cambridge History of China*, Vol. 9, Part 1: *The Ch'ing Dynasty to 1800* (Cambridge, 2002), pp. 73–119.

Dermigny, Louis. *La Chine et l'Occident. Le Commerce à Canton au XVIIIᵉ Siècle.* 3 vols and album. Paris: SEVPEN, 1964.

di Fiore, Giacomo. *La Legazione Mezzabarba in Cina, 1720–1721.* Naples: Istituto Universitario Orientale, 1989.

Ding Zhilin. *Yang Qiyuan xiansheng chao xing shiji.* Late Ming Ed. Courant No. 3370. Paris: Bibliotheque Nationale.

Disney, A. R. *A History of Portugal and the Portuguese Empire: From Beginnings to 1807.* 2 vols. Cambridge: Cambridge University Press, 2009.

Dreyer, Edward L. *Early Ming China: A Political History, 1355–1435.* Stanford, CA: Stanford University Press, 1982.

*Zheng He: China and the Oceans in the Early Ming Dynasty, 1405–1433.* New York: Pearson Longman, 2006.

Dudink, Ad. "Opponents." In Standaert, ed., *Handbook,* pp. 503–533.

"Sympathising Literati and Officials." In Standaert, ed., *Handbook,* pp. 475–491.

Dudink, Adrian, and Nicolas Standaert. "Ferdinand Verbiest's *Qiongli Xue* (1683)." In Golvers, ed., *The Christian Mission in China in the Verbiest Era,* pp. 11–31.

Dunne, George H., S.J. *Generation of Giants: The Story of the Jesuits in China in the Last Decades of the Ming Dynasty.* Notre Dame, IN: Notre Dame University Press, 1962.

Duyvendaak, J. J. L. "The Last Dutch Embassy to the Chinese Court (1794–1795)." *T'oung Pao,* Vol. 34 (1938), pp. 1–137, 223–227; Vol. 35 (1940), pp. 329–353.

Elisonas, Jurgis. "Christianity and the Daimyo." In John Whitney Hall, ed., and James McClain, assistant ed., *The Cambridge History of Japan,* Vol. 4: *Early Modern Japan.* Cambridge: Cambridge University Press, 1991, pp. 301–372.

"The Inseparable Trinity: Japan's Relations with China and Korea." In John Whitney Hall, ed., and James McClain, assistant ed., *The Cambridge History of Japan,* Vol. 4: *Early Modern Japan.* Cambridge: Cambridge University Press, 1991, pp. 235–300.

Elliott, Mark C. *Emperor Qianlong: Son of Heaven, Man of the World.* New York: Longman, 2009.

Elman, Benjamin A. *On Their Own Terms: Science in China, 1550–1900.* Cambridge, MA: Harvard University Press, 2005.

Elvin, Mark. *The Pattern of the Chinese Past.* Stanford, CA: Stanford University Press, 1973.

Empoli, Giovanni da. *Lettere di Giovanni da Empoli.* Edited by A. Bausani. Rome: Instituto Italiano per Il Medio ed Estremo Oriente, 1970.

Engelfriet, Peter M. *Euclid in China: The Genesis of the First Chinese Translation of Euclid's "Elements," Books I–VI (Jihe yuanben, Beijing, 1607) and Its Reception up to 1723.* Leiden: Brill, 1998.

Entenmann, Robert. "Catholics and Society in Eighteenth-Century China." In Daniel H. Bays, ed., *Christianity in China: From the Eighteenth Century to the Present.* Stanford, CA: Stanford University Press, pp. 8–23.

"Chinese Catholic Clergy and Catechists in Eighteenth-Century Szechwan." In Edward Malatesta, S.J., and Yves Raguin, S.J. eds., *Images de la Chine. Le*

*Contexte occidental de la sinologie naissante.* San Francisco: Ricci Institute for Chinese–Western Cultural History and Paris:Institut Ricci, 1995.

*Exotic Printing and the Expansion of Europe.* Bloomington: Lilly Library, Indiana University, 1972.

Fairbank, John K. *Trade and Diplomacy on the China Coast.* Cambridge, MA: Harvard University Press, 1953.

ed. *The Chinese World Order: Traditional China's Foreign Relations.* Cambridge, MA: Harvard University Press, 1968.

Fairbank, John K., and S. Y. Teng, "On the Ch'ing Tributary System." *Harvard Journal of Asiatic Studies*, Vol. 4 (1939), pp. 12–46; reprinted in John K. Fairbank and S. Y. Teng, *Ch'ing Administration: Three Studies.* Harvard-Yenching Institute Studies, No. 19. Cambridge, MA, 1960.

Fang Hao. *Li Zhizao yanjiu.* Taipei, 1966.

"Notes on Matteo Ricci's De Amicitia," *Monumenta Serica*, Vol. 14 (1949–1955), pp. 574–583.

"Wang Zheng zhi shiji ji qi shuru xiyang xueshu zhi gongxian." *Wen Shi Zhe xuebao*, Vol. 13 (1964).

*Zhongguo Tianzhujiao shi renwu zhuan.* 3 vols. Hong Kong: Gongjiao zhenli xuehui, 1967–1973.

Farris, Johnathan A. "Thirteen Factories of Canton: An Architecture of Sino-Western Collaboration and Confrontation." *Buildings & Landscapes: Journal of the Vernacular Architecture Forum*, Vol. 14 (2007), pp. 66–83.

Fei Chengkang. *Aomen sibai nian.* Shanghai: Shanghai renmin, 1988. Translated by Wang Yintong, Fei Chengkang, and Sarah K. Schneewind as *Macao: 400 Years.* Shanghai: Shanghai Academy of Social Sciences, 1996.

Felix, Alfonso, Jr. *The Chinese in the Philippines, 1550–1770.* 2 vols. Manila: Solidaridad, 1966.

Feng Yingjing. "Tianzhu shi yi xu." In Li Zhizao, ed., *Tianxue chu han*, Vol. 1.

Ferguson, Donald. "Letters from Portuguese Captives in Canton, Written in 1534 and 1536. With an Introduction on Portuguese Intercourse with China in the First Half of the Sixteenth Century." *Indian Antiquary*, Vol. 30 (1901), pp. 421–451, 467–491; reprint, Bombay, 1902.

Fichter, James R. *So Great a Profitt: How the East Indies Trade Transformed Anglo-American Capitalism.* Cambridge, MA: Harvard University Press, 2010.

Finlay, Robert. *The Pilgrim Art: Cultures of Porcelain in World History.* Berkeley: University of California Press, 2010.

Fisher, Carney T. *The Chosen One: Succession and Adoption in the Court of Ming Shizong.* London: Allen & Unwin, 1990.

Fletcher, Joseph F. "China and Central Asia, 1368–1884." In Fairbank, ed., *The Chinese World Order*, pp. 206–224, 337–368.

Flynn, Dennis O. *World Silver and Monetary History in the 16th and 17th Centuries.* Aldershot: Variorum, 1996.

Flynn, Dennis O., and Arturo Giráldez. "Born Again: Globalization's Sixteenth Century Origins (Asian/Global Versus European Dynamics)." *Pacific Economic Review*, Vol. 13, No. 3 (2008), pp. 359–387.

"Born With a 'Silver Spoon': World Trade's Origin in 1571." *Journal of World History*, Vol. 6. No. 2 (1995), pp. 201–221; also in Flynn and Giráldez, *Metals and Monies*.

eds. *Metals and Monies in an Emerging Global Economy*. Aldershot: Variorum, 1997.

Foss, Theodore N. "Cartography." In Standaert, ed., *Handbook*, pp. 752–770.

Freitas, Jordão de. *Macau. Materiais para a sua Historia no Seculo XVI*. Macau: Instituto Cultural de Macau, 1988.

Frutuoso, Gaspar. *Livro 2° das Saudades da Terra. Em que se Trata do Descobrimento da Ilha de Madeira e suas Adjacentes e da Vida e Progenie dos Illustres Capitães Dellas*. Introduction and notes by Damião Peres. Porto: F. Machado, 1926.

Fu, Lo-shu. *A Documentary Chronicle of Sino-Western Relations (1644–1820)*. 2 vols. Tucson: University of Arizona Press, 1966.

Fuchs, Walter. *Der Jesuiten-Atlas der Kanghsi-Zeit*. Peking: Fu-Jen Universität, 1943.

Fujita Toyohachi. "Porutogaru-jin Macao senryo ni itaru made no sho mondai." In Fujita Toyohachi, ed., *Tō-Sei Kōshō-shi no kenkyū: Nankai-hen*. Tokyo: Ogihara Seibunkan,1943, pp. 417–491.

Furber, Holden. *Rival Empires of Trade in the Orient, 1600–1800*. Minneapolis: University of Minnesota Press, 1976.

Gaastra, F. S. *The Dutch East India Company: Expansion and Decline*. Translated by Peter Daniels. Zutphen: Walburg, 2003.

Gao Panlong. *Gaozi yishu*. Late Ming Ed. Reprint, Taipei, 1983.

Gardella, Robert. *Harvesting the Mountains: Fujian and the China Tea Trade, 1757–1937*. Berkeley: University of California Press, 1994.

Gaubatz, Piper Rae. *Beyond the Great Wall: Urban Form and Transformation on the Chinese Frontiers*. Stanford, CA: Stanford University Press, 1996.

Gaubil, Antoine, S.J. *Correspondance de Pékin, 1722–1759*. Geneva: Droz, 1970.

Geiss, James. "The Chia-ching Reign, 1522–1566." In Mote and Twitchett, eds., *The Cambridge History of China*, Vol. 7: *The Ming Dynasty, 1368–1644*, pp. 440–510.

Gernet, Jacques. *Chine et Christianisme. Action et Réaction*. Paris: Gallimard, 1982. Translated by Janet Lloyd as *China and the Christian Impact: A Conflict of Cultures*. Cambridge: Cambridge University Press, 1985.

Glamann, Kristof. *Dutch–Asiatic Trade, 1620–1740*. Copenhagen: Danish Science Press and The Hague: M. Nijhoff, 1958.

Goldstein, Jonathan. *Philadelphia and the China Trade, 1682–1846*. University Park: Pennsylvania State University Press, 1978.

Goldstone, Jack A. *Revolution and Rebellion in the Early Modern World*. Berkeley: University of California Press. 1991.

Golvers, Noel. "Verbiest's Introduction of *Aristoteles Latinus* (Coimbra) in China: New Western Evidence." In Golvers, ed., *The Christian Mission in China in the Verbiest Era*, pp. 33–53.

ed. *The Christian Mission in China in the Verbiest Era: Some Aspects of the Missionary Approach.* Louvain Chinese Studies, No. 6. Leuven: Leuven University Press, 1999.

González, José Maria, O.P. *História de las Misiones Dominicanas de China.* 5 vols. Madrid: Juan Bravo, 1964–1966.

*Misiones Dominicanas en China (1700–1750).* Madrid: CSIC Instituto Santo Toribio de Mogrovejo, 1952, 1958.

*El primer obispo chino. Exc.mo Sr. D. Fray Gregorio Lo, o Lopez, O.P.* Pamplona: Editorial OPE, 1966.

Goodrich, L. Carrington, and Chaoying Fang, eds. *Dictionary of Ming Biography,* 1368–1644. 2 vols. New York: Columbia University Press, 1976.

Groeneveldt, W. P. *De Nederlanders in China, Eerste Deel: De eerste Bemoeiinigen om den handel in China en de vestiging in de Pescadores (1601–1624).* The Hague: M. Nijhoff, 1898.

Grootaers, W. A. "Les deux stèles de l'église du Nan-t'ang à Pékin." *Neue Zeitschrift für Missionswissenschaft,* Vol. 6 (1950), pp. 248–251.

Guangzhou Lishi Wenhua Mingcheng Yanjiuhui, Guangzhou Shi Liwan Qu Difangzhi Bianzuan Weiyuanhui, eds. *Guangzhou Shisan Hang Cangsang (The thirteen hongs in Guangzhou).* Guangzhou: Guangdong Sheng Ditu Chubanshe, 2001.

Guerrero, Milagros. "The Chinese in the Philippines, 1570–1770." In Felix, ed., *The Chinese in the Philippines,* Vol. 1, pp. 15–39.

Guimarães, Ângela. *Uma Relação Especial. Macau e as Relações Luso-Chinesas (1780–1840).* Lisbon: Edição CIES, 1996.

Hamilton, Alexander, ed. *A New Account of the East Indies.* 2 vols. Introduction and notes by Sir William Foster. London: Argonaut Press, 1930; reprint, Amsterdam: N. Israel and New York: Da Capo, 1970.

Han Qi. "The Role of the Directorate of Astronomy in the Catholic Mission During the Qing Period." In Golvers, ed., *The Christian Mission in China in the Verbiest Era,* pp. 90–93.

*Zhongguo Kexue Jishu di Xizhuan ji qi Yingxiang.* Shijiazhuang: Hebei Renmin, 1999.

Harris, George, "The Mission of Matteo Ricci, S.J.: A Case Study of an Effort at Guided Cultural Change in China in the Sixteenth Century." *Monumenta Serica,* Vol. 25 (1966), pp. 1–168.

Hart, Roger P. *Proof, Propaganda, and Patronage: A Cultural History of the Dissemination of Western Studies in Seventeenth-Century China.* Ph.D. dissertation, University of California at Los Angeles, 1997.

Hartman, Charles. *Han Yü and the T'ang Search for Unity.* Princeton, NJ: Princeton University Press, 1986.

Hashimoto Keizō. "Chongzhen kaireki to Xu Guangqi no yakuwari." In Li Guohao, Zhang Mengwen, Cao Tianqin, and Hu Daojing, eds., *Explorations in the History of Science and Technology in China: Compiled in Honour of the Eightieth Birthday of Dr. Joseph Needham.* Shanghai: Shanghai Chinese Classics Publishing House, 1982.

"Chongzhen li shu ni miru kagaku kakumei no ikkatei." In *Science and Skills in Asia: A Festschrift for Prof. Yabuuti Kiyoshi* (Kyoto: Dōhōsha, 1982), pp. 370–390.

Heng, Derek. *Sino-Malay Trade and Diplomacy from the Tenth through the Fourteenth Century*. Ohio University Research in International Studies, Southeast Asia Ser., No. 121. Athens: Ohio University Press, 2009.

Hevia, James L. *Cherishing Men from Afar: Qing Guest Ritual and the Macartney Embassy of 1793*. Durham, NC: Duke University Press, 1994.

Heyndrickx, Jerome ed. *Philippe Couplet, S.J. (1623–1693): The Man Who Brought China to Europe*. Monumenta Serica Monograph Series, No. 22. Nettetal: Steyler, 1990.

Hickey, William. *Memoirs*, 4 vols. Edited by Alfred Spencer. London: Hurst & Blackett, 1913–1925. Abridged edition with some material not in the 1913–1925 edition, *The Prodigal Rake: Memoirs of William Hickey*. Edited by Peter Quennell. New York: Dutton, 1962.

Hoang Anh Tuan, "From Japan to Manila and Back to Europe: The Abortive English Trade with Manila in the 1670s." *Itinerario*, Vol. 29, No. 3 (2005), pp. 73–92.

*Silk for Silver: Dutch–Vietnamese Relations, 1637–1700*. TANAP Monographs on the History of the Asian-European Interaction, Vol. 5. Leiden: Brill, 2007.

Hoetink, B. "Soe Bing Kong: Het eerste hoofd der Chinezen te Batavia." *Bijdragen tot de Taal-, Land-, en Volkenkunde van Nederlandsch Indië*, Vol. 73 (1917), pp. 344–415.

Holler, Ursula. "Medicine." In Standaert, ed., *Handbook*, pp. 786–802.

Höllman, Thomas O. "Formosa and the Trade in Venison and Deer Skins." In Roderich Ptak and Dietmar Rothermund, eds., *Emporia, Commodities, and Entrepreneurs in Asian Maritime Trade, c. 1400–1750*. Beiträge zur Südasienforschung, Südasien-Institut, Universität Heidelberg, No. 141. Stuttgart: Franz Steiner, 1991, pp. 263–290.

Hong Weilian [William Hung]. "Kao Li Madou de Shijie Ditu." *Yu Gong*, Vol. 5, No. 3–4 (1936); reprinted in Zhou Kangxie, ed., *Li Madou Yanjiu Lunji*. Hong Kong: 1971.

Hsia, Florence C. *Sojourners in a Strange Land: Jesuits & Their Scientific Missions in Late Imperial China*. Chicago: University of Chicago Press, 2009.

Hsu, Wen-hsiung. "From Aboriginal Island to Chinese Frontier: The Development of Taiwan before 1683." In Ronald G. Knapp, ed., *China's Island Frontier: Studies in the Historical Geography of Taiwan*. Honolulu: University Press of Hawaii, 1980, pp. 3–29.

Hu, Minghui. "Provenance in Contest: Searching for the Origins of Jesuit Astronomy in Early Qing China, 1664–1705." *International History Review*, Vol. 24, No. 1 (March 2002), pp. 1–36.

Huang Bolu. *Zhengjiao fengbao*. 3d ed. Shanghai: Cimutang, 1904.

Huang Guosheng. *Yapian zhanzheng qian de dongnan si sheng haiguan*. Fuzhou: Fujian Renmin, 2000.

Huang, Pei. *Autocracy at Work. A Study of the Yung-cheng Period, 1723–1735*. Bloomington: Indiana University Press, 1974.

Huang, Ray. 1587: *A Year of No Significance: The Ming Dynasty in Decline.* New Haven, CT: Yale University Press, 1981.

"The Lung-ch'ing and Wan-li Reigns, 1567–1620." In Mote and Twitchett, eds., *The Cambridge History of China*, Vol. 7: *The Ming Dynasty, 1368–1644, Part 1*, 1998 pp. 511–584.

Huang Yinong. "Bei hulue di shengyin – Jieshao Zhongguo Tianzhujiao tu dui 'Liyi wenti' taidu di wenxian." *Qinghua Xuebao* (Tsing Hua Journal of Chinese Studies) Vol. 25, No. 2, New Ser. (June 1995), pp. 137–160.

*Liang toushe. Mingmo Qingchu de diyidai Tianzhu jiaotu.* Xinzhu: Guoli Qinghua Daxue chubanshe, 2005; reprint, Shanghai, 2006.

Huard, Pierre, and Ming Wong. *Chinese Medicine.* New York: McGraw-Hill, 1972.

Huber, Johannes. "Chinese Settlers against the Dutch East India Company: The Rebellion Led by Kuo Huai-i on Taiwan in 1652." In E. B. Vermeer, ed., *Development and Decline of Fukien Province in the 17th and 18th Centuries,* Sinica Leidensa, Vol. 22. Leiden: Brill, 1990, pp. 265–296.

Hucker, Charles O. "Hu Tsung-hsien's Campaign Against Hsu Hai, 1556." In Frank A. Kierman, Jr., and John K. Fairbank, eds., *Chinese Ways in Warfare.* Cambridge, MA: Harvard University Press, 1974, pp. 273–307.

Hummel, Arthur W. *Eminent Chinese of the Ch'ing Period.* 2 vols. Washington, DC: U.S. Government Printing Office, 1943–1944.

Hussin, Nordin. *Trade and Society in the Straits of Melaka: Dutch Melaka and English Penang.* Copenhagen: NIAS Press and Singapore: NUS Press, 2007.

Innes, Robert L. *The Door Ajar: Japan's Foreign Trade in the Seventeenth Century.* Ph.D dissertation, University of Michigan, 1980.

*Instrução para o Bispo de Pequim, e Outros Documentos para a História de Macau.* Lisbon: Agência Geral das Colónias, 1943.

Iwao Seiichi. "Kinsei Nisshi bōeki ni kansuru sūryōteki kōsatsu." *Shigaku zasshi,* Vol. 62, No. 1, (1953), pp. 1–40.

"Li Tan, Chief of the Chinese Residents at Hirado, Japan in the Last Days of the Ming Dynasty." *Memoirs of the Research Department of the Toyo Bunko,* Vol. 17 (1958), pp. 27–83.

Jacobs, Els M. *Merchant in Asia: The Trade of the Dutch East India Company during the Eighteenth Century.* Translated by Paul Hulsman. Leiden: CNWS, 2006.

Jami, Catherine, Peter Engelfriet, and Gregory Blue, eds. *Statecraft and Intellectual Renewal in Late Ming China: The Cross-Cultural Synthesis of Xu Guangqi (1562–1633).* Sinica Leidensa, Vol. 50. Leiden, Brill, 2001.

Jin Guo Ping and Wu Zhiuliang, eds. *Correspondência Oficial Trocada Entre as Autoridades de Cantão e os Procuradores do Senado. Fundo das Chapas Sinicas em Português (1749–1847).* 6 vols. Macau: Fundação Macau, 2000.

Johnston, Alastair Iain. *Cultural Realism: Strategic Culture and Grand Strategy in Chinese History.* Princeton, NJ: Princeton University Press, 1995.

Jörg, C. J. A. *Porcelain and the Dutch China Trade.* The Hague: M. Nijhoff, 1982.

Judice Biker, Julio Firmino. *Collecção de Tratados e Concertos de Pazes que o Estado da Índia Portuguesa Fez com os Reis e Senhores com quem Teve*

*Relações nas Partes da Asia e Africa Oriental.* 14 vols. Lisbon: Imprensa Nacional, 1881–1887.

Kajdanski, Edward. *Michal Boym Ostatni Wyslannik Dynastii Ming.* Warsaw: Wydawnictwo Polonia, 1988.

Kammerer, Albert. *La découverte de la Chine par les Portugais au XVIe siècle et la cartographie des Portulans, avec des notes de toponomie chinoise par Paul Pelliot.* T'oung Pao, Supplement to Vol. 39. Leiden: Brill, 1944.

*Kangxi yu Luoma shijie guanxi wenshu. Qianlong yingshi jinjian ji.* Zhongguo shixue congshu, xubian, No. 23. Taipei: Taiwan xuesheng shuju, 1973.

Keevak, Michael. *The Story of a Stele: China's Nestorian Monument and Its Reception in the West, 1625–1916.* Hong Kong: Hong Kong University Press, 2008.

Kelly, Edward Thomas. *The Anti-Christian Persecution of 1616–1617 in Nanking.* Ph.D. dissertation, Columbia University, 1971.

Kepler, Johannes. *Dissertatio cum Nuncio Sidereo.* Translated by J. V. Field in "Astrology in Kepler's Cosmology." In Patrick Curry, ed., *Astrology, Science and Society.* Woodbridge, Suffolk, 1987.

King, Gail. "Couplet's Biography of Madame Candida Xu (1607–1680)." *Sino-Western Cultural Relations Journal,* Vol. 18 (1996), pp. 41–56.

Kowalsky, Nicolas. "Mezzabarba, Carlo Ambrogio." *Enciclopedia Cattolica,* 8:924–25.

Krahl, Joseph. *China Missions in Crisis: Bishop Laimbeckhoven and His Times.* Analecta Gregoriana, No. 137. Rome: Gregorian University Press, 1964.

Kristeller, Paul O. *Eight Philosophers of the Italian Renaissance.* Stanford, CA: Stanford University Press, 1964.

Laamann, Lars Peter. *Christian Heretics in Late Imperial China: Christian Inculturation and State Control, 1720–1850.* London: Routledge, 2006.

Lach, Donald F. *Asia in the Making of Europe.* 2 vols. in 5 books. Chicago: University of Chicago Press, 1965, 1970.

Lach, Donald F., and Edwin J. Van Kley. *Asia in the Making of Europe.* Vol. 3, 4 books. Chicago: University of Chicago Press, 1993.

Lam, Truong Buu. "Intervention versus Tribute in Sino-Vietnamese Relations, 1788–1790." In Fairbank, ed., *The Chinese World Order,* pp. 165–179, 321–326.

Le Comte, Louis, S.J. *Un jésuite à Pékin. Nouveaux mémoires sur l'état présent de la Chine, 1687–1692.* Edited by Frédérique Touboul-Bouyeure. Paris: Phébus, 1990.

Leibniz, G. W. *The Writings on China.* Edited and translated by Daniel J. Cook and Henry Rosemont. La Salle, IL: Open Court, 1994.

Levathes, Louise. *When China Ruled the Seas: The Treasure Fleets of the Dragon Throne, 1405–33.* New York: Simon & Schuster, 1994.

Levenson, Joseph R. *Confucian China and Its Modern Fate: A Trilogy.* Berkeley: University of California Press, 1968.

Lewis, Mark Edward. *China's Cosmopolitan Empire: The Tang Dynasty.* Cambridge, MA: Belknap Press, 2009.

Lewis, Wm. Roger, ed. *The Oxford History of the British Empire.* 5 vols. Oxford: Oxford University Press, 1998–1999.

Liang Jiabin. *Guangdong shisan hang kao.* Shanghai: Guoli bianyi guan, 1937; reprint, Taipei: Donghai daxue, 1960.

Liang Jiamian. *Xu Guangqi nianpu.* Shanghai: Shanghai guji chubanshe, 1981.

Liang Tingnan, *Yuedao gongguo shuo.* Reprint, Taipei: Huawen shuju, 1968.

*Yue haiguan zhi.* n.d; reprint, Taipei: Wenhai, 1975.

Lieberman, Victor. ed., *Beyond Binary Histories: Re-imagining Eurasia to c. 1830.* Ann Arbor: University of Michigan Press, 1999.

*Strange Parallels: Southeast Asia in Global Context, c. 800–1830.* 2 vols. Cambridge: Cambridge University Press, 2003, 2009.

Li Jiubiao. *Kouduo Richao: Li Jiubiao's Diary of Oral Admonitions – A Late Ming Christian Journal.* Translated, edited, and annotated by Erik Zuercher. Monumenta Serica Monograph Series, No. 56. Sankt Augustin: Institut Monumenta Serica and Brescia: Fondazione Civiltà Bresciana, 2007.

Li Lanqin. *Tang Ruowang.* Beijing: Dongfang chubanshe, 1995.

*Li Madou kunyu wanguo quantu.* Beiping, 1936.

Lin Jinshui. "Chinese Literati and the Rites Controversy." In Mungello, ed. *The Chinese Rites Controversy,* pp. 65–82.

Lin Renchuan. *Mingmo Qingchu siren haishang maoyi.* Shanghai: Huadong shifan daxue chubanshe, 1987.

Lin Tong-yang. "Aperçu sur la mappemonde de Ferdinand Verbiest. Le *K'un-yü ch'üan-t'u.*" In Edward Malatesta and Yves Raguin, eds., *Succès et échecs de la rencontre Chine et Occident du XVIe au XXe siècle Varietés Sinologiques,* New. Ser. 74. San Francisco: Ricci Institute, University of San Francisco, and Taipei: Institut Ricci, 1993, pp. 145–173.

Li Qingxin. *Mingdai haiwai maoyi zhidu.* Beijing: Shehui kexueyuan wenxian chubanshe, 2007.

Li Tana. *Nguyễn Cochinchina: Southern Vietnam in the Seventeenth and Eighteenth Centuries.* Ithaca, NY: Cornell University Southeast Asia Program Publications, 1998.

Li Tiangang. *Zhongguo liyi zhi zheng. Lishi wenxian he yiyi.* Shanghai, 1998.

Liu Fang and Zhang Wenqin, eds. *Qingdai Aomen Zhongwen Dangan Huibian.* 2 vols. Macao: Aomen jijinhui, 1999.

Liu, Hui-chen Wang. "An Analysis of Chinese Clan Rules: Confucian Theories in Action." In David S. Nivison and Arthur. F. Wright, eds., *Confucianism in Action.* Stanford, CA: Stanford University Press, 1959, pp. 63–96.

Liu, Yong. *The Dutch East India Company's Tea Trade with China, 1757–1781.* Leiden: Brill, 2007.

Li Zhi. *Xu fen shu.* 1611; reprint, Beijing: Zhonghua shuju, 1959.

Li Zhizao, ed. *Tianxue chu han.* 1628; reprint, Taipei, 1965.

Ljungstedt, Sir Andrew. *An Historical Sketch of the Portuguese Settlements in China; and of the Roman Catholic Church and Missions in China.* Boston, 1836; reprint, Hong Kong: Hong Kong Viking, 1992.

Loehr, George R. "The Sinicization of Missionary Artists and Their Work at the Manchu Court during the Eighteenth Century." *Cahiers d'histoire mondiale,* Vol. 7 (1963), pp. 795–815.

Loureiro, Rui Manuel. *Fidalgos, Missionários, e Mandarins: Portugal e a China no Século XVI.* Lisbon: Fundação Oriente, 2000.

Luk, Bernard. "A Serious Matter of Life and Death: Learned Conversations at Foochow in 1627." In Ronan and Oh, eds., *East Meets West.*

"A Study of Giulio Aleni's Chih-fang wai chi." *Bulletin of the School of Oriental and African Studies,* Vol. 40, No.1 (1977), pp. 58–84.

Lundbaek, Knud. *Joseph de Prémare (1666–1736), S.J.: Chinese Philology and Figurism.* Aarhus: Aarhus University Press, 1991.

"The First Translation from a Confucian Classic in Europe." *China Mission Studies Bulletin,* Vol. 1 (1979), pp. 1–11.

Luo Changpei. "Yesu hui shi tzai yinyunxue shang de gongxian." *Guoli Zhongyang yanjiu yuan lishi yuyan yanjiu suo jikan,* Vol. 1, No. 3 (1930), pp. 267–338.

Macartney, George. *An Embassy to China: Being the Journal Kept by Lord Macartney during His Embassy to the Emperor Ch'ien-lung, 1793–1794.* Edited, annotated, and introduced by J. L. Cranmer-Byng. London, 1962; reprint, St. Clair Shores, MI, 1972.

Mac Sherry, Charles W. *Impairment of the Ming Tribute System as Exhibited in Trade through Fukien.* Ph.D. dissertation, University of California at Berkeley, 1956.

Magalhães, Gabriel de, S.J. *Nouvelle relation de la Chine.* Paris: Barbin, 1688.

Ma Huan. *Ying-yai Sheng-lan: 'The Overall Survey of the Ocean's Shores.'* Edited and translated by J. V. G. Mills. London, 1970; reprint, Bangkok, 1997.

Malatesta, Edward, S.J., and Gao Zhiyu, eds. *Departed, Yet Present: Zhalan, the Oldest Christian Cemetery in Beijing.* Macao: Instituto Cultural de Macau and San Francisco: Ricci Institute, University of San Francisco, 1995.

Mancall, Mark. *Russia and China: Their Diplomatic Relations to 1728.* Cambridge, MA: Harvard University Press, 1971.

Manguin, Pierre-Yves. *Les Nguyen, Macau, et le Portugal. Aspects politiques et commerciaux d'une relation priviliégiée en Mer de Chine, 1773–1800.* Paris: École Française d'Extrême Orient, 1984.

Marshall, P. J. *Bengal: The British Bridgehead – Eastern India, 1740–1828.* In *The New Cambridge History of India,* Vol. 2, Part 2. Cambridge: Cambridge University Press, 1987.

Martini, Martino, S.J. *Novus Atlas Sinensis.* Amsterdam: Blaeu, 1655; reprint, Trent: Museo Tridentino di Scienze Naturali, 1981.

*Opera Omnia.* 3 vols. Edited by Franco Demarchi and Giuliano Bertuccioli. Trent: Università degli Studi di Trento, 1998–2002.

Mazumdar, Sucheta. *Sugar and Society in China: Peasants, Technology, and the World Market.* Cambridge, MA: Harvard University Asia Center, 1998.

Melis, Giorgio. ed. *Martino Martini, geografo, cartografo, storico, teologo,Trento 1614–Hangzhou 1661.* Trent: Museo Tridentino de Scienze Naturali, 1983.

*Mémoires concernant les chinois.* 15 vols. Paris: Nyon, 1777–1791.

Mendes da Luz, Francisco Paulo. *O Conselho da India. Contributo ao Estudo da História da Administração e do Comércio do Ultramar Portugues nos Princípios do Século XVII.* Lisbon: Agencia Geral do Ultramar, 1952.

Mendes Pinto, Fernão. *The Travels of Mendes Pinto.* Edited and translated by Rebecca D. Catz. Chicago: University of Chicago Press, 1989.

Menegon, Eugenio. *Ancestors, Virgins, and Friars: The Localization of Christianity in Late Imperial China.* Cambridge, MA: Harvard East Asian Series, 2009.

*Un Solo Cielo: Giulio Aleni S.J. (1582–1649). Geografia, Arte, Scienza, Religione dall'Europa alla Cina.* Brescia: Grafo, 1994.

"Yang Guangxian's Opposition to Johann Adam Schall: Christianity and Western Science in His Work *Budeyi.*" In Roman Malek, ed., *Western Learning and Christianity in China: The Contribution and Impact of Johann Adam Schall von Bell, S.J. (1592–1666).* 2 vols. Monumenta Serica Monograph Series, No. 35. Nettetal: Steyler Verlag, (1998), pp. 311–337.

Mentz, Søren. *The English Gentleman Merchant at Work: Madras and the City of London, 1660–1740.* Copenhagen: Museum Tusculanum Press, University of Copenhagen, 2005.

Menzies, Gavin. *1421: The Year China Discovered the World.* New York: Bantam, 2002.

Metzler, Josef. *Die Synoden in China, Japan und Korea, 1570–1931.* Paderborn: Ferdinand Schöningh, 1980.

Meynard, Thierry. *Following the Footsteps of the Jesuits in Beijing: A Guide to Sites of Jesuit Work and Influence in Beijing.* St. Louis: Institute of Jesuit Sources, 2006.

Millward, James A. *Beyond the Pass: Economy, Ethnicity, and Empire in Qing Central Asia, 1759–1864.* Stanford, CA: Stanford University Press, 1998.

Minamiki, George. *The Chinese Rites Controversy from Its Beginnings to Modern Times.* Chicago: Loyola University Press, 1985.

*Mingji Helanren qinju Penghu candang.* Taiwan wenxian congkan, No. 154. Taipei: Zhonghua shuju, 1962.

*Ming Qing jinshi timing beilu suoyin.* 3 vols. Taipei: Wen shi zhe chubanshe, 1982.

*Ming Shi.* Bainaben Ed. Taibei: Shangwu, 1967.

*Minhai zengyan.* Taiwan wenxian congkan, No. 56. Taipei: Zhonghua shuju, 1959.

Mish, J. L. "Creating an Image of Europe for China: Aleni's *Hsi-fang ta wen.*" *Monumenta Serica,* Vol. 23 (1964), pp. 1–87.

Moloughney, Brian, and Xia Weizhong. "Silver and the Fall of the Ming: A Reassessment." *Papers in Far Eastern History* (Canberra), No. 40 (1989), pp. 51–78. Also in Flynn and Giráldez, *Metals and Monies.*

Montalto de Jesus, C.A. *Historic Macao.* Shanghai: Kelly and Walsh, 1902.

Morga, Antonio de. *Sucesos de las Islas Filipinas.* Edited and translated by J. S. Cummins. Hakluyt Society, 2d Ser., No. 140. London, 1971.

Morineau, Michel. *Incroyables gazettes et fabuleux métaux. Les retours des trésors américains d'après les gazettes hollandaises (XVIᵉ–XVIIIᵉ siècles).* Cambridge and Paris: Cambridge University Press and Éditions de la Maison des Sciences de l'Homme, 1985.

Morse, H. B. *Chronicles of the East India Company Trading to China.* 5 vols. Oxford: Clarendon Press, 1926–1929; reprint, Taipei: Ch'eng-wen, 1966.

*The International Relations of the Chinese Empire.* 3 vols. London: Longmans, Green, 1910–1918; reprint, Taipei: Wenxing, 1963.

Mui, Hoh-cheung, and Lorna H Mui. *The Management of Monopoly: A Study of the East India Company's Conduct of Its Tea Trade, 1784–1833.* Vancouver: University of British Columbia Press, 1984.

"Smuggling and the British Tea Trade Before 1784." *American Historical Review*, Vol. 74, No. 1 (October 1968), pp. 44–73.

"'Trends in Eighteenth Century Smuggling' Reconsidered." *Economic History Review*, 2d Ser., Vol. 28, No. 1 (February 1975), pp. 28–43.

Mundy, Peter. *The Travels of Peter Mundy in Europe and Asia, 1608–1667*. 5 vols. Edited by Sir Richard C. Temple. Hakluyt Society, New Ser., Vols. 17, 35, 45–46, 55, 78. Cambridge: Cambridge University Press, 1907–1936.

Mungello, David E. *Curious Land: Jesuit Accommodation and the Origins of Sinology*. Studia Leibnitiana Supplementa, No. 25. Stuttgart: Franz Steiner Verlag, 1985; reprint, Honolulu: University of Hawaii Press, 1989.

*The Forgotten Christians of Hangzhou*. Honolulu: University of Hawaii Press, 1994.

*Leibniz and Confucianism: The Search for Accord*. Honolulu: University Press of Hawaii, 1977.

ed. *The Chinese Rites Controversy: Its History and Meaning*. Monumenta Serica Monographs Series, No. 33. Nettetal: Steyler, 1994.

Murray, Dian H. *Pirates of the South China coast, 1790–1810*. Stanford, CA: Stanford University Press, 1987.

in collaboration with Qin Baoqi. *The Origins of the Tiandihui: The Chinese Triads in Legend and History*. Stanford, CA: Stanford University Press, 1994.

Nagtegaal, Luc. *Riding the Dutch Tiger: The Dutch East Indies Company and the Northeast Coast of Java, 1680–1743*. Leiden: KITLV Press, 1996.

Naquin, Susan, and Evelyn Rawski. *Chinese Society in the Eighteenth Century*. New Haven, CT: Yale University Press, 1987.

Needham, Joseph. *Chinese Astronomy and the Jesuit Mission: An Encounter of Cultures*. London: The China Society, 1958.

*Science and Civilisation in China*. 7 vols. in 24 parts. Cambridge: Cambridge University Press, 1954–.

Neuvialle, J. S. de, S.J., "Relação da jornada ... e summaria noticia da embaixada." In E. Brazão, ed., *A Politica Europeia no Extremo Oriente no Seculo XIX e as Nossas Relações Diplomaticas com a China*. Porto: Livraria Civilização, 1938, pp. 60–84.

Niemeijer, Hendrik E. *Batavia: Een Koloniale Samenleving in de 17de Eeuw*. Amsterdam: Balans, 2005.

Noll, Ray, ed. *100 Documents Concerning the Chinese Rites Controversy (1645–1941)*. San Francisco: Ricci Institute, University of San Francisco, 1992.

Ogborn, Miles. *Indian Ink: Script and Print in the Making of the English East India Company*. Chicago: University of Chicago Press, 2007.

Oosterhof, J. L. "Zeelandia, a Dutch Colonial City on Formosa (1624–1662)." In Robert Ross and Gerard J. Telkamp, eds., *Colonial Cities: Essays on Urbanism in a Colonial Context*. Dordrecht: Nijhoff, 1985, pp. 51–63.

Osterhammel, Jürgen. *Die Verwandlung der Welt. Eine Geschichte des 19. Jahrhunderts*. Munich: C. H. Beck, 2009.

Pan Gang'er, Huang Qichen, and Chen Guodong. *Guangdong shisan hang zhi yi: Pan Tongwen (Fu) Hang (One of the thirteen hongs in Canton: Tung-wan/ Tung-fu Hong Puankhequa I–III)*. Guangzhou: Huanan Ligong Daxue Chubanshe, 2006.

Parker, T. M. "The Papacy, Catholic Reform, and Christian Missions." In R. B. Wernham, ed., *The New Cambridge Modern History*, Vol. 8: *The Counter-Reformation and Price Revolution 1559–1610* (Cambridge, 1968).

Pelliot, Paul. "Le Hoja et le Sayyid Husain de l'Histoire des Ming." *T'oung Pao*, Vol. 38 (1948), pp. 81–292.

"Un ouvrage sur les premiers temps de Macao." *T'oung Pao*, Vol. 31 (1935), pp. 58–94.

Peng Zeyi. "Qingdai Guangdong yanghang zhidu qiyuan." *Lishi yanjiu*, Vol. 1 (1957), pp. 1–25.

Perdue, Peter C. *China Marches West: The Qing Conquest of Central Eurasia.* Cambridge, MA: Harvard University Press, 2005.

"Empire and Nation in Comparative Perspective: Frontier Administration in Eighteenth-Century China." In Huri Islamoğlu and Peter C. Perdue, eds., *Shared Histories of Modernity: China, India, and the Ottoman Empire.* London: Routledge, 2009, pp. 21–45.

Peterson, Willard J. *Bitter Gourd: Fang I-chih and the Impetus for Intellectual Change.* New Haven, CT: Yale University Press, 1979.

"Calendar Reform Prior to the Arrival of Missionaries at the Ming Court." *Ming Studies*, Vol. 21 (1986), 49–55.

"Western Natural Philosophy Published in Late Ming China." *Proceedings of the American Philosophical Society*, Vol. 117, No. 4 (1973), pp. 295–322.

"Why Did They Become Christians?" In Ronan and Oh, eds., *East Meets West*, pp. 129–152.

Peyrefitte, Alain. *Un choc des cultures. La vision des Chinois.* Paris: Fayard, 1991.

*The Immobile Empire.* Translated by Jon Rothschild. New York: Knopf, 1992.

Pfister, Louis. *Notices biographiques et bibliographiques sur les Jésuites de l'ancienne mission de Chine.* Shanghai: Mission Catholique, 1932–1934; reprint, Nendeln: Kraus, 1971, and San Francisco: Chinese Materials Center, 1976.

Pih, Irene. *Le père Gabriel de Magalhães. Un Jésuite portugais en Chine.* Cultura Medieval et Moderna, Vol. 14. Paris: Fundação Calouste Gulbenkian Centro Cultural Português, 1979.

Pinot, Virgile. *La Chine et la formation de l'esprit philosophique en France (1640–1740).* Paris: 1932.

Pirazzoli-'t Serstevens, Michèle. "Artistic Issues in the Eighteenth Century." In Standaert, ed., *Handbook*, pp. 823–839.

Pires, Tomé. *The Suma Oriental of Tomé Pires.* Edited and translated by Armando Cortesão. Hakluyt Society, New Ser., Vol. 89–90. London, 1944.

*O Manuscrito de Lisboa da "Suma Oriental" de Tomé Pires (Contribução para uma edição crítica).* Edited and translated by Armando Cortesão. Macau: Instituto Português do Oriente, 1996.

Pomeranz, Kenneth. *The Great Divergence: China, Europe, and the Making of the Modern World Economy.* Princeton, NJ: Princeton University Press, 2000.

Prakash, Om. *The Dutch East India Company and the Economy of Bengal, 1630–1720.* Princeton, NJ: Princeton University Press, 1985.

*European Commercial Enterprise in Pre-Colonial India.* In *The New Cambridge History of India*, Vol. 2, Part 5. Cambridge: Cambridge University Press, 1998.

Prémare, Joseph de, S.J. *Notitia linguae sinicae*. Malacca: Cura Academiae Anglo-Sinensis, 1831; reprint, Hong Kong: Nazareth, 1893.

Pritchard, Earl H. *The Crucial Years of Early Anglo-Chinese Relations, 1750–1800*. New York: Octagon, 1970.

Ptak, Roderich. *Portugal in China: Kurzer Abriss der Portugiesisch-Chinesischen Beziehungen und der Geschichte Macaus*. Bad Boll: Klemmerberg, 1980.

ed. *Portuguese Asia: Aspects in History and Economic History (Sixteenth and Seventeenth Centuries)*. Stuttgart: Steiner Verlag Wiesbaden, 1987.

*[Qinding] Libu zeli*. 1841; reprint, Taipei, 1966.

*Qing shi gao jiaozhu*. 16 vols. Taibei: Guoshiguan, 1986–1991.

Ramos, João de Deus. *História das relações diplomaticas entre Portugal e a China: I. O Padre António de Magalhães, S.J., e a Embaixada de Kangxi a D. João V (1721–1725)*. Macau: Instituto Cultural de Macau, 1991.

Rawski, Evelyn S. *The Last Emperors: A Social History of Qing Imperial Institutions*. Berkeley: University of California Press, 1998.

Ray, Haraprasad. *Trade and Diplomacy in India–China Relations: A Study of Bengal during the Fifteenth Century*. New Delhi: Radiant, 1993.

Reed, Robert R. *Colonial Manila: The Context of Hispanic Urbanism and Process of Morphogenesis*. Berkeley: University of California Press, 1978.

Reid, Anthony. *Southeast Asia in the Age of Commerce, 1450–1680*, 2 vols. New Haven, CT: Yale University Press, 1988–1993.

ed. *The Last Stand of Asian Autonomies: Responses to Modernity in the Diverse States of Southeast Asia and Korea, 1750–1900*. London: Macmillan and New York: St. Martin's, 1997.

ed. *Sojourners and Settlers: Histories of Southeast Asia and the Chinese*. London: Allen & Unwin, 1996, and Honolulu: University of Hawaii Press, 2001.

Reif, Sister Patricia. "Textbooks in Natural Philosophy, 1600–1650." *Journal of the History of Ideas*, Vol. 30 (1969).

Remmelink, Willem. *The Chinese War and the Collapse of the Javanese State, 1725–1743*. Leiden: Koninklijk Instituut voor Taal-, Land-, en Volkenkunde, 1994.

Ricci, Matteo, S.J. *Fonti Ricciane. Documenti originali concernenti Matteo Ricci e la storia delle prime relazioni tra l'Europa e la Cina, 1579–1615*. Edited by Pasquale D' Elia, S.J. 3 vols. Rome, 1942–1949.

*On Friendship: One Hundred Maxims for a Chinese Prince*. Translated by Timothy Billings. New York: Columbia University Press, 2010.

*Opere storiche del P. Matteo Ricci S.J.* Edited by Pietro Tacchi Venturi. 2 vols. Macerata; F. Giorgetti, 1911–1913.

*Qiankun tiyi*. 1614; reprinted in *Siku quanshu zhenben*, 1a, *wu ji*. Taipei, 1974.

*The True Meaning of the Lord of Heaven (T'ien-chu shih-i)*. Translated by Douglas Lancashire and Peter Kuo-chen Hu. St. Louis: Institute of Jesuit Sources, 1985.

Ripa, Matteo. *Giornale (1705–1724)*. Edited by Michele Fattica. 2 vols. Naples: Istituto Universitario Orientale, 1991–1996.

Ronan, Charles E., S.J., and Bonnie B. C. Oh, eds. *East Meets West: The Jesuits in China, 1582–1773*. Chicago: Loyola University Press, 1988.

Rossabi, Morris, "The Ming and Inner Asia." In Twitchett and Mote, eds., *The Cambridge History of China*, Vol. 8: *The Ming Dynasty, 1368–1644, Part 2*, pp. 221–271.

Rosso, Antonio Sisto. *Apostolic Legations to China of the Eighteenth Century*. South Pasadena, CA: P. D. and Ione Perkins, 1948.

Rouleau, Francis A., S.J. "Chinese Rites Controversy." *New Catholic Encyclopedia*, 3:610–611.

"Maillard de Tournon, Papal Legate at the Court of Peking: The First Imperial Audience (31 December 1705)." *Archivum Historicum Societatis Iesu*, Vol. 31 (1962), pp. 264–323.

Rowe, William T. *China's Last Empire: The Great Qing*. Cambridge, MA: Belknap Press, 2009.

*Saving the World: Chen Hongmou and Elite Consciousness in Eighteenth-Century China*. Stanford, CA: Stanford University Press, 2001.

Rubiés, Joan-Pau. *Travel and Ethnology in the Renaissance: South India Through European Eyes, 1250–1625*. Cambridge: Cambridge University Press, 2000.

Rule, Paul A. *K'ung-tzu or Confucius? The Jesuit Interpretation of Confucianism*. Sydney: Allen & Unwin, 1986.

"Louis Fan Shou-I: A Missing Link in the Chinese Rites Controversy." In E. Malatesta, Yves Raguin, and A. Dudink, eds. *Échanges culturels et religieux entre la Chine et l'Occident*. Variétés sinologiques, New Ser., No. 83. San Francisco: Ricci Institute, University of San Francisco, and Taipei: Institut Ricci, 1995, pp. 277–294.

Sá, Isabel dos Guimarães. "Charity, Ritual, and Business at the Edge of Empire: The Misericórdia of Macau." In Liam Matthew Brockey, ed., *Portuguese Colonial Cities in the Early Modern World*. Burlington VT: Ashgate, 2008, pp. 149–173.

Sachsenmaier, Dominic. *Die Aufnahme europäischer Inhalt in die chinesische Kultur durch Zhu Zongyuan (ca. 1616–1660) (Zhu Zongyuan's integration of Western elements into Chinese culture)*. Monumenta Serica Monograph Series, No. 46, Nettetal: Steyler, 2002.

Santamaria, Alberto, O.P. "The Chinese Parian (El Parian de los Sangleyes)." In Felix, *The Chinese in the Philippines*, Vol. 1, pp. 67–118.

Sasaki Masaya. "Etsu kaikan no roki." *Tōyō Gakuhō*, Vol. 34 (1955), pp. 132–61.

Schall von Bell, Johann Adam, S.J. *Lettres et mémoires d'Adam Schall, S.J. Relation historique. Text latin avec traduction française du P. Paul Bornet, S J.* Edited by Henri Bernard. Tientsin: Hautes Études, 1942.

Scheel, J. Ditlev. "Beijing Precursor." In Witek, ed., *Ferdinand Verbiest*, pp. 245–270.

Schottenhammer, Angela. *Das songzeitliche Quanzhou im Spannungsfeld zwischen Zentralregierung und maritimem Handel*. Stuttgart: Steiner, 2002.

ed. *The Emporium of the World: Maritime Quanzhou, 1000–1400.* Leiden: Brill, 2001.

Schurz, W. L. *The Manila Galleon.* New York: Dutton, 1939; paperback, 1959.

Schwarz, Benjamin I. *The World of Thought in Ancient China.* Cambridge, MA: Harvard University Press, 1985.

Seabra, Leonor de. *A Embaixada ao Sião de Pero Vaz de Siqueira (1684–1686).* Macau: Universidade de Macau, 2000. English translation by Custódio Cavaco Martins, Mário Pinharanda Nunes, and Alan Norman Baxter, *The Embassy of Pero Vaz de Siqueira to Siam (1684–1686).* Macau: Universidade de Macau, 2005.

Sebes, Joseph S., S.J. "China's Jesuit Century." *Wilson Quarterly* Vol. 2 (1978), pp. 170–183.

*The Jesuits and the Sino-Russian Treaty of Nerchinsk (1689): The Diary of Thomas Pereira, S.J.* Bibliotheca Instituti Historici Societatis Jesu, No. 18. Rome: Institutum Historicum Societas Iesu, 1961.

"The Precursors of Ricci." In Ronan and Oh, eds., *East Meets West,* pp. 36–37.

Sen, Tansen. *Buddhism, Diplomacy, and Trade: The Realignment of Sino-Indian Relations, 600–1400.* Honolulu: Association for Asian Studies and University of Hawaii Press, 2003.

Shen Defu. *Wanli yehuo bian.* 1619; reprint, Beijing, 1980.

*Shenzong shilu.* In *Ming shilu.* Mid-seventeenth century; reprint, Taipei, 1966.

Shen Yourong et al. *Minhai zengyan, Taiwan wenxian congkan,* No. 56. Taipei, 1959.

Shepherd, John R. *Statecraft and Political Economy on the Taiwan Frontier, 1600–1800.* Stanford, CA: Stanford University Press, 1993.

Shih, Joseph Hsing-san. "The Religious Writings of Father Ferdinand Verbiest." In Witek, ed., *Ferdinand Verbiest,* pp. 421–436.

Shu Liguang. "Ferdinand Verbiest and the Casting of Cannons in the Qing Dynasty." In Witek, ed., *Ferdinand Verbiest,* pp. 227–244.

*Sinica Franciscana.* Edited by Anastasius van den Wyngaert, O.F.M., Fortunato Margiotti, O.F.M., et al. 11 vols. Quaracchi-Firenze: Collegium San Bonaventurae, 1929–2006.

Sivin, Nathan. "Copernicus in China." In *Colloquia Copernica,* II. *Études sur l'audience de la théorie héliocentrique.* Warsaw: Conférences du Symposium de l'Union Internationale d'Histoire et de Philosophie des Sciences, 1973, pp. 63–122.

Smith, Philip Chadwick Foster. *The Empress of China.* Philadelphia: Philadelphia Maritime Museum, 1984.

So, Billy K. L. *Prosperity, Region, and Institutions in Maritime China: The South Fukien Pattern, 946–1368.* Cambridge, MA: Harvard University Asia Center, 2000.

Song, Gang, and Paola Demattè. "Mapping an Acentric World: Ferdinand Verbiest's *Kunyu Quantu.*" In Marcia Reed and Paola Demattè, eds., *China on Paper: European and Chinese Works from the Late Sixteenth to the Early Nineteenth Century.* Los Angeles: Getty Research Institute, 2007, pp. 71–87.

Souza, George Bryan. *The Survival of Empire: Portuguese Trade and Society in China and the South China Sea, 1630–1754.* Cambridge: Cambridge University Press, 1986.

Spalatin, Christopher. "Matteo Ricci's Use of Epictetus' Encheiridion." *Gregorianum*, Vol. 56, No. 3 (1975), pp. 551–557.

Spence, Jonathan. *Emperor of China: Self-Portrait of K'ang-hsi*. New York: Vintage Books, 1974.

"The K'ang-hsi Reign." In Peterson, ed., *The Cambridge History of China*, Vol. 9, Part 2: *The Ch'ing Dynasty to 1800*, pp. 120–182.

*The Memory Palace of Matteo Ricci*. New York: Viking, 1984.

Spence, Jonathan D., and John E. Wills, Jr., eds. *From Ming to Ch'ing: Conquest, Region, and Continuity in Seventeenth-Century China*. New Haven, CT: Yale Univerity Press, 1979.

Standaert, Nicolas. "Associations for Lay-People." In Standaert, ed., *Handbook*, pp. 457–461.

"Chinese Christians: General Characteristics." In Standaert, ed., *Handbook*, pp. 380–399.

"Christianity Shaped by the Chinese." In R. Po-chia Hsia, ed., *The Cambridge History of Christianity*, Vol. 6: *Reform and Expansion, 1500–1600*. Cambridge: Cambridge University Press, 2007, pp. 558–576.

*The Fascinating God: A Challenge to Modern Chinese Theology Presented by a Text on the Name of God Written by a 17th Century Chinese Student of Theology*. Working Papers on Living Faith and Cultures, No. 17. Rome: Pontifical Gregorian University, 1995.

"L'inculturation et la mission en Chine au XVIIᵉ siècle." *Église et Mission*, Vol. 240 (December 1985), pp. 2–24.

*The Interweaving of Rituals: Funerals in the Cultural Exchange Between China and Europe*. Seattle: University of Washington Press, 2008.

"The Investigation of Things and the Fathoming of Principles (*Gewu Qiongli*) in the Seventeenth-Century Contact between Jesuits and Chinese Scholars." In Witek, ed., *Ferdinand Verbiest*, pp. 395–420.

"Rites Controversy." In Standaert, ed., *Handbook*, pp. 680–688.

"Well-Known Individuals." In Standaert, *Handbook*, pp. 404–428.

*Yang Tingyun, Confucian and Christian in Late Ming China: His Life and Thought*. Sinica Leidensa, Vol. 19. Leiden: Brill, 1988. Also in Chinese: Zhong Mingdan, *Yang Tingyun: Ming mo Tianzhujiao ruzhe*. Hong Kong: Shengxue yanjiu zhongxin, 1987.

ed. *Handbook of Christianity in China: Volume One: 635–1800*. Handbook of Oriental Studies, Section Four, China, Vol. 15, No. 1. Leiden: Brill, 2001.

Standaert, Nicolas, and Adrian Dudink, eds. *Chinese Christian Texts from the Roman Archives of the Society of Jesus*. Yesuhui Luoma Dang'anguan Ming Qing Tianzhujiao Wenxian. 12 vols. Taipei: Ricci Institute, 2002.

Standaert, Nicolas, Adrian Dudink, Huang Yinong, and Zhu Pingyi, eds. *Xujiahui cangshulou Ming Qing Tianzhujiao wenxian*. 5 vols. Taipei: Fujen Catholic University, 1996.

Stary, Giovanni. "The 'Manchu Cannons' Cast by Ferdinand Verbiest and the Hitherto Unknown Title of His Instructions." In Witek, ed. *Ferdinand Verbiest*, pp. 215–225.

Struve, Lynn A. *The Southern Ming, 1644–1662*. New Haven, CT: Yale University Press, 1984.

"The Southern Ming, 1644–1662." In Mote and Twitchett, eds., *The Cambridge History of Christianity*, Vol. 7: *The Ming Dynasty, 1368–1644, Part 2*, pp. 641–725.

ed. *The Qing Formation in World-Historical Time*. Cambridge MA: Harvard University Asia Center and Harvard University Press, 2004.

ed. *Time, Temporality, and Imperial Transition: East Asia from Ming to Qing* (Honolulu: Association for Asian Studies and University of Hawaii Press, 2005).

ed. and trans., *Voices from the Ming–Qing Cataclysm: China in Tiger's Jaws*. New Haven, CT: Yale University Press, 1993.

Su Liqun. *Lang Shining Zhuan*. Beijing: Zhongguo wenxue chuban, 1998.

Subrahmanyam, Sanjay. *The Career and Legend of Vasco da Gama*. Cambridge: Cambridge University Press, 1997.

*The Political Economy of Commerce: South India, 1500–1650*. Cambridge: Cambridge University Press, 1990.

*The Portuguese Empire in Asia, 1500–1700: A Political and Economic History*. London: Longman, 1993.

Sullivan, Michael. *The Meeting of Eastern and Western Art*. Rev. Ed. Berkeley: University of California Press, 1989.

Sun Laichen and Geoff Wade, eds. *Southeast Asia in the Fifteenth Century: The China Factor*. Singapore: NUS Press, 2010.

Swope, Kenneth M. *A Dragon's Head and a Serpent's Tail: Ming China and the First Great East Asian War, 1592–1598*. Norman: University of Oklahoma Press, 2009.

Sy, Jarvis Hao. "The Chinese Indigenous Clergy: The Case of the Dominican Gregorio Lo Wen Tsao (1615–1691)." *Philippiniana Sacra*, Vol. 27 (1992), pp. 313–325.

Tam, Laurence C. *Six Masters of Early Qing and Wu Li*. Hong Kong: Hong Kong Museum of Arts, 1986.

Tang Kaijian. *Weiliduo "Baoxiao shimo shu" jianzheng*. Guangzhou: Guangdong Renmin, 2004.

Tarling, Nicholas, ed. *The Cambridge History of Southeast Asia*, Vol. 1, Part 2: *From c.1500 to c. 1800*. Cambridge: Cambridge University Press, 1999.

Thiriez, Régine. "The 'Mission Palais d'Été' and Its Study of the European Palaces of the Yuan-ming-yuan." In Edward Malatesta, S.J., and Yves Raguin, S.J., eds., *Images de la Chine. Le Contexte occidental de la sinologie naissante*. San Francisco: Ricci Institute, 1995, pp. 139–148.

Thomaz, Luis Filipe Ferreira Reis. "The Malay Sultanate of Melaka." In Anthony Reid, ed., *Southeast Asia in the Early Modern World: Trade, Power, and Belief*. Ithaca, NY: Cornell University Press, 1993, pp. 69–90.

Thomaz de Bossierre, Yves de. *François-Xavier Dentrecolles et l'apport de la Chine à l'Europe du XVIIIe siècle*. Paris: Belles Lettres, 1982.

*Jean-François Gerbillon, S.J. (1654–1701). Un des cinq mathématiciens envoyés en Chine par Louis XIV*. Louvain Chinese Studies, No. 2. Leuven: Ferdinand Verbiest Foundation, 1994.

*Tianzhujiao dong chuan wenxian*. Also *Xubian*, 3 vols. Zhongguo shixue congshu, No. 24, 40. Taipei: Xuesheng shuju, 1965.

*Tianzhujiao liuchuan Zhongguo shiliao* (Chinese historical materials on the transmission of Catholicism). In *Wenxian congbian* (Collectanea of historical documents, Qing dynasty). 2 vols. Taipei, 1964.

Titsingh, Isaac. *Isaac Titsingh in China (1794–1796): Het Onuitgegeven Journaal van Zijn Ambassade naar Peking.* Edited by Frank Lequin. Alphen aan den Rijn: Canaletto/Repro Holland, 2005.

Toby, Ronald P. *State and Diplomacy in Early Modern Japan: Asia in the Development of the Tokugawa Bakufu.* Princeton, NJ: Princeton University Press, 1984.

Torbert, Preston M. *The Ch'ing Imperial Household Department: A Study of Its Organization and Principal Functions, 1662–1796.* Cambridge, MA: Harvard East Asian Monographs, 1977.

Twitchett, Denis, and John K. Fairbank, general eds., *The Cambridge History of China.* Vol. 6: *Alien Regimes and Border States, 907–1368,* edited by Herbert Franke and Denis Twitchett; Vol. 7: *The Ming Dynasty, 1368–1644, Part 1,* edited by Frederick W. Mote and Twitchett; Vol. 8: *The Ming Dynasty, 1368–1644, Part 2,* edited by Denis Twitchett and Frederick W. Mote; Vol. 9, Part 1: *The Ch'ing Dynasty to 1800,* edited by Willard J. Peterson; Vol 10: *Late Ch'ing, Part 1,* edited by John Fairbank. Cambridge: Cambridge University Press, 1978, 1988, 1998, 1994, 2002.

Übelhör, Monika. *Hsü Kuang-ch'i (1562–1633) und seine Einstellung zum Christentum. Ein Beitrag zur Geistesgeschichte der Späten Ming-Zeit.* Hamburg: Oriens Extremus, 1969.

Ukers, William H. *All about Tea.* 2 vols. New York: Tea and Coffee Trade Journal Co., 1935.

Vale, A. M. Martins do. *Os Portugueses em Macau (1750–1800).* Macau: Instituto Português do Oriente, 1997.

Van Dyke, Paul A. "Cai and Qiu Enterprises: Merchants of Canton 1730–1784." *Review of Culture,* Int. Ed. No. 15 (July 2005), pp. 60–101.

——— *The Canton–Macao Dagregisters, 1762.* Translated and annotated by Cynthia Viallé. Macao: Cultural Institute, 2006.

——— *The Canton–Macao Dagregisters, 1763.* Translated and annotated by Cynthia Viallé. Macao: Cultural Institute, 2008.

——— *The Canton–Macao Dagregisters, 1764.* Translated and annotated by Cynthia Viallé. Macao: Cultural Institute, 2009.

——— *The Canton Trade: Life and Enterprise on the China Coast, 1700–1845.* Hong Kong: Hong Kong University Press, 2005.

——— *Merchants of Canton and Macao: Politics and Strategies of 18th Century Chinese Trade.* Hong Kong: Hong Kong University Press, in press.

——— *Port Canton and the Pearl River Delta, 1690–1845.* Ph. D. dissertation, University of Southern California, 2002.

——— "A Reassessment of the China Trade: The Canton Junk Trade as Revealed in the Dutch and Swedish Records of the 1750s to the 1770s." In Wang Gungwu and Ng Chin-keong, eds., *Maritime China in Transition, 1750–1850.* Wiesbaden: Harrassowitz Verlag, 2004, pp. 151–167.

——— "The Yan Family: Merchants of Canton, 1734–1780s." *Review of Culture,* Int. Ed., No. 9 (January 2004): 30–85. Translated and published in Chinese as "Yanshi Jiazu: Guangzhou Shangren (1734–1780)." *Review of Culture,* Chinese Ed., No. 57 (Winter 2005), pp. 1–52.

"The Ye Merchants of Canton, 1720–1804." *Review of Culture,* Int. Ed., No. 13 (January 2005), pp. 6–47.

Vasconcelos de Saldanha, Antonio. *De Kangxi para o Papa, pela Via de Portugal.* 3 vols. Lisbon: Instituto Portugues do Oriente, 2002.

Väth, Alfons, S.J. *Johann Adam Schall von Bell, S.J., Missionar in China, kaiserlicher Astronom und Ratgeber am Hofe von Peking, 1592–1666. Ein Lebens- und Zeitbild.* 2d Ed. Monumenta Serica Monograph Series, No. 25. Nettetal: Steyler, 1991.

Verbiest, Ferdinand, S.J. *The Astronomia Europaea of Ferdinand Verbiest, S.J. (Dillingen, 1687).* Translated and with commentaries by Noel Golvers. Monumenta Serica Monograph Series, No. 28. Nettetal, 1993.

*Correspondance de Ferdinand Verbiest de la Compagnie de Jésus (1623–1688).* Edited by H. Josson and L. Willaert. Brussels: Palais des Académies, 1938.

Verhaeren, Hubert. *Catalogue de la Bibliothèque du Pé-T'ang.* Beijing: Imprimerie des Lazaristes, 1949; reprint, Paris: Belles Lettres, 1969.

Verhoeven, F. R. J. *Bijdragen tot de Oudere Koloniale Geschiedenis van het Eiland Formosa.* Leiden dissertation, privately printed. The Hague, 1930.

Vermeer, Eduard B. "Up to the Mountain and Out to the Sea: The Expansion of the Fukienese in the Late Ming Period." In Murray A. Rubinstein, ed., *Taiwan: A History, 1660–1994.* Armonk, NY: Sharpe, 1999, pp. 45–83.

Vermeulen, Johannes T. *De Chinezen te Batavia en de Troebelen van 1740.* Leiden, 1938.

Vertente, Christine. "Nan Huai-Jen's Maps of the World." In Edward Malatesta and Yves Raguin, eds., *Succès et échecs de la rencontre Chine et Occident du XVIᵉ au XXᵉ siècle Variétés Sinologiques,* New Ser., Vol. 74. San Francisco: Ricci Institute, University of San Francisco, and Taipei: Institut Ricci, 1993, pp. 257–263.

Videira Pires, Benjamim. *Embaixada Martir.* Macau: Centro de Informação e Turismo, 1965.

Vink, Markus P. M. "Indian Ocean Studies and the 'New Thalassology.'" *Journal of Global History,* Vol. 2, No. 1 (2007), pp. 41–62.

Viraphol, Sarasin. *Tribute and Profit in Sino-Siamese Trade, 1652–1853.* Harvard East Asian Monographs, No. 76. Cambridge, MA: Council on East Asian Studies, Harvard University, 1977.

Von Collani, Claudia. "Charles Maigrot's Role in the Rites Controversy." In Mungello, ed., *The Chinese Rites Controversy,* pp. 149–184.

"Figurism." In Standaert, ed., *Handbook,* pp. 668–679.

*Joachim Bouvet, S.J. Sein Leben und Sein Werk.* Monumenta Serica Monograph Series, No. 17. Nettetal: Steyler, 1985.

"*Jing tian* – The Kangxi Emperor's Gift to Ferdinand Verbiest in the Rites Controversy." In Witek, ed., *Ferdinand Verbiest,* pp. 453–470.

"Legations and Travelers." In Standaert, ed., *Handbook,* pp. 355–366.

"Missionaries." In Standaert, ed., *Handbook,* pp. 286–354.

Von Glahn, Richard. *Fountain of Fortune: Money and Monetary Policy in China, 1000–1700.* Berkeley: University of California Press, 1996.

"Money Use in China and Changing Patterns of Trade in Monetary Metals, 1500–1800." In Dennis O. Flynn, Arturo Giraldez, and Richard von Glahn, eds., *Global Connections and Monetary History, 1470–1800*. Aldershot: Ashgate, 2003, pp. 187–205.

Von Glahn, Richard, and Paul Jakov Smith, eds. *The Song–Yuan–Ming Conjuncture in Chinese History: Theoretical and Historical Perspectives*. Cambridge, MA: Harvard East Asian Council, 2003.

Wada Sei, ed. *Minshi shokkashi yakuchū*. 2 vols. Tōyō bunko ronsō, No. 44, Tokyo: Tōyō Bunko, 1960.

Wade, Geoff, "Melaka in Ming Dynasty Texts." *Journal of the Malaysian Branch of the Royal Asiatic Society*, Vol. 52, Part 1 (1997), pp. 31–69.

"Southeast Asia in the Ming Shi-lu." Electronic resource, 2005, http://www. epress.nus.edu.sg/msl.

Wakeman, Frederic, Jr., "The Canton Trade and the Opium War." In Fairbank, ed., *The Cambridge History of China*, Vol. 10, *Late Ch'ing, Part 1*, pp. 163–212.

*The Great Enterprise: The Manchu Reconstruction of Imperial Order in Seventeenth-Century China*. 2 vols. Berkeley: University of California Press, 1985.

Waldron, Arthur. *The Great Wall of China: From History to Myth*. Cambridge: Cambridge University Press, 1990.

Walker, D. P. *The Ancient Theology: Studies in Christian Platonism from the Fifteenth to the Eighteenth Century*. Ithaca, NY: Cornell University Press, 1972.

Walter, Chaplain Richard. *Anson's Voyage around the World in the Years 1740–44*. London: Martin Hopkinson, 1928; reprint, New York: Dover, 1974.

Wang Gungwu. "Ming Foreign Relations: Southeast Asia." In Twitchett and Mote, eds., *Cambridge History of China*, Vol. 8: *The Ming Dynasty, 1368–1644, Part 2*, pp. 301–332.

Wang, Xiaochao. *Christianity and Imperial Culture: Chinese Christian Apologetics in the Seventeenth Century and their Latin Patristic Equivalent*. Studies in Christian Mission, Vol. 20. Leiden: Brill, 1998.

Wang Zheng. *Wei Tian ai ren ji lun*. 1628. Courant No. 3368. Paris: Bibliotheque Nationale.

Wang Zhongmin. *Xu Guangqi*. Edited by He Zhaowu. Shanghai, 1981.

Watson, Ian Bruce. *Foundation for Empire: English Private Trade in India, 1659–1760*. New Delhi: Vikas, 1980.

West, S. George, ed. *List of the Writings of Charles Ralph Boxer Published Between 1926 and 1984*. London: Tamesis Books, 1984.

White, Ann. *The Hong Merchants of Canton*. Ph.D. dissertation, University of Pennsylvania, 1976.

Widmaier, Rita, ed. *Leibniz korrespondiert mit China. Der Briefwechsel mit den Jesuitenmissionaren (1689–1714)*. Frankfurt am Main: Vittorio Klostermann, 1990.

Wiethoff, Bodo. *Die chinesische Seeverbotspolitik und der private Überseehandel von 1368 bis 1567*. Mittelungen der Gesellschaft für Natur- und Völkerkunde Ostasiens, Hamburg, No. 45. Wiesbaden: Harrassowitz, 1963.

Wilkinson, Endymion. *The History of Imperial China: A Research Guide.* Cambridge, MA: Harvard University East Asian Research Center, 1973.

Will, Pierre-Étienne, and R. Bin Wong, with James Lee, contributions by Jean Oi and Peter Perdue. *Nourish the People: The State Civilian Granary System in China, 1650–1850.* Ann Arbor: University of Michigan Center for Chinese Studies, 1991.

Willeke, Bernward H. *Imperial Government and Catholic Missions in China During the Years 1784–1785.* Franciscan Institute, Missiology Series 1. St. Bonaventure: Franciscan Institute, 1948.

Williams, Glyn. *The Prize of All the Oceans: The Dramatic True Story of Commodore Anson's Voyage Round the World and How He Seized the Spanish Treasure Ship.* New York: Viking, 2000.

Wills, John E., Jr. "Advances and Archives in Early Sino-Western Relations: An Update." *Ch'ing-shih wen-t'i,* Vol. 4, No. 10 (December 1983), pp. 87–110.

"Brief Intersection: Changing Contexts and Prospects of the Christian–Chinese Encounter from Ricci to Verbiest." In Witek, ed., *Ferdinand Verbiest,* pp. 383–394. In Chinese translation of volume, *Nan Huairen (1623–1688).* Beijing: Shehui kexue wenxian chubanshe, 2001.

"China's Farther Shores: Continuities and Changes in the Destination Ports of China's Foreign Trade, 1680–1690." In Roderick Ptak and Dietmar Rothermund, eds., *Emporia, Commodities, and Entrepreneurs in Asian Maritime Trade, c. 1400–1750.* Beiträge zur Südasienforschung, Südasien-Institut, Universität Heidelberg, No. 141. Stuttgart: Franz Steiner, 1992, pp. 53–77.

*Ch'ing Relations with the Dutch, 1662–1690.* Ph.D.dissertation, Harvard University, 1967.

"Contingent Connections: Fujian, the Empire, and the Early Modern World." In Struve, ed., *The Qing Formation in World-Historical Time,* pp. 167–203.

"Did China Have a Tribute System?" *Asian Studies Newsletter,* Vol. 44, No. 2 (Spring 1999), pp. 12–13.

"Early Sino-European Relations: Problems, Opportunities, and Archives." *Ch'ing-shih wen-t'i,* Vol. 3, No. 2 (December 1974), pp. 50–76.

*Embassies and Illusions: Dutch and Portuguese Envoys to K'ang-hsi, 1666–1687.* Harvard East Asian Monographs, No. 113. Cambridge, MA: Fairbank Center for East Asian Research, 1984.

"European Consumption and Asian Production in the Seventeenth and Eighteenth Centuries." In John Brewer and Roy Porter, eds., *Consumption and the World of Goods* (London: Routledge, 1993), pp. 133–147.

"The First Inhalers: A World-Historical Problem." Paper presented to the World History Association, 2009.

"From Manila to Fuan: Asian Contexts of Dominican Mission Policy." In Mungello, ed., *The Chinese Rites Controversy,* pp. 111–27.

"From Wild Coast to Prefecture: The Transformation of Taiwan in the Seventeenth Century." In E. K. Y. Chen, Jack F. Williams, and Joseph Wong, eds., *Taiwan: Economy, Society and History.* Hong Kong: University of Hong Kong, Centre of Asian Studies, 1991, pp. 374–384.

"Functional, Not Fossilized: Qing Tribute Relations with Annam (Vietnam) and Siam (Thailand), 1700–1820." *T'oung Pao*, in press.

"The Hazardous Missions of a Dominican: Victorio Riccio, O.P. in Amoy, Taiwan, and Manila. Les missions aventureuses d'un Dominicain, Victorio Riccio." In *Actes du IIe Colloque International de Sinologie, Chantilly, 1977*. Paris, 1980, pp. 231–257.

"Interactive Early Modern Asia: Scholarship from a New Generation." *International Journal of Asian Studies* (Japan), Vol. 5, No. 2 (July 2008), pp. 235–245.

"Maritime Asia, 1500–1800: The Interactive Emergence of European Domination." *American Historical Review*, Vol. 98, No. 1 (February 1993), pp. 83–105.

"Maritime China from Wang Chih to Shih Lang: Themes in Peripheral History." In Spence and Wills, eds., *From Ming to Ch'ing*, pp. 204–238.

"Merchants, Brokers, Pioneers, Biculturals: Human Types in the Early Modern History of Maritime China, c. 1550–1850." Paper presented at a seminar on Greater China, University of California, Berkeley, February 1993.

*Pepper, Guns, and Parleys: The Dutch East India Company and China, 1662–1681*. Cambridge MA: Harvard University Press, 1974.

"The Seventeenth-Century Transformation: Taiwan under the Dutch and the Cheng Regime." In Murray A. Rubinstein, ed., *Taiwan: A History, 1600–1994* (Armonk, NY, 1999), pp. 84–106.

*1688: A Global History*. New York: Norton and London: Granta, 2001.

*Toward the Canton System: Maritime Trade and Qing Policy, 1680–1690*. Typescript.

"Tribute, Defensiveness, and Dependency: Uses and Limits of Some Basic Ideas about Mid-Ch'ing Foreign Relations." *Annals of the Southeast Conference of the Association for Asian Studies*, Vol. 8 (1986), pp. 84–90; reprinted in *American Neptune*, Vol. 48, No. 4 (Fall 1988), 225–229.

Witek, John W., S.J. "Chinese Chronology: A Source of Sino-European Widening Horizons in the Eighteenth Century." In *Appréciation par l'Europe de la tradition chinoise à partir du XVIIIe Siècle*. Colloque international de sinologie, 1980. Paris: Belles Lettres, 1983, pp. 223–252.

*Controversial Ideas in China and in Europe: A Biography of Jean-François Foucquet, S.J. (1665–1741)*. Bibliotheca Instituti Historici Societas Iesu, Vol. 43. Rome: Institutum Historicum Societatis Iesu, 1982.

"The Emergence of a Christian Community in Beijing during the Late Ming and Early Qing Period." In Xiaoxin Wu, ed., *Encounters and Dialogues: Changing Perspectives on Chinese–Western Exchanges from the Sixteenth to the Eighteenth Centuries*. Sankt Augustin: Steyler, 2005, pp. 93–116.

"Explaining the Sacrament of Penance in Seventeenth-Century China: An Essay of Ferdinand Verbiest (1623–1688)." In Noel Golvers, ed., *The Christian Mission in China in the Verbiest Era: Some Aspects of the Missionary Approach*. Louvain Chinese Studies, No. 6. Leuven: Leuven University Press, 1999, pp. 55–71.

"Johann Adam Schall von Bell and the Transition from the Ming to the Qing Dynasty." In Roman Malek, ed., *Western Learning and Christianity*

in China: The Contribution and Impact of Johann Adam Schall von Bell,
S.J. (1592–1666). 2 vols. Monumenta Serica Monograph Series, No. 35.
Nettetal: Steyler Verlag, 1998, pp. 109–124.

"Manchu Christians at the Court of Peking in Early Eighteenth-Century
China: A Preliminary Study." In Edward Malatesta, S.J., and Yves Raguin,
S.J., eds., *Succès et échecs de la rencontre Chine et Occident du XVIᵉ au XXᵉ
siècle*. San Francisco Ricci Institute, 1993, pp. 265–279.

"Presenting Christian Doctrine to the Chinese: Reflections on the *Jiaoyao xulun*
of Ferdinand Verbiest." In Witek, ed., *Ferdinand Verbiest*, pp. 437–452.

"Principles of Scholasticism in China: A Comparison of Giulio Aleni's *Wanwu
zhenyuan* with Matteo Ricci's *Tianzhu shiyi*." In Tiziana Lippiello and
Roman Malek, eds., *"Scholar from the West" Giulio Aleni S.J. (1582–1649)
and the Dialogue between Christianity and China*. Nettetal: Steyler, 1977,
pp. 273–290.

"Sent to Lisbon, Paris and Rome: Jesuit Envoys of the Kangxi Emperor." In
Michele Fatica and Francesco D'Arelli, eds., *La missione cattolica tra i secoli
XVIII–XIX. Matteo Ripa e il collegio dei cinesi: atti del colloquio inter-
nazionale, Napoli, 11–12 febbraio 1997*. Naples: Instituto Universitario
Orientale, 1999, pp. 317–340.

"Understanding the Chinese: A Comparison of Matteo Ricci and the French
Jesuit Mathematicians Sent by Louis XIV". In Ronan and Oh, eds., *East
Meets West*, pp. 62–102.

ed. *Ferdinand Verbiest, S.J. (1623–1688): Jesuit Missionary, Scientist,
Engineer and Diplomat*. Monumenta Serica Monograph Series, No. 30.
Nettetal: Steyler, 1994.

Wong, R. Bin. *China Transformed: Historical Change and the Limits of European
Experience*. Ithaca, NY: Cornell University Press, 1997.

Woodside, Alexander. "The Ch'ien-lung Reign." In Peterson, ed., *The Cambridge
History of China*, Vol. 9, Part 2: *The Ch'ing Dynasty to 1800*, pp. 230–309.

Wright, A. D. *The Counter-Reformation: Catholic Europe and the Non-Christian
World*. London: Weidenfeld and Nicolson, 1982.

Wright, Arthur F., ed. *Confucianism and Chinese Civilization*. Stanford, CA:
Stanford University Press, 1957.

Wu, Silas H. L. *Passage to Power: K'ang-hsi and His Heir Apparent, 1661–1722*.
Cambridge, MA: Harvard University Press, 1979.

*Xiangshan xianzhi*. 1750.

Xie Guozhen. *Mingmo Qingchu de xuefeng*. Beijing, 1982.

Xu Changzhi, ed. *Poxie ji*. 1639.

Xu Guangqi. "Xu." In Ricci, *Jihe Yuanben*, in Li Zhizao, ed., *Tianxue chuhan*.

*Xu Guangqi ji*. Edited by Wang Zhongmin. Shanghai, 1963.

Xu Haisong. "Xixue dong jian yu Qingdai Zhedong xuepai." In Xiaoxin Wu,
ed., *Encounters and Dialogues: Changing Perspectives on Chinese–Western
Exchanges from the Sixteenth to Eighteenth Centuries*. Sankt Augustin: Steyler
Verlag, 2005, pp. 141–160.

Xu Zongze. *Ming Qing jian Yesu huishi yizhu tiyao*. Taipei: Zhonghua shuju,
1958; reprint, Beijing: Zhonghua shuju, 1989.

Yang Tingfu and Yang Tongfu, eds. *Qingren shi mingbie cheng zihao suoyin*.
2 vols. Shanghai: Guji chubanshe, 1988.

Yates, Frances A. *Giordano Bruno and the Hermetic Tradition.* Chicago: University of Chicago Press, 1964.

Yazawa Toshihiko. *Chūgoku to Kirisutokyō – Tenrei mondai.* Tokyo: Kondō shuppansha, 1972.

ed. *Chūgoku no igaku to gijutsu. Yezusukaishi Chūgoku shokanshū.* Tokyo: Heibonsha, 1977.

*Yongzheng zhupi yuzhi.* 1738; reprint, Taipei, 1964.

Young, John D. *Confucianism and Christianity: The First Encounter.* Hong Kong: Hong Kong University Press, 1983.

Young, T. Kue-hing. "French Jesuits and the 'Manchu Anatomy': How China Missed the Vesalian Revolution." *Canadian Medical Association Journal,* Vol. 111 (September 21, 1974), pp. 565–68.

Yü Chün-fang. "Ming Buddhism." In Twitchett and Mote, eds., *The Cambridge History of China,* Vol. 8: *The Ming Dynasty, 1368–1644, Part 2,* pp. 893–952.

*The Renewal of Buddhism in China: Chu-hung and the Late Ming Synthesis.* New York: Columbia University Press, 1981.

Yu Dong. *Catalogo delle opere cinesi missionarie della Biblioteca Apostolica Vaticana (XVI–XVIII sec).* Studi e Testi, No. 366. Vatican City: Biblioteca Apostolica Vaticana, 1996.

Zelin, Madeleine. "The Yung-cheng Reign." In Peterson, ed., *The Cambridge History of China,* Vol. 9, Part 2: *The Ch'ing Dynasty to 1800,* pp. 183–229.

Zhang Dawei. "The 'Calendar Case' in the Early Qing Dynasty Re-examined." In Roman Malek, ed., *Western Learning and Christianity in China: The Contribution and Impact of Johann Adam Schall von Bell, S. J. (1592–1666).* 2 vols. Monumenta Serica Monograph Series, No. 35. Nettetal: Steyler Verlag, 1998, pp. 475–495.

Zhang Rulin and Yin Guangren. *Aomen jilue.* 1751; reprinted in *Zhaodai congshu,* n.p., n.d.

Zhang Weihua. *Mingshi Folangji, Lüsong, Helan, Yidaliya sizhuan zhushi.* Yenching Journal of Chinese Studies Monograph Series, No. 7, Peiping, 1934.

Zhang Zengxin. *Mingji dongnan Zhongguo di haishang huodong.* 2 vols. Taipei: Zhongguo xueshu zhuzuo jiangzhu weiyuanhui, 1988.

"Shiliu shiji qianqi Putuoyaren zai Zhongguo yanhai di maoyi judian." In *Zhongguo haiyang fazhanshi lunwen ji (er).* Taipei: Zhongyang yanjiuyuan, Sanmin zhuyi yanjiusuo, 1986, pp. 75–104.

Zhao, Gang. "Geopolitical Integration and Domestic Harmony: Foreign Trade Policy in Qing China, 1684–1757." Typescript, 2009.

Zheng Yangwen. *The Social Life of Opium in China.* Cambridge: Cambridge University Press, 2005.

Zhou Jinglian. *Zhong Pu waijiao shi.* Shanghai: Commercial Press, 1936.

Zhongguo diyi lishi danganguan, ed. *Yingshi Magaerni fang Hua dangan shiliao huibian* Beijing: Guoji wenhua, 1996.

*Yuanmingyuan,* 2 vols. in series *Qingdai dang'an shiliao.* Shanghai: Shanghai Guji chubanshe, 1991.

Zhongguo diyi lishi danganguan, Aomen jijinhui, **and** Jinan daxue guji yanjiusuo, eds. *Ming Qing shiqi Aomen wenti dangan wenxian huibian.* 6 vols. Beijing: Renmin, 1999.

Zhongguo Yuanmingyuan Xuehui choubei weiyuanhui, ed. *Yuanmingyuan.* 4 vols. Beijing: Zhongguo jianzhu gongye chubanshe, 1981–1986.

Zhu Weizheng. *Coming Out of the Middle Ages: Comparative Reflections on China and the West.* Armonk, NY: Sharpe, 1990.

Zürcher, Erik. "Emperors." In Standaert, ed., *Handbook*, pp. 492–502.

——— "The First Anti-Christian Movement in China (Nanjing, 1616–1621)." In P. W. Pestman, ed., *Acta Orientalia Neerlandica, Proceedings of the Congress of the Dutch Oriental Society.* Leiden, 1971, pp. 188–195.

——— "Jesuit Accommodation and the Chinese Cultural Imperative." In Mungello, ed., *The Chinese Rites Controversy*, pp. 42–57.

# Index

For EU product safety concerns, contact us at Calle de José Abascal, 56–1°, 28003 Madrid, Spain or eugpsr@cambridge.org.

www.ingramcontent.com/pod-product-compliance
Ingram Content Group UK Ltd.
Pitfield, Milton Keynes, MK11 3LW, UK
UKHW020806190625
459647UK00032B/2209